DISCOVERING THE AMERICAN PAST

DISCOVERING THE AMERICAN PAST

A LOOK AT THE EVIDENCE

❧ CONCISE EDITION ❧

William Bruce Wheeler
University of Tennessee

Susan D. Becker
University of Tennessee

HOUGHTON MIFFLIN COMPANY   Boston   New York

Sponsoring Editor: Colleen S. Kyle
Senior Project Editor: Christina M. Horn
Editorial Assistant: Leah Mehl
Senior Production/Design Coordinator: Jennifer Waddell
Manufacturing Manager: Florence Cadran
Senior Cover Design Coordinator: Deborah Azerrad Savona
Senior Marketing Manager: Sandra McGuire

Cover Design: Diana Coe / ko Design Studio
Cover Image: Thomas Nast, *Civil War Scrapbook, 1861–1866*. John Hay Library, Brown
University, Providence.

*For permission to use copyrighted material, grateful acknowledgment is made to the
copyright holders listed on pages 365–367, which are hereby considered an extension of
the copyright page.*

Printed in the U.S.A.

Library of Congress Catalog Card Number: 99-71901

ISBN: 0-618-01158-7

2 3 4 5 6 7 8 9-QUF-03 02 01 00

CONTENTS

◎ **CHAPTER THIRTEEN** ◎

PREFACE TO THE CONCISE EDITION

As we began our collaboration on the first edition of *Discovering the American Past*, our first premise was that students actually *were* interested in the past, both their own as well as those of other peoples. Students, we knew, read a great deal of historical fiction, watched films about the past, and tuned in to a number of television miniseries. And yet, curiously, those same students often left that interest outside the classroom when they entered our American history courses.

We therefore fashioned the book "with an urgent desire to tap the already existing interest" in ways that would make students active learners and participants rather than simply passive observers of the historical process. Encouraged to "do history" and to reach their own conclusions based upon a guided examination of evidence concerning a problem or event in the American past, we found our students responded with eagerness, energy, and imagination. With the appearance of the Fourth Edition of *Discovering the American Past* in 1998, we are gratified to know that students throughout the United States as well as in some other nations have found the study of history inside their classrooms as stimulating and exciting as their historical interests outside the academy.

The widespread acceptance of the four editions of *Discovering the American Past* has given rise to this Concise Edition. Many instructors would like to continue using *Discovering the American Past* while at the same time developing *their own* historical problems based on local or regional history or on the instructors' own interests. We congratulate those fellow historians who seek to communicate the excitement of "doing history" to their students. At the same time, several schools have one-term survey courses in American history, courses for which it is often difficult to find appropriate supplementary material for the students to read, study, examine, and analyze. This Concise Edition of *Discovering the American Past* therefore offers instructors (whether in a two-term or one-term course) a great deal of flexibility to organize the American history course as they see fit. We have tried to present a chronologically and thematically balanced set of problems in this briefer edition.

As with previous editions of *Discovering the American Past*, each chapter is divided into five parts: The Problem, Background, The Method, The Evidence, Questions to Consider, and Epilogue. The section entitled "The Problem" begins with a brief discussion of the central issues of the chapter and then states the questions students will explore. A "Background" section follows, designed to help students understand the historical context of the problem. The section called "The Method" gives students suggestions for studying and analyzing the evidence. "The Evidence" is the heart of the chapter, providing a variety of primary source material on a particular historical event or issue. The section called "Questions to Consider" focuses students' attention on specific evidence and on linkages among different evidence material. The "Epilogue" section gives the aftermath of the historical outcome of the evidence—what happened to the people involved, who won the election, the results of a debate, and so on.

This Concise Edition of *Discovering the American Past* is not intended to replace a textbook or other reading material used in class. The "Problem" section in each chapter provides only a minimal factual context, and students are encouraged to return to their texts, readings, or lectures for information that will help them analyze the evidence presented in the chapter. An Instructor's Resource Manual suggests ways that might be useful in guiding students through the evidence, questions students often ask, and a variety of ways in which the students' learning may be evaluated. By the time students complete this book, we believe they will know how to work with a great variety of historical evidence and how to use that evidence to answer historical questions about what happened and why.

Over the years, the staff at Houghton Mifflin Company has become more than just our coworkers: they have become invaluable friends as well. For this Concise Edition of *Discovering the American Past*, our special thanks go to Ms. Colleen Shanley Kyle, who developed this project and saw it through to its successful conclusion.

W. B. W.
S. D. B.

CHAPTER 1

FIRST ENCOUNTERS:
THE CONFRONTATION BETWEEN
CORTÉS AND MONTEZUMA
(1519–1521)

◌⟳ THE PROBLEM ⟳◌

In 1492, Christopher Columbus became the first European to meet Indians[1] and record his observations. In the next few years, Europeans became increasingly fascinated with the New World and its inhabitants. Explorers' accounts were published and widely circulated, as were artistic renderings of the Indians by European artists, many of whom had never traveled to the New World or met a single Indian.

In turn, Native Americans doubtless recorded their own impressions of Europeans. Since most Indian cultures had not developed forms of writing, these impressions were preserved orally, largely through stories and songs. In central Mexico, however, the Aztecs and other peoples did record their observations of Europeans in writing and art. And although the Spanish *conquistadores* (conquerors) attempted to destroy all such records, a few of the written and artistic renderings did survive to tell the Indians' side of the story of the first encounters.[2]

1. Although Europeans quickly realized that the name Columbus conferred on Native Americans was inaccurate, the word *Indian* continued to be used. Alternative names have never replaced it.

2. The major repositories for these written and artistic works are museums in Paris, Florence, and Mexico City.

CHAPTER 1

FIRST
ENCOUNTERS:
THE
CONFRONTATION
BETWEEN
CORTÉS AND
MONTEZUMA
(1519–1521)

There is little doubt that the impressions created by these written and artistic works fostered perceptions that made Indian-white relations confusing, difficult, and ultimately tragic. The European hunger for land and treasure may have made the tragedies that followed almost inevitable, and yet Europeans' early perceptions of Indians were an important factor in how explorers and early colonists dealt with Native American peoples and, in the end, subdued them. At the same time, the early impressions that Indians gained of Europeans (whether passed down orally or by other means) offered to many Native Americans a clear message concerning how they should respond to white encroachment.

In this chapter, you will be concentrating on the conquest of Mexico by Hernando Cortés, which took place between 1519 and 1521. In many ways, that confrontation was typical of the "first encounters" between Europeans and Native Americans. You will be examining and analyzing two separate sets of evidence: (1) selections written by Cortés to King Charles V of Spain, together with some artistic representations of Native Americans by European artists, and (2) selected written and artistic impressions of Cortés and his *conquistadores* by Aztecs and other Native Americans of central Mexico created within a few years of the events they described. Your task is twofold. First, you must use written and artistic accounts to determine the impressions that each side created of the other. Second, you must reach some conclusions about how those impressions (whether totally accurate or inaccurate) might have influenced how Europeans and early colonists dealt with Native Americans and how Native Americans dealt with them.

Before you begin, we would like to issue a note of caution. When dealing with the evidence provided by European conquerors such as Cortés or by European artists, you will *not* be trying to determine what the Native Americans the Europeans encountered were really like, but only what Cortés and selected European artists perceived them to be like. To find out what the diverse peoples collectively known as Indians were really like, you would have to consult the works of archaeologists, cultural anthropologists, and cultural geographers. And yet, if we want to determine how Europeans perceived Indians, Cortés's letters and selected European works of art can provide excellent clues.

This chapter also will give you a revealing look at how historical evidence is created and how the availability—and unavailability—of that evidence influences the ways in which a past event or person is depicted by historians. For example, Cortés and his soldiers attempted to destroy as many of the Native American historical records as they could, for obvious reasons. But some pieces of that evidence survived. Without those pieces of evidence, historians' accounts of the "first encounters" very likely would be dramatically different.

☙ BACKGROUND ☙

By the time Europeans first encountered the various peoples they collectively called Indians, Native Americans had inhabited the Western Hemisphere for approximately 20,000 to 40,000 years.[3] Although there is considerable disagreement about when these people first appeared in the Americas, it is reasonable to assume that they first migrated to the Western Hemisphere sometime in the middle of the Pleistocene Age. During that period (roughly from 75,000 to 8000 B.C.), huge glaciers covered a large portion of North America, the ice cap extending southward to the approximate present border of the United States and Canada. These glaciers, which in some places were more than 9,000 feet thick, interrupted the water cycle because moisture falling as rain or snow was caught by the glaciers and frozen and was thus prevented from draining back into the seas or evaporating into the atmosphere.

This process lowered ocean levels 250 to 300 feet, exposing a natural land bridge spanning the Bering Strait (between present-day Alaska and the former Soviet Union)[4] across which people from Asia could easily migrate,

probably in search of game. It is almost certain that various peoples from Asia did exactly that and then followed an ice-free corridor along the base of the Rocky Mountains southward into the more temperate areas of the American Southwest (which, because of the glaciers, were wetter, cooler, and contained large lakes and forests) and then either eastward into other areas of North America or even farther southward into Central and South America. These migrations took thousands of years, and some Indian peoples were still moving when Europeans first encountered them.

About 8000 B.C., the glacial cap began to retreat fairly rapidly, raising ocean levels to approximately their present-day levels and cutting off further migration from Asia, thus isolating America's first human inhabitants from other peoples for thousands of years. This isolation was almost surely the cause of the inhabitants' extraordinarily high susceptibility to the diseases that Europeans later brought with them, such as measles, tuberculosis, and smallpox, to which the peoples of other continents had built up natural resistance. The glacial retreat also caused large portions of the American Southwest to become hot and arid, thus scattering Indian peoples in almost all directions. Nevertheless, for thousands of years a strong oral tradition enabled Indians to preserve stories of their origins and subsequent isolation. Almost all Indian peoples retained accounts of a long migration from the west and a flood.

3. Other estimates run as high as 70,000 years. Whatever the case, it is almost certain that Indians were not native to the Western Hemisphere because no subhuman remains have ever been found.
4. Today the Bering Strait is only 180 feet deep. Thus a lowering of ocean levels 250 to 300 feet would have exposed a considerable land bridge between Asia and North America.

CHAPTER 1

FIRST
ENCOUNTERS:
THE
CONFRONTATION
BETWEEN
CORTÉS AND
MONTEZUMA
(1519–1521)

The original inhabitants of the Western Hemisphere obtained their food principally by hunting and gathering, killing mammoths, huge bison, deer, elk, antelope, camels, horses, and other game with stone weapons and picking wild fruits and grasses. Beginning about 5000 B.C., however, Indians in present-day Mexico began practicing agriculture. By the time Europeans arrived, most Indians were domesticating plants and raising crops, although their levels of agricultural sophistication were extremely diverse.

The development of agriculture (which occurred about the same time in Europe and the Americas) profoundly affected Indian life. Those peoples who adopted agriculture abandoned their nomadic ways and lived in settled villages (some of the Central American ones became magnificent cities). This more sedentary life permitted them to erect permanent housing, create and preserve pottery and art, and establish more complex political and social institutions. Agriculture also led to a sexual division of labor, with women planting, raising, and harvesting crops and men hunting to supplement their villages' diets with game. With more and better food, most likely Indian populations grew more rapidly, thus furthering the need for more complex political and social structures. The development of agriculture also affected these peoples' religious beliefs and ceremonies, increasing the homage to sun and rain gods who could bring forth good harvests. Contact with other Indian peoples led to trading, a practice with which Indians were quite familiar by the time of European intrusion.

Those Indian cultures that made the transition from food gathering to food producing often attained an impressive degree of economic, political, social, and technological sophistication. In Central America, the Mayas of present-day Mexico and Guatemala built great cities, fashioned elaborate gold and silver jewelry, devised a form of writing, were proficient in mathematics and astronomy, and constructed a calendar that could predict solar eclipses and was more accurate than any system in use in Europe at the time. The conquerors of the Mayas, the Aztecs, built on the achievements of their predecessors, extending their political and economic power chiefly by subjugating other Indian peoples. By the time Cortés and his army of 400 men, 16 horses, and a few cannon landed at Vera Cruz in 1519, the Aztecs had constructed the magnificent city of Tenochtitlán (the site of present-day Mexico City), which rivaled European cities in both size (approximately 300,000 people) and splendor.

Tenochtitlán contained magnificent pyramids and public buildings, a fresh water supply brought to the city by complex engineering, causeways that connected the island city to other islands and the mainland, numerous skilled craftsmen, and even a compulsory education system for all male children (no state in the United States would have such a system for more than 300 years). Raw materials and treasure flowed into Tenochtitlán from all over the Aztec empire, which stretched from the Pacific Ocean to the Gulf of Mexico and from central Mexico to present-day Guatemala. Little wonder that the *conquistadores* with Hernando Cortés were awed and enchanted when they saw it.

In many ways, Cortés was the typical Spanish *conquistador*. Born in 1485 to a respected but poor family (his father had been a career military officer but never rose above the rank of captain), Cortés spent two unsuccessful years studying for the law. Abandoning that goal, he became a soldier and was determined to gain fame and fortune through a military career. In 1504 (when he was but nineteen years old), he boarded a ship bound for the Spanish possessions in the New World. After fourteen years of military service, Cortés finally got his big break in 1518, when he was chosen to command a new armada whose purpose was to conquer Mexico. Earlier, unsuccessful expeditions had given some indications of gold in Mexico, and Cortés was sent to find it (as well as to try to locate members of the earlier expeditions who might still be alive). Since Cortés himself financed a good portion of the new armada (he had to borrow money to do so), he had the opportunity to realize his dreams of wealth if his men found treasure. When Cortés landed at Vera Cruz, he was thirty-four years old.

☞ THE METHOD ☜

In this chapter, you will be working with two distinct types of evidence: (1) written accounts and (2) artistic representations. In addition, the evidence has been divided into two sets: (1) Hernando Cortés's and European artists' perceptions of Indians and (2) Indians' written and artistic accounts of Cortés's invasion of the Aztec capital, Tenochtitlán (1519–1521). As noted previously, Cortés's account comes from letters he wrote to the Spanish king soon after the events he described took place. As for the European artists, some of them undoubtedly used their active imaginations to construct their images of Indians, whereas others relied on explorers' accounts or word-of-mouth reports from those who had seen Native Americans whom the explorers had brought to Europe.

The Indians' accounts of Europeans pose something of a problem. We cannot be sure that all (or any) of the written or artistic representations were done by eyewitnesses to the events they describe. We do know, however, that most of the written selections were completed by 1528 (only seven years after Cortés's conquest of Tenochtitlán) and that all the written and artistic representations were created within the normal lifetimes of eyewitnesses. Therefore, if the writers and artists themselves were not eyewitnesses, they doubtless knew of eyewitnesses who could have reported to them what they saw. Thanks to Roman Catholic missionaries who saved

CHAPTER 1

FIRST
ENCOUNTERS:
THE
CONFRONTATION
BETWEEN
CORTÉS AND
MONTEZUMA
(1519–1521)

these accounts from the *conquistadores,* we have what we can assume are firsthand reactions by Native Americans to European intruders.

Even so, the Native American accounts of Cortés's conquest pose some problems for historians. In addition to the nightmare that Native American place and people names present to non-Indians who attempt to pronounce them, it is not always clear in these accounts precisely what is being described. For example, remember that the Native Americans at first believed that Cortés and his party were some form of gods ("As for their food, it is like human food"), which explains their sacrifices before Cortés, their offering of gifts, and their preparations to "celebrate their god's fiesta." Precisely when they abandoned this notion is unclear, for at the same time that they were conducting their celebration, they simultaneously posted guards at the Eagle Gate. It will take some care and thought to determine exactly what was taking place.

Also, occasionally historical evidence can be contradictory. For instance, Cortés claimed that he attacked the Aztecs only after learning that they were plotting to kill him and his men. Yet the Native American account suggests that no such plot existed and that Cortés's attack was unprovoked. Can you determine from the accounts which explanation is the more nearly correct? Read carefully through both Cortés's and the Native American accounts, and you will see that determining what actually happened is not so difficult as it first appears to be. Also, you will see that both Cortés and the Native American

chroniclers occasionally describe the same events, which can make for some fascinating comparisons.

The two types of evidence in this chapter (written accounts and artistic representations) must be dealt with differently. As you read the written accounts (whether by Cortés or by Native Americans), think of some adjectives that, after reading these accounts, Europeans who read Cortés's letters (some of which were published and widely distributed) might have used to describe Indians. For the Native American written accounts, imagine what adjectives Native Americans who shared the accounts might have used to describe Europeans. How do those adjectives present a collective image of Indians? Of Europeans? How do the stories each author tells reinforce that image? As you read each written account, make a list of adjectives for each set of evidence, then combine them to form a collective image. Be willing to read between the lines. Sometimes, for example, Cortés may simply have been trying to explain a specific incident or practice of the Indians. Yet, intentionally or unintentionally, he was creating an image in the minds of readers. Be equally cautious and sensitive when reading the Indians' written accounts.

The second type of evidence, artistic representations, is quite different from the written accounts. If you think of art as words made into pictures, you will see that you can approach this type of evidence as you did the written accounts. Study each picture carefully, looking especially for how Native Americans or Europeans are portrayed. How are they portrayed physically? How is their supposed nature or character portrayed in their behavior in the works of art? Again, as with the written accounts, create a list of adjectives and deduce the images Europeans would have had of Indians and the images Indians would have had of Europeans. As you analyze the evidence in this chapter, keep two central questions in mind: (1) What images do the written and artistic accounts create of Native Americans and of Europeans? (2) How might those images (or impressions) have influenced how European explorers and early colonists dealt with Native Americans and how Native Americans dealt with them?

♋ THE EVIDENCE ♋

EUROPEAN ACCOUNTS

Source 1 from Francis Augustus MacNutt, *Fernando Cortés: His Five Letters of Relation to the Emperor Charles V* (Cleveland: Arthur H. Clark Co., 1908), Vol. I, pp. 161–166, 211–216.

1. Selections from Cortés's First Letter to Charles I of Spain, July 10, 1519.

. . . According to our judgment, it is credible that there is everything in this country which existed in that from whence Solomon is said to have brought the gold for the Temple, but, as we have been here so short a time, we have not been able to see more than the distance of five leagues inland, and about ten or twelve leagues of the coast length on each side, which we have explored since we landed; although from the sea it must be more, and we saw much more while sailing.

The people who inhabit this country, from the Island of Cozumel, and the Cape of Yucatan to the place where we now are, are a people of middle size, with bodies and features well proportioned, except that in each province their customs differ, some piercing the ears, and putting large and ugly objects in them, and others piercing the nostrils down to the mouth, and putting in large round stones like mirrors, and others piercing their under lips down as far as their gums, and hanging from them large round stones, or pieces of gold, so weighty that they pull down the nether lip, and make it appear very deformed. The clothing which they wear is like long veils, very curiously worked. The men wear breech-cloths about their bodies, and large mantles, very thin, and painted in the style of Moorish draperies. The women of the ordinary people wear, from their waists to their feet, clothes also very much painted, some covering their breasts and leaving the rest of

[7]

CHAPTER 1

FIRST
ENCOUNTERS:
THE
CONFRONTATION
BETWEEN
CORTÉS AND
MONTEZUMA
(1519–1521)

the body uncovered. The superior women, however, wear very thin shirts of cotton, worked and made in the style of *rochets* [blouses with long, straight sleeves]. Their food is maize and grain, as in the other Islands, and *potuyuca*, as they eat it in the Island of Cuba, and they eat it broiled, since they do not make bread of it; and they have their fishing, and hunting, and they roast many chickens, like those of the Tierra Firma, which are as large as peacocks.[5]

There are some large towns well laid out, the houses being of stone, and mortar when they have it. The apartments are small, low, and in the Moorish style, and, when they cannot find stone, they make them of adobes, whitewashing them, and the roof is of straw. Some of the houses of the principal people are very cool, and have many apartments, for we have seen more than five courts in one house, and the apartments very well distributed, each principal department of service being separate. Within them they have their wells and reservoirs for water, and rooms for the slaves and dependents, of whom they have many. Each of these chiefs has at the entrance of his house, but outside of it, a large court-yard, and in some there are two and three and four very high buildings, with steps leading up to them, and they are very well built; and in them they have their mosques and prayer places, and very broad galleries on all sides, and there they keep the idols which they worship, some being of stone, some of gold, and some of wood, and they honour and serve them in such wise, and with so many ceremonies, that much paper would be required to give Your Royal Highnesses an entire and exact description of all of them. These houses and mosques,[6] wherever they exist, are the largest and best built in the town, and they keep them very well adorned, decorated with feather-work and well-woven stuffs, and with all manner of ornaments. Every day, before they undertake any work, they burn incense in the said mosques, and sometimes they sacrifice their own persons, some cutting their tongues and others their ears, and some hacking the body with knives; and they offer up to their idols all the blood which flows, sprinkling it on all sides of those mosques, at other times throwing it up towards the heavens, and practising many other kinds of ceremonies, so that they undertake nothing without first offering sacrifice there.

They have another custom, horrible, and abominable, and deserving punishment, and which we have never before seen in any other place, and it is this, that, as often as they have anything to ask of their idols, in order that their petition may be more acceptable, they take many boys or girls, and

5. These were turkeys, which were unknown in Europe.
6. Temples.

[8]

even grown men and women, and in the presence of those idols they open their breasts, while they are alive, and take out the hearts and entrails, and burn the said entrails and hearts before the idols, offering that smoke in sacrifice to them. Some of us who have seen this say that it is the most terrible and frightful thing to behold that has ever been seen. So frequently, and so often do these Indians do this, according to our information, and partly by what we have seen in the short time we are in this country, that no year passes in which they do not kill and sacrifice fifty souls in each mosque; and this is practised, and held as customary, from the Isle of Cozumel to the country in which we are now settled. Your Majesties may rest assured that, according to the size of the land, which to us seems very considerable, and the many mosques which they have, there is no year, as far as we have until now discovered and seen, when they do not kill and sacrifice in this manner some three or four thousand souls. Now let Your Royal Highnesses consider if they ought not to prevent so great an evil and crime, and certainly God, Our Lord, will be well pleased, if, through the command of Your Royal Highnesses, these peoples should be initiated and instructed in our Very Holy Catholic Faith, and the devotion, faith, and hope, which they have in their idols, be transferred to the Divine Omnipotence of God; because it is certain, that, if they served God with the same faith, and fervour, and diligence, they would surely work miracles.

It should be believed, that it is not without cause that God, Our Lord, has permitted that these parts should be discovered in the name of Your Royal Highnesses, so that this fruit and merit before God should be enjoyed by Your Majesties, of having instructed these barbarian people, and brought them through your commands to the True Faith. As far as we are able to know them, we believe that, if there were interpreters and persons who could make them understand the truth of the Faith, and their error, many, and perhaps all, would shortly quit the errors which they hold, and come to the true knowledge; because they live civilly and reasonably, better than any of the other peoples found in these parts.

To endeavour to give to Your Majesties all the particulars about this country and its people, might occasion some errors in the account, because much of it we have not seen, and only know it through information given us by the natives; therefore we do not undertake to give more than what may be accepted by Your Highnesses as true. Your Majesties may, if you deem proper, give this account as true to Our Very Holy Father, in order that diligence and good system may be used in effecting the conversion of these people, because it is hoped that great fruit and much good may be obtained; also that His Holiness may approve and allow that the wicked and rebellious, being first admonished, may be punished and chastised as

CHAPTER 1

FIRST
ENCOUNTERS:
THE
CONFRONTATION
BETWEEN
CORTÉS AND
MONTEZUMA
(1519–1521)

enemies of Our Holy Catholic Faith, which will be an occasion of punishment and fear to those who may be reluctant in receiving knowledge of the Truth; thereby, that the great evils and injuries they practise in the service of the Devil, will be forsaken. Because, besides what we have just related to Your Majesties about the men, and women, and children, whom they kill and offer in their sacrifices, we have learned, and been positively informed, that they are all sodomites,[7] and given to that abominable sin. In all this, we beseech Your Majesties to order such measures taken as are most profitable to the service of God, and to that of Your Royal Highnesses, and so that we who are here in your service may also be favoured and recompensed. . . .

. . . Along the road we encountered many signs, such as the natives of this province had foretold us, for we found the high road blocked up, and another opened, and some pits, although not many, and some of the city streets were closed, and many stones were piled on the house tops. They thus obliged us to be cautious, and on our guard.

I found there certain messengers from Montezuma, who came to speak with those others who were with me, but to me they said nothing, because, in order to inform their master, they had come to learn what those who were with me had done and agreed with me. These latter messengers departed, therefore, as soon as they had spoken with the first, and even the chief of those who had formerly been with me also left.

During the three days which I remained there I was ill provided for, and every day was worse, and the lords and chiefs of the city came rarely to see and speak to me. I was somewhat perplexed by this, but the interpreter whom I have, an Indian woman of this country whom I obtained in Putunchan, the great river I have already mentioned in the first letter to Your Majesty, was told by another woman native of this city, that many of Montezuma's people had gathered close by, and that those of the city had sent away their wives, and children, and all their goods, intending to fall upon us and kill us all; and that, if she wished to escape, she should go with her, as she would hide her. The female interpreter told it to that Geronimo de Aguilar, the interpreter whom I obtained in Yucatan, and of whom I have written to Your Highness, who reported it to me. I captured one of the natives of the said city, who was walking about there, and took him secretly apart so that no one saw it, and questioned him; and he confirmed all that the Indian woman and the natives of Tascaltecal had told me. As well on account of this information as from the signs I had observed, I determined

7. People who practice anal or oral copulation with members of the opposite (or same) gender or who have sex with animals.

to anticipate them, rather than be surprised, so I had some of the lords of the city called, saying that I wished to speak with them, and I shut them in a chamber by themselves. In the meantime I had our people prepared, so that, at the firing of a musket, they should fall on a crowd of Indians who were near to our quarters, and many others who were inside them. It was done in this wise, that, after I had taken these lords, and left them bound in the chamber, I mounted a horse, and ordered the musket to be fired, and we did such execution that, in two hours, more than three thousand persons had perished.

In order that Your Majesty may see how well prepared they were, before I went out of our quarters, they had occupied all the streets, and stationed all their men, but, as we took them by surprise, they were easily overcome, especially as the chiefs were wanting, for I had already taken them prisoners. I ordered fire to be set to some towers and strong houses, where they defended themselves, and assaulted us; and thus I scoured the city fighting during five hours, leaving our dwelling place which was very strong, well guarded, until I had forced all the people out of the city at various points, in which those five thousand natives of Tascaltecal and the four hundred of Cempoal gave me good assistance. . . .

CHAPTER 1

FIRST
ENCOUNTERS:
THE
CONFRONTATION
BETWEEN
CORTÉS AND
MONTEZUMA
(1519–1521)

Sources 2 through 5 from Hugh Honor, *The European Vision of America* (Cleveland: Cleveland Museum of Art, 1975), plates 3, 8, 64, 65. Source 2 photo: The British Library.

2. German Woodcut, 1509.

3. Portuguese Oil on Panel, 1550.

4. German Engraving, 1590.

CHAPTER 1

FIRST
ENCOUNTERS:
THE
CONFRONTATION
BETWEEN
CORTÉS AND
MONTEZUMA
(1519–1521)

Source 5: Library of Congress/Rare Book Division.

5. German Engraving, 1591.

Sources 6 and 7 from Stefan Lorant, ed., *The New World: The First Pictures of America* (New York: Duell, Sloan & Pearce, 1946), pp. 51, 119. Photos: Metropolitan Museum of Art.

6. German Engraving, 1591.

7. German Engraving, 1591.

Sources 8 and 9 from Honor, *The European Vision of America*, plates 85, 91.
Photos: New York Historical Society.

8. French Engraving, 1575.

CHAPTER 1

FIRST
ENCOUNTERS:
THE
CONFRONTATION
BETWEEN
CORTÉS AND
MONTEZUMA
(1519–1521)

9. **French Engraving, 1579–1600.**

NATIVE AMERICAN ACCOUNTS

Source 10 from Miguel Leon-Portilla, ed., *The Broken Spears: The Aztec Account of the Conquest of Mexico,* trans. Lysander Kemp (Boston: Beacon Press, 1962), pp. viii–ix, 30, 92–93, 128–144.

10. Cortés's Conquest of Tenochtitlán.

Year 1-Canestalk. The Spaniards came to the palace at Tlayacac. When the Captain[8] arrived at the palace, Motecuhzoma[9] sent the Cuetlaxteca[10] to greet him and to bring him two suns as gifts. One of these suns was made of the yellow metal, the other of the white.[11] The Cuetlaxteca also brought him a mirror to be hung on his person, a gold collar, a great gold pitcher, fans and ornaments of quetzal feathers[12] and a shield inlaid with mother-of-pearl.

The envoys made sacrifices in front of the Captain. At this, he grew very angry. When they offered him blood in an "eagle dish," he shouted at the man who offered it and struck him with his sword. The envoys departed at once. . . .

When the sacrifice was finished, the messengers reported to the king. They told him how they had made the journey, and what they had seen, and what food the strangers ate. Motecuhzoma was astonished and terrified by their report, and the description of the strangers' food astonished him above all else.

He was also terrified to learn how the cannon roared, how its noise resounded, how it caused one to faint and grow deaf. The messengers told him: "A thing like a ball of stone comes out of its entrails: it comes out shooting sparks and raining fire. The smoke that comes out with it has a pestilent odor, like that of rotten mud. This odor penetrates even to the brain and causes the greatest discomfort. If the cannon is aimed against a mountain, the mountain splits and cracks open. If it is aimed against a tree, it shatters the tree into splinters. This is a most unnatural sight, as if the tree had exploded from within."

The messengers also said: "Their trappings and arms are all made of iron. They dress in iron and wear iron casques[13] on their heads. Their swords are iron; their bows are iron; their shields are iron; their spears are iron.

---

8. Cortés.
9. Montezuma.
10. The Cuetlaxteca were an Indian people allied with the Aztecs.
11. Gold and silver.
12. Quetzal: A type of bird native to Central America; the male has tail feathers up to 2 feet in length.
13. Helmets.

CHAPTER 1

FIRST
ENCOUNTERS:
THE
CONFRONTATION
BETWEEN
CORTÉS AND
MONTEZUMA
(1519–1521)

Their deer[14] carry them on their backs wherever they wish to go. These deer, our lord, are as tall as the roof of a house.

"The strangers' bodies are completely covered, so that only their faces can be seen. Their skin is white, as if it were made of lime. They have yellow hair, though some of them have black. Their beards are long and yellow, and their moustaches are also yellow. Their hair is curly, with very fine strands.

"As for their food, it is like human food. It is large and white, and not heavy.[15] It is something like straw, but with the taste of a cornstalk, of the pith of a cornstalk. It is a little sweet, as if it were flavored with honey; it tastes of honey, it is sweet-tasting food.

"Their dogs are enormous, with flat ears and long, dangling tongues. The color of their eyes is a burning yellow; their eyes flash fire and shoot off sparks. Their bellies are hollow, their flanks long and narrow. They are tireless and very powerful. They bound here and there, panting, with their tongues hanging out. And they are spotted like an ocelot."

When Motecuhzoma heard this report, he was filled with terror. It was as if his heart had fainted, as if it had shriveled. It was as if he were conquered by despair. . . .

Then the Captain marched to Tenochtitlan. He arrived here during the month called Bird, under the sign of the day 8-Wind. When he entered the city, we gave him chickens, eggs, corn, tortillas and drink. We also gave him firewood, and fodder for his deer. Some of these gifts were sent by the lord of Tenochtitlan, the rest by the lord of Tlatelolco.

Later the Captain marched back to the coast, leaving Don Pedro de Alvarado—The Sun—in command.

During this time, the people asked Motecuhzoma how they should celebrate their god's fiesta. He said: "Dress him in all his finery, in all his sacred ornaments."

During this same time, The Sun commanded that Motecuhzoma and Itzcohuatzin, the military chief of Tlatelolco, be made prisoners. The Spaniards hanged a chief from Acolhuacan named Nezahualquentzin. They also murdered the king of Nauhtla, Cohualpopocatzin, by wounding him with arrows and then burning him alive.

For this reason, our warriors were on guard at the Eagle Gate. The sentries from Tenochtitlan stood at one side of the gate, and the sentries from Tlatelolco at the other. But messengers came to tell them to dress the

14. Horses.
15. Probably pasta.

figure of Huitzilopochtli.[16] They left their posts and went to dress him in his sacred finery: his ornaments and his paper clothing.

When this had been done, the celebrants began to sing their songs. That is how they celebrated the first day of the fiesta. On the second day they began to sing again, but without warning they were all put to death. . . . They ran in among the dancers, forcing their way to the place where the drums were played. They attacked the man who was drumming and cut off his arms. Then they cut off his head, and it rolled across the floor.

They attacked the celebrants, stabbing them, spearing them, striking them with their swords. They attacked some of them from behind, and these fell instantly to the ground with their entrails hanging out. Others they beheaded: they cut off their heads, or split their heads to pieces.

They struck others in the shoulders, and their arms were torn from their bodies. They wounded some in the thigh and some in the calf. They slashed others in the abdomen, and their entrails all spilled to the ground. Some attempted to run away, but their intestines dragged as they ran; they seemed to tangle their feet in their own entrails. No matter how they tried to save themselves, they could find no escape. . . .

The Sun treacherously murdered our people on the twentieth day after the Captain left for the coast. We allowed the Captain to return to the city in peace. But on the following day we attacked him with all our might, and that was the beginning of the war.

The Spaniards attempted to slip out of the city at night, but we attacked furiously at the Canal of the Toltecs, and many of them died. This took place during the fiesta of Tecuilhuitl. The survivors gathered first at Mazatzintamalco and waited for the stragglers to come up.

Year 2-Flint. This was the year in which Motecuhzoma died. Itzcohuatzin of Tlatelolco died at the same time.

The Spaniards took refuge in Acueco, but they were driven out by our warriors. They fled to Teuhcalhueyacan and from there to Zoltepec. Then they marched through Citlaltepec and camped in Temazcalapan, where the people gave them hens, eggs and corn. They rested for a short while and marched on to Tlaxcala.

Soon after, an epidemic broke out in Tenochtitlan. . . . It began to spread during the thirteenth month and lasted for seventy days, striking everywhere in the city and killing a vast number of our people. Sores erupted on our faces, our breasts, our bellies; we were covered with agonizing sores from head to foot.

---

16. The mythical founder of the Aztec people and their supreme god.

CHAPTER 1

FIRST
ENCOUNTERS:
THE
CONFRONTATION
BETWEEN
CORTÉS AND
MONTEZUMA
(1519–1521)

The illness was so dreadful that no one could walk or move. The sick were so utterly helpless that they could only lie on their beds like corpses, unable to move their limbs or even their heads. They could not lie face down or roll from one side to the other. If they did move their bodies, they screamed with pain.

A great many died from this plague, and many others died of hunger. They could not get up to search for food, and everyone else was too sick to care for them, so they starved to death in their beds.[17]

Some people came down with a milder form of the disease; they suffered less than the others and made a good recovery. But they could not escape entirely. Their looks were ravaged, for wherever a sore broke out, it gouged an ugly pockmark in the skin. And a few of the survivors were left completely blind. . . .

[*Here the account describes Cortés's siege of Tenochtitlán, a siege that was successful due in part to bickering among the Aztecs themselves (in which several leaders were put to death), in part to the panic caused by Cortés's cannon, and in part to a number of nearby Indian peoples whom the Aztecs had dominated turning on their former masters and supporting the Spanish. Of course, the devastating smallpox epidemic and general starvation due to the siege also played important roles.*]

Broken spears lie in the roads;
we have torn our hair in our grief.
The houses are roofless now, and their walls
are red with blood.

Worms are swarming in the streets and plazas,
and the walls are splattered with gore.
The water has turned red, as if it were dyed,
and when we drink it,
it has the taste of brine.

We have pounded our hands in despair
against the adobe walls,
for our inheritance, our city, is lost and dead.
The shields of our warriors were its defense,
but they could not save it.

We have chewed dry twigs and salt grasses;
we have filled our mouths with dust and bits of adobe;
we have eaten lizards, rats and worms. . . .

17. The epidemic probably was smallpox.

Cuauhtemoc was taken to Cortes along with three other princes. The Captain was accompanied by Pedro de Alvarado and La Malinche.

When the princes were made captives, the people began to leave, searching for a place to stay. Everyone was in tatters, and the women's thighs were almost naked. The Christians searched all the refugees. They even opened the women's skirts and blouses and felt everywhere: their ears, their breasts, their hair. Our people scattered in all directions. They went to neighboring villages and huddled in corners in the houses of strangers.

The city was conquered in the year 3-House. The date on which we departed was the day 1-Serpent in the ninth month. . . .

[The account next describes Cortés's torture of the remaining Aztec leaders in an attempt to find where the Aztecs' treasures were hidden.]

When the envoys from Tlatelolco had departed, the leaders of Tenochtitlan were brought before the Captain, who wished to make them talk. This was when Cuauhtemoc's feet were burned. They brought him in at daybreak and tied him to a stake.

They found the gold in Cuitlahuactonco, in the house of a chief named Itzpotonqui. As soon as they had seized it, they brought our princes—all of them bound—to Coyoacan.

About this same time, the priest in charge of the temple of Huitzilopochtli was put to death. The Spaniards had tried to learn from him where the god's finery and that of the high priests was kept. Later they were informed that it was being guarded by certain chiefs in Cuauhchichilco and Xaltocan. They seized it and then hanged two of the chiefs in the middle of the Mazatlan road. . . .

They hanged Macuilxochitl, the king of Huitzilopochco, in Coyoacan. They also hanged Pizotzin, the king of Culhuacan. And they fed the Keeper of the Black House, along with several others, to their dogs.

And three wise men of Ehecatl, from Tezcoco, were devoured by the dogs. They had come only to surrender; no one brought them or sent them there. They arrived bearing their painted sheets of paper. There were four of them, and only one escaped; the other three were overtaken, there in Coyoacan. . . .

CHAPTER 1

FIRST
ENCOUNTERS:
THE
CONFRONTATION
BETWEEN
CORTÉS AND
MONTEZUMA
(1519–1521)

Sources 11 through 14 are present-day adaptations of Aztec artistic works that were created not long after the events they depict took place. The modern adaptations can be found in Leon-Portilla, *The Broken Spears,* pp. 21, 82, 75, 143. Illustrations by Alberto Beltran.

11. Native Americans Greet Cortés and His Men.

12. Spanish Response to Native American Greeting.

13. The Massacre at the Fiesta.

CHAPTER 1

FIRST
ENCOUNTERS:
THE
CONFRONTATION
BETWEEN
CORTÉS AND
MONTEZUMA
(1519–1521)

14. Fate of the Wise Men of Ehecatl.

❦ QUESTIONS TO CONSIDER ❦

As you read Cortés's account (Source 1), it helps to look for five factors:

1. Physical appearance (bodies, hair, clothing, jewelry, and so on). This description can provide important clues about Cortés's attitude toward the Indians he confronted.
2. Nature or character (childlike, bellicose, cunning, honest, intellectual, lazy, and so on). Be sure to note the examples Cortés used to provide his analysis of the Indians' nature or character.
3. Political, social, and religious practices (behavior of women, ceremonies, eating habits, government, and so on). Descriptions of these practices can provide excellent insight into the explorer's general perception of the Indians he encountered. Be especially sensitive to Cortés's use of descriptive adjectives.
4. Overall impression of the Indians. What was Cortés's collective image or impression?
5. What did Cortés think should be done with the Indians?

Once you have analyzed Cortés's account using points 1 through 4, you should be able to explain how, based on his overall impression of the Indians, he thought the Indians should be dealt with (point 5). Sometimes Cortés comes right out and tells you, but in other cases you will have to use a little imagination. Ask yourself the following question: If I had been living in Spain in 1522 and read Cortés's account, what would my perception of

Native Americans have been? Based on that perception, how would I have thought those peoples should be dealt with?

You can handle the artistic representations (Sources 2 through 9) in the same way. Each artist tried to convey his notion of the Indians' nature or character. Some of these impressions are obvious, but others are less so. Think of the art as words made into pictures. How are the Indians portrayed? What are they doing? How are they dealing with Europeans? On the basis of these artistic representations, decide how the various artists believed Indians should be dealt with. For example, the Indian woman with child in Source 4 depicts Native Americans in a particular way. What is it? On the basis of this depiction, what would you say was the artist's perception of Indians? Moreover, how would that perception have affected the artist's—and viewer's—opinion of how Indians should be treated? Follow these steps for all the artistic representations.

Finally, put together the two types of evidence. Is there more than one "image" of Native Americans? How might each perception have affected the ways Europeans and early colonists dealt with Indians?

On the surface, the Native Americans' perception of Europeans was one-dimensional and is easily discovered: the Aztec writers and artists portrayed Cortés and his men as brutal and sadistic murderers who were driven mad by their lust for gold. Closer examination of the early sec-

COUNTERS:
THE
CONFRONTATION
BETWEEN
CORTÉS AND
MONTEZUMA
(1519–1521)

tion of the written account (Source 10) and of one of the artistic representations (Source 11), however, reveals other perceptions as well. In the written account, when Montezuma's envoys reported back to him, how did they describe the Europeans (you may use points 1 through 4 above)? What was Montezuma's reaction to the report? The other written and artistic accounts are quite direct, and you should have no difficulty discovering the Indians' overall perception of Europeans. You will, however, have to infer from the accounts how Indians believed Europeans should be dealt with in the future, since none of the written or artistic accounts deals with that question.

⤫ EPILOGUE ⤫

In many respects, the encounter between Cortés and the native peoples of Mexico was typical of many first encounters between Europeans and Native Americans. For one thing, the Indian peoples were terribly vulnerable to the numerous diseases that Europeans unwittingly brought with them. Whether warlike or peaceful, millions of Native Americans fell victim to smallpox, measles, and other diseases against which they had no resistance. Whole villages were wiped out and whole nations decimated as (in the words of one Roman Catholic priest who traveled with Cortés) "they died in heaps."

In addition, Indians were no match for European military technology and modes of warfare. Although many Indian peoples were skillful and courageous warriors, their weaponry was no equal to the European broadsword, pike, musket, or cannon. Moreover, battles between Indian peoples could best be described as skirmishes, in which few lives were lost and several prisoners taken. The Indians could not imagine wholesale slaughtering of their enemies, a practice some Europeans found acceptable as a means of acquiring gold and land. By no means passive peoples in what ultimately would become a contest for a hemisphere, Indians nevertheless had not developed the military technology and tactics to hold Europeans permanently at bay.

Nor were the Indians themselves united against their European intruders. All the explorers and early settlers were able to pit one Indian people against another, thus dividing the opposition and in the end conquering them all. In this practice Cortés was particularly adept; he found a number of villages ready to revolt against Montezuma and used those schisms to his advantage. Brief attempts at Indian unity against European intruders generally proved temporary and therefore unsuccessful.

Sometimes the Native Americans' initial misperceptions of Europeans worked to their own disadvantage. As we have seen, some Central American Indians, including the mighty Aztecs, thought Cortés's men were the "white gods" from the east whom prophets predicted would appear. Cortés's actions quickly disabused them of this notion, but by then much damage had been done. In a somewhat similar vein, Indians of the Powhatan Confederacy in Virginia at first thought the Europeans were indolent because they could not grow their own food. Like the Aztecs' misperception, this mistaken image was soon shattered. In sum, Native Americans' perceptions of Europeans often worked against any notions that they were a threat—until it was too late.

Finally, once Europeans had established footholds in the New World, the Indians often undercut their own positions. For one thing, they rarely were able to unite against the Europeans, fractured as they so often were by intertribal conflicts and jealousies. Therefore, Europeans often were able to enlist Indian allies to fight against those Native Americans who opposed them. Also, after the Indians came to recognize the value of European manufactured goods, they increasingly engaged in wholesale hunting and trapping of animals with the skins and furs Europeans wanted in exchange for those goods. Before the arrival of Europeans, Native Americans saw themselves as part of a complete ecosystem that could sustain all life so long as it was kept in balance. In contrast, Europeans saw the environment as a series of commodities to be exploited, a perception that Indians who desired European goods were quickly forced to adopt. Thus not only did the Indians lose their economic and cultural independence, but they also nearly eliminated certain animal species that had sustained them for so long. An ecological disaster was in the making, driven by the European view of the environment as something to conquer and exploit.

For a number of reasons, Native Americans were extremely vulnerable to the European "invasion" of America. At the same time, however, a major biological "event" was in process that would change life in both the Old World and the New. Called by historians the Columbian exchange, the process involved the transplantation to the New World (sometimes accidentally) of various plants (cabbages, radishes, bananas, wheat, onions, sugar cane), animals (horses, pigs, cattle, sheep, cats), and diseases. At the same time, Europeans returned home with maize, peanuts, squash, sweet potatoes, pumpkins, pineapples, tomatoes, and cocoa. Less beneficial was the possible transportation from the New World to the Old of venereal syphilis. Indeed, some five hundred years later, the Columbian exchange is still going on. In the Great Smoky Mountains of North Carolina and Tennessee, wild boars (imported from Germany in the nineteenth century for sportsmen) threaten the plants, grasses, and small animals of the region. The zebra mussel, released by accident into the Great Lakes in ballast water from Eastern Europe, has spread into the Illinois, Mississippi, Ohio, and Tennessee rivers. An Asian variety of the gypsy moth is chewing its way through the forests of the Pacific Northwest. A recent survey in Olympic National Park has identified 169 species of plants and animals not indigenous to the Western Hemisphere. In the South, the kudzu vine (imported from Japan to combat erosion) was dubbed by the *Los Angeles Times* (July 21, 1992) "the national plant of Dixie." Whether

CHAPTER 1

FIRST
ENCOUNTERS:
THE
CONFRONTATION
BETWEEN
CORTÉS AND
MONTEZUMA
(1519–1521)

purposeful or by accident, whether beneficial or detrimental, the Columbian exchange continues.

Because Europeans ultimately were victorious in their "invasion" of the Western Hemisphere, it is their images of Native Americans that for the most part have survived. Christopher Columbus, who recorded the Europeans' first encounter, depicted Native Americans as innocent, naive children. But he also wrote, "I could conquer the whole of them with fifty men, and govern them as I pleased." For his part, Amerigo Vespucci was less kind, depicting Native Americans as barbarous because "they have no regular time for their meals . . . [and] in making water they are dirty and without shame, for while talking with us they do such things." By placing this badge of inferiority on Indian peoples, most Europeans could justify a number of ways Indians could be dealt with (avoidance, conquest, "civilizing," trading, removal, extermination). Ultimately for the Indian peoples, all methods proved disastrous. Although different European peoples (Spanish,

French, English) often treated Indians differently, in the end the results were the same.

Hernando Cortés returned to Spain in 1528 a fabulously wealthy man. But the ultimate *conquistador* lost most of his fortune in ill-fated expeditions and died in modest circumstances in 1547. In his will, he recognized the four children he had fathered by Native American women while in Mexico (Cortés was married at the time) and worried about the morality of what he had done. In 1562, his body was taken to Mexico to be reburied, but for Hernando Cortés's remains, there would be no rest. In 1794, they were moved again, this time to the chapel of a Mexican hospital that he had endowed. In 1823, Cortés's remains disappeared for good, perhaps as the result of an effort to protect them from politically oriented grave robbers after Mexico declared its independence from Spain. (Rumors abound that they were secretly carried back across the Atlantic, this time to Italy.) The ultimate *conquistador* has vanished, but his legacy lives on.

CHAPTER 2

RHYTHMS OF COLONIAL LIFE:
THE STATISTICS OF
COLONIAL MASSACHUSETTS BAY

∽ THE PROBLEM ∽

An important benefit of studying history is the ability to measure both change over time and people's reactions or adjustments to those changes. Today's world is changing with incredible speed. Recently you probably drove a fuel-injected automobile along an interstate highway while listening to an FM stereo radio station or a cassette tape, exited from the highway for a fast-food snack, continued home and prepared a full meal in a microwave oven, and then watched a film or a previously taped television program on your videocassette recorder or worked with your personal computer. These are all activities that no American could have engaged in thirty years ago. Indeed, we live in a society that expects change, generally welcomes it, and tries to plan for it.

Centuries ago, change took place at a considerably slower pace. Yet change did occur in colonial America, sometimes with what for the colonists must have seemed like startling speed. Colonial Massachusetts Bay was such a society. A child born in that colony in 1650, whether male or female, experienced a profoundly different life from that of a child born in 1750. In some ways, the differences in those two children's lives were dramatic and unwelcome.

What were the differences in the lives of the people of Massachusetts Bay between 1650 and 1750? How can we account for those differences? How might those differences have affected those people's thoughts, attitudes, feelings, and behavior? In this chapter, you will be using statistics to mea-

CHAPTER 2

RHYTHMS OF
COLONIAL LIFE:
THE STATISTICS
OF COLONIAL
MASSACHUSETTS
BAY

sure change over time in colonial Massachusetts Bay and how men, women, and children reacted to and attempted to adapt to those changes. Then, using your historical imagination, you will explain how those changes and adaptations might have affected the emotions and actions of those colonists. More specifically, by the 1760s and early 1770s, an increasing number of Massachusetts Bay colonists were willing to protest and ultimately take up arms against Great Britain. Do the changes in the lives of the people of Massachusetts Bay help explain why these colonists made those momentous decisions?

⨉ BACKGROUND ⨉

The years between the settlement of the colonies and the American Revolution are critical ones in American history. In those years, which in some colonies stretched to more than a century,[1] stability was gradually achieved, economic bases were laid, political institutions were established, social structures and institutions evolved, and intellectual and cultural life eventually thrived. As the population increased and as older settlements matured, new towns and settlements were founded on the edge of the receding wilderness, thus repeating the process of settlement, stability, growth, and maturation. And although most colonists were still tied to England by bonds of language, economics, government, and affection, over the years those bonds gradually loosened until the colonists, many without fully realizing it, had become something distinctly different from simply English men and women who happened to reside in another land. In some ways, then, the American Revolution was the political realization of earlier economic, social, cultural, and political trends and events in colonial life.

These trends and events occurred, with some variations, in all the colonies, especially the Massachusetts Bay colony. Founded in 1630 by Puritans from England, Massachusetts Bay grew rapidly, aided in its first decade by 15,000 to 20,000 immigrants from England, and after that by natural increase.[2] By 1700, Massachusetts Bay's population had risen to almost 56,000 and by 1750, to approximately

1. The following colonies had been in existence for a century or more when the American Revolution broke out in 1775: Virginia, Massachusetts Bay, Rhode Island, Connecticut, Maryland, New York, and New Jersey. Settlements of Europeans also existed in New Hampshire and Delaware areas more than a century before the Revolution, although they did not formally become colonies until later.

2. The outbreak of the English Civil War in 1642 drastically reduced emigration from England to Massachusetts Bay, largely because Puritans in England believed it was important to stay and fight against Charles I. In 1649, when Charles I was deposed and beheaded, a Puritan commonwealth was established in England, which lasted until 1660.

188,000, making it one of Great Britain's most populous North American possessions.

This rapid population growth forced the government of Massachusetts Bay (called the General Court, which included the governor, the deputy governor, the executive council of assistants, and the representatives, all elected annually by the freemen)[3] to organize new towns. Within the first year of settlement, the six original towns of Massachusetts Bay were laid out: Dorchester, Roxbury, Watertown, Newtown (now Cambridge), Charlestown, and Boston, all on the Charles River. By the time Middlesex County (west of Boston) was organized in 1643, there were eight towns in that county alone, and by 1700, there were twenty-two.

The organization of towns was an important way for Puritan leaders to keep control of the rapidly growing population. Unlike settlers in the middle and southern colonies, colonists in Massachusetts Bay could not simply travel to an uninhabited area, select a parcel of land, and receive individual title to the land from the colonial governor. Instead, a group of men who wanted to establish a town had to apply to the General Court for a land grant for the entire town. Leaders of the prospective new town were then selected, and the single church was organized. Having received the grant from the General Court, the new town's leaders apportioned the available land among the male heads of households who were church members, holding in common some land for grazing and other uses (hence the "town common"). In this way, the Puritan leadership retained control of the fast-growing population, ensured Puritan economic and religious domination, and guaranteed that large numbers of dissenters—men and women who might divert the colony from its "holy mission" in the wilderness—would not be attracted to Massachusetts Bay.

Economically, Massachusetts Bay prospered from the very beginning, witnessing no "starving time" as did Virginia. Yet of all the major colonies, Massachusetts Bay fit the least well into England's mercantile system, whereby colonies supplied raw materials to the mother country and in turn purchased the mother country's manufactured products. Because comparatively rocky soil and a short growing season kept crop yields low and agricultural surpluses meager, many people in Massachusetts Bay had to seek other ways of making a living. Many men petitioned the General Court to organize new towns on the frontier; others turned to either the sea as fishermen, traders, shippers, and seamen or native manufacturing enterprises such as iron product manufacturing, rum distilling, shipbuilding, and rope-making. Except for fishing, none of these activities fit into England's mercantile plans for empire, and some undertakings were prohibited outright by the Navigation Acts (1660, 1663, and later, which set up the mercantile system), which most citizens of Massachusetts Bay ignored.

3. A freeman was an adult male who was accepted by his town (hence a landowner) and was a member of the Puritan congregational church.

CHAPTER 2

RHYTHMS OF
COLONIAL LIFE:
THE STATISTICS
OF COLONIAL
MASSACHUSETTS
BAY

The restoration of the English monarchy in 1660 in the person of Charles II greatly concerned the Massachusetts Bay colonists. It was no secret that Charles II loathed Puritanism. The new monarch also made it clear that the Navigation Acts would be enforced. After more than twenty years of wrangling among the colony, the king, and the Lords of Trade, in 1684 the Massachusetts Bay charter was revoked; in 1685, the colony was included in a grand scheme to reorganize the northern colonies into the Dominion of New England, with one royal governor and no elected assembly.[4] The dominion's governor, the undiplomatic Sir Edmund Andros, further alienated Massachusetts Bay colonists by levying taxes on them without consultation or consent, enforcing the Navigation Acts, favoring religious toleration in Massachusetts Bay, and calling their land titles into question. As a result, Massachusetts Bay colonists were only too glad to use the confusion and instability accompanying England's Glorious Revolution of 1688 to stage a bloodless coup that deposed Andros and returned the colony to its original form of government, an act that the mother country ultimately approved. Thus from almost the very beginning, the colonists of Massachusetts Bay were politically aware and jealously guarded their representative government.

Not only were the Massachusetts Bay colonists' political ideas sharp-

ened and refined decades before the American Revolution, but their other ways of thinking also were greatly affected. Two important intellectual movements in Europe, the Enlightenment and the Great Awakening, had an enormous impact in America. The Enlightenment was grounded in the belief that human reason could discover the natural laws that governed the universe, nature, and human affairs; human reason and scientific observation would reveal those natural laws to human beings. Although the Enlightenment's greatest impact was on the well-educated and therefore the wealthier citizens, even the "common" people were affected by it. The Great Awakening was a religious revival that swept through the colonies in the 1740s and 1750s. Touched off by English preacher George Whitefield, the Great Awakening emphasized humanity's utter sinfulness and need for salvation. In hundreds of emotional revival meetings, complete with shouting, moaning, and physical gyrations, thousands were converted. Because the Great Awakening undermined the traditional churches and their leaders, most clergymen (called "Old Lights") opposed the movement, but to little avail.

On the surface, the Enlightenment and the Great Awakening seemed to have nothing in common. The Enlightenment emphasized human reason, whereas the Great Awakening appealed more to emotion than to reason. Both movements, however, contained a strong streak of individualism: The Enlightenment emphasized the potential of the human mind, and the Great Awakening concentrated on

4. The Dominion of New England included the colonies of New Jersey, New York, Connecticut, Rhode Island, Plymouth, and Massachusetts Bay, which included lands that later became New Hampshire and Maine.

the individual soul. Each movement in its own way increased the colonists' sense of themselves as individuals who possessed both individual rights and individual futures. The colonists who once huddled together for protection and mutual assistance in tiny settlements had, by the mid-eighteenth century, grown, changed, and matured, as had the settlements they had built. They harbored new attitudes about themselves, their society, their individual futures, and, almost inevitably, their government. Hence the life and thought of a Massachusetts Bay colonist (or, indeed, any other colonist) born in 1750 was profoundly different from that of one born in 1650.

When most people think of the colonial period in America, they invariably think of the colonial leaders, men and women who held the economic, social, and political reins of the society. But these leaders—the John Winthrops and Anne Hutchinsons, the Jonathan Edwardses and Benjamin Franklins, the William Penns and Nathaniel Bacons—represent only a tiny fraction of the men and women who lived in the colonies between 1607 and 1775. And yet to understand the processes of growth, change, and maturation fully, it is necessary for us to study the lives of the "ordinary" men, women, and children, as well as those of their economic, social, and political "betters." How did the processes of growth, change, and maturation affect small farmers and artisans and their spouses, sons, and daughters? How did the situations of these people change over time? How did they react to those changes? Indeed, if we can learn more about the lives of all Americans, not just those of the prominent colonists, we will be able to understand better the extent to which growth, change, and maturation helped effect the American Revolution.

It is considerably easier to collect information about the leading colonial figures than the "average" men and women. Few of the farmers, artisans, or laborers left diaries or letters to provide clues to their thoughts and behavior; fewer made speeches or participated in decision making; fewer still talked with leaders like Washington and Jefferson, so their thoughts and actions were much less likely to be recorded for us by others. In some ways, then, a curtain has been drawn across a large part of American colonial history, obscuring the lives, thoughts, and feelings of the vast majority of the colonists. Sometimes even their names have been lost.

∽ THE METHOD ∾

How can we hope to reconstruct the lives, thoughts, and feelings of people who left no letters, diaries, sermons, speeches, or votes for us to analyze? Recently, historians have become more imaginative in using the relatively limited records at their disposal to examine the lives of ordinary men, women, and children who lived during the colonial period. Almost every per-

CHAPTER 2

RHYTHMS OF
COLONIAL LIFE:
THE STATISTICS
OF COLONIAL
MASSACHUSETTS
BAY

Table 1

Type of Record	Questions
Census	Is the population growing, shrinking, or stationary? Is the ratio of males to females roughly equal?[5] Does that ratio change over time?
Marriage	At what age are women marrying? Is that age changing over time?
Wills, probate	How are estates divided? Is that method changing over time? Based on real estate and personal property listed, is the collective standard of living rising, falling, or stationary? Based on dates of death, is the population living longer?
Land, tax	What percentage of the adult male population owns land? Is that percentage changing over time? Is the land evenly distributed among the adult male population?

son, even the poorest, left some record that she or he existed. That person's name may appear in any of a number of records, including church records stating when she or he was baptized, marriage records, property-holding records, civil- or criminal-court records, military records, tax records, and death or cemetery records. It is in these records that the lives of the ordinary men, women, and children of colonial America can be examined. An increasing number of historians have been carefully scrutinizing those records to re-create the lives and attitudes of those who left no other evidence.

How is this done? Most historians interested in the lives of the ordinary colonists rely heavily on statistics. Instead of trying to uncover all the rec-

ords relating to one person or family (which might not be representative of the whole population), these historians use statistics to create *collective biographies*—that is, biographies of population groups (farmers in Andover, Massachusetts, for example) rather than biographies of certain individuals. The historians collect all (or a sample of all) the birth, death, and marriage records of a community and look at all (or a sample of all) the wills, probate records,[6] tax and landholding records, and census data. These historians are forming an aggregate or collective picture of a community and how that community has changed over time. Are women marrying later? What percentage of women remain unmarried? Are women having fewer children than they were in another time? Are inheritance patterns (the methods of dividing estates among heirs) changing over time? Are farms

5. Because males and females are born in roughly equal numbers, an unequal ratio of males to females (called a sex ratio) must be explained by events such as wars, out-migration, in-migration, or differing mortality rates for males and females.

6. Probate records are public records of processed wills.

increasing or decreasing in size? To the historian, each statistical summary of records (each set of statistics or *aggregate* picture) contains information that increases understanding of the community being studied.

After the statistics are compiled, what does the historian do next? Each set of statistics is examined separately to see what changes are occurring over time. Table 1 shows the types of questions historians ask of several different types of records.

Having examined each set of statistics, the historian places the sets in some logical order, which may vary depending on the available evidence, the central questions the historian is attempting to answer, and the historian's own preferences. Some historians prefer a "birth-to-death" ordering, beginning with age-at-marriage statistics for females and moving chronologically through the collective life of the community's population. Others prefer to isolate the demographic statistical sets (birth, marriage, migration, and death) from the economic sets (such as landholding and division of estates).

Up to this point, the historian has (1) collected the statistics and arranged them into sets, (2) examined each set and measured tendencies or changes over time, and (3) arranged the sets in some logical order. Now the historian must begin asking "why" for each set. For example:

1. Why does the method of dividing estates change over time?
2. Why are women marrying later?
3. Why are premarital pregnancies increasing?

In many cases, the answer to each question (and other "why" questions) is in one of the other statistical sets. That may cause the historian to alter his or her ordering of the sets to make the story clearer.

The historian is actually linking the sets to one another to form a chain. When two sets have been linked (because one set answers the "why" question of another set), the historian repeats the process until all the sets have been linked to form one chain of evidence. At that point, the historian can summarize the tendencies that have been discovered and, if desired, can connect those trends or tendencies with other events occurring in the period, such as the American Revolution.

One example of how historians link statistical sets together to answer the question "why" is sufficient. Source 1 in the Evidence section shows that the white population growth in Massachusetts Bay was extremely rapid between 1660 and 1770 (the growth rate actually approximates those of many non-Western developing nations today). How can we account for this rapid growth? Look at Source 4, which deals with the survival rate of children born in the town of Andover between 1640 and 1759. Note that between 1640 and 1699, the survival rate was very high (in Sweden between 1751 and 1799, 50 percent of the children born did not reach the age of fifteen). Also examine Source 16, the average number of births per marriage in Andover. Note that between 1655 and 1704, the average number of births per marriage was very high—between 5.3 and 7.6. Thus we can conclude that

CHAPTER 2

RHYTHMS OF
COLONIAL LIFE:
THE STATISTICS
OF COLONIAL
MASSACHUSETTS
BAY

the population grew so rapidly in Massachusetts Bay between 1660 and 1700 because women gave birth to large numbers of children *and* a high percentage of those children survived. By following this process, you will be able to link together all the statistical sets.

Occasionally, however, you will need more information than statistics (some of which are unavailable) can provide. For example, notice in Sources 1 and 2 that the average annual growth rates were generally declining but there was a sharp *increase* in the population growth rates in the 1720s. This increase cannot be explained by the statistics in Sources 4 and 16, so another reason must be found. In fact, beginning in 1713, the number of religious dissenters who immigrated to Massachusetts Bay from Great Britain increased significantly, due to the end of intermittent warfare and to crop failures in northern Ireland. That swelling of immigration lasted for only about twenty years, after which it once again subsided. The town of Andover was host (albeit unwillingly) to some of those immigrants. Thus you can see that population increases in Massachusetts Bay and in Andover between 1713 and 1740 were the results of natural increase *plus* a temporary jump in immigration. If you have similar problems with other statistical sets, consult your instructor for assistance.

Remember that we are dealing with a society that was not as statistically oriented as ours. Several of the statistics you would like to have simply are not obtainable. The statistics we do have, however, provide a fascinating window for us to observe the lives of "ordinary" men, women, and children who lived centuries ago.

In this chapter, you will be using the statistics provided to identify important trends affecting the men, women, and children of Massachusetts Bay in the century preceding the American Revolution. Use the process described below:

1. Examine each statistical set, especially for a change over time.
2. Ask why that change took place.
3. Find the answer in another set, thereby establishing a linkage.
4. Repeat the process until all the sets have been linked together.
5. Then ask the central questions: What important trends affected the men, women, and children of colonial Massachusetts Bay in the century preceding the American Revolution? How were people likely to think and feel about those trends? Finally, how might those trends have contributed to the decision of Massachusetts Bay colonists to revolt against Great Britain?

As you will see, most of the statistical sets deal with Concord and Andover, two older towns in the Massachusetts Bay colony (see the following map). These two towns were chosen because historians Robert Gross and Philip Greven collected much statistical information about Concord and Andover, respectively; we have arranged the data in tabular form. Evidence suggests that these two towns are fairly representative of other towns in the eastern part of the colony. Concord, a farm town founded in 1635, was the first town in Massachu-

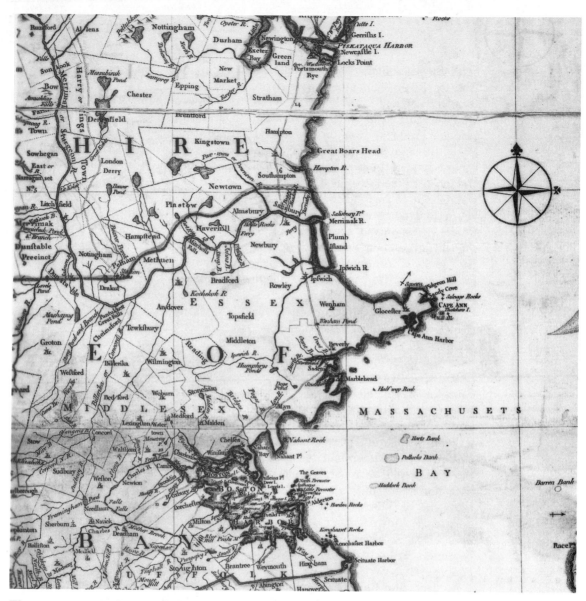

The eastern part of Massachusetts Bay colony, 1755. Reproduced from Thomas Jefferys's "A Map of the Most Inhabited Part of New England, Containing the Provinces of Massachusetts Bay, and New Hampshire, with the Colonies of Connecticut and Rhode Island. November 29, 1755"; in Jefferys's *A General Topography of North America and the West Indies* (London, 1768); courtesy of the Map Division, The New York Public Library, Astor, Lenox and Tilden Foundations.

CHAPTER 2

RHYTHMS OF
COLONIAL LIFE:
THE STATISTICS
OF COLONIAL
MASSACHUSETTS
BAY

setts Bay established away from the Charles River. The area was rich in furs, and settlers initially were able to trap the furs (especially beaver) for income. Andover was organized in 1646, the original settlers mainly from other towns in the colony. In Andover, the people lived in the village and walked out to farm their land, which was organized in the open-field system (landowners owned several strips of land in large open fields and worked the fields in common). In Concord, many settlers lived outside the village and near the fields, building clusters of houses along the Concord River (which was spanned by the soon-to-be-famous Old North Bridge).

As you examine the statistical sets from these two towns, note that the dates for the sets do not always match. Understand both *what* you are examining and *when* that particular factor is being measured. For example, the statistical set on premarital conceptions in Andover records that phenomenon from 1655 to 1739, whereas the same phenomenon in Concord is measured from 1740 to 1774 (see Source 17). Assuming that this trend is similar in both towns, how would you use those two sets of statistics?

At first the statistics appear cold and impersonal and seem to tell us little that is worth knowing. But we cannot just skip this problem and get on to the political events leading up to the American Revolution (such as the Boston Massacre) and the important battles of the Revolution. It is crucial

to remember that some of the men and boys who were on the streets of Boston on the evening of March 5, 1770, are counted in these statistics. And some of the men who participated in the Battles of Lexington and Concord also appear in these statistics. Are there any links between what the statistics represent and the subsequent behaviors of these people? Remember that in this chapter you are dealing not with numbers but with *people:* men, women, and children who had hopes, dreams, problems, and fears not unlike some of your own.

Working with historical statistics is not so difficult as it may first appear. Often it is helpful to establish a small study group with a few of your classmates, if your instructor permits it. As the study group talks through the problem, each individual can contribute something that possibly the other members of the group did not see, thereby broadening the group's understanding of the problem. Analyzing statistics is a challenging undertaking, but the results can be immensely satisfying, as you come to "see" the *people* the statistics represent.

You are bombarded almost daily with statistics—about teen pregnancies, inflation rates, illegal drug use, political polling results, and just about any other subject you can think of. In order to refer to yourself as a truly educated person, you must be able to analyze and understand these numbers, some of which are critical to your own life.

∽ THE EVIDENCE ∽

Source 1 reprinted from U.S. Bureau of the Census, *Historical Statistics of the United States, Colonial Times to 1957* (Washington, D.C.: U.S. Government Printing Office, 1960), p. 756.

1. Growth of White Population, Massachusetts Bay, 1660–1770.

Year	Population	Average Annual Growth Rate (%)
1660	20,082	—
1670	30,000	4.9
1680	39,752	3.3
1690	49,504	2.5
1700	55,941	1.3
1710	62,390	1.2
1720	91,008	4.6
1730	114,116	2.6
1740	151,613	3.3
1750	188,000	2.4
1760	222,600	1.8
1770	235,308	.57

Source 2 data from Philip J. Greven, Jr., *Four Generations: Population, Land, and Family in Colonial Andover, Massachusetts* (Ithaca, N.Y.: Cornell University Press, 1970), p. 179.

2. Growth of White Population, Town of Andover, 1680–1776.

Year	Population	Average Annual Growth Rate (%)
1680	435	—
1685	600	7.6
1695	710	1.8
1705	945	3.3
1715	1,050	1.1
1725	1,305	2.4
1735	1,630	2.5
1745	1,845	1.3
1755	2,135	1.6
1764	2,442	1.6
1776	2,953	1.8

CHAPTER 2

RHYTHMS OF
COLONIAL LIFE:
THE STATISTICS
OF COLONIAL
MASSACHUSETTS
BAY

Source 3 data from Robert A. Gross, *The Minutemen and Their World* (New York: Hill and Wang, 1976), p. 15.

3. Growth of Population, Town of Concord, 1679–1750.

Year	Population	Average Annual Growth Rate (%)
1679	480	—
1706	920	3.3
1710	c. 1,000	2.2
1725	c. 1,500	3.3
1750	c. 2,000	1.3

Sources 4 through 6 data from Greven, *Four Generations: Population, Land, and Family in Colonial Andover, Massachusetts,* pp. 191, 189, 177. Source 6 data also from Gross, *The Minutemen and Their World,* p. 209.

4. Children Born Between 1640 and 1759 Who Lived to at Least Age 10, Andover.

Years	Rate
1640–1669	917 per 1,000
1670–1699	855 per 1,000
1700–1729	805 per 1,000
1730–1759	695 per 1,000

5. Children Who Died Before Reaching Age 20, Andover, 1670–1759.

Years	Number	Mortality Rate[7]
1670–1699	87	225 per 1,000
1700–1729	206	381 per 1,000
1730–1759	142	534 per 1,000

7. The mortality rate is the ratio of the number of deaths per thousand people. It is used to compare the deaths in two or more populations of unequal size, such as those of Andover and Boston.

6. Population Density (persons per square mile), Concord and Andover, 1705–1776 (various years).

Year	Concord	Andover
1705		16.0
1706	14.7	
1754	44.2[8]	
1755		36.2
1764		41.0
1765	48.0	
1776	62.7	50.0

8. In 1729, the town of Bedford was formed from lands originally in Concord. Then, in 1735, the town of Acton was created from lands that had been part of Concord. Finally, in 1754, the town of Lincoln was set off from Concord. These losses of lands were taken into account when computing population density for 1754, 1765, and 1776.

CHAPTER 2

RHYTHMS OF
COLONIAL LIFE:
THE STATISTICS
OF COLONIAL
MASSACHUSETTS
BAY

Source 7 data from James A. Henretta, *The Evolution of American Society,
1700–1815: An Interdisciplinary Approach,* 1st ed. (Lexington, Mass.: D. C.
Heath, 1973), p. 15.

7. Average New England Farm Size, 1650s and 1750s.

1650s: 200–300 acres (3–6 percent cultivated)
1750s: Under 100 acres (10–15 percent cultivated)

Sources 8 through 10 data from Gross, *The Minutemen and Their World,*
pp. 210, 215, 214.

8. Average Landholding, Concord, 1663 and 1749.

Year	Amount of Land
1663	259 acres
1749	56 acres

9. Crop Yields per Acre, Concord, 1749 and 1771.

Year	Grain	Hay
1749	13.2 bushels	0.82 ton
1771	12.2 bushels	0.71 ton

10. Amount of Land Necessary to Pasture One Cow, Concord, 1749 and 1771.

Year	Average
1749	1.4
1771	2.2

Source 11 data from Henretta, *The Evolution of American Society*, p. 19.

11. Average Period of Fallow,[9] New England Farms, 1650 and 1770.

1650: Field left fallow between 7 and 15 years
1770: Field left fallow between 1 and 2 years

Source 12 data from Greven, *Four Generations: Population, Land, and Family in Colonial Andover, Massachusetts*, p. 216.

12. Abbot Family, Andover, Massachusetts, 1650 and 1750.

1650: George Abbot was only adult male Abbot
1750: 25 adult male Abbots in Andover

Source 13 data from Henretta, *The Evolution of American Society*, pp. 29–30.

13. Division of Estates, Andover, Massachusetts.[10]

First generation: 95 percent of all estates divided among all male heirs
Second generation: 75 percent of all estates divided among all male heirs
Third generation: 58 percent of all estates divided among all male heirs
Fourth generation (came to maturity after 1750): under 50 percent of all
  estates divided among all male heirs

Source 14 from Gross, *The Minutemen and Their World*, p. 216.

14. Insolvent Estates, Concord, 1740–1774.

Years	Total Estates	Number of Insolvent Estates
1740–1760	19	1
1760–1774	30	11

9. Fallow land is plowed and tilled but left unseeded during a growing season. Land is left fallow to replenish the soil's nutrients. Colonial farmers as a rule did not use fertilizer.
10. A widow inherited her late husband's estate only if the couple had no male heirs (sons). Otherwise, the land was passed down to the sons. Daughters received personal property (money, silverware, livestock, etc.).

CHAPTER 2

RHYTHMS OF
COLONIAL LIFE:
THE STATISTICS
OF COLONIAL
MASSACHUSETTS
BAY

Sources 15 through 17 data from Greven, *Four Generations: Population, Land, and Family in Colonial Andover, Massachusetts,* pp. 33, 23, 105, 183, 113. Source 17 data also from Gross, *The Minutemen and Their World,* p. 217.

15. Average Age at Marriage for Females, Andover, 1650–1724.

Year	Age
1650–1654	18.0
1660–1664	18.8
1670–1674	20.4
1680–1684	21.6
1690–1694	21.6
1700–1704	21.0
1710–1714	24.0
1720–1724	23.9

16. Average Births per Marriage, Andover, 1655–1764.

Year	Births
1655–1664	5.8
1665–1674	5.3
1675–1684	5.7
1685–1694	6.0
1695–1704	7.6
1705–1714	7.5
1715–1724	5.7
1725–1734	4.8
1735–1744	4.1
1745–1754	4.0
1755–1764	3.9

17. Percentage of Premarital Conceptions,[11] Andover, 1655–1739, and Concord, 1740–1774.

Years	Andover	Concord
1655–1674	0.0	
1675–1699	7.0	
1700–1739	11.3	
1740–1749		19
1750–1759		26
1760–1774		41

11. *Premarital conceptions* refers to first-born children who were born less than nine months from the date of marriage.

Source 18 data from Gary B. Nash, "Urban Wealth and Poverty in Pre-Revolutionary America," *Journal of Interdisciplinary History*, 6 (Spring 1976), pp. 545–584.

18. Percentage of Group Migration[12] into Boston, 1747, 1759, and 1771.

Group	1747	1759	1771
Single men	3.0%	8.5%	23.4%
Single women	4.0	16.8	20.0
Widows and widowers	7.9	8.9	4.4
Married couples	33.6	27.4	27.5
Children	51.5	38.4	24.7
	100.0%	100.0%	100.0%

Source 19 data from Gross, *The Minutemen and Their World*, p. 218.

19. Sex Ratio, Concord, 1765.

88 males to 100 females

Sources 20 through 22 data from Nash, "Urban Wealth and Poverty in Pre-Revolutionary America," pp. 545–584.

20. Distribution of Wealth by Percentage[13] in Boston, 1687 and 1771.

Wealth Distribution	1687	1771
Wealth possessed by the richest 5% of the people	30.2	48.7
Wealth possessed by the next wealthiest 5% of the people	16.1	14.7
Wealth possessed by the next wealthiest 30% of the people	39.8	27.4
Wealth possessed by the next wealthiest 30% of the people	11.3	9.1
Wealth possessed by the poorest 30% of the people	2.6	0.1

12. *Migration* refers to internal migration, not emigration from Europe.
13. See Questions to Consider for assistance in reading this source.

CHAPTER 2

RHYTHMS OF
COLONIAL LIFE:
THE STATISTICS
OF COLONIAL
MASSACHUSETTS
BAY

21. Taxables[14] in Boston, 1728–1771.

Year	Population	Taxables
1728	12,650	c. 3,000
1733	15,100	c. 3,500
1735	16,000	3,637
1738	16,700	3,395
1740	16,800	3,043
1741	16,750	2,972
1745	16,250	2,660
1750	15,800	c. 2,400
1752	15,700	2,789
1756	15,650	c. 2,500
1771	15,500	2,588

22. Poor Relief in Boston, 1700–1775.

Years	Population	Average Annual Expenditure in Pounds Sterling	Expenditure in Pounds Sterling per 1,000 Population
1700–1710	7,500	173	23
1711–1720	9,830	181	18
1721–1730	11,840	273	23
1731–1740	15,850	498	31
1741–1750	16,240	806	50
1751–1760	15,660	1,204	77
1761–1770	15,520	1,909	123
1771–1775	15,500	2,478	156

∞ QUESTIONS TO CONSIDER ∞

When using statistics, first look at each set individually. For each set, ask the following questions:

1. What does this set of statistics measure?
2. How does what is being measured change over time?

14. *Taxables* refers to the number of people who owned a sufficient amount of property (real estate and buildings) to be taxed.

3. Why does that change take place? As noted, the answer to this question can be found in another set or sets. When you connect one set to another, statisticians say that you have made a *linkage*.

A helpful way of examining the statistical sets is to think of three children born in Massachusetts Bay: one in 1650, a second in 1700, and the third in 1750. As you look at the statistical evidence, ask yourself how the lives of these three children (male or female) were different. What factors accounted for those differences?

Begin by examining Sources 1 through 3, which deal with population increase in Massachusetts Bay as a whole, in Andover, and in Concord. How did population growth change over time? How can Sources 4, 5, 15, and 16 help you answer the "why" question for population growth?

Because immigration to Massachusetts Bay from Europe declined drastically in the 1640s and did not resume significantly until the early 1700s, population increases in the period in between can be explained only by migration from other colonies (which was negligible) or by natural increase. How did natural increase change over time (Sources 4, 5, and 16)? How would you explain this change? To answer that question, you will have to use your historical imagination as well as *all* the rest of the sources. For example, how might you explain the dramatic increase in child mortality, as seen in Sources 4 and 5? Look again at Sources 6 through 12 and Source 14, this time with that specific question in mind. As you now see, the same statistics can be used to answer different questions.

We can see that one result of population growth in Andover and Concord was a rise in population density. What were the *results* of that increase in population density? Begin by examining Sources 6 through 11. How did farming change over time? Why was this so (see earlier sources plus Source 12, on the Abbot family)? How did

those changes affect the division of estates (Source 13) and the number of insolvent estates (Source 14), and why? Did economic changes have any effect on the female life cycle? Consider the following demographic changes: the average age at marriage for Andover females (Source 15), the number of births per marriage (Source 16), and the significant increase in premarital conceptions (Source 17).

At this point, it helps to pause and take stock of what you have learned. What was the relationship between population growth and farming? Between changes in farming and social conditions? Would you say that the lifestyle of Massachusetts Bay colonists was improving, declining, or stationary during the first century of the colony's history? How would you prove your answer?

As noted at the beginning of this chapter, one important factor that historians study is the ability of people to adapt to changes in their environment or circumstances. In your view, how were Massachusetts Bay colonists attempting to adapt to these changes? Would you say they were or were not successful?

Many of the people we have been examining chose to adapt by leaving their towns and migrating to the frontier to set up new communities where they could make fresh starts. Many others, however, adapted by migrating to Boston (Source 18). How could you prove this? How did migration to Boston change in character between 1747 and 1771? How did migration affect the towns from which these people migrated (see Source 19)? What were the likely results of that migration?

CHAPTER 2

RHYTHMS OF
COLONIAL LIFE:
THE STATISTICS
OF COLONIAL
MASSACHUSETTS
BAY

Our attention now should follow those migrants to Boston. Were these migrants able to improve their collective situation in that large seaport? How could you prove your answer to that question?

At this point, we are at Source 20, wealth distribution in Boston. Note that Boston was not a farming village like Andover and Concord. Read the set this way: the richest 5 percent of those living in Boston in 1687 owned 30.2 percent of the town's taxable wealth (essentially real estate and buildings), but by 1771 the richest 5 percent owned 48.7 percent of the town's taxable wealth; the poorest 30 percent of those living in Boston in 1687 owned 2.6 percent of the town's taxable wealth, but by 1771 the poorest 30 percent owned 0.1 percent of the town's taxable wealth. Read the chart the same way for the groups in between. As you examine the chart, note which groups were gaining in wealth and which groups were losing in wealth.

Sources 21 and 22 are different ways of looking at the same problem. How are those sources related to one another? How can you link them back to the chain you have made?

At this point, you should be able to answer these central questions:

1. What important trends regarding growth, change, and maturation affected the people of colonial Massachusetts Bay?
2. How were people likely to think and feel about those trends?
3. How might those trends have contributed to the decision of Massachusetts Bay colonists to revolt against Great Britain?

⬅ EPILOGUE ➡

Many of the men who fought on the Patriot side in either Continental Line (the troops under the central government) or the Massachusetts Bay militia came from the towns, farms, and seaports of Massachusetts Bay. If asked why they would endure hardships to fight against the mother country, most probably would have said that they were fighting for liberty and independence—and undoubtedly they were. But we now realize that a number of other factors were present that may very well have provided strong reasons for these men to contest the British. Whether they fully understood these forces can never be known with certainty because very few left any written record that might help us comprehend their thoughts or behavior.

The American Revolution was a momentous event not just for Americans but ultimately for many other people as well. As Ralph Waldo Emerson wrote years later, it was a "shot heard 'round the world." The American Revolution was the first anticolonial rebellion that was successful on the first try, and as such it provided a model for others in Latin America and elsewhere. As a revolt against authority, the American Revolution made many European rulers tremble because if the ideas contained in the Declaration of Independence (especially that of the right of revolution against unjust rulers) ever became widespread, their own tenures might well be doomed. And, beginning with the French Revolution, this is precisely what happened; gradually, crowns began to topple all across the Continent. Indeed, many would have agreed with the Frenchman Turgot, who, writing of America in the 1780s, noted the following:

> This people is the hope of the human race. It may become the model. It ought to show the world, by facts, that men can be free and yet peaceful, and may dispense with the chains in which tyrants and knaves . . . have presumed to bind them. . . . The Americans should be an example of political, religious, commercial and industrial liberty. The asylum they offer to the oppressed of every nation, the avenue of escape they open, will compel governments to be just and enlightened.[15]

The Revolution obviously brought independence and in the long run became one of the significant events in world history. But did it alter or reverse the economic and social trends that, as we have seen, were affecting the men, women, and children of colonial New England? In 1818, the U.S. Congress passed an act providing pensions for impoverished veterans of the War of Independence and their widows. Congressmen believed that there were approximately 1,400 poor veterans and widows who were still alive. Yet an astounding 30,000 applied for pensions, 20,000 of whom were ultimately approved to receive these benefits. Clearly, the American Revolution, although an event that had worldwide significance, did not necessarily change the lives of all the men and women who participated in it. Or did it?

15. Richard Price, *Observations on the Importance of the American Revolution, and the Means of Making It a Benefit to the World* (London: printed for T. Cadell, 1785), pp. 102, 123.

CHAPTER 3

WHAT REALLY HAPPENED IN THE BOSTON MASSACRE? THE TRIAL OF CAPTAIN THOMAS PRESTON

⤷ THE PROBLEM ⤶

On the chilly evening of March 5, 1770, a small group of boys began taunting a British sentry (called a "Centinel" or "Sentinel") in front of the Boston Custom House. Pushed to the breaking point by this goading, the soldier struck one of his tormentors with his musket. Soon a crowd of fifty or sixty gathered around the frightened soldier, prompting him to call for help. The officer of the day, Captain Thomas Preston, and seven British soldiers hurried to the Custom House to protect the sentry.

Upon arriving at the Custom House, Captain Preston must have sensed how precarious his position was. The crowd had swelled to more than one hundred, some anxious for a fight, others simply curiosity seekers, and still others called from their homes by the town's church bells, a traditional signal that a fire had broken out. Efforts by Preston and others to calm the crowd proved useless. And because the crowd had enveloped Preston and his men as it had the lone sentry, escape was nearly impossible.

What happened next is a subject of considerable controversy. One of the soldiers fired his musket into the crowd, and the others followed suit, one by one. The colonists scattered, leaving five dead[1] and six wounded, some of whom were probably innocent bystanders. Preston and his men

1. Those killed were Crispus Attucks (a black seaman in his forties, who also went by the name of Michael Johnson), James Caldwell

quickly returned to their barracks, where they were placed under house arrest. They were later taken to jail and charged with murder.

Preston's trial began on October 24, 1770, delayed by the authorities in an attempt to cool the emotions of the townspeople. Soon after the March 5 event, however, a grand jury had taken sworn depositions from Preston, the soldiers, and more than ninety Bostonians. The depositions leaked out (in a pamphlet, probably published by anti-British extremists), helping to keep emotions at a fever pitch.

John Adams, Josiah Quincy, and Robert Auchmuty had agreed to defend Preston,[2] even though the first two were staunch Patriots. They believed that the captain was entitled to a fair trial and did their best to defend him. After a difficult jury selection,

the trial began, witnesses for the prosecution and the defense being called mostly from those who had given depositions to the grand jury. The trial lasted for four days, an unusually long trial for the times. The case went to the jury at 5:00 P.M. on October 29. Although it took the jury only three hours to reach a verdict, the decision was not announced until the following day.

In this chapter, you will be using portions of the evidence given at the murder trial of Captain Thomas Preston to reconstruct what actually happened on that March 5, 1770, evening in Boston, Massachusetts. Was Preston guilty as charged? Or was he innocent? Only by reconstructing the event that we call the Boston Massacre will you be able to answer these questions.

∽ BACKGROUND ∾

The town of Boston[3] had been uneasy throughout the first weeks of 1770. Tension had been building since the early 1760s because the town was increasingly affected by the forces of migration, change, and maturation. The protests against the Stamp Act had been particularly bitter there, and men such as Samuel Adams were encouraging their fellow Bostonians to be even bolder in their remonstrances. In response, in 1768 the British government ordered two regiments of soldiers to Boston to restore order and enforce the laws of Parliament. "They will not *find* a rebellion," quipped Benjamin Franklin of the soldiers,

---

(a sailor), Patrick Carr (an immigrant from Ireland who worked as a leather-breeches maker), Samuel Gray (a rope-maker), and Samuel Maverick (a seventeen-year-old apprentice).

2. Adams, Quincy, and Auchmuty (pronounced Aŭk′mŭty) also were engaged to defend the soldiers, a practice that would not be allowed today because of the conflict of interest (defending more than one person charged with the same crime).

3. Although Boston was one of the largest urban centers in the colonies, the town was

not incorporated as a city. Several attempts were made, but residents opposed them, fearing they would lose the institution of the town meeting.

CHAPTER 3

WHAT REALLY
HAPPENED IN
THE BOSTON
MASSACRE?
THE TRIAL OF
CAPTAIN
THOMAS
PRESTON

"they may indeed *make* one" (italics added).

Instead of bringing calm to Boston, the presence of soldiers only increased tensions. Incidents between Bostonians and redcoats were common on the streets, in taverns, and at the places of employment of British soldiers who sought part-time jobs to supplement their meager salaries. Known British sympathizers and informers were harassed, and Crown officials were openly insulted. Indeed, the town of Boston seemed to be a powder keg just waiting for a spark to set off an explosion.

On February 22, 1770, British sympathizer and informer Ebenezer Richardson tried to tear down an anti-British sign. He was followed to his house by an angry crowd that proceeded to taunt him and break his windows with stones. One of the stones struck Richardson's wife. Enraged, he grabbed a musket and fired almost blindly into the crowd. Eleven-year-old Christopher Seider[4] fell to the ground with eleven pellets of shot in his chest. The boy died eight hours later. The crowd, by now numbering about one thousand, dragged Richardson from his house and through the streets, finally delivering him to the Boston jail. Four days later, the town conducted a huge funeral for Christopher Seider, probably arranged and organized by Samuel Adams. Seider's casket was carried through the streets by children, and approximately two thousand mourners (one-seventh of Boston's total population) took part.

All through the next week Boston was an angry town. Gangs of men and boys roamed the streets at night looking for British soldiers foolish enough to venture out alone. Similarly, off-duty soldiers prowled the same streets looking for someone to challenge them. A fight broke out at a ropewalk between some soldiers who worked there part time and some unemployed colonists.

With large portions of both the Boston citizenry and the British soldiers inflamed, an incident on March 5 touched off an ugly confrontation that took place in front of the Custom House, a symbol of British authority over the colonies. Both sides sought to use the event to support their respective causes. But Samuel Adams, a struggling attorney with a flair for politics and propaganda, clearly had the upper hand. The burial of the five "martyrs" was attended by almost every resident of Boston, and Adams used the event to push his demands for British troop withdrawal and to heap abuse on the mother country. Therefore, when the murder trial of Captain Thomas Preston finally opened in late October, emotions had hardly diminished.

Crowd disturbances had been an almost regular feature of life, in both England and America. Historian John Bohstedt has estimated that England was the scene of at least one thousand crowd disturbances and riots between 1790 and 1810.[5] Colonial American towns were no more placid; demonstrations and riots were almost regular features of the colonists' lives. De-

---

4. Christopher Seider is sometimes referred to as Christopher Snider.

5. John Bohstedt, *Riots and Community Politics in England and Wales, 1790–1810* (Cambridge, Mass.: Harvard University Press, 1983), p. 5.

struction of property and burning of effigies were common in these disturbances. In August 1765 in Boston, for example, crowds protesting against the Stamp Act burned effigies and destroyed the homes of stamp distributor Andrew Oliver and Massachusetts Lieutenant Governor Thomas Hutchinson. Indeed, it was almost as if the entire community was willing to countenance demonstrations and riots as long as they were confined to parades, loud gatherings, and limited destruction of property. In almost no cases were there any deaths, and the authorities seldom fired on the crowds. Yet on March 5, 1770, both the crowd and the soldiers acted uncharacteristically. The result was the tragedy that colonists dubbed the "Boston Massacre." Why did the crowd and the soldiers behave as they did?

To repeat, your task is to reconstruct the so-called Boston Massacre so as to understand what really happened on that fateful evening. Spelling and punctuation in the evidence have been modernized only to clarify the meaning.

⟨⟩ THE METHOD ⟨⟩

Many students (and some historians) like to think that facts speak for themselves. This is especially tempting when analyzing a single incident like the Boston Massacre, many eyewitnesses of which testified at the trial. However, discovering what really happened, even when there are eyewitnesses, is never quite that easy. Witnesses may be confused at the time, they may see only part of the incident, or they may unconsciously "see" only what they expect to see. Obviously, witnesses also may have some reasons to lie. Thus the testimony of witnesses must be carefully scrutinized, for both what the witnesses *mean* to tell us and other relevant information as well. Therefore, historians approach such testimony with considerable skepticism and are concerned not only with the testimony itself but also with the possible motives of the witnesses.

Neither Preston nor the soldiers testified at the captain's trial because English legal custom prohibited defendants in criminal cases from testifying in their own behalf (the expectation was that they would perjure themselves). One week after the massacre, however, in a sworn deposition, or statement, Captain Preston gave his side of the story. Although the deposition was not introduced at the trial and therefore the jury was not aware of what Preston himself had said, we have reproduced a portion of Preston's deposition for you to examine. How does Preston's deposition agree or disagree with other eyewitnesses' accounts?

No transcript of Preston's trial survives, if indeed one was ever made.

CHAPTER 3

WHAT REALLY
HAPPENED IN
THE BOSTON
MASSACRE?
THE TRIAL OF
CAPTAIN
THOMAS
PRESTON

Trial testimony comes from an anonymous person's summary of what each person said, the notes of Robert Treat Paine (one of the lawyers for the prosecution), and one witness's (Richard Palmes's) reconstruction of what his testimony and the cross-examination had been. Although historians would prefer to use the original trial transcript and would do so if one were available, the anonymous summary, Paine's notes, and one witness's recollections are acceptable substitutes because probably all three people were present in the courtroom (Paine and Palmes certainly were) and the accounts tend to corroborate one another.

Almost all the witnesses were at the scene, yet not all their testimony is of equal merit. First try to reconstruct the scene itself: the actual order in which the events occurred and where the various participants were standing. Whenever possible, look for corroborating testimony: two or more reliable witnesses who heard or saw the same things.

Be careful to use all the evidence. You should be able to develop some reasonable explanation for the conflicting testimony and those things that do not fit into your reconstruction very well.

Almost immediately you will discover that some important pieces of evidence are missing. For example, it would be useful to know the individual backgrounds and political views of the witnesses. Unfortunately, we know very little about the witnesses themselves, and we can reconstruct the political ideas of only about one-third of them. Therefore, you will have to rely on the testimonies given, deducing which witnesses were telling the truth, which were lying, and which were simply mistaken.

The fact that significant portions of the evidence are missing is not disastrous. Historians seldom have all the evidence they need when they attempt to tackle a historical problem. Instead, they must be able to do as much as they can with the evidence that is available, using it as completely and imaginatively as they can. They do so by asking questions of the available evidence. Where were the witnesses standing? Which one seems more likely to be telling the truth? Which witnesses were probably lying? When dealing with the testimony of the witnesses, be sure to determine what is factual and what is a witness's opinion. A rough sketch of the scene has been provided. How can it help you?

Also included in the evidence is Paul Revere's famous engraving of the incident, probably plagiarized from a drawing by artist Henry Pelham. It is unlikely that either Pelham or Revere was an eyewitness to the Boston Massacre, yet Revere's engraving gained widespread distribution, and most people—in 1770 and today—tend to recall that engraving when they think of the Boston Massacre. Do not examine the engraving until you have read the trial account closely. Can Revere's engraving help you find out what really happened that night? How does the engraving fit the eyewitnesses' accounts? How do the engraving and the accounts differ? Why?

Keep the central question in mind: What really happened in the Boston Massacre? Throughout this exercise, you will be trying to determine whether an order to fire was actually given. If so, by whom? If not, how can you explain why shots were fired? As commanding officer, Thomas Preston was held responsible and charged with murder. You might want to consider the evidence available to you as either a prosecution or defense attorney. Which side had the stronger case?

THE EVIDENCE

1. Site of the Boston Massacre, Town House Area, 1770.

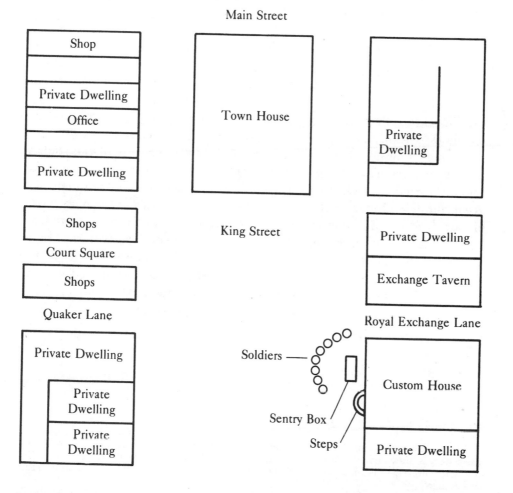

CHAPTER 3

WHAT REALLY
HAPPENED IN
THE BOSTON
MASSACRE?
THE TRIAL OF
CAPTAIN
THOMAS
PRESTON

Source 2 from *Publications of The Colonial Society of Massachusetts,* Vol. VII
(Boston: The Colonial Society of Massachusetts, 1905), pp. 8–9.

2. Deposition of Captain Thomas Preston, March 12, 1770 (Excerpt).

The mob still increased and were outrageous, striking their clubs or blud-
geons one against another, and calling out, come on you rascals, you bloody
backs, you lobster scoundrels, fire if you dare, G-d damn you, fire and be
damned, we know you dare not, and much more such language was used.
At this time I was between the soldiers and the mob, parleying with, and
endeavoring all in my power to persuade them to retire peaceably, but to
no purpose. They advanced to the points of the bayonets, struck some of
them and even the muzzles of the pieces, and seemed to be endeavoring to
close with the soldiers. On which some well behaved persons asked me if
the guns were charged. I replied yes. They then asked me if I intended to
order the men to fire. I answered no, by no means, observing to them that
I was advanced before the muzzles of the men's pieces, and must fall a
sacrifice if they fired; that the soldiers were upon the half cock[6] and charged
bayonets, and my giving the word fire under those circumstances would
prove me to be no officer. While I was thus speaking, one of the soldiers
having received a severe blow with a stick, stepped a little to one side and
instantly fired. . . . On this a general attack was made on the men by a
great number of heavy clubs and snowballs being thrown at them, by which
all our lives were in imminent danger, some persons at the same time from
behind calling out, damn your bloods—why don't you fire. Instantly three
or four of the soldiers fired. . . . On my asking the soldiers why they fired
without orders, they said they heard the word fire and supposed it came
from me. This might be the case as many of the mob called out fire, fire,
but I assured the men that I gave no such order; that my words were, don't
fire, stop your firing. . . .[7]

6. The cock of a musket had to be fully drawn back (cocked) for the musket to fire. In half cock,
the cock was drawn only halfway back so that priming powder could be placed in the pan. The
musket, however, would not fire at half cock. This is the origin of "Don't go off half cocked."
See Source 5.
7. Depositions also were taken from the soldiers, three of whom claimed, "We did our Captain's
orders and if we don't obey his commands should have been confined and shot." As with
Preston's deposition, the jury was not aware of that statement. In addition, ninety-six depositions were taken from townspeople.

Source 3 from Hiller B. Zobel, ed., *The Legal Papers of John Adams* (Cambridge, Mass.: Belknap Press of Harvard University Press, 1965), Vol. III, pp. 46–98.

3. The Trial of Captain Thomas Preston (*Rex v. Preston*), October 24–29 (Excerpt).

Witnesses for the King (Prosecution)

Edward Gerrish (or Garrick)

I heard a noise about 8 o'clock and went down to Royal Exchange Lane. Saw some Persons with Sticks coming up Quaker Lane. I said [to the sentry] Capt. Goldsmith owed my fellow Apprentice. He said he was a Gentleman and would pay every body. I said there was none in the Regiment.[8] He asked for me. I went to him, was not ashamed of my face. . . . The Sentinel left his Post and Struck me. I cried. My fellow Apprentice and a young man came up to the Sentinel and called him Bloody back.[9] He called to the Main Guard. . . . There was not a dozen people when the Sentinel called the Guard.

Ebenezer Hinkley

Just after 9 o'clock heard the Cry of Fire. I saw the party come out of the Guard House. A Capt. cried out of the Window "fire upon 'em damn 'em." I followed 'em down before the Custom House door. Capt. Preston was out and commanded 'em. They drew up and charged their Bayonets. Montgomery[10] pushed at the people advancing. In 2 or 3 minutes a Boy threw a small stick over hand and hit Montgomery on Breast. Then I heard the word fire in ¼ minute he fired. I saw some pieces of Snow as big as Egg thrown. 3 or 4 thrown at the same time of pushing on the other End of the file, before 1st gun fired. The body of People about a Rod[11] off. People said Damn 'em they durst not fire don't be afraid. No threats . . . I was a Rod from Capt. Preston. Did not hear him give Order to fire. ½ minute from 1st Gun to 2d. same to 3d. The others quicker. I saw no people striking the Guns or Bayonets nor pelting 'em. I saw Preston between people and Soldiers. I did not see him when 1st firing.

8. To say that there was no gentleman in the regiment was an insult to the sentry's superior officer, Captain Goldsmith.
9. British soldiers' coats were red.
10. Montgomery, one of the soldiers, undoubtedly fired the first shot.
11. A rod equals 16.5 feet.

CHAPTER 3

WHAT REALLY
HAPPENED IN
THE BOSTON
MASSACRE?
THE TRIAL OF
CAPTAIN
THOMAS
PRESTON

Peter Cunningham

Upon the cry of fire and Bells ringing went into King Street, heard the Capt. say Turn out the Guard.[12] Saw the Centinel standing on the steps of the Custom house, pushing his Bayonet at the People who were about 30 or 40. Captain came and ordered the Men to prime and load.[13] He came before 'em about 4 or 5 minutes after and put up their Guns with his Arm. They then fired and were priming and loading again. I am pretty positive the Capt. bid 'em Prime and load. I stood about 4 feet off him. Heard no Order given to fire. The Person who gave Orders to Prime and load stood with his back to me, I did not see his face only when he put up their Guns. I stood about 10 or 11 feet from the Soldiers, the Captain about the midway between.

William Wyatt

I heard the bell, . . . saw People running several ways. The largest part went down to the North of the Townhouse. I went the South side, saw an officer leading out 8 or 10 Men. Somebody met the officer and said, Capt. Preston for Gods sake mind what you are about and take care of your Men. He went down to the Centinel, drew up his Men, bid them face about, Prime and load. I saw about 100 People in the Street huzzaing, crying fire, damn you fire. In about 10 minutes I heard the Officer say fire. The Soldiers took no notice. His back was to me. I heard the same voice say fire. The Soldiers did not fire. The Officer then stamped and said Damn your bloods fire be the consequences what it will. Immediately the first Gun was fired. I have no doubt the Officer was the same person the Man spoke to when coming down with the Guard. His back was to me when the last order was given. I was then about 5 or 6 yards off and within 2 yards at the first. He stood in the rear when the Guns were fired. Just before I heard a Stick, which I took to be upon a Gun. I did not see it. The Officer had to the best of my knowledge a cloth coloured Surtout[14] on. After the firing the Captain stepd forward before the Men and struck up their Guns. One was loading again and he damn'd 'em for firing and severely reprimanded 'em. I did not mean the Capt. had the Surtout but the Man who spoke to him when coming with the Guard.

12. To dress and equip so as to be ready for duty.
13. Muskets were loaded from the muzzle with powder, wadding, a ball, and more wadding. The hammer was drawn back halfway, and powder was poured into the small pan under the hammer. There was a small piece of flint attached to the cock (see Source 5) so that when the trigger was pulled, the cock would come down and the flint would spark and ignite the gunpowder in the pan. The fire would then ignite the gunpowder in the breech and fire the gun. If the powder in the pan exploded but did not ignite the powder in the breech, the result was a "flash in the pan" and a musket that did not fire.
14. A type of overcoat.

Theodore Bliss

At home. I heard the Bells for fire.[15] Went out. Came to the Town House. The People told me there was going to be a Rumpus[16] with the Soldiers. Went to the Custom house. Saw Capt. Preston there with the Soldiers. Asked him if they were loaded. He said yes. If with Ball. He said nothing. I saw the People throw Snow Balls at the Soldiers and saw a Stick about 3 feet long strike a Soldier upon the right. He sallied[17] and then fired. A little time a second. Then the other[s] fast after one another. One or two Snow balls hit the Soldier, the stick struck, before firing. I know not whether he sallied on account of the Stick or step'd back to make ready. I did not hear any Order given by the Capt. to fire. I stood so near him I think I must have heard him if he had given an order to fire before the first firing. I never knew Capt. Preston before. I can't say whether he had a Surtout on, he was dressed in red. I know him to be the Man I took to be the Officer. The Man that fired first stood next to the Exchange lane. I saw none of the People press upon the Soldiers before the first Gun fired. I did after. I aimed a blow at him myself but did not strike him. I am sure the Captain stood before the Men when the first Gun was fired. I had no apprehension[18] the Capt. did give order to fire when the first Gun was fired. I thought, after the first Gun, the Capt. did order the Men to fire but do not certainly know.

Benjamin Burdick

When I came into King Street about 9 o'Clock I saw the Soldiers round the Centinel. I asked one if he was loaded and he said yes. I asked him if he would fire, he said yes by the Eternal God and pushd his Bayonet at me. After the firing the Captain came before the soldiers and put up their Guns with his arm and said stop firing, dont fire no more or dont fire again. I heard the word fire and took it and am certain that it came from behind the Soldiers. I saw a man passing busily behind who I took to be an Officer. The firing was a little time after. I saw some persons fall. Before the firing I saw a stick thrown at the Soldiers. The word fire I took to be a word of Command. I had in my hand a highland broad Sword which I brought from home. Upon my coming out I was told it was a wrangle[19] between the Soldiers and people, upon that I went back and got my Sword. I never used to go out with a weapon. I had not my Sword drawn till after the Soldier

15. Colonial American towns did not have fire departments. When fires broke out, church bells would be rung, and citizens were expected to come out with buckets to help extinguish the fire.
16. A disturbance.
17. Leaped forward suddenly.
18. Had no doubt.
19. A quarrel.

CHAPTER 3

WHAT REALLY
HAPPENED IN
THE BOSTON
MASSACRE?
THE TRIAL OF
CAPTAIN
THOMAS
PRESTON

pushed his Bayonet at me. I should have cut his head off if he had stepd out of his Rank to attack me again. At the first firing the People were chiefly in Royal Exchange lane, there being about 50 in the Street. After the firing I went up to the Soldiers and told them I wanted to see some faces that I might swear to them another day. The Centinel in a melancholy tone said perhaps Sir you may.

Diman Morton

Between 9 and 10 I heard in my house the cry of fire but soon understood there was no fire but the Soldiers were fighting with the Inhabitants. I went to King Street. Saw the Centinel over the Gutter, his Bayonet breast high. He retired to the steps—loaded. The Boys dared him to fire. Soon after a Party came down, drew up. The Captain ordered them to load. I went across the Street. Heard one Gun and soon after the other Guns. The Captain when he ordered them to load stood in the front before the Soldiers so that the Guns reached beyond him. The Captain had a Surtout on. I knew him well. The Surtout was not red. I think cloth colour. I stood on the opposite corner of Exchange lane when I heard the Captain order the Men to load. I came by my knowledge of the Captain partly by seeing him lead the Fortification Guard.

Nathaniel Fosdick

Hearing the Bells ring, for fire I supposed I went out and came down by the Main Guard. Saw some Soldiers fixing their Bayonets on. Passed on. Went down to the Centinel. Perceived something pass me behind. Turned round and saw the Soldiers coming down. They bid me stand out of the way and damnd my blood. I told them I should not for any man. The party drew up round the Centinel, faced about and charged their Bayonets. I saw an Officer and said if there was any disturbance between the Soldiers and the People there was the Officer present who could settle it soon. I heard no Orders given to load, but in about two minutes after the Captain step'd across the Gutter. Spoke to two Men—I don't know who—then went back behind his men. Between the 4th and 5th men on the right. I then heard the word fire and the first Gun went off. In about 2 minutes the second and then several others. The Captain had a Sword in his hand. Was dressd in his Regimentals. Had no Surtout on. I saw nothing thrown nor any blows given at all. The first man on the right who fired after attempting to push the People slipped down and drop'd his Gun out of his hand. The Person who stepd in between the 4th and 5th Men I look upon it gave the orders to fire. His back was to me. I shall always think it was him. The Officer had a Wig on. I was in such a situation that I am as well satisfied there were no blows given as that the word fire was spoken.

Witnesses for the Prisoner (Preston)

Edward Hill

After all the firing Captain Preston put up the Gun of a Soldier who was going to fire and said fire no more you have done mischief enough.

Richard Palmes

Somebody there said there was a Rumpus in King Street. I went down. When I had got there I saw Capt. Preston at the head of 7 or 8 Soldiers at the Custom house drawn up, their Guns breast high and Bayonets fixed. Found Theodore Bliss talking with the Captain. I heard him say why don't you fire or words to that effect. The Captain answered I know not what and Bliss said God damn you why don't you fire. I was close behind Bliss. They were both in front. Then I step'd immediately between them and put my left hand in a familiar manner on the Captains right shoulder to speak to him. Mr. John Hickling then looking over my shoulder I said to Preston are your Soldiers Guns loaded. He answered with powder and ball. Sir I hope you dont intend the Soldiers shall fire on the Inhabitants. He said by no means. The instant he spoke I saw something resembling Snow or Ice strike the Grenadier[20] on the Captains right hand being the only one then at his right. He instantly stepd one foot back and fired the first Gun. I had then my hand on the Captains shoulder. After the Gun went off I heard the word fire. The Captain and I stood in front about half between the breech and muzzle of the Guns. I dont know who gave the word fire. I was then looking on the Soldier who fired. The word was given loud. The Captain might have given the word and I not distinguish it. After the word fire in about 6 or 7 seconds the Grenadier on the Captains left fired and then the others one after another. . . .

Q. Did you situate yourself before Capt. Preston, in order that you might be out of danger, in case they fired?
A. I did not apprehend myself in any danger.
Q. Did you hear Captain Preston give the word *Fire?*
A. I have told your Honors, that after the first gun was fired, I heard the word, *fire!* but who gave it, I know not.

20. A soldier in the British Grenadier Guards.

CHAPTER 3

WHAT REALLY
HAPPENED IN
THE BOSTON
MASSACRE?
THE TRIAL OF
CAPTAIN
THOMAS
PRESTON

Matthew Murray

I heard no order given. I stood within two yards of the Captain. He was in front talking with a Person, I don't know who. I was looking at the Captain when the Gun was fired.

Andrew, a Negro servant to Oliver Wendell[21]

I jump'd back and heard a voice cry fire and immediately the first Gun fired. It seemed to come from the left wing from the second or third man on the left. The Officer was standing before me with his face towards the People. I am certain the voice came from beyond him. The Officer stood before the Soldiers at a sort of a corner. I turned round and saw a Grenadier who stood on the Captain's right swing his Gun and fire. . . .

Jane Whitehouse

A Man came behind the Soldiers walked backwards and forward, encouraging them to fire. The Captain stood on the left about three yards. The man touched one of the Soldiers upon the back and said fire, by God I'll stand by you. He was dressed in dark colored clothes. . . . He did not look like an Officer. The man fired directly on the word and clap on the Shoulder. I am positive the man was not the Captain. . . . I am sure he gave no orders. . . . I saw one man take a chunk of wood from under his Coat throw it at a Soldier and knocked him. He fell on his face. His firelock[22] was out of his hand. . . . This was before any firing.

Newton Prince, a Negro, a member of the South Church

Heard the Bell ring. Ran out. Came to the Chapel. Was told there was no fire but something better, there was going to be a fight. Some had buckets and bags and some Clubs. I went to the west end of the Town House where [there] were a number of people. I saw some Soldiers coming out of the Guard house with their Guns and running down one after another to the Custom house. Some of the people said let's attack the Main Guard, or the Centinel who is gone to King street. Some said for Gods sake don't lets touch the main Guard. I went down. Saw the Soldiers planted by the Custom house two deep. The People were calling them Lobsters, daring 'em to fire saying damn you why don't you fire. I saw Capt. Preston out from behind the Soldiers. In the front at the right. He spoke to some people.

21. Andrew was actually Wendell's slave, and Wendell appeared in court to testify that Andrew was honest and truthful.
22. Musket.

The Capt. stood between the Soldiers and the Gutter about two yards from the Gutter. I saw two or three strike with sticks on the Guns. I was going off to the west of the Soldiers and heard the Guns fire and saw the dead carried off. Soon after the Guard Drums beat to arms.[23] The People whilst striking on the Guns cried fire, damn you fire. I have heard no Orders given to fire, only the people in general cried fire.

James Woodall

I saw one Soldier knocked down. His Gun fell from him. I saw a great many sticks and pieces of sticks and Ice thrown at the Soldiers. The Soldier who was knocked down took up his Gun and fired directly. Soon after the first Gun I saw a Gentleman behind the Soldiers in velvet of blue or black plush trimmed with gold. He put his hand toward their backs. Whether he touched them I know not and said by God I'll stand by you whilst I have a drop of blood and then said fire and two went off and the rest to 7 or 8. . . . The Captain, after, seemed shocked and looked upon the Soldiers. I am very certain he did not give the word fire.

Cross-Examination of Captain James Gifford

Q. Did you ever know an officer order men to fire with their bayonets charged?

A. No, Officers never give order to fire from charged bayonet. They would all have fired together, or most of them.

---

23. A special drumbeat that signaled soldiers to arm themselves.

CHAPTER 3

WHAT REALLY
HAPPENED IN
THE BOSTON
MASSACRE?
THE TRIAL OF
CAPTAIN
THOMAS
PRESTON

Source 4 from Anthony D. Darling, *Red Coat and Brown Bess,* Historical Arms Series, No. 12 (Bloomfield, Ontario). Courtesy of Museum Restoration Service, © 1970, 1981.

4. The Position of "Bayonets Charged."

Source 5 from Robert Helm, *Age of Firearms* (1957), p. 93. Drawing by Nancy Jenkins. Reprinted by permission of the author.

5. Detail of a Musket.

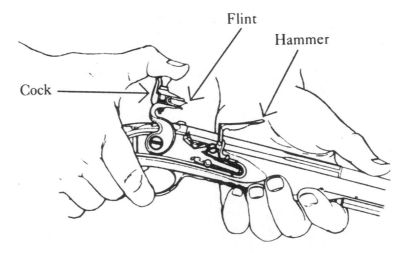

Source 6: Library of Congress.

6. Paul Revere's Engraving of the Boston Massacre.
[*Notice how he dubbed the Custom House "Butcher's Hall."*]

∽ QUESTIONS TO CONSIDER ∽

In reconstructing the event, begin by imagining the positions of the various soldiers and witnesses. Where were the soldiers standing? Where was Captain Preston standing? Which witnesses were closest to Preston (that is, in the best positions to see and hear what happened)? Where were the other witnesses? Remember that the event took place around 9:00 P.M., when Boston was totally dark.

Next, read closely Preston's deposition and the trial testimony. What major points did Preston make in his own defense? Do you find those points plausible? More important, do the wit-

CHAPTER 3

WHAT REALLY
HAPPENED IN
THE BOSTON
MASSACRE?
THE TRIAL OF
CAPTAIN
THOMAS
PRESTON

nesses who were closest to Preston agree or disagree with his recounting, or with each other's? On what points? Be as specific as possible.

Now consider the other witnesses, those who were not so near. What did they hear? What did they see? To what degree do their testimonies agree or disagree, both with each other and with Preston and those closest to him?

Lawyers for both sides spent considerable time trying to ascertain what Captain Preston was wearing on that evening. Why did they consider this important? Based on the evidence, what do you think Preston was wearing on the evening of March 5, 1770? What conclusions could you draw from that?

The attorneys also were particularly interested in the crowd's behavior *prior to* the firing of the first musket. Why did they consider that important? How would you characterize the crowd's behavior? Are you suspicious of testimony that is at direct odds with your conclusion about this point?

Several witnesses (especially Jane Whitehouse) tell a quite different story. To what extent is her recounting of the event plausible? Is it corroborated by other witnesses?

We included Paul Revere's engraving, even though he probably was not an eyewitness, because by the time of Preston's trial, surely all the witnesses would have seen it and, more important, because later Americans have obtained their most lasting visual image of the event from that work. How does the engraving conform to what actually happened? How does it conflict with your determination of what actually took place? If there are major discrepancies, why do you think this is so? (Revere certainly knew a number of the eyewitnesses and could have ascertained the truth from them.)

After you have answered these questions and carefully weighed the eyewitnesses' evidence, answer the central question: What really happened in the Boston Massacre?

⚬ EPILOGUE ⚬

In his closing arguments in defense of Captain Preston, John Adams noted that the crowd not only had been harassing the soldiers but also had actually threatened to attack them. Yet there was no reliable evidence to prove that Preston had ordered his men to fire into the crowd, Adams insisted. In such doubtful cases, he concluded, the jury must vote for an acquittal. The prosecution's closing summary portrayed Preston as a murderer. The

crowd's actions, the prosecution maintained, were "a few Snow-balls, thrown by a parcel of *Boys*." According to the prosecution, the rest of the people who gathered in the square were peaceful and simply curious about what was happening.

In the trial of Thomas Preston, the jury took only three hours to reach its verdict: not guilty. Some of the jurors were sympathetic to the British, and thus were determined to find

Preston innocent no matter what evidence was presented. Also, the leaking of the grand jury depositions ultimately helped Preston's defense, since defense attorneys knew in advance what the potentially most damaging witnesses would say in court. Finally, defense attorney John Adams's tactics (to create so much confusion in the minds of the jurors that they could not be certain what actually had taken place) were extremely effective. As it turned out, Preston had the advantage from the very beginning.

As for Thomas Preston himself, the British officer was quickly packed off to England, where he received a pension of £200 per year from the king "to compensate him for his suffering." He did not participate in the American Revolution and died in 1781. Of the eight soldiers (the sentry plus the seven men Preston brought to the Custom House), six were acquitted, and two were convicted of manslaughter and punished by being branded on the thumb. From there they disappeared into the mists of history.

On the road to the American Revolution, many events stand out as important or significant. The Boston Massacre is one such event. However, we must be careful in assessing its importance. After all, the colonists and the mother country did not finally resort to arms until five years after this dramatic event. By that time, most of those killed on King Street on March 5 had been forgotten.

Yet the Boston Massacre and other events have helped shape Americans' attitudes as to what their own Revolution was all about. To most Americans, the British were greedy, heartless tyrants who terrorized a peaceful citizenry. More than one hundred years after the event, the Massachusetts legislature authorized a memorial honoring the "martyrs" to be placed on the site of the "massacre." The Bostonians' convictions were bolstered by Irish immigrants whose ancestors had known British "tyranny" firsthand, and the Bostonians remained convinced that the American Revolution had been caused by Britain's selfishness and oppression. As we can see in the Boston Massacre, the road to the Revolution was considerably more complicated than that.

Today the site of the Boston Massacre is on a traffic island beside the Old State House (formerly called the Town House and seen in the background of Paul Revere's famous engraving) in the midst of Boston's financial district. With the exception of the State House (now a tasteful museum), the site is ringed by skyscrapers that house, among other institutions, BankBoston and Fleet Bank of Massachusetts. Thousands of Bostonians and tourists stand on the Boston Massacre site every day, waiting for the traffic to abate.

Many years ago, John Adams said that "the foundation of American independence was laid" on the evening of March 5, 1770. Although he may have overstated the case, clearly many Americans have come to see the event as a crucial one in the coming of their Revolution against Great Britain.

Now that you have examined the evidence, do you think the Boston Massacre of March 5, 1770, was a justifiable reason for rebellion against the mother country? Could the crowd

CHAPTER 3

WHAT REALLY
HAPPENED IN
THE BOSTON
MASSACRE?
THE TRIAL OF
CAPTAIN
THOMAS
PRESTON

action on that evening secretly have been directed by the Patriot elite, or was it a spontaneous demonstration of anti-British fury? Why was Paul Revere's engraving at such variance with what actually took place?

Few Americans have stopped to ponder what actually happened on that fateful evening. Like the American Revolution itself, the answer to that question may well be more complex than we think.

CHAPTER 4

AWAY FROM HOME: THE WORKING GIRLS OF LOWELL

⌒ THE PROBLEM ⌒

Just before the War of 1812, the successful New England merchant Francis Cabot Lowell toured Great Britain. Among other things, Lowell was very interested in the English textile industry. The invention of the power loom enabled spinning and weaving operations to be combined within one factory, but the factory system had spawned mill towns with overcrowded slums, horrible living conditions, and high death rates. The potential profits the new technology offered were great, yet Lowell knew that Americans already feared the Old World evils that seemed to accompany the factory system.

Back in Boston once again, Lowell and his brother-in-law built a power loom, patented it, raised money, formed a company, and built a textile factory. Realizing that their best source of available labor would be young women from the surrounding New England rural areas and that farm families would have to be persuaded to let their daughters work far from home in the new factories, the company managers developed what came to be known as the Lowell system.

In this chapter, you will be looking at what happened when people's ideas about women's "proper place" conflicted with the labor needs of the new factory system. What did the general public fear? How did the working girls react?

∽ BACKGROUND ∽

By the end of the eighteenth century, the American economy began undergoing a process that historians call modernization. This process involves a number of changes, including the rapid expansion of markets, commercial specialization, improved transportation networks, the growth of credit transactions, the proliferation of towns and cities, and the rise of manufacturing and the factory system. Quite obviously, all these factors are interrelated. Furthermore, such changes always have profound effects on people's lifestyles as well as on the pace of life itself.

While the frontier moved steadily westward, the South was primarily agrarian—tied to cash crops such as cotton and tobacco. New England's economy, however, quickly became modernized. Although agriculture was never completely abandoned in New England, by the early 1800s it was increasingly difficult to obtain land, and many small New England farms suffered from soil exhaustion. Young men, of course, could go west—in fact, so many of them left New England that soon there was a "surplus" of young women in the area. In addition, the transformation of New England agriculture and the demise of much of the "putting-out" system of the first local textile manufacturing left many single female workers underemployed or unemployed. What were these farmers' daughters supposed to do? What were their options?

At the same time that these economic developments were occurring, ideas about white middle-class women and their place in society also were changing. Even before the American Revolution, sharp distinctions between the "better sort" and the "poorer sort" were noticeable, especially in cities like Boston. The Revolution itself, with its emphasis on "republican virtues," drew many women away from their purely domestic duties and into patriotic work for the cause. The uncertainties of the early national period, which followed the Revolution, only intensified the concern about the new Republic: How could such a daring experiment in representative government succeed? An important part of the answer to this question was the concept of "republican motherhood": Women would take on the important task of raising children to be responsible citizens who possessed the virtues (and value system) necessary for the success of the newly independent nation.

Those who study women's history disagree on the question of whether women's status improved or declined as a result of the emphasis on republican motherhood. Nevertheless, it was clear that the new focus on motherhood and child rearing would not only reduce the variety of roles women could play but also limit women's proper place to their own homes.

As historian Alice Kessler-Harris notes in her study of wage-earning women in the United States, there was a direct conflict for poorer or unmarried women between their need to earn money and the ideology that home and family should be central to *all* women's lives.[1] This emphasis on domestic ideology, Kessler-Harris concludes, sharpened class divisions and eroded any possibility of real independence for women. Historian Christine Stansell reaches many of the same conclusions in her study of gender and class in New York City.[2] In addition, according to Stansell, young unmarried working women often dressed and behaved in ways that directly challenged domestic ideology and women's place within the home. Such alternative ways of living, especially on the part of young, white, native-born, Protestant women, were deeply disturbing to many Americans, both male and female.

In periods of rapid change, people often try to cling to absolute beliefs and even create stereotypes that implicitly punish those who do not conform. Such a stereotype began to emerge after the American Revolution. According to this stereotype, every "true" woman was a "lady" who behaved in certain ways because of her female nature. Historian Barbara Welter has called this phenomenon the "cult of true womanhood."[3] True women possessed four virtues: piety, purity, submissiveness, and domesticity. These characteristics, it was thought, were not so much learned as

they were biologically natural, simply an inherent part of being born female. Women's magazines, etiquette books for young ladies, sermons and religious tracts, and popular short stories and novels all told women what they were like and how they should feel about themselves. Such sources are called "prescriptive literature" because they literally prescribe how people should—and should not—behave.

What, then, was expected of New England farmers' daughters and other respectable (white) women? They were supposed to be pious, more naturally religious than men (real men might occasionally swear, but real women never did). Because they were naturally logical and rational, men might pursue education, but true women should not because they might be led into error if they strayed from the Bible. As daughters, wives, or even sisters, women had the important responsibility of being the spiritual uplifters to whom men could turn when necessary.

Just as important as piety was the true woman's purity. This purity was absolute because whereas a man might "sow his wild oats" and then be saved by the love of a good woman, a "fallen woman" could never be saved. In the popular fiction of the period, a woman who had been seduced usually became insane, died, or did both. If she had a baby, it also came to a bad end. Only on her wedding night did a true woman surrender her virginity, and then out of duty rather than passion, because it was widely believed that pure women were not sexually responsive. In fact, many young women of

1. Alice Kessler-Harris, *Out to Work: A History of America's Wage-Earning Women* (New York: Oxford, 1982).
2. Christine Stansell, *City of Women: Sex and Class in New York, 1789–1860* (New York: Knopf, 1986).
3. Barbara Welter, "The Cult of True Womanhood, 1820–1860," *American Quarterly* 18 (Summer 1966): 151–174.

this era knew nothing at all about their own bodies or the nature of sexual intercourse until they married.

Submission and domesticity were perhaps not as vital as piety and purity. Although women who did not submit to men's leadership were destined to be unhappy (according to the thought of the day), they could correct their mistaken behavior. Men were, after all, stronger and more intelligent, the natural protectors of women. A true woman, wrote then-popular author Grace Greenwood, should be like a "perpetual child," who is always "timid, doubtful, and clingingly dependent." Such pious, pure, submissive women were particularly well suited to the important task of creating a pleasant, cheerful home—a place where men could escape from their worldly struggles and be fed, clothed, comforted, and nursed if they were ill. Even a woman who did not have very much money could create such a haven, people believed, simply by using her natural talents of sewing, cooking, cleaning, and flower arranging.

Simultaneously, then, two important trends were occurring in the early 1800s: the northern economy was modernizing, and sexual stereotypes that assigned very different roles to men and women were developing. Whereas a man should be out in the world of education, work, and politics, a woman's place was in the home, a sphere where she could be sheltered. But what would happen if the economic need for an increased supply of labor clashed with the new ideas about women's place in society? If a young unmarried woman went to work in a factory far away from her parents' farm, would she still be respectable? Where would she live? Who would protect her? Perhaps the experience of factory work itself would destroy those special feminine characteristics all true women possessed. All these fears and more would have to be confronted in the course of the development of the New England textile industry during the 1830s and 1840s.

Although the first American textile mill using water-powered spinning machines was built in 1790, it and the countless other mills that sprang up throughout New England during the next thirty years depended heavily on the putting-out system. The mills made only the yarn, which was then distributed ("put out") to women who wove the cloth in their own homes and returned the finished products to the mills. In 1820, two-thirds of all American cloth was still being produced by women working at home. But the pace of modernization accelerated sharply with the formation of the Boston Manufacturing Company, a heavily capitalized firm that purchased a large tract of rural land in the Merrimack River valley. The Boston Associates adopted the latest technology and, more important, concentrated all aspects of cloth production inside their factories. Because they no longer put out work, they had to attract large numbers of workers, especially young women from New England farms, to their mills. Lowell, Massachusetts (the "City of Spindles"), and the Lowell mills became a kind of model, an experiment that received a good deal of attention in both Europe and America. As historian Thomas Dublin has shown, most of the young women at the Lowell mills were fifteen to thirty years old, unmarried, and from farm families that were neither the richest nor the poorest in their area. Although some of the Lowell girls occasionally sent small amounts of money back to their families, most used their wages for new clothes, education, and dowries.[4] These wages were significantly higher than those for teaching, farm labor, or domestic services, the three other major occupations open to women.

The factory girls were required to live and eat in boardinghouses run according to company rules and supervised by respectable landladies. The company partially subsidized the cost of room and board and also encouraged the numerous lecture series, evening schools, and church-related activities in Lowell. Girls worked together in the mills, filling the unskilled and semiskilled positions, and men (about one-fourth of the work force) performed the skilled jobs and served as overseers (foremen). Work in the mills also was characterized by strict regulations and an elaborate system of bells that signaled mealtimes and work times.

During the 1840s, factory girls occasionally published their own magazines, the most famous of which was the *Lowell Offering*. This journal grew out of a working woman's self-improvement society and was sponsored by a local Lowell minister. When the minister was transferred, the mill owners partially subsidized the magazine. The female editors, who were former mill workers, insisted that the magazine was for "literary" work rather than for labor reform. The Evidence section presents a description of Lowell mills and boardinghouses and several selections from the *Lowell Offering* and other sources. The conflict between economic modernization and the cult of true womanhood was indirectly recognized by many New Englanders and directly experienced by the Lowell mill girls. What forms did this conflict take? What fears and anxieties did it reveal? How did the mill girls attempt to cope with this tension?

☙ THE METHOD ❧

When historians use prescriptive literature as evidence, they ask (1) what message is being conveyed, (2) who is sending the message, (3) why it is being sent, and (4) for whom it is intended. All the evidence you are using in this chapter is in some ways prescriptive—that is, it tells people how women *should* behave.

An early major criticism of the effects of factory work on young women was written by Orestes Brownson, a well-known New England editor and reformer. A sharply contrasting view appears in the excerpts from a brief, popular book about Lowell written by Reverend Henry Mills in 1845. Rever-

4. A dowry is the money, goods, or property that a woman brings into her marriage.

[73]

a good point about the source of the writers' information

end Mills was a local Protestant minister who was asked by the textile company owners to conduct surveys into the workers' habits, health, and moral character. Depending heavily on information provided by company officials, overseers, and landladies, Reverend Mills published *Lowell, As It Was, and As It Is*.

Yet the controversy continued, because only one year later, the journal owned by the Lowell Female Labor Reform Association, *Voice of Industry,* painted a much darker picture of the factory girls' "slavery." Although purchased by a militant group of women factory workers, the *Voice* had originated as a labor reform paper. Its editorial policy always addressed larger, worker-oriented issues such as a shorter workday and dedicated a special column to women workers' concerns.

The young women who worked in the textile mills also actively participated in the debate. The evidence in the selections from the *Lowell Offering* was written by factory girls during the years 1840 to 1843. Also presented is an excerpt from a book written by Lucy Larcom, one of the few children (under age fifteen) employed in the Lowell mills in the late 1830s. She was a factory girl for more than ten years, after which she went west and obtained a college education. She became a well-known teacher and author when she returned to New England. Larcom published the book about her New England girlhood when she was

sixty-five years old. The final set of evidence includes two pictures of "typical" mill girls in 1860 and letters written by mill girls and their families.

First read through the evidence, looking for elements of the cult of true womanhood in the factory girls' writings and in the Lowell system itself. Be sure to consider all four questions: What message is being conveyed? Who is sending the message? Why is it being sent? For whom is it intended? This will tell you a great deal not only about the social standards for respectable young white women but also about the fears and anxieties aroused by a factory system that employed women away from their homes.

Reading about how people *should* behave, however, does not tell us how people actually behaved. Remember that the central question of this problem involves a clash: a conflict between ideas (the cult) and reality (the factory system). Go through the evidence again, this time trying to reconstruct what it was really like for the young women who lived and worked in Lowell. Ask yourself to what degree and in what ways they might have deviated from the ideal of "true" women. Also ask whether they could have achieved this ideal goal—and whether they really wanted to—while working and living in Lowell. In other words, try to clarify in your own mind the forms of the conflict and the reactions (of both society and the young women) to that conflict.

Is there firsthand evidence from women who were not virtuous? Why or Why not? Can we surmise that those women were less inclined to write about their lives? Thus, is there a bulwark of evidence missing?

∞ THE EVIDENCE ∞

Source 1 from Orestes A. Brownson, *Boston Quarterly Review* 3 (July 1840): 368–370.

1. Slave Labor Versus Free Labor.

In regard to labor, two systems obtain: one that of slave labor, the other that of free labor. Of the two, the first is, in our judgment, except so far as the feelings are concerned, decidedly the least oppressive. If the slave has never been a free man, we think, as a general rule, his sufferings are less than those of the free laborer at wages. As to actual freedom, one has just about as much as the other. The laborer at wages has all the disadvantages of freedom and none of its blessings, while the slave, if denied the blessings, is freed from the disadvantages.

We are no advocates of slavery. We are as heartily opposed to it as any modern abolitionist can be. But we say frankly that, if there must always be a laboring population distinct from proprietors and employers, we regard the slave system as decidedly preferable to the system at wages.

It is no pleasant thing to go days without food; to lie idle for weeks, seeking work and finding none; to rise in the morning with a wife and children you love, and know not where to procure them a breakfast; and to see constantly before you no brighter prospect than the almshouse. . . .

It is said there is no want in this country. There may be less in some other countries. But death by actual starvation in this country is, we apprehend, no uncommon occurrence. The sufferings of a quiet, unassuming but useful class of females in our cities, in general seamstresses, too proud to beg or to apply to the almshouse, are not easily told. They are industrious; they do all that they can find to do. But yet the little there is for them to do, and the miserable pittance they receive for it, is hardly sufficient to keep soul and body together. . . .

The average life—working life, we mean—of the girls that come to Lowell, for instance, from Maine, New Hampshire, and Vermont, we have been assured, is only about three years. What becomes of them then? Few of them ever marry[5]; fewer still ever return to their native places with repu-

5. According to historian Thomas Dublin in *Women at Work* (New York: Columbia University Press, 1979), the working women of Lowell tended to marry in about the same proportion as nonworking New England women, although the Lowell women married three to five years later in life and had a distinct tendency to marry men who were tradesmen or skilled workers rather than farmers.

tations unimpaired. "She has worked in a factory" is almost enough to damn to infamy the most worthy and virtuous girl. . . .

One thing is certain: that, of the amount actually produced by the operative, [the worker] retains a less proportion than it costs the master to feed, clothe, and lodge his slave. Wages is a cunning device of the devil, for the benefit of tender consciences who would retain all the advantages of the slave system without the expense, trouble, and odium of being slaveholders.

Source 2 from Reverend Henry A. Mills, *Lowell, As It Was, and As It Is* (Lowell, Mass.: Powers, Bagley, and Dayton, 1845).

2. A Lowell Boardinghouse.

[*Reverend Mills began by describing the long blocks of boardinghouses, each three stories high, which were built in a style reminiscent of country farmhouses. Clean, well painted, and neat, these houses contained common eating rooms, parlors, and sleeping rooms for two to six boarders. The boarders, Reverend Mills observed, were sometimes a bit crowded but actually lived under better conditions than seamstresses and milliners in other towns.*]

As one important feature in the management of these houses, it deserves to be named that male operatives and female operatives do not board in the same tenement; and the following Regulations, printed by one of the companies, and given to each keeper of their houses, are here subjoined, as a simple statement of the rules generally observed by all the Corporations.

Regulations to be observed by persons occupying the Boarding-houses belonging to the Merrimack Manufacturing company.

They must not board any persons not employed by the company, unless by special permission.

No disorderly or improper conduct must be allowed in the houses.

The doors must be closed at 10 o'clock in the evening; and no person admitted after that time, unless a sufficient excuse can be given.

Those who keep the houses, when required, must give an account of the number, names, and employment of their boarders; also with regard to their general conduct and whether they are in the habit of attending public worship.

The buildings, both inside and out, and the yards about them, must be kept clean and in good order. If the buildings or fences are injured, they will be repaired and charged to the occupant.

No one will be allowed to keep swine.

[*The meals might seem rushed, Mills noted, but that was common among all Americans, particularly businesspeople. Working girls could choose whichever boardinghouses they preferred, rents were very low, and their living arrangements were very respectable.*]

No tenant is admitted who has not hitherto borne a good character, and who does not continue to sustain it. In many cases the tenant has long been keeper of the house, for six, eight, or twelve years, and is well known to hundreds of her girls as their adviser and friend and second mother. . . .

The influence which this system of boarding-houses has exerted upon the good order and good morals of the place, has been vast and beneficent. . . . By it the care and influence of the superintendent are extended over his operatives, while they are out of the mill, as well as while they are in it. Employing chiefly those who have no permanent residence in Lowell, but are only temporary boarders, upon any embarrassment of affairs they return to their country homes, and do not sink down here a helpless caste, clamouring for work, starving unless employed, and hence ready for a riot, for the destruction of property, and repeating here the scenes enacted in the manufacturing villages of England. To a very great degree the future condition of Lowell is dependent upon a faithful adhesion to this system; and it will deserve the serious consideration of those old towns which are now introducing steam mills, whether, if they do not provide boarding-houses, and employ chiefly other operatives than resident ones, they be not bringing in the seeds of future and alarming evil. . . .

To obtain this constant importation of female hands from the country, it is necessary to secure *the moral protection of their characters while they are resident in Lowell*. This, therefore, is the chief object of that moral police referred to, some details of which will now be given.

It should be stated, in the outset, that no persons are employed on the Corporations who are addicted to intemperance, or who are known to be guilty of any immoralities of conduct. As the parent of all other vices, intemperance is most carefully excluded. Absolute freedom from intoxicating liquors is understood, throughout the city, to be a prerequisite to obtaining employment in the mills, and any person known to be addicted to their use is at once dismissed. This point has not received the attention, from writers upon the moral conditions of Lowell, which it deserves; and we are surprised that the English traveller and divine, Dr. Scoresby, in his recent book upon Lowell, has given no more notice to this subject. A more strictly and universally temperate class of persons cannot be found, than the nine thousand operatives of this city; and the fact is as well known to all others living here, as it is of some honest pride among themselves. In relation to other immoralities, it may be stated, that the suspicion of criminal conduct, association with suspected persons, and general and habitual light behavior and conversation, are regarded as sufficient reasons for dismissions, and for which delinquent operatives are discharged.

[*Reverend Mills also described the discharge system at the factories. For those girls whose conduct was satisfactory and who had worked at least a year, honorable discharges were issued. Discharge letters could be used as recommendations for another job. Those who received dishonorable discharges for infractions such as stealing, lying, leaving the job without permission, or other "improper conduct" would have difficulty finding other employment.*]

This system, which has been in operation in Lowell from the beginning, is of great and important effect in driving unworthy persons from our city, and in preserving the high character of our operatives.

[*Male overseers, or foremen, also were closely screened and had to possess good moral character. In response to Reverend Mills's questions about the male overseers, one factory owner responded as follows.*]

Lowell, May 10, 1841

Dear Sir:—

I employ in our mills, and in the various departments connected with them, thirty overseers, and as many second overseers. My overseers are married men, with families, with a single exception, and even he has engaged a tenement, and is to be married soon. Our second overseers are younger men, but upwards of twenty of them are married, and several others are soon to be married. Sixteen of our overseers are members of some regular church, and four of them are deacons. Ten of our second overseers are also members of the church, and one of them is the Superintendent of a Sunday School. I have no hesitation in saying that in all the sterling requisites of character, in native intelligence, and practical good sense, in sound morality, and as active, useful, and exemplary citizens, they may, as a class, safely challenge comparison with any class in our community. I know not, among them all, an intemperate man, nor, at this time, even what is called a moderate drinker.

[*Furthermore, the girls were expected to obey numerous rules.*]

Still another source of trust which a Corporation has, for the good character of its operatives, is the moral control which they have over one another. Of course this control would be nothing among a generally corrupt and degraded class. But among virtuous and high-minded young women, who feel that they have the keeping of their characters, and that any stain upon their associates brings reproach upon themselves, the power of opinion becomes an ever-present, and ever-active restraint. A girl, *suspected* of immoralities, or serious improprieties of conduct, at once loses caste. Her fellow-boarders will at once leave the house, if the keeper does not dismiss the offender. In self-protection, therefore, the matron is obliged to put the offender away. Nor will her former companions walk with, or work with her; till at length, finding herself everywhere talked about, and pointed at, and shunned, she is obliged to relieve her fellow-operatives of a presence which they feel brings disgrace. From this power of opinion, there is no appeal; and as long as it is exerted in favor of propriety of behavior and purity of life, it is one of the most active and effectual safeguards of character.

It may not be out of place to present here the regulations, which are observed alike on all the Corporations, which are given to the operatives when they are first employed, and are posted up conspicuously in all the mills. They are as follows:—

Regulations to be observed by all persons employed by the _____
Manufacturing Company, in the Factories.

Every overseer is required to be punctual himself, and to see that those employed under him are so.

The overseers may, at their discretion, grant leave of absence to those employed under them, when there are sufficient spare hands to supply their place; but when there are not sufficient spare hands, they are not allowed to grant leave of absence unless in cases of absolute necessity.

All persons are required to observe the regulations of the room in which they are employed. They are not allowed to be absent from their work without the consent of their overseer, except in case of sickness, and then they are required to send him word of the cause of their absence.

All persons are required to board in one of the boarding-houses belonging to the company, and conform to the regulations of the house in which they board.

All persons are required to be constant in attendance on public worship, at one of the regular places of worship in this place.

Persons who do not comply with the above regulations will not be employed by the company.

Persons entering the employment of the company are considered as engaging to work one year.

All persons intending to leave the employment of the company, are required to give notice of the same to their overseer, at least two weeks previous to the time of leaving.

[Handwritten margin note: Thus, an "easy" victim for sexual impropriety or adultery. Why would the girls speak or write of this?]

Any one who shall take from the mills, or the yard, any yarn, cloth, or other article belonging to the company, will be considered guilty of STEALING—and prosecuted accordingly.

The above regulations are considered part of the contract with all persons entering the employment of the _____ MANUFACTURING COMPANY. All persons who shall have complied with them, on leaving the employment of the company, shall be entitled to an honorable discharge, which will serve as a recommendation to any of the factories in Lowell. No one who shall not have complied with them will be entitled to such a discharge.

_____ _____, Agent

Do we have any evidence from discharged women? Those honorably discharged vs. those _not_ honorably discharged ... _supposedly_, those w/ "good" discharges were fine in society — not so?

Source 3 courtesy of the American Textile History Museum.

3. Timetable of the Lowell Mills.

TIME TABLE OF THE LOWELL MILLS,

Arranged to make the working time throughout the year average 11 hours per day.

TO TAKE EFFECT SEPTEMBER 21st., 1853.

The Standard time being that of the meridian of Lowell, as shown by the Regulator Clock of AMOS SANBORN, Post Office Corner, Central Street.

From March 20th to September 19th, inclusive.

COMMENCE WORK, at 6.30 A. M.   LEAVE OFF WORK, at 6.30 P. M., except on Saturday Evenings.
BREAKFAST at 6 A. M.   DINNER, at 12 M.   Commence Work, after dinner, 12.45 P. M.

From September 20th to March 19th, inclusive.

COMMENCE WORK at 7.00 A. M.   LEAVE OFF WORK, at 7.00 P. M., except on Saturday Evenings.
BREAKFAST at 6.30 A. M.   DINNER, at 12.30 P. M.   Commence Work, after dinner, 1.15 P. M.

BELLS.

From March 20th to September 19th, inclusive.

Morning Bells.	Dinner Bells.	Evening Bells.
First bell,..........4.30 A. M.	Ring out,..............12.00 M.	Ring out,...........6.30 P. M.
Second, 5.30 A. M.; Third, 6.20.	Ring in,..........12.35 P. M.	Except on Saturday Evenings.

From September 20th to March 19th, inclusive.

Morning Bells.	Dinner Bells.	Evening Bells.
First bell,..........5.00 A. M.	Ring out,..........12.30 P. M.	Ring out at...........7.00 P. M.
Second, 6.00 A. M.; Third, 6.50.	Ring in,..........1.05 P. M.	Except on Saturday Evenings.

SATURDAY EVENING BELLS.

During APRIL, MAY, JUNE, JULY, and AUGUST, Ring Out, at 6.00 P. M.
The remaining Saturday Evenings in the year, ring out as follows :

SEPTEMBER.
First Saturday, ring out 6.00 P. M.
Second   "   "   5.45   "
Third   "   "   5.30   "
Fourth   "   "   5.20   "

OCTOBER.
First Saturday, ring out 5.05 P. M.
Second   "   "   4.55   "
Third   "   "   4.45   "
Fourth   "   "   4.35   "
Fifth   "   "   4.25   "

NOVEMBER.
First Saturday, ring out 4.15 P. M.
Second   ".   "   4.05   "

NOVEMBER.
Third Saturday ring out 4.00 P. M.
Fourth   "   "   3.55   "

DECEMBER.
First Saturday, ring out 3.50 P. M.
Second   "   "   3.55   "
Third   "   "   3.55   "
Fourth   "   "   4.00   "
Fifth   "   "   4.00   "

JANUARY.
First Saturday, ring out 4.10 P. M.
Second   "   "   4.15   "

JANUARY.
Third Saturday, ring out 4.25 P. M.
Fourth   "   "   4.35   "

FEBRUARY.
First Saturday, ring out 4.45 P. M.
Second   "   "   4.55   "
Third   "   "   5.00   "
Fourth   "   "   5.10   "

MARCH.
First Saturday, ring out 5.25 P. M.
Second   "   "   5.30   "
Third   "   "   5.35   "
Fourth   "   "   5.45   "

YARD GATES will be opened at the first stroke of the bells for entering or leaving the Mills.

.   *SPEED GATES commence hoisting three minutes before commencing work.*

Penhallow, Printer, Wyman's Exchange, 28 Merrimack St.

Source 4 from *Voice of Industry,* January 2, 1846, in H. R. Warfel et al., eds., *The American Mind* (New York: American Book Company, 1937), p. 392.

4. "Slaver" Wagons.

We were not aware, until within a few days, of the *modus operandi* of the factory powers in this village of forcing poor girls from their quiet homes to become their tools and, like the Southern slaves, to give up their life and liberty to the heartless tyrants and taskmasters.

Observing a singular-looking "long, low, black" wagon passing along the street, we made inquiries respecting it, and were informed that it was what we term a "slaver." She makes regular trips to the north of the state [Massachusetts], cruising around in Vermont and New Hampshire, with a "commander" whose heart must be as black as his craft, who is paid a dollar a head for all he brings to the market, and more in proportion to the distance—if they bring them from such a distance that they cannot easily get back.

This is done by "hoisting false colors," and representing to the girls that they can tend more machinery than is possible, and that the work is so very neat, and the wages such that they can dress in silks and spend half their time in reading. Now, is this true? Let those girls who have been thus deceived, answer.

Let us say a word in regard to the manner in which they are stowed in the wagon, which may find a similarity only in the manner in which slaves are fastened in the hold of a vessel. It is long, and the seats so close that it must be very inconvenient.

Is there any humanity in this? Philanthropists may talk of Negro slavery, but it would be well first to endeavor to emancipate the slaves at home. Let us not stretch our ears to catch the sound of the lash on the flesh of the oppressed black while the oppressed in our very midst are crying out in thunder tones, and calling upon us for assistance.

Source 5 from *Lowell Offering,* Series I, Issue 1 (1840). Courtesy of the American Textile History Museum.

5. Title Page of *Lowell Offering*.

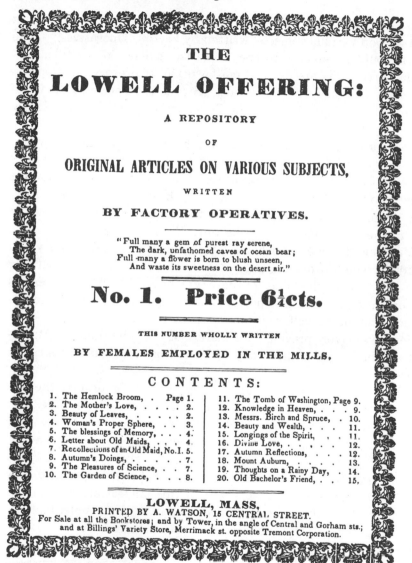

THE
LOWELL OFFERING:

A REPOSITORY

OF

ORIGINAL ARTICLES ON VARIOUS SUBJECTS,

WRITTEN

BY FACTORY OPERATIVES.

"Full many a gem of purest ray serene,
The dark, unfathomed caves of ocean bear;
Full many a flower is born to blush unseen,
And waste its sweetness on the desert air."

No. 1. Price 6¼cts.

THIS NUMBER WHOLLY WRITTEN

BY FEMALES EMPLOYED IN THE MILLS.

CONTENTS:

LOWELL, MASS,
PRINTED BY A. WATSON, 15 CENTRAL STREET.
For Sale at all the Bookstores; and by Tower, in the angle of Central and Gorham sts.;
and at Billings' Variety Store, Merrimack st. opposite Tremont Corporation.

Source 6 from *Lowell Offering,* Series I, Issue 1 (1840), p. 16.

6. Editorial Corner.

The Lowell Offering is strictly what it purports to be, a "Repository of original articles on various subjects, written by Factory Operatives."—The objects of the publication are, to encourage the cultivation of talent; to preserve such articles as are deemed most worthy of preservation; and to correct an erroneous idea which generally prevails in relation to the intelligence of persons employed in the Mills. This number is wholly the offering of Females. . . .

We are persuaded that the citizens generally, and those engaged in the Mills particularly, will feel and manifest a lively interest in the prosperity of the Lowell Offering. That it is faultless—that the severe and captious critic will find no room for his vocation, is not to be expected. Nevertheless, while the work makes no noisy pretensions to superior excellency, it would claim no unusual indulgences. It asks only that, all the circumstances incident to its peculiar character being duly weighed, it shall be fairly and candidly judged. The Editors do not hesitate to say, that they anticipate for a favorable reception at the hands of those who have at heart the interests of that important and interesting portion of our population, whose intellectual elevation and moral welfare it aims to promote. . . .

An opinion extensively prevails, not merely beyond the limits of Massachusetts, that the Manufacturing city of Lowell is a nucleus of depravity and ignorance.

Confessedly, wherever there exists *any* depravity or ignorance, there is *too much* of it. We have this to testify however, that they who know least of the people of Lowell, including the Factory Operatives, entertain the most unworthy and unjust opinions of them. Close personal observation has satisfied us, that in respect of morality and intelligence, they will not suffer in comparison with the inhabitants of any part of moral and enlightened New England. We shall have occasion to speak of this subject at considerable length hereafter. We shall note the unsurpassed (if not unequaled) advantages of education enjoyed by our population; and the extensive means of information and piety furnished by popular lectures and religious institutions. We shall note the absence of theatres and kindred abominations; the care taken to exclude unworthy persons from the Corporations, &c.

And as to the intelligence of our people, we may safely present the pages of the Offering as a testimony against all revilers "who know not whereof they affirm." Editors who think proper to copy any thing therefrom, are requested to give due credit, and thus assist in the correction of an unwarranted and injurious error.

Sources 7 and 8 from *Lowell Offering,* Series II, Vol. II (1842), p. 192; Series II, Vol. III (1842), pp. 69–70.

7. Dignity of Labor.

From whence originated the idea, that it was derogatory to a lady's dignity, or a blot upon the female character, to labor? and who was the first to say, sneeringly, "Oh, she *works* for a living"? Surely, such ideas and expressions ought not to grow on republican soil. The time has been, when ladies of the first rank were accustomed to busy themselves in domestic employment.

Homer tells us of princesses who used to draw water from the springs, and wash with their own hands the finest of the linen of their respective families. The famous Lucretia used to spin in the midst of her attendants; and the wife of Ulysses, after the siege of Troy, employed herself in weaving, until her husband returned to Ithaca. And in later times, the wife of George the Third of England, has been represented as spending a whole evening in hemming pocket-handkerchiefs, while her daughter Mary sat in the corner, darning stockings.

Few American fortunes will support a woman who is above the calls of her family; and a man of sense, in choosing a companion to jog with him through all the up-hills and down-hills of life, would sooner choose one who *had* to work for a living, than one who thought it beneath her to soil her pretty hands with manual labor, although she possessed her thousands. To be able to earn one's own living by laboring with the hands, should be reckoned among female accomplishments; and I hope the time is not far distant when none of my countrywomen will be ashamed to have it known that they are better versed in useful, than they are in ornamental accomplishments.

C.B.

8. Editorial: Home in a Boardinghouse.

[*Factory boardinghouses were not really like homes, the editor pointed out. A place to eat and lodge, the boardinghouses often seemed crowded and impersonal.*]

But these are all trifles, compared with the perplexities to which we are subjected in other ways; and some of these things might be remedied by the girls themselves. We now allude to the importunities of evening visitors, such as peddlers, candy and newspaper boys, shoe-dealers, book-sellers, &c., &c., breaking in upon the only hours of leisure we can call our own, and proffering their articles with a pertinacity which will admit of no denial. . . . And then they often forget, if they ever knew, the rules of politeness which should regulate all transient visitors. . . .

The remedy is entirely with the girls. Treat all of these comers with a politeness truly lady-like, when they appear as gentlemen, but let your manners change to stern formality when they forget that they are in the company of respectable females. . . .

C.B.

Sources 9 through 11 from *Lowell Offering,* Series I (1840), pp. 17–19, 61, 44–46.

9. Factory Girls.

"She has worked in a factory, *is sufficient to damn to infamy the most worthy and virtuous girl.*"

So says Mr. Orestes A. Brownson; and either this horrible assertion is true, or Mr. Brownson is a slanderer. I assert that it is *not* true, and Mr. B. may consider himself called upon to prove his words, if he can.

This gentleman has read of an Israelitish boy who, with nothing but a stone and sling, once entered into a contest with a Philistine giant, arrayed in brass, whose spear was like a weaver's beam; and he may now see what will probably appear to him quite as marvellous; and that is, that a *factory girl* is not afraid to oppose herself to the *Editor of the Boston Quarterly Review.* True, he has upon his side fame, learning, and great talent; but I have what is better than either of these, or all combined, and that is *truth.* Mr. Brownson has not said that this thing should be so; or that he is glad it is so; or that he deeply regrets such a state of affairs; but he has said it *is* so; and *I* affirm that it is *not.*

And whom has Mr. Brownson slandered? A class of girls who in this city alone are numbered by thousands, and who collect in many of our smaller towns by hundreds; girls who generally come from quiet country homes, where their minds and manners have been formed under the eyes of the worthy sons of the Pilgrims, and their virtuous partners, and who return again to become the wives of the free intelligent yeomanry of New England and the mothers of quite a portion of our future republicans. Think, for a moment, how many of the next generation are to spring from mothers doomed to infamy! "Ah," it may be replied, "Mr. Brownson acknowledges that you may still be worthy and virtuous." Then we must be a set of worthy and virtuous idiots, for no virtuous girl of common sense would choose for an occupation one that would consign her to infamy. . . .

That there has been prejudice against us, we know; but it is wearing away, and has never been so deep nor universal as Mr. B's statement will lead many to believe. Even now it may be that "the mushroom aristocracy" and "would-be fashionables" of Boston, turn up their eyes in horror at the sound of those vulgar words, *factory girls;* but *they* form but a small part of the community, and theirs are not the opinions which Mr. Brownson intended to represent. . . .

[*The prejudice against factory girls was connected to the degraded and exploited conditions of European workers, the angry letter writer asserted. "Yankee girls," she said, are independent, and although the work is hard, the wages are better than those in other kinds of employment. It is no wonder, she concluded, that so many intelligent, worthy, and virtuous young women have been drawn to Lowell.*]

The erroneous idea, wherever it exists, must be done away, that there is in factories but one sort of girls, and *that* the baser and degraded sort. There are among us *all* sorts of girls. I believe that there are few occupations which can exhibit so many gradations of piety and intelligence; but the majority may at least lay claim to as much of the former as females in other stations of life. . . . The Improvement Circles, the Lyceum and Institute, the social religious meetings, the Circulating and other libraries, can bear testimony that the little time they have is spent in a better manner. Our well filled churches and lecture halls and the high character of our clergymen and lecturers, will testify that the state of morals and intelligence is not low.

Mr. Brownson, I suppose, would not judge of our moral characters by our church-going tendencies; but as many do, a word on this subject may not be amiss. That there are many in Lowell who do not regularly attend any meeting, is as true as the correspondent of the Boston Times once represented it; but for this there are various reasons. . . .

There have also been nice calculations made, as to the small proportion which the amount of money deposited in the Savings Bank bears to that earned in the city; but this is not all that is saved. Some is deposited in Banks at other places, and some is put into the hands of personal friends. Still, much that is earned is immediately, though not foolishly, spent. Much that none but the parties concerned will ever know of, goes to procure comforts and necessaries for some lowly home, and a great deal is spent for public benevolent purposes. . . .

And now, if Mr. Brownson is a *man,* he will endeavor to retrieve the injury he has done; he will resolve that "the dark shall be light, and the wrong made right," and the assertion he has publicly made will be as publicly retracted. If he still doubts upon the subject let him come among us: let

him make himself as well acquainted with us as our pastors and superin-
tendents are; and though he will find error, ignorance, and folly among us,
(and where would he find them not?) yet he would not see worthy and
virtuous girls consigned to infamy, because they work in a factory.

A FACTORY GIRL

10. A Familiar Letter.

Friends and Associates:—

With indescribable emotions of pleasure, mingled with feelings of deepest
gratitude to Him who is the Author of every good and perfect gift, I have
perused the second and third numbers of the Lowell Offering.

As a laborer among you, (tho' least of all) I rejoice that the time has
arrived when a class of laboring females (who have long been made a
reproach and byword, by those whom fortune or pride has placed above the
avocation by which we have subjected ourselves to the sneers and scoffs of
the idle, ignorant and envious part of community,) are bursting asunder the
captive chains of prejudice. . . .

I know it has been affirmed, to the sorrow of many a would-be lady, that
factory girls and ladies could not be distinguished by their apparel. What a
lamentable evil! and no doubt it would be a source of much gratitude to
such, if the awful name of "factory girl!" were branded on the forehead of
every female who is, or ever was, employed in the Mills. Appalling as the
name may sound in the delicate ears of a sensitive lady, as she contrasts
the music of her piano with the rumblings of the factory machinery, we
would not shrink from such a token of our calling, could the treasures of
the mind be there displayed, and merit, in her own unbiased form be
stamped there also. . . .

Yours, in the bonds of affection,

DOROTHEA

11. Gold Watches.

It is now nearly a year since an article appeared in the Ladies' Book, in
the form of a tale, though it partakes more of the character of an essay. It
was written by Mrs. Hale, and exhibits her usual judgment and talent. Her
object evidently was to correct the many erroneous impressions which exist

in society, with regard to the folly of extravagance in dress, and all outward show. I was much pleased with all of it, with the exception of a single sentence. Speaking of the impossibility of considering dress a mark of distinction, she observed,—(addressing herself, I presume, to the *ladies* of New England,)—"How stands the difference now? Many of the factory girls wear gold watches, and an imitation, at least, of all the ornaments which grace the daughters of our most opulent citizens."

O the times! O the manners! Alas! how very sadly the world has changed! The time was when the *lady* could be distinguished from the *no-lady* by her dress, as far as the eye could reach; but now, you might stand in the same room, and judging by their outward appearance, you could not tell "which was which." Even gold watches are now no *sure* indication—for they have been worn by the lowest, even by "many of the factory girls." No *lady* need carry one now, for any other than the simple purpose of easily ascertaining the time of day, or night, if she so please! . . .

Those who do not labor for their living, have more time for the improvement of their minds, for the cultivation of conversational powers, and graceful manners; but if, with these advantages, they still need richer dress to distinguish them from *us,* the fault must be their own, and they should at least learn to honor merit, and acknowledge talent wherever they see it. . . .

And now I will address myself to my sister operatives in the Lowell factories. Good advice should be taken, from whatever quarter it may come, whether from friend or foe; and part of the advice which Mrs. Hale has given to the readers of the Ladies' Book, may be of advantage to us. Is there not among us, as a class, too much of this striving for distinction in dress? Is it not the only aim and object of too many of us, to wear something a little better than others can obtain? Do we not sometimes see the girl who has half a dozen silk gowns, toss her head, as if she felt herself six times better than her neighbor who has none? . . .

We all have many opportunities for the exercise of the kindly affections, and more than most females. We should look upon one another something as a band of orphans should do. We are fatherless and motherless: we are alone, and surrounded by temptation. Let us caution each other; let us watch over and endeavor to improve each other; and both at our boarding-houses and in the Mill, let us strive to promote each other's comfort and happiness. Above all, let us endeavor to improve ourselves by making good use of the many advantages we here possess. I say let us at least strive to do this; and if we succeed, it will finally be acknowledged that Factory Girls shine forth in ornaments far more valuable than *Gold Watches.*

A FACTORY GIRL

Source 12 from *Lowell Offering*, Series II, Vol. II (1842), p. 380.

12. Editor's Valedictory.

It has been the object of the editor to encourage the cultivation of talent, and thus open and enlarge the sources of enjoyment in the midst of a toilsome life. In this way he has done something toward modifying the privations and other evils incident to employment in the Mills; and it must be acknowledged, that even if no other good be effected, something is gained by retarding the progress of decay.

We hoped ere this to have seen a spacious room, with a Library, &c., established on each Corporation, for the accommodation of the female operatives in the evenings. The example, we trust, will shortly be set by the Merrimack. And why should not bathing-rooms be fitted up in the basement of each Mill? The expense would not be felt by the Company, and the means of health and comfort thus provided, would be gratefully acknowledged. We suggest, in addition, a better ventilation of the boarding-houses. Diminution of the hours of mill-labor, and the entire abrogation of premiums to Overseers, should also be included in the list of improvements.

There is another matter, some time since presented to the operatives, and now repeated, namely, the payment of a small sum monthly, say 8 or 10 cents, to consitute a fund for the relief of the sick. The amount might be deducted by the pay-master, as agent of the Superintendent. The details of the plan could readily be agreed upon. Two cents each week would surely be well spent as insurance against the expenses of sickness, to be fixed at about three dollars weekly—to be received, not as *charity*, but as a lawful demand.

Source 13 from *Lowell Offering*, Series II, Vol. V (1845), p. 96.

13. Editorial: The Ten-Hour Movement.

[*The editor begins by reviewing the work of the Massachusetts legislature's Committee upon the Hours of Labor. Although she understands why the demand for a ten-hour workday was not accepted, she believes there were other improvements that might have been made.*]

It seems to have been generally conceded, that the time allotted to meals is very short—where the operatives have tolerable appetites: and this is usually the case with persons who *work so regularly* and indefatigably. Why not have compromised then with the petitioners, and allowed them one hour for dinner through the year, and three-quarters of an hour for breakfast? The dinner *hour* is given in some manufacturing places, therefore the plea with regard to competition is not unanswerable. We believe also that Lowell is expected to take the lead in all improvements of this nature, and, should she amend her present system, it is more probable that she would be imitated than successfully contended against. . . .

[The editor then addresses employers' argument that there are girls waiting at the factory gate before the work bell rings, eager to get in and begin work. The author concedes that some girls compete with each other for the overseer's favors. But what of the others? she asks.]

. . . They feel that they are unable to work all these hours, and "work upon the stretch," as they say. They are older, or weaker, or more heavily moulded, or unwilling, if not unable. Therefore they are not favorites with their overseer. They are not so "profitable servants," and the kind look and word, or obliging act, is not so often bestowed upon them. This is one instance where the testimony is liable to misconstruction, and had we space, we might find many more.

The Legislature seem to have doubted the propriety of their commencing action upon this subject. Where should it commence? How is it to be done? When, where, and by whom? All, connected with manufacturing establishments, feel confident that, "as surely as there is benevolence and justice in the heart of man," this wrong will be righted. But objections are brought against every movement. Of late the efforts of the dissatisfied operatives have been of a quiet nature. This petition to the Legislature is both proper and dignified. Picknicks, if *conducted with propriety,* would be unobjectionable, as demonstrations of public sentiment. Conventions, as affording opportunity for a free expression of opinion, should also be favored; notwithstanding there may be much bombast and rhodomontade, with a little injustice and demagoguism.

No effort originating among a promiscuous number of laborers, and conducted wholly by them, can be expected to be free from every imputation. So far we should be gratified that the dissatisfied and "despised" have conducted so quietly and well.

Source 14 from *Lowell Offering,* Series II, Vol. I (1841), p. 32. Courtesy of the American Textile History Museum.

14. "Song of the Spinners."

SONG OF THE SPINNERS.

1. The day is o'er, nor lon-ger we toil and spin; For ev'ning's hush withdraws from the dai-ly din. And

2. We spin all day, and then, in the time for rest, Sweet peace is found, A joyous and welcome guest. Des -

now we sing, with gladsome hearts, The theme of the spinner's song, That la-bor to lei-sure a zest imparts, Unknown to the i - - dle throng.

- pite of toil we all agree, or out of the Mills, or in, De-pen-dent on others we ne'er will be. So long as we're a-ble to spin.

Source 15 from Lucy Larcom, *A New England Girlhood* (Boston: Houghton Mifflin, 1889).

15. Selection from *A New England Girlhood.*

[After her husband's death, Lucy Larcom's mother moved to Lowell to run a boarding-house. Because her mother could not earn enough to support the family, Lucy, age eleven, and her older sister went to work in the mills.]

So I went to my first day's work in the mill with a light heart. The novelty of it made it seem easy, and it really was not hard, just to change the bobbins on the spinning-frames every three quarters of an hour or so, with half a dozen other little girls who were doing the same thing. When I came back at night, the family began to pity me for my long, tiresome day's work, but I laughed, and said,—

"Why, it is nothing but fun. It is just like play."

And for a little while it was only a new amusement; I liked it better than going to school and "making believe" I was learning when I was not. And there was a great deal of play mixed with it. We were not occupied more than half the time. The intervals were spent frolicking around among the spinning-frames, teasing and talking to the older girls, or entertaining ourselves with games and stories in a corner, or exploring, with the over-seer's permission, the mysteries of the carding-room, the dressing-room, and the weaving-room. . . .

There were compensations for being shut in to daily toil so early. The mill itself had its lessons for us. But it was not, and could not be, the right sort of life for a child, and we were happy in the knowledge that, at the longest, our employment was only to be temporary. . . .

[*Lucy loved elementary school and wanted to continue her studies, but her family needed her mill wages.*]

In the older times it was seldom said to little girls, as it always has been said to boys, that they ought to have some definite plan, while they were children, what to be and do when they were grown up. There was usually but one path open before them, to become good wives and housekeepers. And the ambition of most girls was to follow their mothers' footsteps in this direction; a natural and laudable ambition. But girls, as well as boys, must often have been conscious of their own peculiar capabilities,—must have desired to cultivate and make use of their individual powers. When I was growing up, they had already begun to be encouraged to do so. We were often told that it was our duty to develop any talent we might possess, or at least learn how to do some one thing which the world needed, or which would make it a pleasanter world. . . .

At this time I had learned to do a spinner's work, and I obtained permission to tend some frames that stood directly in front of the river-windows, with only them and the wall behind me, extending half the length of the mill,—and one young woman beside me, at the farther end of the row. She was a sober, mature person, who scarcely thought it worth her while to speak often to a child like me; and I was, when with strangers, rather a reserved girl; so I kept myself occupied with the river, my work, and my thoughts. . . .

The printed regulations forbade us to bring books into the mill, so I made my window-seat into a small library of poetry, pasting its side all over with newspaper clippings. In those days we had only weekly papers, and they had always a "poet's corner," where standard writers were well repre-sented, with anonymous ones, also. I was not, of course, much of a critic. I chose my verses for their sentiment, and because I wanted to commit them to memory; sometimes it was a long poem, sometimes a hymn, sometimes only a stray verse. . . .

Some of the girls could not believe that the Bible was meant to be counted among forbidden books. We all thought that the Scriptures had a right to go wherever we went, and that if we needed them anywhere, it was at our work. I evaded the law by carrying some leaves from a torn Testament in my pocket.

[*In spite of the regulations, girls brought poetry and plants into the factory.*]

One great advantage which came to these many stranger girls through being brought together, away from their own homes, was that it taught them to go out of themselves, and enter into the lives of others. Home-life, when one always stays at home, is necessarily narrowing. That is one reason why so many women are petty and unthoughtful of any except their own family's interests. We have hardly begun to live until we can take in the idea of the whole human family as the one to which we truly belong. To me, it was an incalculable help to find myself among so many working-girls, all of us thrown upon our own resources, but thrown much more upon each others' sympathies. . . .

My grandfather came to see my mother once at about this time and visited the mills. When he had entered the room, and looked around for a moment, he took off his hat and made a low bow to the girls, first toward the right, and then toward the left. We were familiar with his courteous habits, partly due to his French descent; but we had never seen anybody bow to a roomful of mill girls in that polite way, and some one of the family afterwards asked him why he did so. He looked a little surprised at the question, but answered promptly and with dignity, "I always take off my hat to ladies."

His courtesy was genuine. Still, we did not call ourselves ladies. We did not forget that we were working-girls, wearing coarse aprons suitable to our work, and that there was some danger of our becoming drudges. I know that sometimes the confinement of the mill became very wearisome to me. In the sweet June weather I would lean far out of the window, and try not to hear the unceasing clash of sound inside. Looking away to the hills, my whole stifled being would cry out

"Oh, that I had wings!"

Still I was there from choice, and

"The prison unto which we doom ourselves,
No prison is."

Source 16 courtesy of the Mildred Tunis Tracey Memorial Library, New London, New Hampshire.

16. A "Typical" Factory Girl, Delia Page, at Age 18 or 19 (c. 1860).

Source 17 courtesy of the American Textile History Museum.

17. Two Weavers, c. 1860.

Sources 18 through 22 from Thomas Dublin, ed., *Farm to Factory: Women's Letters, 1830–1860* (New York: Columbia University Press, 1981), pp. 42, 100–104, 170–172.

18. Letter from Sarah Hodgdon.

[*In 1830, Sarah Hodgdon, age sixteen, and two friends went to Lowell to work in the textile mills. After approximately ten years of working in various factories, Hodgdon married a shoemaker from her home town. This is one of her early letters to her mother.*]

[June 1830]

Dear mother

I take this oppertunity to write to you to informe you that I have gone into the mill and like [it] very well. I was here one week and three days before I went into the mill to work for my board. We boord t[o]gether. I like my boording place very well. I enjoy my health very well. I do not enjoy my mind so well as it is my desire to. I cant go to any meetings except I hire a seat therefore I have to stay home on that account.[6] I desire you pay that it may not be said of me when I come home that I have sold my soul for the gay vanitys of this world. Give my love to my father and tell him not to forget me and to my dear sister and to my brothers and to my grammother tell her I do not forget her and to my Aunts and to all my enquiring friends. I want that you should write to me as soon as you can and when you write to me I want that you should write to me the particulars about sister and Aunt Betsy. Dont fail writing. I bege you not to let this scrabling be seen.

Sarah Hodgdon

Mary Hodgdon

19. Letter from Mary Paul.

[*Mary Paul left home in 1845 at age fifteen. She worked briefly and unsuccessfully as a domestic servant and then went to Lowell as a factory girl for four years. After leaving the mills, she returned home for a short while and then worked as a seamstress. Next she joined a utopian community, and finally she took a job as a housekeeper. In 1857, Paul married the son of the woman who ran the boarding-house where she had lived in Lowell.*]

6. Urban churches in this period often charged people who attended services a fee called pew rent.

Saturday, Sept. 13th 1845

Dear Father

I received your letter this afternoon by Wm Griffith. . . . I am very glad you sent my shoes. They fit very well indeed they [are] large enough.

I want you to consent to let me go to Lowell if you can. I think it would be much better for me than to stay about here. I could earn more to begin with than I can any where about here. I am in need of clothes which I cannot get if I stay about here and for that reason I want to go to Lowell or some other place. We all think if I could go with some steady girl that I might do well. I want you to think of it and make up your mind. Mercy Jane Griffith is going to start in four or five weeks. Aunt Miller and Aunt Sarah think it would be a good chance for me to go if you would consent—which I want you to do if possible. I want to see you and talk with you about it.

Aunt Sarah gains slowly.

Mary

Bela Paul

20. Letter from Mary Paul.

Lowell Dec 21st 1845

Dear Father

I received your letter on Thursday the 14th with much pleasure. I am well which is one comfort. My life and health are spared while others are cut off. Last Thursday one girl fell down and broke her neck which caused instant death. She was going in or coming out of the mill and slipped down it being very icy. The same day a man was killed by the cars. Another had nearly all of his ribs broken. Another was nearly killed by falling down and having a bale of cotton fall on him. Last Tuesday we were paid. In all I had six dollars and sixty cents paid four dollars and sixty-eight cents for board. With the rest I got me a pair of rubbers and a pair of 50.cts shoes. . . . Perhaps you would like something about our regulations about going in and coming out of the mill. At 5 o'clock in the morning the bell rings for the folks to get up and get breakfast. At half past six it rings for the girls to get up and at seven they are called into the mill. At half past 12 we have dinner are called back again at one and stay till half past seven. I get along very well with my work. I can doff[7] as fast as any girl in our room. I think I shall have frames before long. The usual time allowed for learning is six months

7. A doffer replaced empty bobbins on the spinning frames with full ones.

but I think I shall have frames before I have been in three as I get along so fast. I think that the factory is the best place for me and if any girl wants employment I advise them to come to Lowell. Tell Harriet that though she does not hear from me she is not forgotten. I have little time to devote to writing that I cannot write all I want to. . . .

This from
Mary S Paul

Bela Paul
Henry S Paul

21. Letter to Delia Page.[8]

[Delia Page lived with a foster family, the Trussells, because she did not get along well with her stepmother. In 1859, at age eighteen, she went to work at a textile mill in Manchester, New Hampshire, where she fell in love with a mill worker who had evidently deserted his wife and child in Lowell. When reports of Delia's "affair" reached home, her foster family wrote her urgent letters trying to persuade her to reconsider. Eventually, in 1866, she married an eligible, respectable single man.]

New London Sept. 7, 1860

Dear Delia,

I should thank you for your very good letter. I am glad to know your health is good. I trust I shall ever feel a deep interest in your welfare.

You say you are not so much in love as we imagine; if so I am very glad of it. Not that I should not be willing you should love a worthy object but the one referred to is no doubt an *unworthy* one; and should you fix you[r] affections on him, it will cause you sorrow such as you never knew; indeed we believe it would be *your ruin*. We have no reason to think, his pretensions notwithstanding, that he has any *real love for you*. Your father Trussell has told or rather written you what he has learned about him. I fear it will be hard for you to believe it, but if you will take the trouble to inquire, I think you will find it all true. He probably is incapable of even friendship, and in his apparent regard for you, is actuated by *low, base, selfish* motives.

I think you will sooner or later come to this conclusion respecting him. The sooner the better. Your reputation your happiness all you hold dear are I fear at stake. You have done well, let not your high hopes be blasted. Do the best you can, keep no company but good and you stand fair to get a good husband, one who has a real regard for you. But if you keep this man's

8. Delia Page's photograph is shown in Source 16.

company, the virtuous must shun you. You will not like to read this. My only excuse for writing is that I am very anxious about you. If my anxiety is unfounded so much the better. Unfounded it cannot be if you are keeping the company of an unprincipled libertine.

Your affectionate Mother Trussell

22. Letter to Delia Page.

[Sept. 7 1860]

My Dear Delia,

I am going to trouble you a little longer (I speak for the whole family now). In your situation you must necessarily form many new acquaintance[s] and amongst them there will be not a few who will assure you of their friendship and seek your confidence. The less worthy they are the more earnestly they will seek to convince you of their sincerity. You spoke of one girl whom you highly prised. I hope she is all that you think her to be. If so you are certainly fortunate in making her acquaintance.

But the best have failings & I should hardly expect one of her age a safe counciler in all cases. You must in fact rely upon a principal of morality within your own bosom and if you [are] at a loss you may depend upon the council of Mrs. Piper.[9] A safe way is not to allow yourself to say or do anything that you would not be willing anyone should know if necessary. You will say Humpf think I cant take care of myself. I have seen many who thought so and found their mistake when ruined. My dear girl. We fear much for those we love much, or the fear is in porportion [sic] to the Love. And although I have no reason to think that you go out nights or engage in anything that will injure your health or morrals [sic] yet the love I have for you leads me to fear lest among so much that is pleasant but evil you may be injured before you are aware of danger.

And now my Dear Girl I will finish by telling you what you must do for me.

You must take care of my little factory girl. Dont let her expose her health if you do she will be sick and loose [sic] all she has earned. Don't let her do any thing any time that she would be ashamed to have her father know. If you do she may loose her charracter [sic]. Try to have her improve some every day that she may be the wealthiest most respected & best beloved of all her sisters, brothers & kindred & so be fitted to make the best of husbands the best of wives.

[Luther M Trussell]

9. The Pipers were Trussell family friends who lived in Manchester.

∽ QUESTIONS TO CONSIDER ∾

Why did Brownson (Source 1) believe that slaves were better off than free laborers? What did he imply about women who worked? What major advantages did Reverend Mills observe in the Lowell system (Source 2)? In what important ways did the system (the factories and the boardinghouses) regulate the girls' lives? How did it protect the morals of its female employees? Of course, not all girls lived up to these standards. What did they do? How were they punished? Do you think Reverend Mills presented a relatively unbiased view? Why or why not? In what ways did the author of the article in *Voice of Industry* (Source 4) believe factory girls were being exploited?

Look carefully at the title page (Source 5) and the first editorial of the *Lowell Offering* (Source 6). What do they tell you about the factory girls, their interests, and their concerns? Was C.B. (Source 7) upholding the cult of true womanhood in her article about the dignity of labor? How did "home" in the boardinghouse (Source 8) differ from the girls' real homes? Based on what you read in Reverend Mills's account, in what ways might a boardinghouse have been similar to the girls' real homes?

The next three letters were written by girls who were rather angry. How did "a factory girl" (Source 9) try to disprove Brownson's view? What fears and anxieties do this letter and the one from Dorothea (Source 10) reveal? What were these two girls trying to prove? The third letter writer (Source 11) retained her sense of humor, but she also was upset. In this case, the offensive remark to which she referred appeared in *Godey's Lady's Book,* the most popular American women's magazine of the period, and was written by the highly respected Sarah Josepha Hale, the magazine's editor and author of "Mary Had a Little Lamb." What had Mrs. Hale written? What was the factory girl's response? What advice did she give her coworkers about fashion? About being a true woman? Both the editor's valedictory and the editorial about the ten-hour-day petitions (Sources 12 and 13) want changes. What were they? How does the editor believe these changes can be achieved? Even "Song of the Spinners" (Source 14) contains a message. What do the lyrics tell you about the spinners' values and attitudes toward work?

What were the other realities of factory girls' lives? What does the bell schedule (Source 3) tell you? How would you describe the image that the pictures of the mill girls present (Sources 16 and 17)? What hopes (and fears) does the correspondence between the mill girls and their families (Sources 18 through 22) express? Why did Lucy Larcom (Source 15) have to go to work in the mills when she was so young? How did she feel about the work when she was a child? What contrast did she draw between young boys' and young girls' upbringing in the early nineteenth century? Did she and the other girls always obey the factory rules? What advantages did she discover in her factory experience? What were the disadvantages?

Now that you are thoroughly familiar with the ideas about how the working girls of Lowell were supposed to behave and the realities of the system under which they lived, you are ready to frame an answer to the central question: How did people react when the needs of a modernizing economy came into conflict with the ideas about women's place in society?

☙ EPILOGUE ❧

The Lowell system was a very real attempt to prevent the spread of the evils associated with the factory system and to make work in the textile mills "respectable" for young New England women. Working conditions in Lowell were considerably better than in most other New England mill towns. However, several major strikes (or "turnouts," as they were called) occurred in the Lowell mills in the mid-1830s, and by the mid-1840s Lowell began to experience serious labor problems. To remain competitive yet at the same time maximize profits, companies introduced the "speedup" (a much faster work pace) and the "stretch-out" (one worker was put in charge of more machinery—sometimes as many as four looms). The mills also cut wages, even though boardinghouse rents were rising. In Lowell, workers first tried to have the length of the workday reduced and, as did many other American workers, united in support of the Ten-Hour Movement. When women workers joined such protests, they further challenged the ideas embodied in the cult of true womanhood, especially that of submissiveness.

Even before the strikes, the Lowell system was breaking down, as more and more mills, far larger than their predecessors, were built. Construction of private housing (especially tenements) expanded, and a much smaller proportion of mill hands lived in boardinghouses. Both housing and neighborhoods became badly overcrowded. By 1850, mill owners were looking for still other ways besides the speedup and stretch-out to reduce the cost of labor. They found their answer in the waves of Irish immigrating to America to escape the economic hardships so widespread in their own country. Fewer and fewer "Yankee girls" were recruited for work in the textile mills. At one Lowell company, the number of native-born girls declined from 737 in 1836 to 324 in 1860, although the total number of female workers remained constant. Irish men, women, and increasing numbers of children filled the gap, because as wages declined, a family income became a necessity.

By 1860, what Reverend Mills had characterized as "the moral and intellectual advantages" of the Lowell system had come to an end. Indeed, many Americans could see little or no difference between our own factory towns and those of Europe.

CHAPTER 5

THE "PECULIAR INSTITUTION": SLAVES TELL THEIR OWN STORY

∞ THE PROBLEM ∞

With the establishment of its new government in 1789, the United States became a virtual magnet for foreign travelers, perhaps never more so than during the three decades immediately preceding our Civil War. Middle to upper class, interested in everything from politics to prison reform to botanical specimens to the position of women in American society, these curious travelers fanned out across the United States, and almost all wrote about their observations in letters, pamphlets, and books widely read on both sides of the ocean. Regardless of their special interests, however, few travelers failed to notice—and comment on—the "peculiar institution" of African American slavery.

As were many nineteenth-century women writers, English author Harriet Martineau was especially interested in those aspects of American society that affected women and children. She was appalled by the slave system, believing it degraded marriage by allowing southern white men to exploit female slaves sexually, a practice that often produced mulatto children born into slavery.

The young Frenchman Alexis de Tocqueville came to study the American penitentiary system and stayed to investigate politics and society. In his book *Democracy in America* (1842), Tocqueville expressed his belief that American slaves had completely lost their African culture—their customs, languages, religions, and even the memories of their countries. An English novelist who was enormously popular in the United States, the crusty Charles Dickens, also visited in 1842. He spent very little time in the

CHAPTER 5

THE "PECULIAR
INSTITUTION":
SLAVES TELL
THEIR OWN
STORY

South but collected (and published) advertisements for runaway slaves that contained gruesome descriptions of their burns, brandings, scars, and iron cuffs and collars. As Dickens departed for a steamboat trip to the West, he wrote that he left "with a grateful heart that I was not doomed to live where slavery was, and had never had my senses blunted to its wrongs and horrors in a slave-rocked cradle."[1]

In the turbulent 1850s, Fredrika Bremer, a Swedish novelist, traveled throughout the United States for two years and spent considerable time in South Carolina, Georgia, and Louisiana. After her first encounters with African Americans in Charleston, Bremer wrote to her sister that "they are ugly, but appear for the most part cheerful and well-fed."[2] Her subsequent trips to the plantations of the backcountry, however, increased her sympathy for slaves and her distrust of white southerners' assertions that "slaves are the happiest people in the world."[3] In fact, by the end of her stay, Bremer was praising the slaves' morality, patience, talents, and religious practices.

These travelers—and many more—added their opinions to the growing literature about the nature of American slavery and its effects. But the overwhelming majority of this literature was written by white people. What did the slaves themselves think? How did they express their feelings about the peculiar institution of slavery?

ᏏᎧ BACKGROUND ᏏᎧ

By the time of the American Revolution, what had begun in 1619 as a trickle of Africans intended to supplement the farm labor of indentured servants from England had swelled to a slave population of approximately 500,000 people, the majority concentrated on tobacco, rice, and cotton plantations in the South. Moreover, as the African American population grew, what apparently had been a fairly loose and unregimented labor system gradually evolved into an increasingly harsh, rigid, and complete system of chattel slavery that tried to control nearly every aspect of the slaves' lives. By 1775, African American slavery had become a significant (some would have said indispensable) part of southern life.

The American Revolution did not reverse those trends. Although northern states in which African American slavery was not so deeply rooted began instituting gradual emancipation, after the Revolution, the slave system—as well as its harshness—increased in the South. The invention of the cotton gin, which enabled seeds to be removed from the easily grown short staple cotton, permitted southerners

1. Charles Dickens, *American Notes and Pictures from Italy* (London: Oxford University Press, 1957), p. 137.

2. Fredrika Bremer, *America of the Fifties: Letters of Fredrika Bremer,* ed. Adolph B. Benson (New York: American Scandinavian Foundation, 1924), p. 96.
3. Ibid., p. 100.

to cultivate cotton on the uplands, thereby spurring the westward movement of the plantation system and slavery. As a result, slavery expanded along with settlement into nearly every area of the South: the Gulf region, Tennessee, Kentucky, and ultimately Texas. Simultaneously, the slave population burgeoned, roughly doubling every thirty years (from approximately 700,000 in 1790 to 1.5 million in 1820 to more than 3.2 million in 1850). Because importation of slaves from Africa was banned in 1808 (although there was some illegal slave smuggling), most further gains in the slave population were from natural increase.

But as the slave population grew, the fears and anxieties of southern whites grew correspondingly. In 1793, a slave rebellion in the Caribbean caused tremendous consternation in the white South. Rumors of uprisings plotted by slaves were numerous. And the actual rebellion of Nat Turner in Virginia in 1831 (in which fifty-five whites were killed, many of them while asleep) only increased white insecurities and dread. In response, southern states passed a series of laws that made the system of slavery even more restrictive. Toward the end of his life, Thomas Jefferson (who did not live to see Nat Turner's uprising) agonized:

> But as it is, we have the wolf by the ears, and we can neither hold him, nor safely let him go. Justice is in one scale, and self-preservation in the other. . . . I regret that I am now to die in the belief, that the useless sacrifice of themselves by the generation of 1776, to acquire self-government

and happiness to their country, is to be thrown away by the unwise and unworthy passions of their sons.

By this time, however, Jefferson was nearly alone among white southerners. Most did not question the assertion that slavery was a necessity, that it was good for both the slave and the owner, and that it must be preserved at any cost.

It often has been pointed out that the majority of white southerners did not own slaves. In fact, the proportion of white southern families who did own slaves was actually declining in the nineteenth century, from one-third in 1830 to roughly one-fourth by 1860. Moreover, nearly three-fourths of these slaveholders owned fewer than ten slaves. Slaveholders, then, were a distinct minority of the white southern population, and those slaveholders with large plantations and hundreds of slaves were an exceedingly small group.

How, then, did the peculiar institution of slavery, as one southerner called it, become so embedded in the Old South? First, even though only a minority of southern whites owned slaves, nearly all southern whites were somehow touched by the institution of slavery. Fear of black uprisings prompted many nonslaveholders to support an increasingly rigid slave system that included night patrols, written passes for slaves away from plantations, supervised religious services for slaves, a law prohibiting teaching slaves to read or write, and other measures to keep slaves ignorant, dependent, and always under the eyes of whites. Many nonslaveholders also were afraid that emancipation would

CHAPTER 5

THE "PECULIAR
INSTITUTION":
SLAVES TELL
THEIR OWN
STORY

bring them into direct economic competition with blacks, who, it was assumed, would drive down wages. Finally, although large planters represented only a fraction of the white population, they virtually controlled the economic, social, and political institutions and were not about to injure either themselves or their status by eliminating the slave system that essentially supported them.

To defend their peculiar institution, white southerners constructed a remarkably complete and diverse set of arguments. Slavery, they maintained, was actually a far more humane system than northern capitalism. After all, slaves were fed, clothed, sheltered, cared for when they were ill, and supported in their old age, whereas northern factory workers were paid pitifully low wages, used, and then discarded when no longer useful. Furthermore, many white southerners maintained that slavery was a positive good because it had introduced the "barbarous" Africans to civilized American ways and, more importantly, to Christianity. Other southern whites stressed what they believed was the childlike, dependent nature of African Americans, insisting that they could never cope with life outside the paternalistic and "benevolent" institution of slavery. In such an atmosphere, in which many of the white southern intellectual efforts went into the defense of slavery, dissent and freedom of thought were not welcome. Hence those white southerners who disagreed and might have challenged the South's dependence on slavery remained silent, were hushed up, or decided to leave the region. In many

ways, then, the enslavement of African Americans partly rested on the limitation of rights and freedoms for southern whites as well.

But how did the slaves react to an economic and social system that meant that neither they nor their children would ever experience freedom? Most white southerners assumed that slaves were happy and content. Northern abolitionists (a minority of the white population) believed that slaves continually yearned for freedom. Both groups used oceans of ink to justify and support their claims. But evidence of how the slaves felt and thought is woefully sparse. Given the restrictive nature of the slave system (which included enforced illiteracy among slaves), this pitiful lack of evidence is hardly surprising.

How, then, can we learn how slaves felt and thought about the peculiar institution? Slave uprisings were almost nonexistent, but does that mean most slaves were happy with their lot? Runaways were common, and some, such as Frederick Douglass and Harriet Jacobs, actually reached the North and wrote about their experiences as slaves. Yet how typical were their experiences? Most slaves were born, lived, and died in servitude, did not participate in organized revolts, and did not run away. How did they feel about the system of slavery?

Although most slaves did not read or write, did not participate in organized revolts, and did not attempt to run away, they did leave a remarkable amount of evidence that can help us understand their thoughts and feelings. Yet we must be imaginative in how we approach and use that evidence.

In an earlier chapter, you discovered that statistical information (about births, deaths, age at marriage, farm size, inheritance, tax rolls, and so forth) can reveal a great deal about ordinary people, such as the New Englanders on the eve of the American Revolution. Such demographic evidence can help the historian form a picture of who these people were and the socioeconomic trends of the time, even if the people themselves were not aware of those trends. In this exercise, you will be using another kind of evidence and asking different questions. Your evidence will not come from white southerners (whose stake in maintaining slavery was enormous), foreign travelers (whose own cultural biases often influenced what they reported), or even white abolitionists in the North (whose urgent need to eradicate the "sin" of slavery sometimes led them to gross exaggerations for propaganda purposes). You will be using anecdotes, stories, and songs from the rich oral tradition of African American slaves, supplemented by the narratives of two runaway slaves, to investigate the human dimensions of the peculiar institution.

Some of the oral evidence was collected and transcribed by people soon after emancipation. However, much of the evidence did not come to light until many years later, when the former slaves who were still alive were very old men and women. In fact, not until the 1920s did concerted efforts to preserve the reminiscences of these people begin. In the 1920s, Fisk University collected a good deal of evidence. In the 1930s, the government-financed Federal Writers' Project accumulated more than two thousand narratives from ex-slaves in every southern state except Louisiana and deposited them in the Library of Congress in Washington, D.C.

Much of the evidence, however, is in the form of songs and stories that slaves created and told to one another. Like the narratives of former slaves, these sources also must be used with imagination and care.

The central question you are to answer is this: How did the slaves themselves view the peculiar institution? How did they endure under a labor system that, at its very best, was still based on the total ownership of one human being by another?

historian Ken Stampp's term from 1950

∞ THE METHOD ∞

Historians must always try to be aware of the limitations of their evidence. In the Federal Writers' Project, most of the former slaves were in their eighties or nineties (quite a few were older than one hundred) at the time they were interviewed. In other words, most of the interviewees had been children or young people in 1860. It is also important to know that although some of the interviewers were black, the overwhelming majority were white. Last, although many of the former slaves had moved to another location or a different state after the Civil War, many others were still

CHAPTER 5

THE "PECULIAR
INSTITUTION":
SLAVES TELL
THEIR OWN
STORY

living in the same county (sometimes even on the same land) where they had been slaves. In what ways might the age of the former slave, the race of the interviewer, or the place where the former slave was living have affected the narratives?

These narratives reveal much about these people's thoughts and feelings about slavery. What direct reactions did the ex-slaves give? Why did many of them choose to be indirect? Some chose to answer questions by telling stories. Why? Remember that although some of the stories or anecdotes may not actually be true, they can be taken as representative of what the former slaves wished had happened or what they really thought about an incident. Therefore, often you must pull the true meaning from a narrative, inferring what the interviewee meant as well as what he or she said.

As for slave songs and other contemporary evidence, most slaves could never have spoken their thoughts or vented their feelings directly. Instead, they often hid their true meanings through the use of symbols, metaphors, and allegories. Here again, you must be able to read between the lines, extracting thoughts, attitudes, and feelings that were purposely hidden or concealed from all but other slaves.

Included in the evidence are two accounts of runaway slaves who escaped to the North before the Civil War.

Frederick Bailey (who later changed his name to Douglass) ran away when he was about nineteen years old, but he was captured and returned. Two years later, he was able to escape, and he moved to Massachusetts, where he worked as a laborer. After joining an antislavery society and becoming a successful speaker, he published his autobiography (1845) and edited his own abolitionist newspaper, the *North Star*. Harriet Jacobs (who used the pen name Linda Brent) was twenty-seven years old when she ran away in 1845, but her narrative was not published until the beginning of the Civil War. Throughout her story, Jacobs used fictitious names and places to protect those who had helped her and to conceal the escape route she had used. Both Douglass and Jacobs were self-educated people who wrote their own books, although the abolitionist writer Lydia Maria Child made minor editorial revisions in Jacobs's manuscript.

As you examine each piece of evidence, jot down enough notes to allow you to recall that piece of evidence later. But also (perhaps in a separate column) write down the *attitude* that each piece of evidence communicates about the peculiar institution of slavery. What is the hidden message?

After you have examined each piece of evidence, look back over your notes. What attitudes about slavery stand out? What did the slaves think about the slave system?

❧ THE EVIDENCE ❧

Sources 1 through 16 from B. A. Botkin, Federal Writers' Project, *Lay My Burden Down: A Folk History of Slavery* (Chicago: University of Chicago Press, 1945).

1. Hog-Killing Time.

. . . I remember Mammy told me about one master who almost starved his slaves. Mighty stingy, I reckon he was.

Some of them slaves was so poorly thin they ribs would kinda rustle against each other like corn stalks a-drying in the hot winds. But they gets even one hog-killing time, and it was funny, too, Mammy said.

They was seven hogs, fat and ready for fall hog-killing time. Just the day before Old Master told off they was to be killed, something happened to all them porkers. One of the field boys found them and come a-telling the master: "The hogs is all died, now they won't be any meats for the winter."

When the master gets to where at the hogs is laying, they's a lot of Negroes standing round looking sorrow-eyed at the wasted meat. The master asks: "What's the illness with 'em?"

"Malitis," they tells him, and they acts like they don't want to touch the hogs. Master says to dress them anyway for they ain't no more meat on the place.

He says to keep all the meat for the slave families, but that's because he's afraid to eat it hisself account of the hogs' got malitis.

"Don't you all know what is malitis?" Mammy would ask the children when she was telling of the seven fat hogs and seventy lean slaves. And she would laugh, remembering how they fooled Old Master so's to get all them good meats.

"One of the strongest Negroes got up early in the morning," Mammy would explain, "long 'fore the rising horn called the slaves from their cabins. He skitted to the hog pen with a heavy mallet in his hand. When he tapped Mister Hog 'tween the eyes with the mallet, 'malitis' set in mighty quick, but it was a uncommon 'disease,' even with hungry Negroes around all the time."

2. The Old Parrot.

The mistress had an old parrot, and one day I was in the kitchen making cookies, and I decided I wanted some of them, so I tooks me out some and put them on a chair; and when I did this the mistress entered the door. I

CHAPTER 5

THE "PECULIAR
INSTITUTION":
SLAVES TELL
THEIR OWN
STORY

picks up a cushion and throws [it] over the pile of cookies on the chair, and Mistress came near the chair and the old parrot cries out, "Mistress burn, Mistress burn." Then the mistress looks under the cushion, and she had me whupped, but the next day I killed the parrot, and she often wondered who or what killed the bird.

3. The Coon and the Dog.

Every time I think of slavery and if it done the race any good, I think of the story of the coon and dog who met. The coon said to the dog, "Why is it you're so fat and I am so poor, and we is both animals?" The dog said: "I lay round Master's house and let him kick me and he gives me a piece of bread right on." Said the coon to the dog: "Better, then, that I stay poor." Them's my sentiment. I'm like the coon, I don't believe in 'buse.

4. The Partridge and the Fox.

. . . A partridge and a fox 'greed to kill a beef. They kilt and skinned it. Before they divide it, the fox said, "My wife says send her some beef for soup." So he took a piece of it and carried it down the hill, then come back and said, "My wife wants more beef for soup." He kept this up till all the beef was gone 'cept the liver. The fox come back, and the partridge says, "Now let's cook this liver and both of us eat it." The partridge cooked the liver, et its parts right quick, and then fell over like it was sick. The fox got scared and said that beef is pizen, and he ran down the hill and started bringing the beef back. And when he brought it all back, he left, and the partridge had all the beef.

5. The Rabbit and the Tortoise.

I want to tell you one story 'bout the rabbit. The rabbit and the tortoise had a race. The tortoise git a lot of tortoises and put 'em 'long the way. Ever' now and then a tortoise crawl 'long the way, and the rabbit say, "How you now, Br'er Tortoise?" And he say, "Slow and sure, but my legs very short." When they git tired, the tortoise win 'cause he there, but he never run the race, 'cause he had tortoises strowed out all 'long the way. The tortoise had other tortoises help him.

6. Same Old Thing.

The niggers didn't go to the church building; the preacher came and preached to them in their quarters. He'd just say, "Serve your masters. Don't steal your master's turkey. Don't steal your master's chickens. Don't steal your master's hogs. Don't steal your master's meat. Do whatsomever your master tells you to do." Same old thing all the time.

7. Freedom.

I been preaching the gospel and farming since slavery time. I jined the church 'most 83 years ago when I was Major Gaud's slave, and they baptizes me in the spring branch close to where I finds the Lord. When I starts preaching I couldn't read or write and had to preach what Master told me, and he say tell them niggers iffen they obeys the master they goes to Heaven; but I knowed there's something better for them, but daren't tell them 'cept on the sly. That I done lots. I tells 'em iffen they keeps praying, the Lord will set 'em free.

8. Prayers.

My master used to ask us children, "Do your folks pray at night?" We said "No," 'cause our folks had told us what to say. But the Lord have mercy, there was plenty of that going on. They'd pray, "Lord, deliver us from under bondage."

9. Hoodoo Doctor.

My wife was sick, down, couldn't do nothing. Someone got to telling her about Cain Robertson. Cain Robertson was a hoodoo doctor in Georgia. They [say] there wasn't nothing Cain couldn't do. She says, "Go and see Cain and have him come up here."

I says, "There ain't no use to send for Cain. Cain ain't coming up here because they say he is a 'two-head' nigger." (They called all them hoodoo men "two-head" niggers; I don't know why they called them two-head.) "And you know he knows the white folks will put him in jail if he comes to town."

But she says, "You go and get him."

CHAPTER 5

THE "PECULIAR
INSTITUTION":
SLAVES TELL
THEIR OWN
STORY

So I went.

I left him at the house, and when I came back in, he said, "I looked at your wife and she had one of them spells while I was there. I'm afraid to tackle this thing because she has been poisoned, and it's been going on a long time. And if she dies, they'll say I killed her, and they already don't like me and looking for an excuse to do something to me."

My wife overheard him and says, "You go on, you got to do something."

So he made me go to town and get a pint of corn whiskey. When I brought it back he drunk a half of it at one gulp, and I started to knock him down. I'd thought he'd get drunk with my wife lying there sick.

Then he said, "I'll have to see your wife's stomach." Then he scratched it, and put three little horns on the place he scratched. Then he took another drink of whiskey and waited about ten minutes. When he took them off her stomach, they were full of blood. He put them in the basin in some water and sprinkled some powder on them, and in about ten minutes more he made me get them and they were full of clear water and there was a lot of little things that looked like wiggle tails swimming around it.

He told me when my wife got well to walk in a certain direction a certain distance, and the woman that caused all the trouble would come to my house and start a fuss with me.

I said, "Can't you put this same thing back on her?"

He said, "Yes, but it would kill my hand." He meant that he had a curing hand and that if he made anybody sick or killed them, all his power to cure would go from him.

I showed the stuff he took out of my wife's stomach to old Doc Matthews, and he said, "You can get anything into a person by putting it in them." He asked me how I found out about it, and how it was taken out, and who did it.

I told him all about it, and he said, "I'm going to see that that nigger practices anywhere in this town he wants to and nobody bothers him." And he did.

10. Buck Brasefield.

They was pretty good to us, but old Mr. Buck Brasefield, what had a plantation 'jining us'n, was so mean to his'n that 'twa'n't nothing for 'em to run away. One nigger, Rich Parker, runned off one time, and whilst he gone he seed a hoodoo man, so when he got back Mr. Brasefield took sick and stayed sick two or three weeks. Some of the darkies told him, "Rich been to the hoodoo doctor." So Mr. Brasefield got up outen that bed and come a-yelling in the field, "You thought you had old Buck, but by God he rose again." Them niggers was so scared they squatted in the field just like partridges, and some of 'em whispered, "I wish to God he had-a died."

11. The White Lady's Quilts.

Now I'll tell you another incident. This was in slave times. My mother was a great hand for nice quilts. There was a white lady had died, and they were going to have a sale. Now this is true stuff. They had the sale, and Mother went and bought two quilts. And let me tell you, we couldn't sleep under 'em. What happened? Well, they'd pinch your toes till you couldn't stand it. I was just a boy and I was sleeping with my mother when it happened. Now that's straight stuff. What do I think was the cause? Well, I think that white lady didn't want no nigger to have them quilts. I don't know what Mother did with 'em, but that white lady just wouldn't let her have 'em.

12. Papa's Death.

My papa was strong. He never had a licking in his life. He helped the master, but one day the master says, "Si, you got to have a whopping," and my poppa says, "I never had a whopping and you can't whop me." And the master says, "But I can kill you," and he shot my papa down. My mama took him in the cabin and put him on a pallet. He died.

13. Forbidden Knowledge.

None of us was 'lowed to see a book or try to learn. They say we git smarter than they was if we learn anything, but we slips around and gits hold of that Webster's old blue-back speller and we hides it till 'way in the night and then we lights a little pine torch, and studies that spelling book. We learn it too. I can read some now and write a little too.

They wasn't no church for the slaves, but we goes to the white folks' arbor on Sunday evening, and a white man he gits up there to preach to the niggers. He say, "Now I takes my text, which is, Nigger obey your master and your mistress, 'cause what you git from them here in this world am all you ever going to git, 'cause you just like the hogs and the other animals—when you dies you ain't no more, after you been throwed in that hole." I guess we believed that for a while 'cause we didn't have no way finding out different. We didn't see no Bibles.

CHAPTER 5

THE "PECULIAR
INSTITUTION":
SLAVES TELL
THEIR OWN
STORY

14. Broken Families.

I seen children sold off and the mammy not sold, and sometimes the mammy sold and a little baby kept on the place and give to another woman to raise. Them white folks didn't care nothing 'bout how the slaves grieved when they tore up a family.

15. Burning in Hell.

We was scared of Solomon and his whip, though, and he didn't like frolicking. He didn't like for us niggers to pray, either. We never heard of no church, but us have praying in the cabins. We'd set on the floor and pray with our heads down low and sing low, but if Solomon heared he'd come and beat on the wall with the stock of his whip. He'd say, "I'll come in there and tear the hide off you backs." But some the old niggers tell us we got to pray to God that He don't think different of the blacks and the whites. I know that Solomon is burning in hell today, and it pleasures me to know it.

16. Marriage.

After while I taken a notion to marry and Massa and Missy marries us same as all the niggers. They stands inside the house with a broom held crosswise of the door and we stands outside. Missy puts a little wreath on my head they kept there, and we steps over the broom into the house. Now, that's all they was to the marrying. After freedom I gits married and has it put in the book by a preacher.

Sources 17 and 18 from Gilbert Osofsky, comp., *Puttin' on Ole Massa* (New York: Harper & Row, 1969), p. 22.

17. Pompey.

Pompey, how do I look?
O, massa, mighty.
What do you mean "mighty," Pompey?
Why, massa, you look noble.

[114]

What do you mean by "noble"?
Why, sar, you just look like one *lion*.
Why, Pompey, where have you ever seen a lion?
I see one down in yonder field the other day, massa.
Pompey, you foolish fellow, that was a *jackass*.
Was it, massa? Well you look just like him.

18. A Grave for Old Master.

Two slaves were sent out to dig a grave for old master. They dug it very deep. As I passed by I asked Jess and Bob what in the world they dug it so deep for. It was down six or seven feet. I told them there would be a fuss about it, and they had better fill it up some. Jess said it suited him exactly. Bob said he would not fill it up; he wanted to get the old man as near *home* as possible. When we got a stone to put on his grave, we hauled the largest we could find, so as to fasten him down as strong as possible.

Sources 19 through 21 from Lawrence W. Levine, "Slave Songs and Slave Consciousness: An Exploration in Neglected Sources," in *Anonymous Americans: Explorations in Nineteenth Century Social History,* ed. Tamara K. Hareven (Englewood Cliffs, N.J.: Prentice Hall, 1971), pp. 112, 113, 121.

19.

We raise de wheat,
Dey gib us de corn;
We bake de bread,
Dey gib us de crust;
We sif de meal,
Dey gib us de huss;
We [peel] de meat,
Dey gib us de skin;
And dat's de way
Dey take us in;
We skim de pot,
Dey gib us de liquor,
And say dat's good enough for nigger.

CHAPTER 5

THE "PECULIAR
INSTITUTION":
SLAVES TELL
THEIR OWN
STORY

20.

My old Mistiss promise me,
W'en she died, she'd set me free,
She lived so long dat 'er head got bal',
An, she give out'n de notion a dyin' at all.

21.

He delivered Daniel from the lion's den,
Jonah from de belly ob de whale,
And de Hebrew children from de fiery furnace,
And why not every man?

Sources 22 and 23 from Sterling Stuckey, "Through the Prism of Folklore: The Black Ethos in Slavery," *Massachusetts Review* 9 (1968): 421, 422.

22.

When I get to heaven, gwine be at ease,
Me and my God gonna do as we please.
Gonna chatter with the Father, argue with the Son,
Tell um 'bout the world I just come from.

23.

[*A song about Samson and Delilah*]

He said, 'An' if I had-'n my way,'
He said, 'An' if I had-'n my way,'
He said, 'An' if I had-'n my way,
I'd tear the build-in' down!'

Source 24 from Frederick Douglass, *Narrative of the Life of Frederick Douglass* (New York: Anchor Books, Doubleday, 1963), pp. 1–3, 13–15, 36–37, 40–41, 44–46, 74–75.

24. Autobiography of Frederick Douglass.

I was born in Tuckahoe, near Hillsborough, and about twelve miles from Easton, in Talbot county, Maryland. I have no accurate knowledge of my age, never having seen any authentic record containing it. By far the larger part of the slaves know as little of their ages as horses know of theirs, and it is the wish of most masters within my knowledge to keep their slaves thus ignorant. I do not remember to have ever met a slave who could tell of his birthday. They seldom come nearer to it than planting-time, harvesting-time, cherry-time, spring-time, or fall-time. A want of information concerning my own was a source of unhappiness to me even during childhood. The white children could tell their ages. I could not tell why I ought to be deprived of the same privilege. I was not allowed to make any inquiries of my master concerning it. He deemed all such inquiries on the part of a slave improper and impertinent, and evidence of a restless spirit. The nearest estimate I can give makes me now between twenty-seven and twenty-eight years of age. I come to this, from hearing my master say, some time during 1835, I was about seventeen years old.

My mother was named Harriet Bailey. She was the daughter of Isaac and Betsey Bailey, both colored, and quite dark. My mother was a darker complexion than either my grandmother or grandfather.

My father was a white man. He was admitted to be such by all I ever heard speak of my parentage. The opinion was also whispered that my master was my father; but of the correctness of this opinion, I know nothing; the means of knowing was withheld from me. . . .

[*His mother, a field hand, lived twelve miles away and could visit him only at night.*]

. . . I do not recollect of ever seeing my mother by the light of day. She was with me in the night. She would lie down with me, and get me to sleep, but long before I waked she was gone. Very little communication ever took place between us. Death soon ended what little we could have while she lived, and with it her hardships and suffering. She died when I was about seven years old, on one of my master's farms, near Lee's Mill. I was not allowed to be present during her illness, at her death, or burial. She was gone long before I knew any thing about it. Never having enjoyed, to any considerable extent, her soothing presence, her tender and watchful care, I received the tidings of her death with much the same emotions I should have probably felt at the death of a stranger. . . .

The slaves selected to go to the Great House Farm,[4] for the monthly allowance for themselves and their fellow-slaves, were peculiarly enthusiastic. While on their way, they would make the dense old woods, for miles around, reverberate with their wild songs, revealing at once the highest joy and the deepest sadness. They would compose and sing as they went along,

4. Great House Farm was the huge "home plantation" that belonged to Douglass's owner.

CHAPTER 5

THE "PECULIAR
INSTITUTION":
SLAVES TELL
THEIR OWN
STORY

consulting neither time nor tune. The thought that came up, came out—if not in the word, in the sound;—and as frequently in the one as in the other. . . .

I did not, when a slave, understand the deep meaning of those rude and apparently incoherent songs. I was myself within the circle; so that I neither saw nor heard as those without might see and hear. They told a tale of woe which was then altogether beyond my feeble comprehension; they were tones loud, long, and deep; they breathed the prayer and complaint of souls boiling over with the bitterest anguish. Every tone was a testimony against slavery, and a prayer to God for deliverance from chains.

I have often been utterly astonished, since I came to the north, to find persons who could speak of the singing, among slaves, as evidence of their contentment and happiness. It is impossible to conceive of a greater mistake. Slaves sing most when they are most unhappy. The songs of the slave represent the sorrows of his heart; and he is relieved by them, only as an aching heart is relieved by its tears. At least, such is my experience. I have often sung to drown my sorrow, but seldom to express my happiness. Crying for joy, and singing for joy, were alike uncommon to me while in the jaws of slavery. . . .

[*Douglass was hired out as a young boy and went to live in Baltimore.*]

Very soon after I went to live with Mr. and Mrs. Auld, she very kindly commenced to teach me the A, B, C. After I had learned this, she assisted me in learning to spell words of three or four letters. Just at this point of my progress, Mr. Auld found out what was going on, and at once forbade Mrs. Auld to instruct me further, telling her, among other things, that it was unlawful, as well as unsafe, to teach a slave to read. To use his own words, further, he said, "If you give a nigger an inch, he will take an ell.[5] A nigger should know nothing but to obey his master—to do as he is told to do. Learning would *spoil* the best nigger in the world. Now," said he, "if you teach that nigger (speaking of myself) how to read, there would be no keeping him. It would forever unfit him to be a slave. He would at once become unmanageable, and of no value to his master. As to himself, it could do him no good, but a great deal of harm. It would make him discontented and unhappy." These words sank deep into my heart, stirred up sentiments within that lay slumbering, and called into existence an entirely new train of thought. . . .

5. An ell was an English unit of measure for cloth, approximately 45 inches.

[Douglass came to believe that education could help him gain his freedom.]

The plan which I adopted, and the one by which I was most successful, was that of making friends of all the little white boys whom I met in the street. As many of these as I could, I converted into teachers. With their kindly aid, obtained at different times and in different places, I finally succeeded in learning to read. When I was sent on errands, I always took my book with me, and by doing one part of my errand quickly, I found time to get a lesson before my return. I used also to carry bread with me, enough of which was always in the house, and to which I was always welcome; for I was much better off in this regard than many of the poor white children in our neighborhood. This bread I used to bestow upon hungry little urchins, who, in return, would give me that more valuable bread of knowledge. I am strongly tempted to give the names of two or three of those little boys, as a testimonial of the gratitude and affection I bear them; but prudence forbids;—not that it would injure me, but it might embarrass them; for it is almost an unpardonable offence to teach slaves to read in this Christian country. . . .

I was now about twelve years old, and the thought of being a *slave for life* began to bear heavily upon my heart. . . . After a patient waiting, I got one of our city papers, containing an account of the number of petitions from the north, praying for the abolition of slavery in the District of Columbia, and of the slave trade between the States. From this time I understood the words *abolition* and *abolitionist,* and always drew near when that word was spoken, expecting to hear something of importance to myself and fellow-slaves. The light broke in upon me by degrees. . . .

[After talking with two Irish laborers who advised him to run away, Douglass determined to do so.]

. . . I looked forward to a time at which it would be safe for me to escape. I was too young to think of doing so immediately; besides, I wished to learn how to write, as I might have occasion to write my own pass.[6] I consoled myself with the hope that I should one day find a good chance. Meanwhile, I would learn to write.

The idea as to how I might learn to write was suggested to me by being in Durgin and Bailey's ship-yard, and frequently seeing the ship carpenters, after hewing, and getting a piece of timber ready for use, write on the timber the name of that part of the ship for which it was intended. When a piece of timber was intended for the larboard side, it would be marked

6. In many areas, slaves were required to carry written passes stating that they had permission from their owners to travel to a certain place.

CHAPTER 5

THE "PECULIAR
INSTITUTION":
SLAVES TELL
THEIR OWN
STORY

thus—"L." When a piece was for the starboard side, it would be marked thus—"S." A piece for the larboard side forward, would be marked thus—"L. F." When a piece was for starboard side forward, it would be marked thus—"S. F." For larboard aft, it would be marked thus—"L. A." For starboard aft, it would be marked thus—"S. A." I soon learned the names of these letters, and for what they were intended when placed upon a piece of timber in the ship-yard. I immediately commenced copying them, and in a short time was able to make the four letters named. After that, when I met with any boy who I knew could write, I would tell him I could write as well as he. The next word would be, "I don't believe you. Let me see you try it." I would then make the letters which I had been so fortunate as to learn, and ask him to beat that. In this way I got a good many lessons in writing, which it is quite possible I should never have gotten in any other way. During this time, my copy-book was the board fence, brick wall, and pavement; my pen and ink was a lump of chalk. With these, I learned mainly how to write. I then commenced and continued copying the Italics in Webster's Spelling Book, until I could make them all without looking on the book. By this time, my little Master Thomas had gone to school, and learned how to write, and had written over a number of copy-books. These had been brought home, and shown to some of our near neighbors, and then laid aside. My mistress used to go to class meeting at the Wilk Street meeting-house every Monday afternoon, and leave me to take care of the house. When left thus, I used to spend the time in writing in the spaces left in Master Thomas's copy-book, copying what he had written. I continued to do this until I could write a hand very similar to that of Master Thomas. Thus, after a long, tedious effort for years, I finally succeeded in learning how to write. . . .

[*After the death of his owner, Douglass was recalled to the plantation and put to work as a field hand. Because of his rebellious attitude, he was then sent to work for a notorious "slave-breaker" named Covey. When Covey tried to whip Douglass, who was then about sixteen years old, Douglass fought back.*]

We were at it for nearly two hours. Covey at length let me go, puffing and blowing at a great rate, saying that if I had not resisted, he would not have whipped me half so much. The truth was, that he had not whipped me at all. I considered him as getting entirely the worst end of the bargain; for he had drawn no blood from me, but I had from him. The whole six months afterwards, that I spent with Mr. Covey, he never laid the weight of his finger upon me in anger. He would occasionally say, he didn't want to get hold of me again. "No," thought I, "you need not; for you will come off worse than you did before."

This battle with Mr. Covey was the turning point in my career as a slave. It rekindled the few expiring embers of freedom, and revived within me a sense of my own manhood. It recalled the departed self-confidence, and inspired me again with a determination to be free. The gratification afforded by the triumph was a full compensation for whatever else might follow, even death itself. He only can understand the deep satisfaction which I experienced, who has himself repelled by force the bloody arm of slavery. I felt as I never felt before. It was a glorious resurrection, from the tomb of slavery, to the heaven of freedom. My long-crushed spirit rose, cowardice departed, bold defiance took its place; and I now resolved that, however long I might remain a slave in form, the day had passed forever when I could be a slave in fact. I did not hesitate to let it be known of me, that the white man who expected to succeed in whipping, must also succeed in killing me.

From this time I was never again what might be called fairly whipped, though I remained a slave four years afterwards. I had several fights, but was never whipped.

It was for a long time a matter of surprise to me why Mr. Covey did not immediately have me taken by the constable to the whipping-post, and there regularly whipped for the crime of raising my hand against a white man in defense of myself. And the only explanation I can now think of does not entirely satisfy me; but such as it is, I will give it. Mr. Covey enjoyed the most unbounded reputation for being a first-rate overseer and negro-breaker. It was of considerable importance to him. That reputation was at stake; and had he sent me—a boy about sixteen years old—to the public whipping-post, his reputation would have been lost; so, to save his reputation, he suffered me to go unpunished. . . .

[*During the Civil War, Douglass actively recruited African American soldiers for the Union, and he worked steadfastly after the war for African American civil rights. Douglass also held a series of federal jobs that culminated in his appointment as the U.S. minister to Haiti in 1888. He died in 1895 at the age of seventy-eight.*]

Source 25 from Linda Brent, *Incidents in the Life of a Slave Girl* (New York: Harcourt Brace Jovanovich, 1973), pp. xiii–xiv, 7, 9–10, 26–28, 48–49, 54–55, 179, 201–203, 207.

25. Autobiography of Linda Brent (Harriet Jacobs).

I wish I were more competent to the task I have undertaken. But I trust my readers will excuse deficiencies in consideration of circumstances. I was

CHAPTER 5

THE "PECULIAR
INSTITUTION":
SLAVES TELL
THEIR OWN
STORY

born and reared in Slavery; and I remained in a Slave State twenty-seven years. Since I have been at the North, it has been necessary for me to work diligently for my own support, and the education of my children. This has not left me much leisure to make up for the loss of early opportunities to improve myself; and it has compelled me to write these pages at irregular intervals, whenever I could snatch an hour from household duties. . . .

[*Brent explains that she hopes her story will help northern women realize the suffering of southern slave women.*]

I was born a slave; but I never knew it till six years of happy childhood had passed away. My father was a carpenter, and considered so intelligent and skilful in his trade, that when buildings out of the common line were to be erected, he was sent for from long distances, to be head workman. On condition of paying his mistress two hundred dollars a year, and supporting himself, he was allowed to work at his trade, and manage his own affairs. His strongest wish was to purchase his children; but, though he several times offered his hard earnings for that purpose, he never succeeded. In complexion my parents were a light shade of brownish yellow, and were termed mulattoes. They lived together in a comfortable home; and, though we were all slaves, I was so fondly shielded that I never dreamed I was a piece of merchandise, trusted to them for safe keeping, and liable to be demanded of them at any moment. I had one brother, William, who was two years younger than myself—a bright, affectionate child. I had also a great treasure in my maternal grandmother, who was a remarkable woman in many respects. . . .

[*When Linda Brent was six years old, her mother died, and six years later the kind mistress to whom Brent's family belonged also died. In the will, Brent was bequeathed to the mistress's five-year-old niece, Miss Emily Flint.*]

Dr. Flint, a physician in the neighborhood, had married the sister of my mistress, and I was now the property of their little daughter. It was not without murmuring that I prepared for my new home; and what added to my unhappiness, was the fact that my brother William was purchased by the same family. My father, by his nature, as well as by the habit of transacting business as a skilful mechanic, had more of the feelings of a freeman than is common among slaves. My brother was a spirited boy; and being brought up under such influences, he early detested the name of master and mistress. One day, when his father and his mistress both happened to call him at the same time, he hesitated between the two; being perplexed to know which had the strongest claim upon his obedience. He finally concluded to go to his mistress. When my father reproved him for it, he said, "You both called me, and I didn't know which I ought to go to first."

"You are *my* child," replied our father, "and when I call you, you should come immediately, if you have to pass through fire and water."

Poor Willie! He was now to learn his first lesson of obedience to a master. Grandmother tried to cheer us with hopeful words, and they found an echo in the credulous hearts of youth. . . .

My grandmother's mistress had always promised her that, at her death, she would be free; and it was said that in her will she made good the promise. But when the estate was settled, Dr. Flint told the faithful old servant that, under existing circumstances, it was necessary she should be sold. . . .

[*Brent's grandmother, widely respected in the community, was put up for sale at a local auction.*]

. . . Without saying a word, she quietly awaited her fate. No one bid for her. At last, a feeble voice said, "Fifty dollars." It came from a maiden lady, seventy years old, the sister of my grandmother's deceased mistress. She had lived forty years under the same roof with my grandmother; she knew how faithfully she had served her owners, and how cruelly she had been defrauded of her rights; and she resolved to protect her. The auctioneer waited for a higher bid; but her wishes were respected; no one bid above her. She could neither read nor write; and when the bill of sale was made out, she signed it with a cross. But what consequence was that, when she had a big heart overflowing with human kindness? She gave the old servant her freedom. . . .

During the first years of my service in Dr. Flint's family, I was accustomed to share some indulgences with the children of my mistress. Though this seemed to me no more than right, I was grateful for it, and tried to merit the kindness by the faithful discharge of my duties. But I now entered on my fifteenth year—a sad epoch in the life of a slave girl. My master began to whisper foul words in my ear. Young as I was, I could not remain ignorant of their import. I tried to treat them with indifference or contempt. The master's age, my extreme youth, and the fear that his conduct would be reported to my grandmother, made him bear this treatment for many months. He was a crafty man, and resorted to many means to accomplish his purposes. . . . The mistress, who ought to protect the helpless victim, has no other feelings towards her but those of jealousy and rage. . . . Even the little child, who is accustomed to wait on her mistress and her children,

CHAPTER 5

THE "PECULIAR
INSTITUTION":
SLAVES TELL
THEIR OWN
STORY

will learn, before she is twelve years old, why it is that her mistress hates such and such a one among the slaves. . . . She listens to violent outbreaks of jealous passion, and cannot help understanding what is the cause. She will become prematurely knowing in evil things. Soon she will learn to tremble when she hears her master's footfall. She will be compelled to realize that she is no longer a child. If God has bestowed beauty upon her, it will prove her greatest curse. That which commands admiration in the white woman only hastens the degradation of the female slave. . . .

[*Afraid to tell her grandmother about Dr. Flint's advances, Brent kept silent. But Flint was enraged when he found out that Brent had fallen in love with a young, free, African American carpenter. The doctor redoubled his efforts to seduce Brent and told her terrible stories about what happened to slaves who tried to run away. For a long time, she was afraid to try to escape because of stories such as the one she recounts here.*]

In my childhood I knew a valuable slave, named Charity, and loved her, as all children did. Her young mistress married, and took her to Louisiana. Her little boy, James, was sold to a good sort of master. He became involved in debt, and James was sold again to a wealthy slaveholder, noted for his cruelty. With this man he grew up to manhood, receiving the treatment of a dog. After a severe whipping, to save himself from further infliction of the lash, with which he was threatened, he took to the woods. He was in a most miserable condition—cut by the cowskin, half naked, half starved, and without the means of procuring a crust of bread.

Some weeks after his escape, he was captured, tied, and carried back to his master's plantation. This man considered punishment in his jail, on bread and water, after receiving hundreds of lashes, too mild for the poor slave's offence. Therefore he decided, after the overseer should have whipped him to his satisfaction, to have him placed between the screws of the cotton gin, to stay as long as he had been in the woods. This wretched creature was cut with the whip from his head to his feet, then washed with strong brine, to prevent the flesh from mortifying. . . . He was then put into the cotton gin, which was screwed down, only allowing him room to turn on his side when he could not lie on his back. Every morning a slave was sent with a piece of bread and bowl of water, which were placed within reach of the poor fellow. The slave was charged, under penalty of severe punishment, not to speak to him.

Four days passed, and the slave continued to carry the bread and water. On the second morning, he found the bread gone, but the water untouched. When he had been in the press four days and five nights, the slave informed his master that the water had not been used for four mornings, and that a horrible stench came from the gin house. The overseer was sent to examine into it. When the press was unscrewed, the dead body was found partly eaten by rats and vermin. . . .

[*Dr. Flint's jealous wife watched his behavior very closely, so Flint decided to build a small cabin out in the woods for Brent, who was now sixteen years old. Still afraid to run away, she became desperate.*]

And now, reader, I come to a period in my unhappy life, which I would gladly forget if I could. The remembrance fills me with sorrow and shame. It pains me to tell you of it; but I have promised to tell you the truth, and I will do it honestly, let it cost me what it may. I will not try to screen myself behind the plea of compulsion from a master; for it was not so. Neither can I plead ignorance or thoughtlessness. For years, my master had done his utmost to pollute my mind with foul images, and to destroy the pure principles inculcated by my grandmother, and the good mistress of my childhood. The influences of slavery had had the same effect on me that they had on other young girls; they had made me prematurely knowing, concerning the evil ways of the world. I knew what I did, and I did it with deliberate calculation. . . .

I have told you that Dr. Flint's persecutions and his wife's jealousy had given rise to some gossip in the neighborhood. Among others, it chanced that a white unmarried gentleman had obtained some knowledge of the circumstances in which I was placed. He knew my grandmother, and often spoke to me in the street. He became interested for me, and asked questions about my master, which I answered in part. He expressed a great deal of sympathy, and a wish to aid me. He constantly sought opportunities to see me, and wrote to me frequently. I was a poor slave girl, only fifteen years old.

So much attention from a superior person was, of course, flattering; for human nature is the same in all. I also felt grateful for his sympathy, and encouraged by his kind words. It seemed to me a great thing to have such a friend. By degrees, a more tender feeling crept into my heart. He was an educated and eloquent gentleman; too eloquent, alas, for the poor slave girl who trusted in him. Of course I saw whither all this was tending. I knew the impassable gulf between us; but to be an object of interest to a man who is not married, and who is not her master, is agreeable to the pride and feelings of a slave, if her miserable situation has left her any pride or sentiment. It seems less degrading to give one's self, than to submit to compulsion. There is something akin to freedom in having a lover who has no control over you, except that which he gains by kindness and attach-

CHAPTER 5

THE "PECULIAR
INSTITUTION":
SLAVES TELL
THEIR OWN
STORY

ment. A master may treat you as rudely as he pleases, and you dare not speak; moreover, the wrong does not seem so great with an unmarried man, as with one who has a wife to be made unhappy. There may be sophistry in all this; but the condition of a slave confuses all principles of morality, and, in fact, renders the practice of them impossible.

[*Brent had two children, Benjy and Ellen, as a result of her relationship with Mr. Sands, the white "gentleman." Sands and Brent's grandmother tried to buy Brent, but Dr. Flint rejected all their offers. However, Sands was able (through a trick) to buy his two children and Brent's brother, William. After he was elected to Congress, Sands married a white woman. William escaped to the North, and Brent spent seven years hiding in the tiny attic of a shed attached to her grandmother's house. Finally, Brent and a friend escaped via ship to Philadelphia. She then went to New York City, where she found work as a nursemaid for a kind family, the Bruces, and was reunited with her two children. However, as a fugitive slave, she was not really safe, and she used to read the newspapers every day to see whether Dr. Flint or any of his relatives were visiting New York.*]

But when summer came, the old feeling of insecurity haunted me. It was necessary for me to take little Mary[7] out daily, for exercise and fresh air, and the city was swarming with Southerners, some of whom might recognize me. Hot weather brings out snakes and slaveholders, and I like one class of the venomous creatures as little as I do the other. What a comfort it is, to be free to *say* so! . . .

I kept close watch of the newspapers for arrivals; but one Saturday night, being much occupied, I forgot to examine the Evening Express as usual. I went down into the parlor for it, early in the morning, and found the boy about to kindle a fire with it. I took it from him and examined the list of arrivals. Reader, if you have never been a slave, you cannot imagine the acute sensation at my heart, when I read the names of Mr. and Mrs. Dodge,[8] at a hotel in Courtland Street. It was a third-rate hotel, and that circumstance convinced me of the truth of what I had heard, that they were short of funds and had need of my value, as *they* valued me; and that was by dollar and cents. I hastened with the paper to Mrs. Bruce. Her heart and hand were always open to every one in distress, and she always warmly sympathized with mine. It was impossible to tell how near the enemy was. He might have passed and repassed the house while we were sleeping. He might at that moment be waiting to pounce upon me if I ventured out of doors. I had never seen the husband of my young mistress, and therefore I could not distinguish him from any other stranger. A carriage was hastily ordered; and, closely veiled, I followed Mrs. Bruce, taking the baby again

7. Mary was the Bruces' baby.
8. Emily Flint and her husband.

with me into exile. After various turnings and crossings, and returnings, the carriage stopped at the house of one of Mrs. Bruce's friends, where I was kindly received. Mrs. Bruce returned immediately, to instruct the domestics what to say if any one came to inquire for me.

It was lucky for me that the evening paper was not burned up before I had a chance to examine the list of arrivals. It was not long after Mrs. Bruce's return to her house, before several people came to inquire for me. One inquired for me, another asked for my daughter Ellen, and another said he had a letter from my grandmother, which he was requested to deliver in person.

They were told, "She *has* lived here, but she has left."

"How long ago?"

"I don't know, sir."

"Do you know where she went?"

"I do not, sir." And the door was closed. . . .

[*Mrs. Bruce was finally able to buy Brent from Mr. Dodge, and she immediately gave Brent her freedom.*]

Reader, my story ends with freedom; not in the usual way, with marriage. I and my children are now free! We are as free from the power of slaveholders as are the white people of the north; and though that, according to my ideas, is not saying a great deal, it is a vast improvement in *my* condition. The dream of my life is not yet realized. I do not sit with my children in a home of my own. I still long for a hearthstone of my own, however humble. I wish it for my children's sake far more than for my own. But God so orders circumstances as to keep me with my friend Mrs. Bruce. Love, duty, gratitude, also bind me to her side. It is a privilege to serve her who pities my oppressed people, and who has bestowed the inestimable boon of freedom on me and my children. . . .

[*Harriet Jacobs's story was published in 1861, and during the Civil War she did relief work with the newly freed slaves behind the Union army lines. For several years after the war ended, she worked tirelessly in Georgia to organize orphanages, schools, and nursing homes. Finally, she returned to the North, where she died in 1897 at the age of eighty-four.*]

❧ QUESTIONS TO CONSIDER ❧

The evidence in this chapter falls into three categories: reminiscences from former slaves, culled from interviews conducted in the 1930s (Sources 1

CHAPTER 5

THE "PECULIAR
INSTITUTION":
SLAVES TELL
THEIR OWN
STORY

through 18); songs transcribed soon after the Civil War, recalled by runaway slaves, or remembered years after (Sources 19 through 23); and the autobiographies of two slaves who escaped to the North: Frederick Douglass and Harriet Jacobs (Sources 24 and 25).

These categories are artificial at best, and you might want to rearrange the evidence in a way that may suit your purposes better.

The evidence contains a number of subtopics, and arrangement into those subtopics may be profitable. For example:

1. How did slaves feel about their masters and/or mistresses?
2. How did slaves feel about their work? Their families? Their religion?
3. How did they feel about freedom?
4. How did slaves feel about themselves?

By regrouping the evidence into subtopics and then using each piece of evidence to answer the question for that subtopic, you should be able to answer the central question: What did slaves (or former slaves) think and feel about the peculiar institution of slavery?

As mentioned, some of the slaves and former slaves chose to be direct in their messages (see, for example, Source 19), but many more chose to communicate their thoughts and feelings more indirectly or obliquely. Several of the symbols and metaphors used are easy to figure out (see Source 23), but others will take considerably more care. The messages are there, however.

Frederick Douglass and Harriet Jacobs wrote their autobiographies for northern readers. Furthermore, both of these runaway slaves were active in abolitionist work. Do these facts mean that this evidence is worthless? Not at all, but the historian must be very careful when analyzing such obviously biased sources. Which parts of Douglass's and Jacobs's stories seem to be exaggerated or unlikely to be true? What do these writers say about topics such as their work, religious beliefs, and families? Does any other evidence from the interviews, tales, or songs corroborate what Douglass and Jacobs wrote?

One last point you might want to consider: Why have historians neglected this kind of evidence for so long?

⮔ EPILOGUE ⮔

Even before the Civil War formally ended, thousands of African Americans began casting off the shackles of slavery. Some ran away to meet the advancing Union armies (who often treated them no better than their former masters and mistresses). Others drifted into cities, where they hoped to find work opportunities for themselves and their families. Still others stayed on the land, perhaps hoping to become free farmers. At the end of the war, African Americans were quick to establish their own churches and enrolled in schools established by the Freedmen's Bureau. For most former slaves, the impulse seems to have been to look forward and not backward into the agonizing past of slavery.

Yet memories of slavery were not forgotten and often were passed down orally, from generation to generation. In 1976, Alex Haley's book *Roots* and the twelve-part television miniseries based on it stunned an American public that had assumed that blacks' memories of their origins and of slavery had been for the most part either forgotten or obliterated.[9] Although much of Haley's work contains the author's artistic license, the skeleton of the book was the oral tradition transmitted by his family since the capture of his ancestor Kunta Kinte in West Africa in the late eighteenth century. Not only had Haley's family remembered its African origins, but stories about slavery had not been lost; they had been passed down through the generations.

While Haley was engaged in his twelve years of research and writing, historian Henry Irving Tragle proposed to compile a documentary history of the Nat Turner rebellion of 1831. Talking to black people in 1968 and 1969 in Southampton County, Virginia, where the rebellion occurred, Tragle discovered that in spite of numerous attempts to obliterate Turner from the area's historical memory,

Turner's action had become part of the oral history of the region. As the surprised Tragle wrote, "I believe it possible to say with certainty that Nat Turner did exist as a folk-hero to several generations of black men and women who have lived and died in Southampton County since 1831."[10] Again, oral history had persisted and triumphed over time, and professional historians began looking with a new eye on what in the past many had dismissed as unworthy of their attention.

Folk music, customs, religious practices, stories, and artifacts also received new attention. Increasingly, students of history have been able to reconstruct the lives, thoughts, and feelings of people once considered inarticulate. Of course, these people were not inarticulate, but it took imagination to let their evidence speak.

Many people have argued about the impact of slavery on blacks and whites alike, and that question may never be answered fully. What we *do* know is that an enormous amount of historical evidence about slavery exists, from the perspectives of both African Americans and whites. And the memory of that institution lingers. It is part of what one southern white professional historian calls the "burden of southern history," a burden to be overcome but never completely forgotten.

---

9. A condensed version of *Roots* appeared in 1974 in *Reader's Digest*.

10. Henry Irving Tragle, *The Southampton Slave Revolt of 1831: A Compilation of Source Material* (Amherst: University of Massachusetts Press, 1971), p. 12.

CHAPTER 6

THE PRICE FOR VICTORY:
THE DECISION TO USE
AFRICAN AMERICAN TROOPS

∽ THE PROBLEM ∽

With the outbreak of war at Fort Sumter in April 1861, many northern African Americans volunteered for service in the Union army. President Abraham Lincoln initially rejected black petitions to become soldiers. On April 29, Secretary of War Simon Cameron wrote one of many letters to African American volunteers; it curtly stated that "this Department has no intention at present to call into the service of the Government any colored soldiers."[1] Later, in July 1862, when Congress passed the Confiscation Act (part of which authorized the presi-

dent to use escaped slaves for the suppression of the rebellion "in such manner as he may judge best") and the Militia Act (which authorized him to enroll African Americans for military service), Lincoln virtually ignored both laws, arguing that the two acts *authorized* him to recruit blacks but did not *require* him to do so.

Curiously, in the South, too, free blacks and some slaves petitioned to be included in the newly formed Confederate army, perhaps hoping that such service might improve their conditions or even win them freedom. Like Lincoln, Confederate president Jefferson Davis rejected African American volunteers for military service and consistently opposed their use. Yet ultimately both chief executives changed their minds and accepted Af-

1. The letter was addressed to "Jacob Dodson (colored)" and is in *The War of the Rebellion: A Compilation of the Official Records of the Union and Confederate Armies* (Washington, D.C.: U.S. Government Printing Office, 1899), Series III, Vol. I, p. 133.

rican Americans into the armed forces, although in Davis's case, the policy reversal came too late for black units to see action on the Confederate side. And although the recruitment of African American soldiers by the South might have prolonged the conflict, it probably would not have altered the ultimate outcome. In this chapter, you will examine the evidence so as to answer the following questions:

1. What were the arguments in the North and South against arming African Americans and using them as regular soldiers? What were the arguments in favor of this move? How did the reasons in the North and South differ? How were they similar?

2. What do you think were the principal reasons that both the United States and the Confederate States of America changed their policies? How did the reasons in the North and South differ? How were they similar?

∽ BACKGROUND ∽

Although many leaders in both the North and South studiously tried to avoid public discussion of the issue, the institution of slavery unquestionably played a major role in bringing on the American Civil War. As slavery intruded into the important issues and events of the day (such as westward expansion, the Mexican War, the admission of new states to the Union, the course charted for the proposed transcontinental railroad, and the right of citizens to petition Congress), as well as into all the major institutions (churches and schools, for example), an increasing number of northerners and southerners came to feel that the question of slavery must be settled, and settled on the battlefield. Therefore, when news arrived of the firing on Fort Sumter, many greeted the announcement with relief. Lincoln's call for seventy-five thousand volunteers was answered with an enormous response. A wave of patriotic fervor swept across the northern states, as crowds greeted Union soldiers marching south to "lick the rebels." In the South, too, the outbreak of war was greeted with great enthusiasm. In Charleston, South Carolina, a day of celebration was followed by a night of parades and fireworks. Many southerners compared the upcoming war with the American Revolution, when, so the thinking went, an outnumbered but superior people had been victorious over the tyrant.

Yet for a number of reasons, most northern and southern leaders carefully avoided the slavery issue even after the war had begun. To Abraham Lincoln, the debate over the abolition of slavery threatened to divert northerners from what he considered the war's central aim: preserving the Union and denying the South's right to secede. In addition, Lincoln realized

CHAPTER 6

THE PRICE FOR
VICTORY: THE
DECISION TO
USE AFRICAN
AMERICAN
TROOPS

that a great number of northern whites, including himself, did not view African Americans as equals and might well oppose a war designed to liberate slaves from bondage. Finally, in large parts of Virginia, North Carolina, Kentucky, and Tennessee and in other pockets in the South, Union sentiment was strong, largely because of the antiplanter bias in these states. But anti-Negro sentiment also was strong in these same areas. With the border states so crucial to the Union both politically and militarily (as points of invasion into the South), it is not surprising that Lincoln purposely discouraged any notion that the war was for the purpose of emancipating slaves. Therefore, when influential editor Horace Greeley publicly called on Lincoln in August 1862 to make the Civil War a war for the emancipation of slaves, the president replied that the primary purpose of the war was to preserve the Union. "My paramount object in this struggle," Lincoln wrote, "is *not* either to save or destroy slavery" (italics added):

> If I could save the Union without freeing *any* slave I would do it, and if I could save it by freeing *all* the slaves I would do it; and if I could save it by freeing some and leaving others alone I would also do that. What I do about slavery, and the colored race, I do because I believe it helps to save the Union; and what I forbear, I forbear because I do *not* believe it would help to save the Union.[2]

2. Lincoln to Greeley, August 22, 1862, in Roy P. Basler, ed., *The Collected Works of Abraham Lincoln* (New Brunswick, N.J.: Rutgers University Press, 1953), Vol. V, pp. 388–389. Italics added.

Hence President Lincoln, in spite of his "*personal* wish that all men everywhere could be free" (italics added), strongly resisted all efforts to turn the Civil War into a moral crusade to, in his words, "destroy slavery."

On the Confederate side, President Jefferson Davis also had reasons to avoid making slavery (in this case, its preservation) a primary war aim. Davis feared, correctly, that foreign governments would be unwilling to recognize or aid the Confederacy if the preservation of slavery was the most important southern reason for fighting. In addition, the majority of white southerners did not own slaves, often disliked people who did, and, Davis feared, might not fight if the principal war aim was to defend the peculiar institution. Therefore, while Lincoln was explaining to northerners that the war was being fought to preserve the Union, Davis was trying to convince southerners that the struggle was for independence and the defense of constitutional rights.

Yet as it became increasingly clear that the Civil War was going to be a long and costly conflict, issues concerning slavery and the use of African Americans in the war effort continually came to the surface. In the North, reports of battle casualties in 1862 caused widespread shock and outrage, and some feared that the United States would be exhausted before the Confederacy was finally subdued—if it was to be subdued at all.[3] Also, many

3. The following is an estimate of Union casualties (the sum of those killed, wounded, and missing) for the principal engagements of 1862: Shiloh (April, 13,000 casualties), Seven Pines (May, 6,000), Seven Days (June, 16,000), Antietam (September, 12,400), Fredericksburg (December, 12,000).

northerners came to feel that emancipation could be used as both a political and a diplomatic weapon. Those European nations (especially England, which had ended slavery throughout its own empire in 1833) that had been technically neutral but were leaning toward the Confederacy might, northerners reasoned, be afraid to oppose a government committed to such a worthy cause as emancipation. Some northerners also hoped that a proclamation of emancipation would incite widespread slave rebellions in the South that would cripple the Confederacy. Not to be overlooked, however, are those northerners (a minority) who sincerely viewed slavery as a stain on American society and whose eradication was a moral imperative.

Gradually, President Lincoln came to favor the emancipation of slaves, although never to the extent that the abolitionists wanted. In early 1862, the president proposed the gradual emancipation of slaves by the states, with compensation for the slave owners and colonization of the former slaves outside the boundaries of the United States. When Congress mandated that Lincoln go further than that, by passing the Confiscation Act of 1862, which explicitly called for the permanent emancipation of all slaves in the Confederacy, the president simply ignored the law, choosing not to enforce it.[4] But political and diplomatic considerations prompted Lincoln to alter his course and support the issuing of the Preliminary Emancipation Proclamation in September 1862. So that his action would not be interpreted as one of desperation, the president waited until after the Union "victory" at the Battle of Antietam. Although the proclamation (scheduled to take effect on January 1, 1863) actually freed slaves only in areas still under Confederate control (hence immediately freeing no one), the act was a significant one regarding a shift in war aims. The final Emancipation Proclamation was issued on January 1, 1863.[5]

The second important issue that Lincoln and other northern leaders had to face was whether to arm African Americans and make them regular soldiers in the Union army. Blacks had seen service in the American Revolution and the War of 1812, prompting abolitionist Frederick Douglass, a former slave, to criticize the United States' initial policy of excluding African Americans from the army in the Civil War, saying in February 1862,

> Colored men were good enough to fight under Washington. They are not good enough to fight under McClellan. They were good enough to fight under Andrew Jackson. They are not good enough to fight under Gen. Halleck. They were good enough to help win American Independence, but they are not good enough to help preserve that independence against treason and rebellion.[6]

---

4. It was this action by Lincoln that prompted the exchange between Greeley and the president in August 1862.

5. The Preliminary Emancipation Proclamation was issued to test public opinion in the North and to give southern states the opportunity to retain slavery by returning to the Union before January 1, 1863. No state in the Confederacy took advantage of Lincoln's offer, and the final proclamation was issued and took effect on January 1, 1863.

6. Quoted in James M. McPherson, *The Negro's Civil War: How American Negroes Felt*

CHAPTER 6

THE PRICE FOR
VICTORY: THE
DECISION TO
USE AFRICAN
AMERICAN
TROOPS

Emancipation of slaves in the South was one thing, but making blacks United States soldiers was another. Such a decision would imply that white northerners recognized African Americans as equals. Although most abolitionists preached the dual message of emancipation and racial equality, most northern whites did not look on African Americans as equals, a belief that they shared with their president. Would whites fight alongside blacks even in racially separated units? Were blacks, many northern whites asked, courageous enough to stand and hold their positions under fire? What would African Americans want as a price for their aid? Throughout 1862, northern leaders carried on an almost continual debate over whether to accept African Americans into the Union army, an issue that had a number of social, ideological, and moral implications.

In the Confederacy, the issue of arming African Americans for the southern war effort was also a divisive one. The northern superiority in population, supplemented by continued immigration from Europe, put the South at a terrific numerical disadvantage, a disadvantage that could be lessened by the enlistment of at least a portion of the approximately four million slaves. Southern battle casualties also had been fearfully high, in some battles higher than those of the Union.[7] How long could the Confederacy hold out as its numbers continually eroded? If the main goal of the war was southern independence, shouldn't Confederate leaders use all available means to secure that objective? It was known that some northern whites, shocked by Union casualty figures, were calling on Lincoln to let the South go in peace. If the Confederacy could hold out, many southerners hoped, northern peace sentiments might grow enough to force the Union to give up. If slaves could help in that effort, some reasoned, why not arm them? Yet, as in the North, the question of whether to arm African Americans had significance far beyond military considerations. Except for the promise of freedom, what would motivate the slaves to fight for their masters? If freedom was to be offered, then what, many surely would argue, was the war being fought over in the first place? Would southern whites fight with blacks? Would some African Americans, once armed, then turn against their masters? And finally, if southern whites were correct in their insistence that African Americans were essentially docile, childlike creatures, what conceivable support could they give to the war effort? Interestingly, there were some remarkable similarities in the points debated by the northern and southern policymakers and citizens.

and Acted During the War for the Union (New York: Pantheon Books, 1965), p. 163.

7. The following are estimates of Confederate casualties for the principal engagements of 1862–1863: Seven Days (June 1862, 20,000), Antietam (September 1862, 13,700), Fredericksburg (December 1862, 5,000), Gettysburg (July 1863, 28,000).

⊗ THE METHOD ⊗

In this chapter, you are confronted with two sets of evidence: private and official correspondence, reports, newspaper articles and editorials, and laws and proclamations. One set concerns the argument in the North over whether to arm blacks, and the other set deals with the same question in the South. Read and analyze each series separately. Take notes as you go along, always being careful not to lose track of your central objectives.

By now you should be easily able to identify and list the major points, pro and con, in a debate. Jotting down notes as you read the evidence is extremely helpful. Be careful, however, because some reports, articles, and letters contain more than one argument.

Several earlier chapters required that you read between the lines—that is, identify themes and issues that are implied though never directly stated.

What emotional factors can you identify on both sides of the question? How important would you say these factors were in the final decision? For example, you will see from the evidence that at no time in the debate being carried on in the North were battle casualties mentioned. Were casualties therefore of no importance in the debate? How would you go about answering this question?

In some cases, the identity of the author of a particular piece (if known) can give you several clues as to that person's emotions, fears, anxieties, and needs. Where the identity of the author is not known, you may have to exercise a little historical imagination. What might this person really have meant when he or she said (or failed to say) something? Can you infer from the context of the argument any emotions that are not explicitly stated?

⊗ THE EVIDENCE ⊗

NORTH

Source 1 from James M. McPherson, *The Negro's Civil War: How American Negroes Felt and Acted During the War for the Union* (New York: Pantheon Books, 1965), p. 33.

1. Petition of Some Northern Blacks to President Lincoln, October 1861.

We, the undersigned, respectfully represent to Your Excellency that we are native citizens of the United States, and that, notwithstanding much injustice and oppression which our race have suffered, we cherish a strong attachment for the land of our birth and for our Republican Government.

CHAPTER 6

THE PRICE FOR
VICTORY: THE
DECISION TO
USE AFRICAN
AMERICAN
TROOPS

We are filled with alarm at the formidable conspiracy for its overthrow, and lament the vast expense of blood and treasure which the present war involves. . . . We are anxious to use our power to give peace to our country and permanence to our Government.

We are strong in numbers, in courage, and in patriotism, and in behalf of our fellow countrymen of the colored race, we offer to you and to the nation a power and a will sufficient to conquer rebellion, and establish peace on a permanent basis. We pledge ourselves, upon receiving the sanction of Your Excellency, that we will immediately proceed to raise an efficient number of regiments, and so fast as arms and equipments shall be furnished, we will bring them into the field in good discipline, and ready for action.

Source 2 from Bell Irvin Wiley, *The Life of Billy Yank: The Common Soldier of the Union* (Baton Rouge: Louisiana State University Press, 1971), p. 109.

2. A. Davenport (a Union Soldier from New York) to His Home Folk, June 19, 1861.

I think that the best way to settle the question of what to do with the darkies would be to shoot them.

Source 3 from McPherson, *The Negro's Civil War,* p. 162.

3. Newspaper Editorial by Frederick Douglass, *Douglass' Monthly,* September 1861.

Our Presidents, Governors, Generals and Secretaries are calling, with almost frantic vehemence, for men—"Men! men! send us men!" they scream, or the cause of the Union is gone; . . . and yet these very officers, representing the people and Government, steadily and persistently refuse to receive the very class of men which have a deeper interest in the defeat and humiliation of the rebels, than all others. . . . What a spectacle of blind, unreasoning prejudice and pusillanimity[8] is this! The national edifice is on fire. Every man who can carry a bucket of water, or remove a brick, is wanted; but those who have the care of the building, having a profound respect for the feeling of the national burglars who set the building on fire,

8. Cowardice.

are determined that the flames shall only be extinguished by Indo-Caucasian[9] hands, and to have the building burnt rather than save it by means of any other. Such is the pride, the stupid prejudice and folly that rules the hour.

Why does the Government reject the negro? Is he not a man? Can he not wield a sword, fire a gun, march and countermarch, and obey orders like any other? . . . If persons so humble as we can be allowed to speak to the President of the United States, we should ask him if this dark and terrible hour of the nation's extremity is a time for consulting a mere vulgar and unnatural prejudice? . . . We would tell him that this is no time to fight with one hand, when both are needed; that this is no time to fight only with your white hand, and allow your black hand to remain tied. . . . While the Government continues to refuse the aid of colored men, thus alienating them from the national cause, and giving the rebels the advantage of them, it will not deserve better fortunes than it has thus far experienced.—Men in earnest don't fight with one hand, when they might fight with two, and a man drowning would not refuse to be saved even by a colored hand.

Source 4 from Roy P. Basler, ed., *The Collected Works of Abraham Lincoln* (New Brunswick, N.J.: Rutgers University Press, 1953), Vol. V, p. 222.

4. Lincoln's Proclamation Revoking General Hunter's Order of Military Emancipation of May 9, 1862.[10]

May 19, 1862

I, Abraham Lincoln, president of the United States, proclaim and declare, that the government of the United States, had no knowledge, information, or belief, of an intention on the part of General Hunter to issue such a proclamation; nor has it yet, any authentic information that the document is genuine. And further, that neither General Hunter, nor any other commander, or person, has been authorized by the Government of the United States, to make proclamations declaring the slaves of any State free; and that the supposed proclamation, now in question, whether genuine or false, is altogether void, so far as respects such declaration.

9. Douglass meant European American.
10. On April 12, 1862, General David Hunter organized the first official regiment of African American soldiers. On May 9, Hunter proclaimed that slaves in Georgia, Florida, and South Carolina were free. Lincoln overruled both proclamations, and the regiment was disbanded without pay. Observers reported that the regiment, composed of former slaves, was of poor quality. Do you think those reports influenced Lincoln's thinking? Lincoln also overruled similar proclamations by General John C. Frémont in Missouri.

CHAPTER 6

THE PRICE FOR
VICTORY: THE
DECISION TO
USE AFRICAN
AMERICAN
TROOPS

Sources 5 and 6 from *Diary and Correspondence of Salmon P. Chase*,[11] in *Annual Report of the American Historical Association for the Year 1902* (Washington, D.C.: U.S. Government Printing Office, 1903), Vol. II, pp. 45–46, 48–49.

5. Diary of Salmon P. Chase, Entry for July 21, 1862.

. . . I went at the appointed hour, and found that the President had been profoundly concerned at the present aspect of affairs, and had determined to take some definitive steps in respect to military action and slavery. He had prepared several Orders, the first of which contemplated authority to Commanders to subsist their troups in the hostile territory—the second, authority to employ negroes as laborers—the third requiring that both in the case of property taken and of negroes employed, accounts should be kept with such degrees of certainty as would enable compensation to be made in proper cases—another provided for the colonization of negroes in some tropical country.

A good deal of discussion took place upon these points. The first Order was universally approved. The second was approved entirely; and the third, by all except myself. I doubted the expediency of attempting to keep accounts for the benefit of the inhabitants of rebel States. The Colonization project was not much discussed.

The Secretary of War presented some letters from Genl. Hunter in which he advised the Department that the withdrawal of a large proportion of his troups to reinforce Genl. McClellan,[12] rendered it highly important that he should be immediately authorized to enlist all loyal persons without reference to complexion. Messrs. Stanton,[13] Seward[14] and myself, expressed ourselves in favor of this plan, and no one expressed himself against it. (Mr. Blair[15] was not present.) The President was not prepared to decide the question but expressed himself as averse to arming negroes. The whole matter was postponed until tomorrow. . . .

6. Diary of Salmon P. Chase, Entry for July 22, 1862.

. . . The question of arming slaves was then brought up and I advocated it warmly. The President was unwilling to adopt this measure, but proposed to issue a proclamation, on the basis of the Confiscation Bill, calling upon

11. Chase was Lincoln's secretary of the treasury from 1861 until 1864.
12. George McClellan (1826–1885) was commander of the Army of the Potomac in 1862. Lincoln removed him because of his excessive caution and lack of boldness.
13. Edwin Stanton (1814–1869), secretary of war.
14. William Seward (1801–1872), secretary of state.
15. Montgomery Blair (1813–1883), postmaster general.

the States to return to their allegiance—warning the rebels the provisions of the Act would have full force at the expiration of sixty days adding on his own part, a declaration of his intention to renew, at the next session of Congress, his recommendation of compensation to States adopting the gradual abolishment of slavery and proclaiming the emancipation of all slaves within States remaining in insurrection on the first of January, 1863.

I said that I should give to such a measure my cordial support: but I should prefer that no new expression on the subject of compensation should be made, and I thought that the measure of Emancipation could be much better and more quietly accomplished by allowing Generals to organize and arm the slaves (thus avoiding depredation and massacre on the one hand, and support to the insurrection on the other) and by directing the Commanders of Departments to proclaim emancipation within their Districts as soon as practicable; but I regarded this as so much better than inaction on the subject, that I should give it my entire support.

The President determined to publish the first three Orders forthwith, and to leave the other for some further consideration. The impression left upon my mind by the whole discussion was, that while the President thought that the organization, equipment and arming of negroes, like other soldiers, would be productive of more evil than good, he was not willing that Commanders should, at their discretion, arm, for purely defensive purposes, slaves coming within their lines.

Mr. Stanton brought forward a proposition to draft 50,000 men. Mr. Seward proposed that the number should be 100,000. The President directed that, whatever number were drafted, should be a part of the 3,000,000 already called for. No decision was reached, however.

Source 7 from Basler, ed., *The Collected Works of Abraham Lincoln*, Vol. V, p. 338.

7. Lincoln's Memorandum on Recruiting Negroes.

[July 22, 1862?]

To recruiting free negroes, no objection.

To recruiting slaves of disloyal owners, no objection.

To recruiting slaves of loyal owners, *with their consent,* no objection.

To recruiting slaves of loyal owners *without* consent, objection, *unless the necessity is urgent.*

To conducting offensively, while recruiting, and to carrying away slaves not suitable for recruits, objection.

CHAPTER 6

THE PRICE FOR
VICTORY: THE
DECISION TO
USE AFRICAN
AMERICAN
TROOPS

Source 8 from *Diary and Correspondence of Salmon P. Chase,* pp. 53–54.

8. Diary of Salmon P. Chase, Entry for August 3, 1862.

. . . There was a good deal of conversation on the connection of the Slavery question with the rebellion. I expressed my conviction for the tenth or twentieth time, that the time for the suppression of the rebellion without interference with slavery had passed; that it was possible, probably, at the outset, by striking the insurrectionists wherever found, strongly and decisively; but we had elected to act on the principles of a civil war, in which the whole population of every seceding state was engaged against the Federal Government, instead of treating the active secessionists as insurgents and exerting our utmost energies for their arrest and punishment;— that the bitternesses of the conflict had now substantially united the white population of the rebel states against us; that the loyal whites remaining, if they would not prefer the Union without Slavery, certainly would not prefer Slavery to the Union; that the blacks were really the only loyal population worth counting; and that, in the Gulf States at least, their right to Freedom ought to be at once recognized, while, in the Border States, the President's plan of Emancipation might be made the basis of the necessary measures for their ultimate enfranchisement;—that the practical mode of effecting this seemed to me quite simple;—that the President had already spoken of the importance of making of the freed blacks on the Mississippi, below Tennessee, a safeguard to the navigation of the river;—that Mitchell, with a few thousand soldiers, could take Vicksburgh;—assure the blacks freedom on condition of loyalty; organize the best of them in companies, regiments etc. and provide, as far as practicable for the cultivation of the plantations by the rest:—that Butler should signify to the slaveholders of Louisiana that they must recognize the freedom of their workpeople by paying them wages;—and that Hunter should do the same thing in South-Carolina.

Mr. Seward expressed himself as in favor of any measures likely to accomplish the results I contemplated, which could be carried into effect without Proclamations; and the President said he was pretty well cured of objections to any measure except want of adaptedness to put down the rebellion; but did not seem satisfied that the time had come for the adoption of such a plan as I proposed. . . .

Source 9 from Basler, ed., *The Collected Works of Abraham Lincoln,* Vol. V, pp. 356–357.

9. President Lincoln, "Remarks to Deputation of Western Gentlemen," August 4, 1862. From an article in the *New York Tribune,* August 5, 1862.

A deputation of Western gentlemen waited upon the President this morning to offer two colored regiments from the State of Indiana. Two members of Congress were of the party. The President received them courteously, but stated to them that he was not prepared to go the length of enlisting negroes as soldiers. He would employ all colored men offered as laborers, but would not promise to make soldiers of them.

The deputation came away satisfied that it is the determination of the Government not to arm negroes unless some new and more pressing emergency arises. The President argued that the nation could not afford to lose Kentucky at this crisis, and gave it as his opinion that to arm the negroes would turn 50,000 bayonets from the loyal Border States against us that were for us. . . .

Source 10 from McPherson, *The Negro's Civil War,* pp. 163–164.

10. Letter to the Editor, *New York Tribune,* August 16, 1862.[16]

I am quite sure there is not one man in ten but would feel himself degraded as a volunteer if negro equality is to be the order in the field of battle. . . . I take the liberty of warning the abettors of fraternizing with the blacks, that one negro regiment, in the present temper of things, put on equality with those who have the past year fought and suffered, will withdraw an amount of life and energy in our army equal to disbanding ten of the best regiments we can now raise.

16. This was a letter to the editor and did not reflect the opinion of Horace Greeley, editor of the *Tribune* and supporter of racial equality for African Americans.

CHAPTER 6

THE PRICE FOR
VICTORY: THE
DECISION TO
USE AFRICAN
AMERICAN
TROOPS

Source 11 from William Wells Brown,[17] *The Negro in the American Rebellion: His Heroism and His Fidelity* (Boston: Lee & Shepard, 1867), pp. 101–104.

11. Reminiscence of a Black Man of the Threat to Cincinnati, September 1862.[18]

The mayor's proclamation, under ordinary circumstances, would be explicit enough. "Every man, of every age, be he citizen or alien," surely meant the colored people. . . . Seeking to test the matter, a policeman was approached, as he strutted in his new dignity of provostguard. To the question, humbly, almost trembling, put, "Does the mayor desire colored men to report for service in the city's defence?" he replied, "You know d——d well he doesn't mean you. Niggers ain't citizens."—"But he calls on all, citizens and aliens. If he does not mean all, he should not say so."—"The mayor knows as well as you do what to write, and all he wants is for you niggers to keep quiet." This was at nine o'clock on the morning of the second. The military authorities had determined, however, to impress the colored men for work upon the fortifications. The privilege of volunteering, extended to others, was to be denied to them. Permission to volunteer would imply some freedom, some dignity, some independent manhood. . . .

If the guard appointed to the duty of collecting the colored people had gone to their houses, and notified them to report for duty on the fortifications, the order would have been cheerfully obeyed. But the brutal ruffians who composed the regular and special police took every opportunity to inflict abuse and insult upon the men whom they arrested. . . .

The captain of these conscripting squads was one William Homer, and in him organized ruffianism had its fitting head. He exhibited the brutal malignity of his nature in a continued series of petty tyrannies. Among the first squads marched into the yard was one which had to wait several hours before being ordered across the river. Seeking to make themselves as comfortable as possible, they had collected blocks of wood, and piled up bricks, upon which they seated themselves on the shaded side of the yard. Coming into the yard, he ordered all to rise, marched them to another part, then issued the order, "D—n you, squat." Turning to the guard, he added, "Shoot the first one who rises." Reaching the opposite side of the river, the same squad were marched from the sidewalk into the middle of the dusty road, and again the order, "D—n you, squat," and the command to shoot the first one who should rise. . . .

17. Brown was an African American who ultimately served in the Union army and recorded his experiences.
18. In early September 1862, the citizens of Cincinnati, Ohio, feared a raid on the city by Confederates. Mayor George Hatch issued a proclamation calling on "every man of every age" to take part in the defense of the city.

Calling up his men, he would address them thus: "Now, you fellows, hold up your heads. Pat, hold your musket straight; don't put your tongue out so far; keep your eyes open: I believe you are drunk. Now, then, I want you fellows to go out of this pen, and bring all the niggers you can catch. Don't come back here without niggers: if you do, you shall not have a bit of grog. Now be off, you shabby cusses, and come back in forty minutes, and bring me niggers; that's what I want." This barbarous and inhuman treatment of the colored citizens of Cincinnati continued for four days, without a single word of remonstrance, except from the "Gazette."

Source 12 from John G. Nicolay and John Hay, eds., *Abraham Lincoln—Complete Works* (New York: Century Co., 1894), Vol. II, pp. 234–235, 242–243.

12. Lincoln's Reply to a Committee from the Religious Denominations of Chicago, Asking the President to Issue a Proclamation of Emancipation, September 13, 1862.

The subject presented in the memorial is one upon which I have thought much for weeks past, and I may even say for months. I am approached with the most opposite opinions and advice, and that by religious men who are equally certain that they represent the divine will. I am sure that either the one or the other class is mistaken in that belief, and perhaps in some respects both. I hope it will not be irreverent for me to say that if it is probable that God would reveal his will to others on a point so connected with my duty, it might be supposed he would reveal it directly to me; for, unless I am more deceived in myself than I often am, it is my earnest desire to know the will of Providence in this matter. And if I can learn what it is, I will do it. These are not, however, the days of miracles, and I suppose it will be granted that I am not to expect a direct revelation. I must study the plain physical facts of the case, ascertain what is possible, and learn what appears to be wise and right. . . .

I admit that slavery is the root of the rebellion, or at least its *sine qua non*.[19] The ambition of politicians may have instigated them to act, but they would have been impotent without slavery as their instrument. I will also concede that emancipation would help us in Europe, and convince them that we are incited by something more than ambition. I grant, further, that it would help somewhat at the North, though not so much, I fear, as you

19. An essential element or condition; a necessary ingredient.

CHAPTER 6

THE PRICE FOR
VICTORY: THE
DECISION TO
USE AFRICAN
AMERICAN
TROOPS

and those you represent imagine. Still, some additional strength would be added in that way to the war, and then, unquestionably, it would weaken the rebels by drawing off their laborers, which is of great importance; but I am not so sure we could do much with the blacks. If we were to arm them, I fear that in a few weeks the arms would be in the hands of the rebels; and, indeed, thus far we have not had arms enough to equip our white troops. I will mention another thing, though it meet only your scorn and contempt. There are fifty thousand bayonets in the Union armies from the border slave States. It would be a serious matter if, in consequence of a proclamation such as you desire, they should go over to the rebels. I do not think they all would—not so many, indeed, as a year ago, or as six months ago—not so many to-day as yesterday. Every day increases their Union feeling. They are also getting their pride enlisted, and want to beat the rebels.

Sources 13 through 15 from Basler, ed., *The Collected Works of Abraham Lincoln,* Vol. V, pp. 444, 509, 28–30.

13. Lincoln to Vice President Hannibal Hamlin.

(Strictly private.)   Executive Mansion,
                                   Washington, September 28, 1862.

My Dear Sir:

Your kind letter of the 25th is just received. It is known to some that while I hope something from the proclamation,[20] my expectations are not as sanguine as are those of some friends. The time for its effect southward has not come; but northward the effect should be instantaneous.

It is six days old, and while commendation in newspapers and by distinguished individuals is all that a vain man could wish, the stocks have declined, and troops came forward more slowly than ever. This, looked soberly in the face, is not very satisfactory. We have fewer troops in the field at the end of six days than we had at the beginning—the attrition among the old outnumbering the addition of the new. The North responds to the proclamation sufficiently in breath; but breath alone kills no rebels.

I wish I could write more cheerfully; nor do I thank you the less for the kindness of your letter. Yours very truly,

A. LINCOLN

20. Lincoln was referring to his Preliminary Emancipation Proclamation, which he issued on September 22, 1862. Lincoln's hope was that the threat of emancipation would cause the South to surrender so as to keep slavery intact. See again Lincoln's letter to Horace Greeley, August 22, 1862, on page 226.

14. Lincoln to Carl Schurz.

Gen. Carl Schurz

Executive Mansion,
Washington, Nov. 24, 1862.

My dear Sir

I have just received, and read your letter of the 20th. The purport of it is that we lost the late elections,[21] and the administration is failing, because the war is unsuccessful; and that I must not flatter myself that I am not justly to blame for it. I certainly know that if the war fails, the administration fails, and that I *will* be blamed for it, whether I deserve it or not. And I ought to be blamed, if I could do better. You think I could do better; therefore you blame me already. I think I could not do better; therefore I blame you for blaming me. . . .

15. The Emancipation Proclamation.

January 1, 1863

By the President of the United States of America:
A Proclamation. . . .

Now, therefore I, Abraham Lincoln, President of the United States, by virtue of the power in me vested as Commander-in-Chief, of the Army and Navy of the United States in time of actual armed rebellion against authority and government of the United States, and as a fit and necessary war measure for suppressing said rebellion, do, on this first day of January, in the year of our Lord one thousand eight hundred and sixty three, and in accordance with my purpose so to do publicly proclaimed for the full period of one hundred days, from the day first above mentioned, order and designate as the States and parts of States wherein the people thereof respectively, are this day in rebellion against the United States, the following, to wit: . . .

[*Here Lincoln identified the geographic areas of the South still under the control of the Confederacy.*]

And by virtue of the power, and for the purpose aforesaid, I do order and declare that all persons held as slaves within said designated States, and

21. In the congressional elections of 1862, the Republicans lost three seats in the House of Representatives, although they were still the majority party. Senators were not elected by the people until the Seventeenth Amendment to the Constitution was ratified in 1913.

CHAPTER 6

THE PRICE FOR
VICTORY: THE
DECISION TO
USE AFRICAN
AMERICAN
TROOPS

parts of States, are, and henceforward shall be free; and that the Executive government of the United States, including the military and naval authorities thereof, will recognize and maintain the freedom of said persons.

And I hereby enjoin upon the people so declared to be free to abstain from all violence, unless in necessary self-defence; and I recommend to them that, in all cases when allowed, they labor faithfully for reasonable wages.

And I further declare and make known, that such persons of suitable condition, will be received into the armed services of the United States to garrison forts, positions, stations, and other places, and to man vessels of all sorts in said service.[22]

And upon this act, sincerely believed to be an act of justice, warranted by the Constitution, upon military necessity, I invoke the considerate judgment of mankind, and the gracious favor of Almighty God.

In witness whereof, I have hereunto set my hand and caused the seal of the United States to be affixed.

Done at the City of Washington, this first day of January, in the year of our Lord one thousand eight hundred and sixty three, and of the Independence of the United States of America the eighty-seventh. By the President:

ABRAHAM LINCOLN

Source 16 from George Washington Williams, *A History of the Negro Troops in the War of the Rebellion, 1861–65* (New York: Harper and Brothers, 1888), pp. 66–67, 90–91.

16. Reminiscence of a Former Black Soldier in the Union Army.

At first the faintest intimation that Negroes should be employed as soldiers in the Union Army was met with derision. By many it was regarded as a joke. The idea of arming the ex-slaves seemed ridiculous to most civil and military officers. . . .

Most observing and thoughtful people concluded that centuries of servitude had rendered the Negro slave incapable of any civil or military service. . . . Some officers talked of resigning if Negroes were to be called upon to fight the battles of a free republic. The privates in regiments from large cities and border States were bitter and demonstrative in their opposition. The Negro volunteers themselves were subjected to indignities from rebel civilians within the Union lines, and obtained no protection from the white troops. . . .

22. This paragraph was not part of the preliminary proclamation issued by Lincoln on September 22, 1862. See Basler, ed., *The Collected Works of Abraham Lincoln*, Vol. V, pp. 433–436.

Source 17 from Lawrence Frederick Kohl and Margaret Cosse Richard, eds., *Irish Green and Union Blue: The Civil War Letters of Peter Welsh, Color Sergeant, 28th Regiment, Massachusetts Volunteers* (New York: Fordham University Press, 1986), p. 62.

17. Fragment of a Letter from a Union Soldier, Early 1863.

I see by late papers that the governor of Massachusetts has been autheured to raise nigar regiments. i hope he may succeed but i doubt it very much if they can raise a few thousand and sent them out here i can assure you that whether they have the grit to go into battle or not if they are placed in front and any brigade of this army behind them they will have to go in or they will meet as hot a reception in their retreat as in their advance[.] The feeling against nigars is intensly strong in this army as is plainly to be seen wherever and whenever they meet them[.] They are looked upon as the principal cause of this war and this feeling is especially strong in the Irish regiments[.]

Source 18 from *The War of the Rebellion*, Series III, Vol. III, p. 16.

18. L. Thomas to Governor of Rhode Island, January 15, 1863.

ADJUTANT-GENERAL'S OFFICE,
Washington, D.C., January 15, 1863.

GOVERNOR OF RHODE ISLAND
Providence, R. I.:

SIR: I am directed to say that the President will accept into the service of the United States an infantry regiment of volunteers of African descent, if offered by your State and organized according to the rules and regulations of the service.

I am, very respectfully,

L. THOMAS,
Adjutant-General.

CHAPTER 6

THE PRICE FOR
VICTORY: THE
DECISION TO
USE AFRICAN
AMERICAN
TROOPS

Source 19 from Glenn W. Sunderland, *Five Days to Glory* (South Brunswick, N.J.: A. S. Barnes & Co., 1970), pp. 97–98.

19. Letter from Tighlman Jones (a Union Soldier) to Brother Zillman Jones, October 6, 1863.

You have heard of Negroes being enlisted to fight for Uncle Sam. If you would like to know what the soldiers think about the idea I can almost tell you. Why, that is just what they desire. There is some soldiers who curse and blow and make a great noise about it but we set him as a convalescent who is like a man who is afraid of the smallpox who curses the works of a power he can in no way avoid, but will kick and rail and act the part of a fool, but of no avail, nature will have its own course, or to say that this war will free the Negroes and that they will enlist and fight to sustain the Government. I think more of a Negro Union soldier than I do of all the cowardly Copperhead trash of the north[23] and there is no soldier but what approves of the course of the present administration and will fight till the Rebels unconditionally surrender and return to their allegiance.

Source 20 from Dudley Cornish, *The Sable Arm: Negro Troops in the Union Army, 1861–1865* (New York: W. W. Norton, 1966), pp. ix–x.

20. Editorial, *New York Times*, March 7, 1864.

There has been no more striking manifestation of the marvelous times that are upon us than the scene in our streets at the departure of the first of our colored regiments. Had any man predicted it last year he would have been thought a fool, even by the wisest and most discerning. History abounds with strange contrasts. It always has been an ever-shifting melodrama. But never, in this land at least, has it presented a transition so extreme and yet so speedy as what our eyes have just beheld.

Eight months ago the African race in this City were literally hunted down like wild beasts.[24] They fled for their lives. When caught, they were shot down in cold blood, or stoned to death, or hung to the trees or the lampposts. Their homes were pillaged; the asylum which Christian charity had

---

23. Copperheads were northerners who opposed the war and advocated peace at any price.
24. In mid-1863, demonstrations against conscription in New York City turned into an ugly mob action against African Americans, partly because of their connection, through the Emancipation Proclamation of January 1, 1863, to the war and partly because of economic competition with the poorer whites who constituted most of the rioters.

provided for their orphaned children was burned; and there was no limit to the persecution but in the physical impossibility of finding further material on which the mob could wreak its ruthless hate. Nor was it solely the raging horde in the streets that visited upon the black man the nefarious wrong. Thousands and tens of thousands of men of higher social grade, of better education, cherished precisely the same spirit. . . .

How astonishingly has all this been changed. The same men who could not have shown themselves in the most obscure street in the City without peril of instant death, even though in the most suppliant attitude, now march in solid platoons, with shouldered muskets, slung knapsacks, and buckled cartridge boxes down through our gayest avenues and our busiest thoroughfares to the pealing strains of martial music and are everywhere saluted with waving handkerchiefs, with descending flowers, and with the acclamations and plaudits of countless beholders. They are halted at our most beautiful square, and amid an admiring crowd, in the presence of many of our most prominent citizens, are addressed in an eloquent and most complimentary speech by the President of our chief literary institution, and are presented with a gorgeous stand of colors in the names of a large number of the first ladies of the City, who attest on parchment, signed by their own fair hands, that they "will anxiously watch your career, glorifying in your heroism, ministering to you when wounded and ill, and honoring your martyrdom with benedictions and with tears."

It is only by such occasions that we can at all realize the prodigious revolution which the public mind everywhere is experiencing. Such developments are infallible tokens of a new epoch.

SOURCES

SOUTH

Sources 21 and 22 from *The War of the Rebellion,* Series IV, Vol. I, pp. 482, 529.

21. Correspondence Between W. S. Turner and the Confederate War Department, July 17, 1861.

HELENA, ARK., *July 17, 1861.*

Hon. L. P. WALKER[25]:

DEAR SIR: I wrote you a few days since for myself and many others in this district to ascertain if we could get negro regiments received for Confederate service, officered, of course, by white men. All we ask is arms, clothing, and provisions, and usual pay for officers and not one cent pay for negroes.

25. Walker was the Confederate secretary of war from February to September 1861.

CHAPTER 6

THE PRICE FOR
VICTORY: THE
DECISION TO
USE AFRICAN
AMERICAN
TROOPS

Our negroes are too good to fight Lincoln hirelings, but as they pretend to love negroes so much we want to show them how much the true Southern cotton-patch negro loves them in return. The North cannot complain at this. They proclaim negro equality from the Senate Chamber to the pulpit, teach it in their schools, and are doing all they can to turn the slaves upon master, mistress, and children. And now, sir, if you can receive the negroes that can be raised we will soon give the Northern thieves a gorge of the negroes' love for them that will never be forgotten. As you well know, I have had long experience with negro character. I am satisfied they are easy disciplined and less trouble than whites in camp, and will fight desperately as long as they have a single white officer living. I know one man that will furnish and arm 100 of his own and his son for their captain. The sooner we bring a strong negro force against the hirelings the sooner we shall have peace, in my humble judgment. Let me hear from you.

Your old friend,

W. S. TURNER

22. Correspondence Between W. S. Turner and the Confederate War Department, August 2, 1861.

CONFEDERATE STATES OF AMERICA, WAR DEPARTMENT,

Richmond, August 2, 1861.

W. S. TURNER,

Helena, Ark.:

SIR: In reply to your letter of the 17th of July I am directed by the Secretary of War to say that this Department is not prepared to accept the negro regiment tendered by you, and yet it is not doubted that almost every slave would cheerfully aid his master in the work of hurling back the fanatical invader. Moreover, if the necessity were apparent there is high authority for the employment of such forces. Washington himself recommended the enlistment of two negro regiments in Georgia, and the Congress sanctioned the measure. But now there is a superabundance of our own color tendering their services to the Government in its day of peril and ruthless invasion, a superabundance of men when we are bound to admit the inadequate supply of arms at present at the disposal of the Government.

Respectfully,

A. T. BLEDSOE
Chief of Bureau of War.

Sources 23 through 26 from Robert F. Durden, *The Gray and the Black: The Confederate Debate on Emancipation* (Baton Rouge: Louisiana State University Press, 1972), pp. 30–31, 54–58, 61, 66–67.

23. *Montgomery* (Ala.) *Weekly Mail*, "Employment of Negroes in the Army," September 9, 1863.

. . . We must either employ the negroes ourselves, or the enemy will employ them against us. While the enemy retains so much of our territory, they are, in their present avocation and status, a dangerous element, a source of weakness. They are no longer negative characters, but subjects of volition as other people. They must be taught to know that this is peculiarly the country of the black man—that in no other is the climate and soil so well adapted to his nature and capacity. He must further be taught that it is his duty, as well as the white man's, to defend his home with arms, if need be.

We are aware that there are persons who shudder at the idea of placing arms in the hands of negroes, and who are not willing to trust them under any circumstances. The negro, however, is proverbial for his faithfulness under kind treatment. He is an affectionate, grateful being, and we are persuaded that the fears of such persons are groundless.

There are in the slaveholding States four millions of negroes, and out of this number at least six hundred thousand able-bodied men capable of bearing arms can be found. Lincoln proposes to free and arm them against us. There are already fifty thousand of them in the Federal ranks. Lincoln's scheme has worked well so far, and if no[t] checkmated, will most assuredly be carried out. The Confederate Government must adopt a counter policy. It must thwart the enemy in this gigantic scheme, at all hazards, and if nothing else will do it—if the negroes cannot be made effective and trustworthy to the Southern cause in no other way, we solemnly believe it is the duty of this Government to forestall Lincoln and proceed at once to take steps for the emancipation or liberation of the negroes itself. Let them be declared free, placed in the ranks, and told to fight for their homes and country. . . .

Such action on the part of our Government would place our people in a purer and better light before the world. It would disabuse the European mind of a grave error in regard to the cause of our separation. It would prove to them that there were higher and holier motives which actuated our people than the mere love of property. It would show that, although slavery is one of the principles that we started to fight for, yet it falls far short of being the chief one; that, for the sake of our liberty, we are capable

CHAPTER 6

THE PRICE FOR
VICTORY: THE
DECISION TO
USE AFRICAN
AMERICAN
TROOPS

of any personal sacrifice; that we regard the emancipation of slaves, and the consequent loss of property as an evil infinitely less than the subjugation and enslavement of ourselves; that it is not a war exclusively for the privilege of holding negroes in bondage. It would prove to our soldiers, three-fourths of whom never owned a negro, that it is not "the rich man's war and the poor man's fight," but a war for the most sacred of all principles, for the dearest of all rights—the right to govern ourselves. It would show them that the rich man who owned slaves was not willing to jeopardize the precious liberty of the country by his eagerness to hold on to his slaves, but that he was ready to give them up and sacrifice his interest in them whenever the cause demanded it. It would lend a new impetus, a new enthusiasm, a new and powerful strength to the cause, and place our success beyond a peradventure. It would at once remove all the odium which attached to us on account of slavery, and bring us speedy recognition, and, if necessary, intervention.

24. General Patrick Cleburne to General Joseph Johnston, January 2, 1864.

We have now been fighting for nearly three years, have spilled much of our best blood, and lost, consumed, or thrown to the flames an amount of property equal in value to the specie currency of the world. . . . Our soldiers can see no end to this state of affairs except in our own exhaustion; hence, instead of rising to the occasion, they are sinking into a fatal apathy, growing weary of hardships and slaughters which promise no results. In this state of things it is easy to understand why there is a growing belief that some black catastrophe is not far ahead of us, and that unless some extraordinary change is soon made in our condition we must overtake it. . . .

In view of the state of affairs what does our country propose to do? In the words of President Davis "no effort must be spared to add largely to our effective force as promptly as possible. The sources of supply are to be found in restoring to the army all who are improperly absent, putting an end to substitution, modifying the exemption law, restricting details, and placing in the ranks such of the able-bodied men now employed as wagoners, nurses, cooks, and other employees, as are doing service for which the negroes may be found competent.". . . [W]e propose, in addition to a modification of the President's plans, that we retain in service for the war all troops now in service, and that we immediately commence training a large reserve of the most courageous of our slaves, and further that we guarantee freedom within a reasonable time to every slave in the South who shall remain true to the Confederacy in this war. As between the loss of independence and the loss of slavery, we assume that every patriot will freely give up the latter—give up the negro slave rather than be a slave himself. If we are correct in this assumption it only remains to show how this great national sacrifice is, in all human probabilities, to change the current of success and sweep the invader from our country.

Our country has already some friends in England and France, and there are strong motives to induce these nations to recognize and assist us, but they cannot assist us without helping slavery, and to do this would be in conflict with their policy for the last quarter of a century. . . . But this barrier once removed, the sympathy and the interests of these and other nations will accord with their own, and we may expect from them both moral support and material aid. . . .

Will the slaves fight? . . . The negro slaves of Saint Domingo, fighting for freedom, defeated their white masters and the French troops sent against them.[26] The negro slaves of Jamaica revolted, and under the name of Maroons held the mountains against their masters for 150 years; and the experience of this war has been so far that half-trained negroes have fought as bravely as many other half-trained Yankees. If, contrary to the training of a lifetime, they can be made to face and fight bravely against their former masters, how much more probable is it that with the allurement of a higher reward, and led by those masters, they would submit to discipline and face dangers.

25. President Jefferson Davis to General Walker, January 13, 1864—Reaction to Cleburne's Proposal.

I have received your letter, with its inclosure, informing me of the propositions [Cleburne's proposal] submitted to a meeting of the general officers on the 2d instant, and thank you for the information. Deeming it to be injurious to the public service that such a subject should be mooted, or even known to be entertained by persons possessed of the confidence and

26. On August 23, 1791, thousands of slaves in the French colony of Saint Dominigue (in Spanish, Santo Domingo; now Haiti) revolted against their white masters. Ultimately led by Toussaint Louverture (often spelled L'Ouverture), the slaves overthrew their masters, beat back invasions from both Britain and France, and declared Haiti an independent republic in 1804. Whites who fled from Haiti to the United States reported atrocities that filled white southerners with alarm for years after. See especially Alfred N. Hunt, *Haiti's Influence on Antebellum America* (Baton Rouge: Louisiana State University Press, 1988).

CHAPTER 6

THE PRICE FOR
VICTORY: THE
DECISION TO
USE AFRICAN
AMERICAN
TROOPS

respect of the people, I have concluded that the best policy under the circumstances will be to avoid all publicity, and the Secretary of War has therefore written to General Johnston requesting him to convey to those concerned my desire that it should be kept private. If it be kept out of public journals its ill effect will be much lessened.

26. General Joseph Johnston to General Hardee et al., January 31, 1864—Reaction to Cleburne's Proposal.

Lieutenant-General Hardee, Major-Generals Cheatham, Hindman, Cleburne, Stewart, Walker, Brigadier-Generals Bate and P. Anderson:

GENERAL:

I have just received a letter from the Secretary of War in reference to Major-General Cleburne's memoir read in my quarters about the 2d instant. In this letter the Honorable Secretary expresses the earnest conviction of the President "that the dissemination or even promulgation of such opinions under the present circumstances of the Confederacy, whether in the Army or among the people, can be productive only of discouragement, distraction, and dissension." The agitation and controversy which must spring from the presentation of such views by officers high in the public confidence are to be deeply deprecated, and while no doubt or mistrust is for a moment entertained of the patriotic intents of the gallant author of the memorial, and such of his brother officers as may have favored his opinions, it is requested that you communicate to them, as well as all others present on the occasion, the opinions, as herein expressed, of the President, and urge on them the suppression, not only of the memorial itself, but likewise of all discussion and controversy respecting or growing out of it. . . .

Source 27 from Bell Irvin Wiley, ed., *Letters of Warren Akin, Confederate Congressman* (Athens: University of Georgia Press, 1959), pp. 32–33.

27. Letter from Warren Akin to Nathan Land, October 31, 1864.

As to calling out the negro men and placing them in the army, with the promise that they shall be free at the end of the war, I can only say it is a question of fearful magnitude. Can we prevent subjugation, confiscation, degradation and slavery without it? If not, will our condition or that of the negro, be any worse by calling them into service?

On the other hand: Can we feed our soldiers and their families if the negro men are taken from the plantations? Will our soldiers submit to having our negroes along side them in the ditches, or in line of battle? When the negro is taught the use of arms and the art of war, can we live in safety with them afterwards? Or if it be contemplated to send them off to another country, when peace is made, will it be right to force them to a new, distant and strange land, after they have fought for and won the independence of this? Would they go without having another war? Involving, perhaps a general insurrection of all the negroes? To call forth the negroes into the army, with the promise of freedom, will it not be giving up the great question involved by doing the very thing Lincoln is now doing? The Confederate States may take private property for public use, by paying for it; but can we ever pay for 300,000 negro men at present prices, in addition to our other indebtedness? The Confederate Government may buy the private negro property of the Citizens, but can it set them free among us, to corrupt our slaves, and place in peril our existence? These are some of the thoughts that have passed th[r]ough my mind on the subject. But I can not say that I have a definite and fixed opinion. If I were convinced that we will be subjugated, with the long train of horrors that will follow it, unless the negroes be placed in the army, I would not hesitate to enrol our slaves and put them to fighting. Subjugation will give us free negroes in abundance— enemies at that—while white slaves will be more numerous than free negroes. We and our children will be slaves, while our freed negroes will lord it over us. It is impossible for the evils resulting from placing our slaves in the army to be greater than those that will follow subjugation. We may (if necessary) put our slaves in the army, win our independence, and have liberty and homes for ourselves and children. But subjugation will deprive us of our homes, houses, property, liberty, honor, and every thing worth living for, leaving for us and our posterity only the chains of slavery, tenfold more galling and degrading than that now felt by our negroes. But I will not enlarge, I have made suggestions merely for your reflection.

Source 28 from McPherson, *The Negro's Civil War,* pp. 243–244.

28. Judah P. Benjamin (Secretary of War, Confederacy) to Fred A. Porcher (an Old Friend and Former Classmate), December 21, 1864.

For a year past I have seen that the period was fast approaching when we should be compelled to use every resource of our command for the defense of our liberties. . . . The negroes will certainly be made to fight against us

CHAPTER 6

THE PRICE FOR
VICTORY: THE
DECISION TO
USE AFRICAN
AMERICAN
TROOPS

if not armed for our defense. The drain of that source of our strength is steadily fatal, and irreversible by any other expedient than that of arming the slaves as an auxiliary force.

I further agree with you that if they are to fight for our freedom they are entitled to their own. Public opinion is fast ripening on the subject, and ere the close of the winter the conviction on this point will become so widespread that the Government will have no difficulty in inaugurating the policy [of recruiting Negro soldiers].

. . . It is well known that General Lee, who commands so largely the confidence of the people, is strongly in favor of our using the negroes for defense, and emancipating them, if necessary, for that purpose. Can you not yourself write a series of articles in your papers, always urging this point as the true issue, viz, is it better for the negro to fight for us or against us?

Source 29 from Durden, *The Gray and the Black,* pp. 89–91.

29. *Richmond Enquirer,* November 4, 1864, Letter to the Editor in Reply to the Editorial of October 6, 1864.

Can it be possible that you are serious and earnest in proposing such a step to be taken by our Government? Or were you merely discussing the matter as a something which might be done? An element of power which might be used—meaning thereby to intimidate or threaten our enemy with it as a weapon of offence which they may drive us to use? Can it be possible that a Southern man—editor of a Southern journal—recognizing the right of property in slaves, admitting their inferiority in the scale of being and also their social inferiority, would recommend the passage of a law which at one blow levels all distinctions, deprives the master of a right to his property, and elevates the negro to an equality with the white man?—for, disguise it as you may, those who fight together in a common cause, and by success win the *same* freedom, enjoy equal rights and equal position, and in this case, are distinguished only by color. Are we prepared for this? Is it for this we are contending? Is it for this we would seek the aid of our slaves? . . . When President Davis said: "We are not fighting for slavery, but independence," he meant that the question and subject of slavery was a matter settled amongst ourselves and one that admitted of no dispute—that he intended to be independent of all foreign influences on this as well as on other matters—free to own slaves if he pleased—free to lay our own taxes—free to govern ourselves. He never intended to ignore the question of slavery or to do aught else but express the determination to be *independent* in this as well as in all other matters. What has embittered the feelings of the two sections of the old Union? What has gradually driven them to the final separation? What is it that has made two nationalities of them, if it is not slavery?

The Yankee *steals* my slave, and makes a soldier and freeman of him to *destroy* me. You *take* my slave, and make a soldier and freeman of him to *defend* me. The difference in your intention is very great; but is not the practice of both equally pernicious to the slave and destruction to the country? And at the expiration of ten years after peace what would be the relative difference between my negro *stolen* and freed by the Yankee and my negro taken and freed by you? Would they not be equally worthless and vicious? How would you distinguish between them? How prevent the return of him whose hand is red with his master's blood, and his enjoyment of those privileges which you so lavishly bestow upon the faithful freedman?

Have you thought of the influence to be exerted by these half or quarter million of free negroes in the midst of slaves as you propose to leave them at the end of the war; these men constitute the bone and sinew of our slaves, the able-bodied between 18 and 45. They will be men who know the value and power of combination; they will be well disciplined, trained to the use of arms, with the power and ability of command; at the same time they will be grossly and miserably ignorant, without any fixed principle of life or the ability of acquiring one. . . .

Sources 30 and 31 from McPherson, *The Negro's Civil War,* p. 244.

30. Howell Cobb, Speech in the Confederate Senate, 1864.

. . . If slaves will make good soldiers our whole theory of slavery is wrong. . . . The day you make soldiers of them is the beginning of the end of the revolution.

31. Robert Toombs, Speech in the Confederate Senate, 1864.

. . . The worst calamity that could befall us would be to gain our independence by the valor of our slaves. . . . The day that the army of Virginia allows a negro regiment to enter their lines as soldiers they will be degraded, ruined, and disgraced.

CHAPTER 6

THE PRICE FOR
VICTORY: THE
DECISION TO
USE AFRICAN
AMERICAN
TROOPS

Source 32 from Durden, *The Gray and the Black,* pp. 93–94.

32. *Lynchburg* (Va.) *Republican,* November 2, 1864.

The proposition is so strange—so unconstitutional—so directly in conflict with all of our former practices and teachings—so entirely subversive of our social and political institutions—and so completely destructive of our liberties, that we stand completely appalled [and] dumfounded [*sic*] at its promulgation.

They propose that Congress shall conscribe two hundred and fifty thousand slaves, arm, equip and fight them in the field. As an inducement of them to be faithful, it is proposed that, at the end of the war, they shall have their freedom and live amongst us. "The conscription of negroes," says the *Enquirer,* "should be accompanied with freedom and the privilege of remaining in the States." This is the monstrous proposition. The South went to war to defeat the designs of the abolitionists, and behold! in the midst of the war, we turn abolitionists ourselves! We went to war because the Federal Congress kept eternally meddling with our domestic institutions, with which we contended they had nothing to do, and now we propose to end the war by asking the Confederate Congress to do precisely what Lincoln proposes to do—free our negroes and make them the equals of the white man! We have always been taught to believe that slaves are property, and under the exclusive control of the States and the courts. This new doctrine teaches us that Congress has a right to free our negroes and make them the equals of their masters. . . .

Source 33 from Wiley, ed., *Letters of Warren Akin,* p. 117.

33. Mary V. Akin to Warren Akin, January 8, 1865.

. . . Every one I talk to is in favor of putting negros in the army and that *immediately.* Major Jones speaks very strongly in favor of it. I think slavery is now gone and what little there is left of it should be rendered as serviceable as possible and for that reason the negro men ought to be put to fighting and where some of them will be killed, if it is not done there will soon be more negroes than whites in the country and they will be the free race. I want to see them *got rid of soon.* . . .

Sources 34 through 36 from Durden, *The Gray and the Black,* pp. 163, 195, 202–203.

34. *Macon* (Ga.) *Telegraph and Confederate,* January 11, 1865.

Mr. Editor:

A lady's opinion may not be worth much in such an hour as this, but I cannot resist the temptation of expressing my approbation of "The crisis—the Remedy," copied from the Mobile Register. Would to God our Government would act upon its suggestions at once. The women of the South are not so in love with their negro property, as to wish to see husbands, fathers, sons, brothers, slain to protect it; nor would they submit to Yankee rule, could it secure to them a thousand waiting maids, whence now they possess one. . . .

35. *Richmond Whig,* February 28, 1865.

Mobile, Feb. 14—One of the largest meetings ever assembled in Mobile was held at the Theatre last night, which was presided over by Hon. Judge Forsyth.

Resolutions were unanimously adopted declaring our unalterable purpose to sustain the civil and military authorities to achieve independence—that our battle-cry henceforth should be—"Victory or Death"—that there is now no middle-ground between treachery and patriotism—that we still have an abiding confidence in our ability to achieve our independence—that the Government should immediately place one hundred thousand negroes in the field—that reconstruction is no longer an open question.

36. Confederate Congress, "An Act to Increase the Military Force of the Confederate States," March 13, 1865.

The Congress of the Confederate States of America do enact, That in order to provide additional forces to repel invasion, maintain the rightful possession of the Confederate States, secure their independence, and preserve their institutions, the President be, and he is hereby, authorized to ask for and accept from the owners of slaves, the services of such number of able-bodied negro men as he may deem expedient, for and during the war, to perform military service in whatever capacity he may direct.

CHAPTER 6

THE PRICE FOR
VICTORY: THE
DECISION TO
USE AFRICAN
AMERICAN
TROOPS

Sec. 2. That the General-in-Chief be authorized to organize the said slaves into companies, battalions, regiments and brigades, under such rules and regulations as the Secretary of War may prescribe, and to be commanded by such officers as the President may appoint.

Sec. 3. That while employed in the service the said troops shall receive the same rations, clothing and compensation as are allowed to other troops in the same branch of the service.

Sec. 4. That if, under the previous sections of this act, the President shall not be able to raise a sufficient number of troops to prosecute the war successfully and maintain the sovereignty of the States and the independence of the Confederate States, then he is hereby authorized to call on each State, whenever he thinks it expedient, for her quota of 300,000 troops, in addition to those subject to military service under existing laws, or so many thereof as the President may deem necessary to be raised from such classes of the population, irrespective of color, in each State, as the proper authorities thereof may determine: *Provided,* that no more than twenty-five per cent of the male slaves between the ages of eighteen and forty-five, in any State, shall be called for under the provisions of this act.

Sec. 5. That nothing in this act shall be construed to authorize a change in the relation which the said slaves shall bear toward their owners, except by consent of the owners and of the States in which they may reside, and in pursuance of the laws thereof.

Approved March 13, 1865.

QUESTIONS TO CONSIDER

Begin by examining the evidence from the North. For each piece of evidence, answer the following questions:

1. Is the writer for or against using African Americans as soldiers?
2. What are the principal reasons for taking this position? (A piece of evidence may have more than one reason, as does Lincoln's September 13, 1862, reply to a delegation of Chicago Christians, Source 12.)

At this point, you will confront your first problem. Some pieces of evidence do not speak directly to the issue of enlisting African Americans as soldiers (two such examples are A. Davenport's letter and William Wells Brown's recollections, Sources 2 and 11, respectively). Yet are there implied reasons for or against arming African Americans? Included in these reasons may be unstated racial feelings (look again at Lincoln's September 13, 1862, remarks in Source 12), casualty figures (note when the casualties were suffered and consult the evidence for any shifts in the argument at that time), or political considerations.

The central figure in the decision of whether the United States should arm African Americans was Abraham Lincoln. In July 1862, Congress gave the president the authority to do so, yet Lincoln hesitated. How did members of Lincoln's cabinet attempt to influence his opinion in July–August 1862? What was Lincoln's reply?

President Lincoln's memorandum (Source 7), probably written after the July 22 cabinet meeting, appears to show a shift in his opinion. How does this compare with his remarks on August 4, 1862 (Source 9), and September 13, 1862? How would you explain this shift?

By January 1, 1863, the president had changed his public stance completely and was on record as favoring taking African Americans into the United States Army (Source 15). Because President Lincoln did not live to write his memoirs and kept no diary,

we are not sure what arguments or circumstances were responsible for the shift in his position. Yet a close examination of the evidence and some educated guesswork will allow you to come very close to the truth. Do Lincoln's letters to Hamlin and Schurz (Sources 13 and 14) provide any clues?

The remaining evidence from the North deals with northern reactions to Lincoln's decision (Sources 16 through 20). Was the decision a popular one in the army? Among private citizens? Can you detect a shift in northern white public opinion? Can you explain this shift?

Now repeat the same steps for the South (Sources 21 through 36). In what ways was the debate in the South similar to that in the North? In what ways was it different? Which reasons do you think were most influential in the Confederacy's change of mind about arming African Americans? How would you prove this?

↶ EPILOGUE ↷

Even after northern leaders adopted the policy that blacks would be recruited as soldiers in the Union army, many white northerners still doubted whether blacks would volunteer and, if they did, whether they would fight. Yet the evidence overwhelmingly demonstrates that African Americans rushed to the colors and were an effective part of the Union war effort. By the end of the Civil War, approximately 190,000 African American men had served in the United States army

and navy, a figure that represents roughly 10 percent of all the North's fighting men throughout the war. Former slaves who had come within the Union lines during the war made up the majority of African American soldiers, and Louisiana, Kentucky, and Tennessee contributed the most African American soldiers to the Union cause (approximately 37 percent of the total), probably because these states had been occupied the longest by Union troops.

CHAPTER 6

THE PRICE FOR
VICTORY: THE
DECISION TO
USE AFRICAN
AMERICAN
TROOPS

Although, as we have seen, Lincoln initially opposed the use of black soldiers, once he changed his mind, he pursued the new policy with vigor. Moreover, the president was determined to be fair to those African Americans who had volunteered to serve the Union. In an August 19, 1864, interview, Lincoln said, "There have been men who have proposed to me to return to slavery the black warriors . . . to their masters to conciliate the South. I should be damned in time & in eternity for so doing. The world shall know that I will keep my faith."[27]

Black soldiers were employed by the Union largely in noncombat roles (to garrison forts, protect supply dumps and wagons, load and unload equipment and supplies, guard prison camps, and so on). Nevertheless, a number of black regiments saw combat, participating in approximately four hundred engagements, including thirty-nine major battles. One of the most famous battles was the ill-fated assault on Fort Wagner (near Charleston, South Carolina), led by the 54th Massachusetts Infantry, the first black regiment recruited in the North. Almost half the regiment, including its commander, Colonel Robert Gould Shaw, was lost in the frontal attack, but the troops fought valiantly in the losing effort. The *Atlantic Monthly* reported, "Through the cannon smoke of that dark night, the manhood of the colored race shines before many eyes." Over a century later, the regiment was immortalized in the film *Glory.*[28]

27. Basler, ed., *The Collected Works of Abraham Lincoln,* Vol. VII, pp. 506–508.
28. The Confederates refused to return Shaw's body to his parents for burial, saying, "We have buried him with his niggers."

Overall, African American casualties were high: more than one-third of the African American soldiers were killed or wounded, although the majority of deaths, as with white soldiers, came from disease rather than battle wounds. The percentage of desertions among African Americans was lower than for the army as a whole. Moreover, twenty-one black soldiers and sailors were awarded the Congressional Medal of Honor, the nation's most distinguished award to military personnel.

Yet there is another side to the story of African American service in the Union army and navy. African American volunteers were rigidly segregated, serving in all-black regiments, usually under white officers. At first, black troops received less pay than their white counterparts. However, after many petitions and protests by African American soldiers, Congress at last established the principle of equal pay for African American soldiers in June 1864. Unfortunately, racial incidents within the Union army and navy were common.

Confederate reaction to the Union's recruitment of African American troops was predictably harsh. The Confederate government announced that any blacks taken as prisoners of war would be either shot on the spot or returned to slavery. In retaliation, Lincoln stated that he would order a Confederate prisoner of war executed for every African American prisoner shot by the South and would order a southern prisoner to do hard labor for every African American prisoner returned to slavery. Most Confederates treated black prisoners of war the same as they did whites. Nevertheless, in several instances, surrendering African Americans were murdered, the most notable instance occurring at Fort Pillow, Tennessee, where apparently several dozen African American prisoners of war and their white commander, Major William Bradford, were shot "while attempting to escape." After another engagement, one Confederate colonel bragged, "I then ordered every one shot, and with my Six Shooter I assisted in the execution of the order." Yet in spite of his warning, Lincoln did not retaliate, even though a United States Senate investigating committee charged that about three hundred African American Union soldiers had been murdered. The president probably felt that any action on his part would only further inflame the Confederates.

Within the Confederacy, the adoption of the policy to recruit African American soldiers came too late, the last gasp of a dying nation that had debated too long between principle and survival. In the month between the approval of the policy and the end of the war at Appomattox Court House, some black companies were organized, but there is no record that they ever saw action. For a conflict that had raged for four agonizingly long years, the end came relatively quickly.

The debate over the use of African American troops points out what many abolitionists had maintained for years: Although slavery was a moral concern that consumed all who touched it, the institution of slavery was but part of the problem facing black—and white—Americans. More insidious and less easily eradicated was racism, a set of assumptions, feelings, and emotions that has survived long after slavery was destroyed. The debate in both the North and the South over the use of African American troops clearly demonstrates that the true problem confronting many people of the Civil War era was their own feelings, anxieties, and fears.

CHAPTER 7

RECONSTRUCTING RECONSTRUCTION: THE POLITICAL CARTOONIST AND THE NATIONAL MOOD

∽ THE PROBLEM ∽

The Civil War took a tremendous toll on North and South alike. In the defeated South, more than one-fourth of all men who had borne arms for the Confederacy died, and an additional 15 percent were permanently disabled. Indeed, in 1865 Mississippi spent one-fifth of the state's total revenue on artificial arms and legs for Confederate veterans. Combined with the damage to agriculture, industry, and railroads, the human cost of the Civil War to the South was nearly catastrophic. For its part, the North had suffered frightful human losses as well, although proportionately less than those of the South.

And yet the Civil War, although appalling in its human, physical, and psychological costs, did settle some important issues that had plagued the

nation for decades before that bloody conflict. First, the triumph of Union arms had established the United States as "one nation indivisible," from which no state could secede.[1] No less important, the "peculiar institution" of slavery was eradicated, and African Americans at last were free. In truth, although the Civil War had been costly, the issues it settled were momentous.

---

1. In response to President Benjamin Harrison's 1892 appeal for schoolchildren to mark the four hundredth anniversary of Columbus's discovery with patriotic exercises, Bostonian Francis Bellamy composed the pledge of allegiance to the American flag, from which the phrase "one nation indivisible" comes. In 1942, Congress made it the official pledge to the flag, and in 1954 Congress added the words "under God" in the middle of Bellamy's phrase.

The victory of the United States, however, raised at least as many questions as it settled. There was the question of what should happen to the defeated South. Should the states of the former Confederacy be permitted to take their natural place in the Union as quickly and smoothly as possible, with minimum concessions to their northern conquerors? Or should the North insist on a thorough reconstruction of the South, with new economic and social institutions to replace the old? Tied to this issue was the thorny constitutional question of whether the South actually had left the Union at all in 1861. If so, then the southern states in 1865 were territories, to be governed and administered by Congress. If not, then the Civil War had been an internal insurrection and the president, as commander in chief, would administer the South's re-entry into the Union.

Perhaps the most difficult question the Union's victory raised was the status of the former slaves. To be sure, they were no longer in bondage. But should they possess all the rights that whites had? Should they be assisted in becoming landowners; if not, how would they earn a living? Should they be allowed to vote and run for elective office? Indeed, no more complex and difficult issue confronted the country than the "place" of the newly freed slaves in the nation.

In all these questions, public opinion in the victorious North was a critical factor in shaping or altering the policies designed to reconstruct the South. Earlier democratic reforms made it unlikely that either the president or Congress could defy public opinion successfully. Yet public opinion can shift with remarkable speed, and political figures forever must be sensitive to its sometimes fickle winds.

Among the many influences on public opinion in the second half of the nineteenth century were writers and artists who worked for newspapers and magazines. In this chapter, you will be examining and analyzing the work of one man who attempted to shape public opinion in the North: editorial cartoonist Thomas Nast (1840–1902). Nast was not the only person who attempted to influence public opinion in the North, but at the peak of his career, he and his cartoons were well-known and widely appreciated. What were Nast's views on the controversial issues of the Reconstruction era, and how did he try to influence public opinion?

⤳ BACKGROUND ⤳

By early 1865, it was evident to most northerners and southerners that the Civil War was nearly over. While Grant was hammering at Lee's depleted forces in Virginia, Union general William Tecumseh Sherman broke the back of the Confederacy with his devastating march through Georgia and then northward into the Carolinas. Atlanta fell to Sherman's troops in September 1864, Savannah in December, and Charleston and Co-

CHAPTER 7

RECONSTRUCTING
RECONSTRUCTION:
THE POLITICAL
CARTOONIST
AND THE
NATIONAL MOOD

lumbia, South Carolina, in February 1865. Two-thirds of Columbia lay in ashes. Meanwhile, General Philip Sheridan had driven the Confederates out of the Shenandoah Valley of Virginia, thus blocking any escape attempts by Lee and further cutting southern supply routes. The Union naval blockade of the South was taking its fearful toll, as parts of the dying Confederacy were facing real privation. Hence, although northern armies had suffered terrible losses, by 1865 they stood poised on the brink of victory.

In the South, all but the extreme die-hards recognized that defeat was inevitable. The Confederacy was suffering in more ways than militarily. The Confederate economy had almost completely collapsed, and Confederate paper money was nearly worthless. Slaves were abandoning their masters and mistresses in great numbers, running away to Union armies or roaming through the South in search of better opportunities. In many areas, civilian morale had almost totally deteriorated, and one Georgian wrote, "The people are soul-sick and heartily tired of the hateful, hopeless strife. . . . We have had enough of want and woe, of cruelty and carnage, enough of cripples and corpses."[2] As the Confederate government made secret plans to evacuate Richmond, most southerners knew that the end was very near.

Yet even with victory almost in hand, many northerners had given little thought to what should happen after the war. Would southerners accept the changes that defeat would almost inevitably force on them (especially the end of slavery)? What demands should the victors make on the vanquished? Should the North assist the South in rebuilding after the devastation of war? If so, should the North dictate how that rebuilding, or reconstruction, should take place? What efforts should the North make to ensure that the former slaves were receiving the rights of free men and women? During the war, few northerners had seriously considered these questions. Now that victory was within their grasp, they could not avoid them.

One person who had been wrestling with these questions was Abraham Lincoln. In December 1863, the president announced his own plan for reconstructing the South, a plan in keeping with his later hope, as expressed in his second inaugural address, for "malice toward none; with charity for all; . . . Let us . . . bind up the nation's wounds."[3] In Lincoln's plan, a southern state could resume its normal activities in the Union as soon as 10 percent of the voters of 1860 had taken an oath of loyalty to the United States. High-ranking Confederate leaders would be excluded, and some blacks might gain the right to vote. No mention was made of protecting the civil rights of former slaves; it was presumed that this matter would be left

2. The letter probably was written by Georgian Herschel V. Walker. See Allan Nevins, *The Organized War to Victory, 1864–1865,* Vol. IV of *The War for the Union* (New York: Charles Scribner's Sons, 1971), p. 221.

3. The full text of Lincoln's second inaugural address, delivered on March 4, 1865, can be found in Roy P. Basler, ed., *The Collected Works of Abraham Lincoln,* Vol. VIII (New Brunswick, N.J.: Rutgers University Press, 1953), pp. 332–333.

to the slaves' former masters and mistresses.

To many northerners, later known as Radical Republicans, Lincoln's plan was much too lenient. In the opinion of these people, a number of whom had been abolitionists, the South, when conquered, should not be allowed to return to its former ways. Not only should slavery be eradicated, they claimed, but freed blacks should be assisted in their efforts to attain economic, social, and political equity. Most of the Radical Republicans favored education for African Americans, and some advocated carving the South's plantations into small parcels to be given to the freedmen. To implement these reforms, Radical Republicans wanted detachments of the United States Army to remain in the South and favored the appointment of provisional governors to oversee the transitional governments in the southern states. Lincoln approved plans for the Army to stay and supported the idea of provisional governors. But he opposed the more far-reaching reform notions of the Radical Republicans, and as president he was able to block them.

In addition to having diametrically opposed views of Reconstruction, Lincoln and the Radical Republicans differed over the constitutional question of which branch of the federal government would be responsible for the reconstruction of the South. The Constitution made no mention of secession, reunion, or reconstruction. But Radical Republicans, citing passages in the Constitution giving Congress the power to guarantee each state a republican government, insisted that

the reconstruction of the South should be carried out by Congress.[4] For his part, however, Lincoln maintained that as chief enforcer of the law and as commander in chief, the president was the appropriate person to be in charge of Reconstruction. Clearly, a stalemate was in the making, with Radical Republicans calling for a more reform-minded Reconstruction policy and Lincoln continuing to block them.

President Lincoln's death on April 15, 1865 (one week after Lee's surrender at Appomattox Court House),[5] brought Vice President Andrew Johnson to the nation's highest office. At first, Radical Republicans had reason to hope that the new president would follow policies more to their liking. A Tennessean, Johnson had risen to political prominence from humble circumstances, had become a spokesperson for the common white men and women of the South, and had opposed the planter aristocracy. Upon becoming president, he excluded from amnesty all former Confederate political and military leaders as well as all southerners who owned taxable property worth more than $20,000 (an obvious slap at his old planter-aristocrat foes). Moreover, Johnson issued a proclamation setting up provisional military governments in the conquered South and told his cabinet he favored

4. See Article IV, Section 4, of the Constitution. Later Radical Republicans also justified their position using the Thirteenth Amendment, adopted in 1865, which gave Congress the power to enforce the amendment ending slavery in the South.
5. The last Confederate army to give up, commanded by General Joseph Johnston, surrendered to Sherman at Durham Station, North Carolina, on April 18, 1865.

CHAPTER 7

RECONSTRUCTING
RECONSTRUCTION:
THE POLITICAL
CARTOONIST
AND THE
NATIONAL MOOD

black suffrage, although as a states' rightist he insisted that states adopt the measure voluntarily. At the outset, then, Johnson appeared to be all the Radical Republicans wanted, preferable to the more moderate Lincoln.

Yet it did not take Radical Republicans long to realize that President Johnson was not one of them. Although he spoke harshly, he pardoned hundreds of former Confederates, who quickly captured control of southern state governments and congressional delegations. Many northerners were shocked to see former Confederate generals and officials, and even former Confederate vice president Alexander Stephens, returned to Washington. The new southern state legislatures passed a series of laws, known collectively as black codes, that so severely restricted the rights of former slaves that they were all but slaves again. Moreover, Johnson privately told southerners that he opposed the Fourteenth Amendment to the Constitution, which was intended to confer full civil rights on the newly freed slaves. He also used his veto power to block Radical Republican Reconstruction measures in Congress and seemed to do little to combat the general defiance of the former Confederacy (exhibited in many forms, including insults thrown at Union occupation soldiers, the desecration of the United States flag, and the formation of organized resistance groups such as the Ku Klux Klan).

To an increasing number of northerners, the unrepentant spirit of the South and Johnson's acquiescence to it were nothing short of appalling. Had the Civil War been fought for nothing? Had more than 364,000 federal soldiers died in vain? White southerners were openly defiant, African Americans were being subjugated by white southerners and virtually ignored by President Johnson, and former Confederates were returning to positions of power and prominence. Radical Republicans had sufficient power in Congress to pass harsher measures, but Johnson kept vetoing them, and the Radicals lacked the votes to override his vetoes.[6] Indeed, the impasse that had existed before Lincoln's death continued.

In such an atmosphere, the congressional elections of 1866 were bitterly fought campaigns, especially in the northern states. President Johnson traveled throughout the North, defending his moderate plan of Reconstruction and viciously attacking his political enemies. However, the Radical Republicans were even more effective. Stirring up the hostilities of wartime, they "waved the bloody shirt" and excited northern voters by charging that the South had never accepted its defeat and that the 364,000 Union dead and 275,000 wounded would be for nothing if the South was permitted to continue its arrogant and stubborn behavior. Increasingly, Johnson was greeted by hostile audiences as the North underwent a major shift in public opinion.

The Radical Republicans won a stunning victory in the congressional elections of 1866 and thus broke the stalemate between Congress and the

6. Congress was able to override Johnson's vetoes of the Civil Rights Act and a revised Freedmen's Bureau bill.

president. Armed with enough votes to override Johnson's vetoes almost at will, the new Congress proceeded rapidly to implement the Radical Republican vision of Reconstruction. The South was divided into five military districts to be ruled by martial law. Southern states had to ratify the Fourteenth Amendment and institute black suffrage before being allowed to take their formal places in the Union. The Freedmen's Bureau, founded earlier, was given additional federal support to set up schools for African Americans, negotiate labor contracts, and, with the military, help monitor elections. Only the proposal to give land to blacks was not adopted, being seen as too extreme even by some Radical Republicans. Congressional Reconstruction had begun.

President Johnson, however, had not been left completely powerless. Determined to undercut the Radical Republicans' Reconstruction policies, he issued orders increasing the powers of civil governments in the South and removed military officers who were enforcing Congress's will, replacing them with commanders less determined to protect black voting rights and more willing to turn the other way when disqualified white southerners voted. Opposed most vigorously by his own secretary of war, Edwin Stanton, Johnson tried to discharge Stanton. To an increasing number of Radicals, it became clear that the president would have to be removed from office.

In 1868, the House of Representatives voted to impeach Andrew Johnson. Charged with violating the Tenure of Office Act and the Command of the Army Act (both of which had been passed over Johnson's ve-

toes), the president was tried in the Senate, where two-thirds of the senators would have to vote against Johnson for him to be removed.[7] The vast majority of senators disagreed with the president's Reconstruction policies, but they feared that impeachment had become a political tool that, if successful, threatened to destroy the balance of power between the branches of the federal government. The vote on removal fell one short of the necessary two-thirds, and Johnson was spared the indignity of removal. Nevertheless, the Republican nomination of General Ulysses Grant and his subsequent landslide victory (running as a military hero, Grant carried twenty-six out of thirty-four states) gave Radical Republicans a malleable president, one who, although not a Radical himself, could ensure the continuation of their version of Reconstruction.[8]

The Democratic party, however, was not dead, even though the Republican party dominated national politics in the immediate aftermath of the Civil War. In addition to white farmers and planters in the South and border states, the Democratic party contained many northerners who favored conservative ("sound money") policies, voters who opposed Radical Reconstruction, and first- and second-generation Irish immigrants who had settled in urban areas and had established powerful political machines

7. See Article I, Sections 2 and 3, of the Constitution.
8. In 1868, southern states, where the Democratic party had been strong, either were not in the Union or were under the control of Radical Reconstruction governments. Grant's victory, therefore, was not as sweeping as it may first appear.

CHAPTER 7

RECONSTRUCTING
RECONSTRUCTION:
THE POLITICAL
CARTOONIST
AND THE
NATIONAL MOOD

such as Tammany Hall in New York City.

By 1872, a renewed Democratic party believed it had a chance to oust Grant and the Republicans. The Grant administration had been rocked by a series of scandals, some involving men quite close to the president. Although honest himself, Grant had lost a good deal of popularity by defending the culprits and naively aiding in a cover-up of the corruption. These actions, along with some of his other policies, triggered a revolt within the Republican party, in which a group calling themselves Liberal Republicans bolted the party ranks and nominated well-known editor and reformer Horace Greeley to oppose Grant for the presidency.[9] Hoping for a coalition to defeat Grant, the Democrats also nominated the controversial Greeley.

Greeley's platform was designed to attract as many different groups of voters as possible to the Liberal Republican-Democratic fold. He favored civil service reform, the return to a "hard money" fiscal policy, and the reservation of western lands for settlers rather than for large land companies. He vowed an end to corruption in government. But the most dramatic part of Greeley's message was his call for an end to the bitterness of the Civil War, a thinly veiled promise to bring an end to Radical Reconstruction in the South. "Let us," he said, "clasp hands over the bloody chasm."

For their part, Radical Republicans attacked Greeley as the tool of diehard southerners and labeled him as

the candidate of white southern bigots and northern Irish immigrants manipulated by political machines. By contrast, Grant was labeled as a great war hero and a friend of blacks and whites alike. The incumbent Grant won easily, capturing 55 percent of the popular vote. Greeley died soon after the exhausting campaign.

Gradually, however, the zeal of Radical Republicanism began to fade. An increasing number of northerners grew tired of the issue. Their commitment to full civil rights for African Americans had never been strong, and they had voted for Radical Republicans more out of anger at southern intransigence than out of any lofty notions of black equality. Thus northerners did not protest when, one by one, southern Democrats returned to power in the states of the former Confederacy.[10] As an indication of how little their own attitudes had changed, white southerners labeled these native Democrats "Redeemers."

Although much that was fruitful and beneficial was accomplished in the South during the Reconstruction period (most notably black suffrage and public education), some of this was to be temporary, and many opportunities for progress were lost. By the presidential election of 1876, both candidates (Rutherford B. Hayes and Samuel Tilden) promised an end to Reconstruction, and the Radical Re-

9. See Volume I, Chapter 10, for a discussion of Greeley's position on the emancipation of slaves in 1862.

10. Southerners regained control of the state governments in Tennessee and Virginia in 1869, North Carolina in 1870, Georgia in 1871, Arkansas and Alabama in 1874, and Mississippi in early 1876. By the presidential election of 1876, only South Carolina, Louisiana, and Florida were still controlled by Reconstruction governments.

publican experiment, for all intents and purposes, was over.

It is clear that northern public opinion from 1865 to 1876 was not static but was almost constantly shifting. This public opinion was influenced by a number of factors, among them speeches, newspapers, and word of mouth. Especially influential were editorial cartoons, which captured the issues visually, often simplifying them so that virtually everyone could understand them. Perhaps the master of this style was Thomas Nast, a political cartoonist whose career, principally with *Harper's Weekly,* spanned the tumultuous years of the Civil War and Reconstruction. Throughout his career, Nast produced more than three thousand cartoons, illustrations for books, and paintings. He is credited with originating the modern depiction of Santa Claus, the Republican elephant, and the Democratic donkey. Congratulating themselves for having hired Nast, the editors of *Harper's Weekly* once exclaimed that each of Nast's drawings was at once "a poem and a speech."

Apparently, Thomas Nast developed his talents early in life. Born in the German Palatinate (one of the German states) in 1840, Nast was the son of a musician in the Ninth Regiment Bavarian Band. The family moved to New York City in 1846, at which time young Thomas was enrolled in school. It seems that art was his only interest. One teacher admonished him, "Go finish your picture. You will never learn to read or figure." After unsuccessfully trying to interest their son in music, his parents eventually encouraged the development of his artistic talent. By the age of fifteen, Thomas Nast was drawing illustrations for *Frank Leslie's Illustrated Newspaper.* He joined *Harper's Weekly* in 1862 (at the age of twenty-two), where he developed the cartoon style that was to win him a national reputation, as well as enemies. He received praise from Abraham Lincoln, Ulysses Grant, and Samuel Clemens (also known as Mark Twain, who in 1872 asked Nast to do the illustrations for one of his books so that "then I will have good pictures"). In contrast, one of Nast's favorite targets, political boss William Marcy Tweed of New York's Tammany Hall, once shouted, "Let's stop these damn pictures. I don't care so much what the papers say about me—my constituents can't read; but damn it, they can see pictures!"

It is obvious from his work that Nast was a man of strong feelings and emotions. In his eyes, those people whom he admired possessed no flaws. Conversely, those whom he opposed were, to him, capable of every conceivable villainy. As a result, his characterizations often were terribly unfair, gross distortions of reality and more than occasionally libelous. In his view, however, his central purpose was not to entertain but to move his audience, to make them scream out in outrage or anger, to prod them to action. The selection of Nast's cartoons in this chapter is typical of the body of his work for *Harper's Weekly:* artistically inventive and polished, blatantly slanted, and brimming with indignation and emotion.

Your tasks in this chapter are (1) to identify the principal issues and events of the Reconstruction era, (2)

CHAPTER 7

RECONSTRUCTING
RECONSTRUCTION:
THE POLITICAL
CARTOONIST
AND THE
NATIONAL MOOD

to analyze Nast's cartoons to determine what he thought about each issue or event, and (3) to trace any changes in Nast's beliefs between 1865 (Source 1) and the end of Reconstruction in 1876 (Source 13).

∽ THE METHOD ∽

Although Thomas Nast developed the political cartoon into a true art form, cartoons and caricatures had a long tradition in both Europe and America before Nast. English artists helped bring forth the cartoon style that eventually made *Punch* (founded in 1841) one of the liveliest illustrated periodicals on both sides of the Atlantic. In America, Benjamin Franklin is traditionally credited with publishing the first newspaper cartoon in 1754—the multidivided snake (each part of the snake representing one colony) with the ominous warning "Join or Die." By the time Andrew Jackson sought the presidency, the political cartoon had become a regular and popular feature of American political life. Crude by modern standards, these cartoons influenced some people far more than did the printed word.

As we noted, the political cartoon, like the newspaper editorial, is intended to do more than objectively report events. It is meant to express an opinion, a point of view, approval or disapproval. Political cartoonists want to move people, to make them laugh, to anger them, or to move them to action. In short, political cartoons do not depict exactly what is happening; rather, they portray popular reaction to what is happening and try to persuade people to react in a particular way.

How do you analyze political cartoons? First, using your text and the Problem and Background sections of this chapter, make a list of the most important issues and events (including elections) of the period between 1865 and 1876. As you examine the cartoons in this chapter, try to determine what event or issue is being portrayed. Often a cartoon's caption, dialogue, or date will help you discover its focus.

Next, look closely at each cartoon for clues that will help you understand the message that Nast was trying to convey. People who saw these cartoons more than one hundred years ago did not have to study them so carefully, of course. The individuals and events shown in each cartoon were immediately familiar to them, and the message was obvious. But you are historians, using these cartoons as evidence to help you understand how people were reacting to important events many years ago.

As you can see, Nast was a talented artist. Like many political cartoonists, he often explored the differences between what he believed was the ideal (justice, fairness) and the reality (his view of what was actually happening). To "read" Nast's cartoons, you should identify the issue or event on which the cartoon is based. Then look at the *imagery* Nast used: the situation, the setting, the clothes people are wearing, and the objects in the picture. It is especially important to note how people are portrayed: Do they look handsome and noble, or do they look like animals? Are they happy or sad? Intelligent or stupid?

Political cartoonists often use *symbolism* to make their point, sometimes in the form of an *allegory*. In an allegory, familiar figures are shown in a situation or setting that everyone knows—for example, a setting from the Bible, a fairy tale, or another well-known source. For instance, a cartoon showing a tiny president of the United States holding a slingshot, dressed in sandals and rags, and fighting a giant, muscular man labeled "Congress" would remind viewers of the story of David and Goliath. In that story, the small man won. The message of the cartoon is that the president will win in his struggle with Congress.

Other, less complicated symbolism is often used in political cartoons. In Nast's time, as today, the American flag was an important symbol of the ideals of our democratic country, and an olive branch or dove represented the desire for peace. Some symbols have changed, however. Today, the tall, skinny figure we call Uncle Sam represents the United States. In Nast's time, Columbia, a tall woman wearing a long classical dress, represented the United States. Also in Nast's time, an hourglass, rather than a clock, symbolized that time was running out. And military uniforms, regardless of the fact that the Civil War had ended in 1865, were used to indicate whether a person had supported the Union (and, by implication, was a Republican) or the Confederacy (by implication, a Democrat).

As you can see, a political cartoon must be analyzed in detail to get the full meaning the cartoonist was trying to convey. From that analysis, one can discover the message of the cartoon, along with the cartoonist's views on the subject and the ways in which the cartoonist was trying to influence public opinion. Now you are ready to begin your analysis of the Reconstruction era through the cartoons of Thomas Nast.

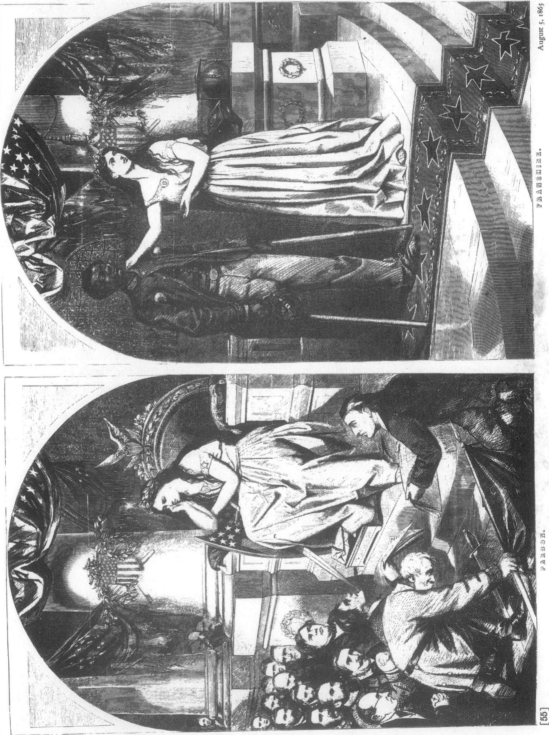

Sources 1 through 12 from Morton Keller, *The Art and Politics of Thomas Nast* (New York: Oxford University Press, 1968), plates 55 and 56, 22, 17, 27, 32, 47, 50, 38, 196, 197, 155, 209. Courtesy of the publisher.

1.

[55]

FRANCHISE.

Columbia.—"Shall I Trust These Men,

FRANCHISE.

And Not This Man?"

August 5, 1865

THE CONTRAST OF SUFFERING: ANDERSONVILLE & FORTRESS MONROE.

TREASON MUST BE MADE ODIOUS.

June 30, 1866

March 30, 1867

Amphitheatrum Johnsonianum.—Massacre of the Innocents
At New Orleans, July 30, 1866.

September 5, 1868

"This Is a White Man's Government."

"We regard the Reconstruction Acts (so called) of Congress as usurpations, and unconstitutional, revolutionary, and void."—*Democratic Platform.*

[177]

The Modern Samson.

August 3, 1872

Baltimore 1861–1872.

"Let Us Clasp Hands over the Bloody Chasm."

CHAPTER 7

RECONSTRUCTING
RECONSTRUCTION:
THE POLITICAL
CARTOONIST
AND THE
NATIONAL MOOD

7.

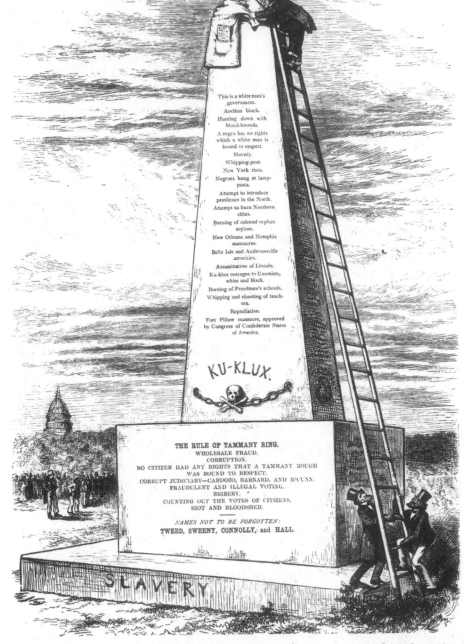

September 7, 1872

The Whited Sepulchre.

Covering the monument of infamy with his white hat and coat.

April 13, 1872

The Republic Is Not Ungrateful.

"It is not what is *charged* but what is *proved* that damages the party defendant. Any one may be accused of the most heinous offenses; the Saviour of mankind was not only arraigned but convicted; but what of it? Facts alone are decisive."—*New York Tribune*, March 13, 1872.

CHAPTER 7

RECONSTRUCTING
RECONSTRUCTION:
THE POLITICAL
CARTOONIST
AND THE
NATIONAL MOOD

9.

March 14, 1874

Colored Rule in a Reconstructed (?) State.

(THE MEMBERS CALL EACH OTHER THIEVES, LIARS, RASCALS, AND COWARDS.)

COLUMBIA. "You are aping the lowest whites. If you disgrace your race in this way you had better take back seats."

September 26, 1874

The Commandments in South Carolina.

"We've pretty well smashed that; but I suppose, Massa Moses, you can get another one."

CHAPTER 7

RECONSTRUCTING
RECONSTRUCTION:
THE POLITICAL
CARTOONIST
AND THE
NATIONAL MOOD

11.

December 9, 1876

The Ignorant Vote—Honors Are Easy.

October 24, 1874

A Burden He Has To Shoulder.

And they say, "He wants a third term."

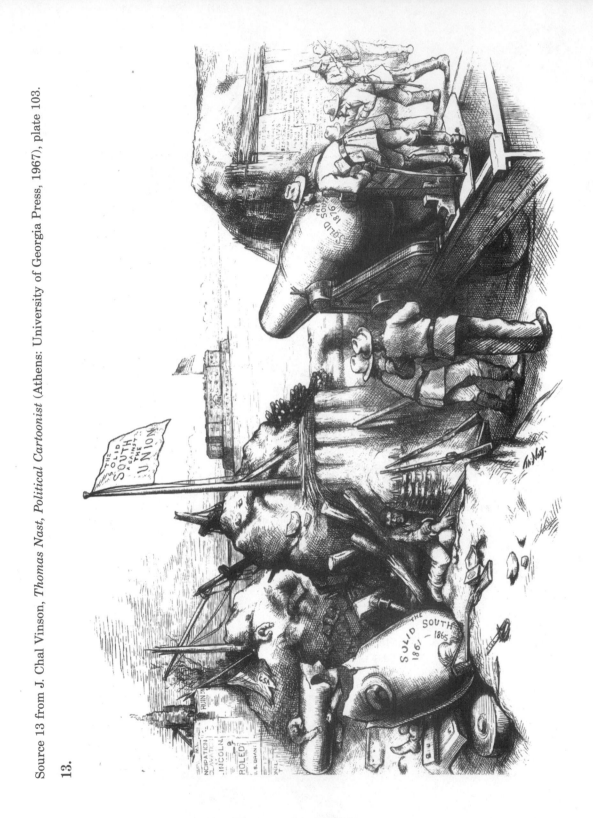

Source 13 from J. Chal Vinson, *Thomas Nast, Political Cartoonist* (Athens: University of Georgia Press, 1967), plate 103.

13.

⬲ QUESTIONS TO CONSIDER ⬲

Begin by reviewing your list of the important issues and events of the Reconstruction era. Then systematically examine the cartoons, answering the following questions for each one:

1. What issue or event is represented by this cartoon?
2. Who are the principal figures, and how are they portrayed?
3. What *imagery* is used?
4. Is this cartoon an *allegory*? if so, what is the basis of the allegory?
5. What *symbols* are used?
6. How was Nast trying to influence public opinion through this cartoon?

You may find that making a chart is the easiest way to do this.

Sources 1 through 3 represent Nast's views of Reconstruction under President Andrew Johnson. Sources 4 and 5 deal with an issue crucial to Radical Republicans. Sources 6 and 7 focus on the presidential election of 1872, and Sources 8 through 12 evaluate Radical Reconstruction in its later years. The cartoons are roughly in chronological order, and you should watch for any changes in Nast's portrayal of the major issues between the end of the Civil War in 1865 and the end of Radical Reconstruction after the election of 1876.

Who is the woman in Source 1? What emotions do her two different poses suggest? Who are the people asking for pardon in the first frame? Look carefully at the black man in the second frame. Who does he represent? Can you formulate one sentence that

summarizes the message of both parts of Source 1?

Source 2 is more complex: two drawings within two other drawings. If you do not already know what purpose Andersonville and Fortress Monroe served, consult a text on this time period, an encyclopedia, or a good Civil War history book. Then look at the upper left and upper right outside drawings. Contrast the appearance of the man entering with the man leaving. Now examine the lower left and lower right outside drawings the same way. What was Nast trying to tell? The larger inside drawings explain the contrast. What were the conditions like at Andersonville? At Fortress Monroe? What did the cartoonist think were the physical and psychological results?

On July 30, 1866, several blacks attending a Radical Republican convention in New Orleans were shot and killed by white policemen. Who is the emperor in Source 3, and how is he portrayed? What kind of setting is used in this cartoon? Who is the person in the lower left intending to represent? What did Nast think caused this event? What was his own reaction to it?

Each of the three people standing in Source 4 represents part of the Democratic party coalition, and each has something to contribute to the party. Can you identify the groups that the man on the right and the man in the center represent? What do they offer the party? Notice the facial features of the man on the left as well as his dress, particularly the hatband from

[187]

CHAPTER 7

RECONSTRUCTING
RECONSTRUCTION:
THE POLITICAL
CARTOONIST
AND THE
NATIONAL MOOD

Five Points (a notorious slum section of New York City). Who is this man supposed to represent, and what does he give the party? Notice what the black man lying on the ground has dropped. What does he represent? What is he reaching for? What is happening in the background of the cartoon?

What issue does Source 5 explore? What story are people supposed to remember when they see this cartoon? Who is the woman, and what has she done? Who are her supporters at the left? What other things do they advocate? Who is the figure in the upper right-hand corner? What has he promised African Americans? What has he done?

Sources 6 and 7 were published just before the presidential election of 1872. Who is the plump little man with the white beard and glasses who appears in both cartoons? What part of this man's campaign did Nast find especially objectionable? Why? What is wrong with what the character is trying to do? Who is portrayed in Source 8? Why is the woman protecting him from attack?

Sources 9 through 12 reflect Nast's thinking in the later years of Reconstruction. Sources 9 and 10 portray his opinion of Reconstruction in South Carolina, presided over by Radical Republican governor Franklin J. Moses (caricatured in Source 10). How are African Americans pictured (compare to Sources 1, 4, and 5)? To whom are African Americans compared in Source 11? What does this say about Nast's opinion of Reconstruction? Source 12 portrays President Ulysses Grant (compare to Sources 3 and 8). How is he pictured?

The last cartoon (Source 13) shows Nast's opinion of the South in 1876, near the end of Reconstruction. What scene was Nast re-creating? What is the significance of this scene? How is the black man depicted? What was Nast trying to show? How would you compare or contrast this cartoon with Sources 9 through 12? How did Nast's views change? In the final analysis, what did he think had been accomplished by more than a decade of Reconstruction?

Now return to the central questions asked earlier. What significant events took place during Reconstruction? How did Nast try to influence public opinion on the important issues of the era? How did Nast's own views change between 1865 and 1876? Why did Reconstruction finally end?

∞ EPILOGUE ∞

Undoubtedly, Nast's work had an important impact on northern opinion of Reconstruction, the Democratic party, Horace Greeley, the Irish Americans, and other issues. Yet gradually, northern ardor began to decline as other issues and concerns eased Reconstruction out of the limelight and as it appeared that the crusade to reconstruct the South would be an endless one. Radical Republicans, who insisted on equality for the freed slaves, received less and less attention, and southern Democrats, who regained control of southern state governments, were essentially allowed a free hand as long as they did not obviously violate the Constitution and federal law. By 1877, the South was once again in the hands of white Democrats.

As long as African Americans did not insist on their rights, white southern leaders allowed them to retain, in principle, all that the Civil War and Reconstruction had won. In other words, as long as black voters did not challenge the "Redeemers," they were allowed to retain their political rights. Economically, many African Americans gradually slipped into the status of tenant farmer, sharecropper, or even peon. The political structure, local courts, and law-enforcement agencies tended to support this arrangement. For his part, African American leader Booker T. Washington was praised by white southerners for urging that blacks seek education and economic opportunities but not "rock the boat" politically in the white-controlled South. Finally, in the late 1880s, when white southerners realized that the Reconstruction spirit had waned in the North, southern state legislatures began instituting rigid segregation of schools, public transportation and accommodations, parks, restaurants and theaters, ele-vators, drinking fountains, and so on. Not until the 1950s did those chains begin to be broken.

As the reform spirit waned in the later years of Reconstruction, Nast's popularity suffered. The public appeared to tire of his anger, his self-righteousness, his relentless crusades. The new publisher of *Harper's Weekly* sought to make the magazine less political, and in that atmosphere there was no place for Nast. He resigned in 1886.

Nast continued to free-lance for a number of magazines and tried unsuccessfully to start his own periodical, *Nast's Weekly*. Financially struggling, he appealed to friends, who influenced President Theodore Roosevelt to appoint Nast to a minor consular post in Ecuador. He died there of yellow fever in 1902.

Thomas Nast was a pioneer of a tradition and a political art form. His successors, people such as Herbert Block (Herblock), Bill Mauldin, Oliphant, and even Garry Trudeau ("Doonesbury"), have continued to prick the American conscience, fret and irritate newspaper readers, and assert through their art the proposition that no evildoer can escape the scrutiny and ultimate justice of the popular will. Sometimes these successors are effective, sometimes not.

CHAPTER 8

HOW THEY LIVED: MIDDLE-CLASS LIFE, 1870–1917

⤜ THE PROBLEM ⤛

In the 1870s, Heinrich Schliemann, a middle-aged German archaeologist, astonished the world with his claim that he had discovered the site of ancient Troy. As all educated people of the time knew, Troy was the golden city of heroes that the blind poet Homer (seventh century B.C.) made famous in his *Iliad* and *Odyssey*. Although archaeologists continued to argue bitterly about whether it was really Troy or some other ancient city that Schliemann was excavating, the general public was fascinated with the vases, gold and silver cups, necklaces, and earrings that were unearthed.

Not only the relics and "treasure" interested Americans, however. As the magazine *Nation* pointed out in 1875, these discoveries offered an opportunity to know about Troy as it had actually existed and to understand something about the daily lives of the inhabitants. Nineteenth-century Americans were intensely curious about the art, religion, burial customs, dress, and even the foods of the ancient Greeks. "Real Trojans," noted a magazine editor in 1881, "were very fond of oysters." (He based his conclusion on the large amounts of oyster shells uncovered at the archaeological digs.)

Material culture study is the use of artifacts to understand people's lives. In this chapter, you will be looking at some artifacts of the late nineteenth and early twentieth centuries—advertisements and house plans—to try to reconstruct the lives of middle-class white Americans during a period when the country was changing rapidly. What were Americans' hopes and fears during this era? What were their values?

∽ BACKGROUND ∽

The age from approximately 1870 to 1900 was characterized by enormous and profound changes in American life. Unquestionably, the most important changes were the nation's rapid industrialization and urbanization. Aided and accelerated by the rapid growth of railroads, emerging industries could extend their tentacles throughout the nation, collecting raw materials and fuel for the factories and distributing finished products to the growing American population. By 1900, that industrial process had come to be dominated by a few energetic and shrewd men, captains of industry to their friends and robber barons to their enemies. Almost every conceivable industry, from steel and oil to sugar refining and meat packing, was controlled by one or two gigantic corporations that essentially had the power to set prices on the raw materials bought and the finished products sold. In turn, the successes of those corporations created a new class of fabulously rich industrialists, and names like Swift, Armour, Westinghouse, Pillsbury, Pullman, Rockefeller, Carnegie, and Duke literally became almost household words, as much for the notoriety of the industrialists as for the industries and products they created.

As America became more industrialized, it also became more urban. In the past, the sizes of cities had been limited by the availability of nearby food, fuel, and employment opportunities. But the network of railroads and the rise of large factories had removed those limitations, and American cities grew phenomenally. Between 1860 and 1910, urban population increased sevenfold, and by 1920 more than half of all Americans lived in cities.[1] These urban complexes not only dominated the regions in which they were located but eventually set much of the tone for the entire nation as well.

Both processes—industrialization and urbanization—profoundly altered nearly every facet of American life. Family size began to decrease; the woman who might have had five or six children in 1860 was replaced by the "new" woman of 1900 who had only three or four children. The fruits of industrialization, distributed by new marketing techniques, could be enjoyed by a large portion of the American population. Electric lights, telephones, and eventually appliances virtually revolutionized the lives of the middle and upper classes, as did Ford's later mass production of the Model T automobile.

The nature of the work also was changed because factories required a higher degree of regimentation than did farm work or the "putting-out" system. Many industries found it more profitable to employ women and children than adult males, thus altering the home lives of many of the nation's working-class citizens. Moreover, the lure of employment brought millions of immigrants to the United States, most of whom huddled together in

---

1. The census defined *city* as a place with a population over twenty-five hundred people. Thus, many of the cities referred to in this exercise are what we would call towns, or even small towns.

cities, found low-paying jobs, and dreamed of the future. And as the cities grew grimy with factory soot and became increasingly populated by laborers, immigrants, and what one observer referred to as the "dangerous classes," upper- and middle-class Americans began to abandon the urban cores and retreat to fashionable suburbs on the peripheries, to return to the cities either in their automobiles or on streetcars only for work or recreation. In fact, the comforts of middle-class life were made possible, in part, by the exploitation of industrial workers.

Industrialization and urbanization not only changed how most Americans lived but how they *thought* as well. Faith in progress and technology was almost boundless, and there was widespread acceptance of the uneven distribution of wealth among Americans. Prior to the turn of the century, many upper- and middle-class Americans believed that life was a struggle in which the fittest survived. This concept, which applied Charles Darwin's discoveries about biological evolution to society, was called social Darwinism. The poor, especially the immigrant poor, were seen as biologically and morally inferior. It followed, then, that efforts to help the less fortunate through charity or government intervention were somehow tampering with both God's will and Darwinian evolution. In such a climate of opinion, the wealthy leaders of gigantic corporations became national heroes, superior in prestige to both preachers and presidents.

The response of the working classes varied; although many workers rejected the concepts of social Darwinism and Victorian morality, others aspired to middle-class status. In spite of long hours, low pay, and hazardous conditions, the men and women of the working classes engaged in a series of important labor protests and strikes during this period. A rich working-class culture developed in the saloons, vaudeville theaters, dance halls, and streets of medium-size and larger cities. Many workers sought alternatives in some form of socialism; many others, however, strove to achieve the standard of living of the rapidly expanding middle class. Across the country, young boys read the rags-to-riches tales of Horatio Alger, and girls learned to be "proper ladies" so that they would not embarrass their future husbands as they rose in society together.

Social critics and reformers of the time were appalled by the excesses of the "fabulously rich" and the misery of the "wretchedly poor." And yet a persistent belief in the opportunity to better oneself (or one's children's position) led many people to embrace an optimistic attitude and to focus on the acquisition of material possessions. New consumer goods were pouring from factories, and the housing industry was booming. Middle-class families emulated the housing and furnishing styles of the wealthy, and skilled blue-collar workers and their families aspired to own modest suburban homes on the streetcar line.

After 1900, widespread concern about the relationship of wages to the cost of maintaining a comfortable standard of living led to numerous studies of working-class families in various parts of the country. Could workers realistically hope to own homes and achieve decent standards of living as a result of their labor? In 1909, economist Robert Coit Chapin estimated that a family of five needed an annual income of about $900 to live in a decent home or apartment in New York City. A follow-up study of Philadelphia in 1917 estimated that same standard of living at approximately $1,600. Yet the average annual pay of adult male wage workers during these years ranged from only $600 to $1,700. Several other factors affected family income, however. Average wages are misleading, since skilled workers earned significantly more than unskilled or semiskilled workers. Even within the same industry and occupation, midwestern workers earned more than northeastern workers, and southern workers earned the lowest wages of all. Adult women workers, 80 percent of whom lived with families as wives or unmarried daughters, added their wages (approximately $300 to $600 a year) to the family income, as did working children. Many families, especially those of recent immigrants, also took in boarders and lodgers, who paid rent.

Finally, the cost of land and building materials was much more expensive in large cities than in smaller cities and towns. In his investigation of New York, Chapin found that 28 percent of working-class families in nine upstate cities owned their own homes, compared with only 1 percent in New York City. Another study in 1915 also sharply illustrated regional differences in home ownership. Twenty percent of Paterson, New Jersey, silk

workers were homeowners, but only 10 percent of Birmingham, Alabama, steelworkers owned homes. Nineteen percent of Milwaukee's working-class families owned their own homes, compared to 4.4 percent of Boston's working-class families. Nor were all these homes in the central city. Working-class suburbs expanded along streetcar lines or were developed near industries on the fringes of a city, such as the suburb of Oakwood just outside Knoxville, Tennessee.[2] In this community near textile mills and a major railroad repair shop, house lots measuring 50 by 140 feet sold for less than one hundred dollars; most homes were built for under one thousand dollars. Nearly half of the one thousand families who moved to Oakwood between 1902 and 1917 came from the older industrial sections of Knoxville.

Completely reliable income and cost statistics for early twentieth-century America do not exist, but it seems reasonable to estimate that at least one-fourth of working-class families owned or were paying for homes and that many more aspired to homeownership. But fully half of all working-class families, usually concentrated in large cities, lived in or near poverty and could not hope to own their own homes. Those with middle-class white-collar occupations were more fortunate. Lawyers, doctors, businessmen, ministers, bank tellers, newspaper editors, and even schoolteachers could—through careful budgeting and saving—realistically expect to buy or build a house.

2. Knoxville's population in 1900 was 32,637; the city had experienced a 237 percent growth in population from 1880 to 1900.

Although technological advances and new distribution methods put many modern conveniences and new products within the reach of all but the poorest Americans, the economic growth of the period was neither constant nor steady. The repercussions from two major depressions—one in 1873 and one in 1894—made "getting ahead" difficult, if not impossible, for many lower-middle-class and blue-collar families. Furthermore, at times everything seemed to be changing so rapidly that many people felt insecure. Yet within middle-class families, this sense of insecurity and even fear often coexisted with optimism and a faith in progress.

One way to understand the lives of middle-class Americans during the post–Civil War era is to look at the *things* with which they surrounded themselves: their clothes, the goods and services they bought, and even their houses. Why did such fashions and designs appeal to Americans of the late nineteenth and early twentieth centuries? What kind of an impression were these people trying to make on other people? How did they really feel about themselves? Sometimes historians, like archaeologists, use artifacts such as clothes, furniture, houses, and so forth to reconstruct the lives of Americans in earlier times. Indeed, each year many thousands of tourists visit historic homes such as Jefferson's Monticello, retrace the fighting at Gettysburg, or stroll through entire restored communities such as Colonial Williamsburg. But historians of the post–Civil War period also may use advertisements (instead of the products or services themselves) and house plans (instead of the actual houses) to understand how middle-class Americans lived and what their values and concerns were.

Every day, Americans are surrounded, even bombarded, by advertising that tries to convince them to buy some product, use some service, or compare brand X with brand Y. Television, radio, billboards, magazines, and newspapers spread the message to potential consumers of a variety of necessary—and unnecessary—products. Underlying this barrage of advertisements is an appeal to a wide range of emotions: ambition, elitism, guilt, and anxiety. A whole new "science" has arisen, called market research, that analyzes consumers' reactions and predicts future buying patterns.

Yet advertising is a relatively new phenomenon, one that began to develop after the Civil War and did not assume its modern form until the 1920s. P. T. Barnum, the promoter and impresario of mid-nineteenth-century entertainment, pointed the way with publicity gimmicks for his museum and circuses and, later, for the relatively unknown Swedish singer Jenny Lind. (Barnum created such a demand for Lind's concert tickets that they sold for as much as two hundred dollars each.) But at the time of the Civil War, most merchants still announced special sales of their goods in simple newspaper notices, and brand names were virtually unknown.

Businesses, both large and small, expanded enormously after the Civil War. Taking advantage of the country's greatly improved transportation and communication systems, daring business leaders established innovative ways to distribute products, such as the mail-order firm and the department store. Sears Roebuck & Co. was founded in 1893, and its "wish book," or catalogue, rapidly became popular reading for millions of people, especially those who lived in rural areas. Almost one thousand pages long, these catalogues offered a dazzling variety of consumer goods and were filled with testimonial letters from satisfied customers. Lewis Thomas from Jefferson County, Alabama, wrote in 1897,

> I received my saddle and I must say that I am so pleased and satisfied with my saddle, words cannot express my thanks for the benefit that I received from the pleasure and satisfaction given me. I know that I have a saddle that will by ordinary care last a lifetime, and all my neighbors are pleased as well, and I am satisfied so well that you shall have more of my orders in the near future.

And from Granite, Colorado, Mrs. Laura Garrison wrote, "Received my suit all right, was much pleased with it, will recommend your house to my friends."

For those who lived in cities, the department store was yet another way to distribute consumer goods. The massive, impressively decorated buildings erected by department store owners were often described as consumer "cathedrals" or "palaces." In fact, no less a personage than President William Howard Taft dedicated the new Wanamaker's department store in Philadelphia in 1911. "We are here," Taft told the crowd, "to celebrate the completion of one of the most important instrumentalities in modern life for the promotion of comfort among the people."

Many of the products being manufactured in factories in the late nineteenth and early twentieth centuries represented items previously made at home. Tinned meats and biscuits, "store-bought" bread, ready-made clothing, and soap all represent the impact of technology on the functions of the homemaker. Other products were new versions of things already being used. For example, the bathtub was designed solely for washing one's body, as opposed to the large bucket or tub in which one collected rainwater, washed clothes, and, every so often, bathed. Still other products and gadgets (such as the phonograph and the automobile) were completely new, the result of a fertile period of inventiveness (1860 to 1890) that saw more than ten times more patents issued than were issued during the entire period up to 1860 (only 36,000 patents were issued prior to the Civil War, but 440,000 were granted during the next thirty years).

There was no question that American industry could produce new products and distribute them nationwide. But there *was* a problem: how could American industry overcome the traditional American ethic of thrift and create a demand for products that might not have even existed a few years earlier? It was this problem that the new field of advertising set out to solve.

America in 1865 was a country of widespread, if uneven, literacy and a vast variety of newspapers and magazines, all competing for readership.

Businesses quickly learned that mass production demanded a national, even an international, market, and money spent on national advertising in newspapers and magazines rose from $27 million in 1860 to more than $95 million in 1900. By 1929, the amount spent on advertising had climbed to more than $1 billion. Brand names and catchy slogans vied with one another to capture the consumer's interest. Consumers could choose from among many biscuit manufacturers, as the president of National Biscuit Company reported to his stockholders in 1901: "We do not pretend to sell our standard goods cheaper than other manufacturers of biscuits sell their goods. They always undersell us. Why do they not take away our business?" His answer was fourfold: efficiency, quality goods, innovative packaging, and advertising. "The trademarks we adopted," he concluded, "their value we created."

Advertising not only helped differentiate one brand of a product from another, but it also helped break down regional differences as well as differences between rural and urban lifestyles. Women living on farms in Kansas could order the latest "New York–style frocks" from a mail-order catalogue, and people in small towns in the Midwest or rural areas in the South could find the newest furniture styles, appliances, and automobiles enticingly displayed in mass-circulation magazines. In this era, more and more people abandoned the old ways of doing things and embraced the new ways of life that resulted from the application of modern technology, mass production, and efficient distribution of products. Thus, some historians have argued that advertising accelerated the transition of American society from one that emphasized production to one that stressed consumption.

The collective mentality, ideas, mood, and values of the rapidly changing society were reflected in nearly everything the society created, including its architecture. During the period from approximately 1865 to 1900, American architects designed public buildings, factories, banks, apartment houses, offices, and residential structures, aided by technological advances that allowed them to do things that had been impossible in the past. For instance, as American cities grew in size and population density, the value of real estate soared. Therefore, it made sense to design higher and higher buildings, taking advantage of every square foot of available land. The perfection of central heating systems; the inventions of the radiator, the elevator, and the flush toilet; and the use of steel framing allowed architects such as William Le Baron Jenney, Louis Sullivan, and others of the Chicago school of architecture to erect the modern skyscraper, a combined triumph of architecture, engineering, ingenuity, and construction.

At the same time, the new industrial elite were hiring these same architects to build their new homes—homes that often resembled huge Italian villas, French chateaux, and even Renaissance palaces. Only the wealthy, however, could afford homes individually designed by professional architects. Most people relied on contractors, builders, and carpenters who adapted drawings from books or magazines to suit their clients' needs and tastes. Such "pattern books," published by men like Henry Holly, the Palliser brothers, Robert Shoppell, and the Radford Architectural Company, were extremely popular. It is estimated that in the mid-1870s, at least one hundred homes a year were being built from plans published in one women's magazine, *Godey's Lady's Book,* and thousands of others were built from pamphlets provided by lumber and plumbing fixture companies and architectural pattern books. Eventually, a person could order a complete home through the mail; all parts of the prefabricated house were shipped by railroad for assembly by local workers on the owner's site. George Barber of Knoxville, Tennessee, the Aladdin Company of Bay City, Michigan, and even Sears Roebuck & Co. were all prospering in mail-order homes around the turn of the century.

From the historian's viewpoint, both advertising and architecture created a wealth of evidence that can be used to reconstruct our collective past.

By looking at and reading advertisements, we can trace Americans' changing habits, interests, and tastes. And by analyzing the kinds of emotional appeals used in the advertisements, we can begin to understand the aspirations and goals as well as the fears and anxieties of the people who lived in the rapidly changing society of the late nineteenth and early twentieth centuries.

Unfortunately, most people, including professional historians, are not used to looking for values and ideas in architecture. Yet every day we pass by houses and other buildings that could tell us a good deal about how people lived in a particular time period, as well as something about the values of the time. In this chapter, you will be examining closely both advertisements and house plans to reconstruct partially how middle-class Americans of the late nineteenth and early twentieth centuries lived.

THE METHOD

No historian would suggest that the advertisements of preceding decades (or today's advertisements, for that matter) speak for themselves—that they tell you how people actually lived. Like almost all other historical evidence, advertisements must be carefully analyzed for their messages. Advertisements are intended to make people want to buy various products and services. They can be positive or negative. Positive advertisements show the benefits—direct or indirect, explicit or implicit—that would come

from owning a product. Such advertisements depict an ideal. Negative or "scare" advertisements demonstrate the disastrous consequences of not owning the product. Some of the most effective advertisements combine both negative and positive approaches ("I was a lonely 360-pound woman before I discovered Dr. Quack's Appetite Suppressors—now I weigh 120 pounds and am engaged to be married!"). Advertisements also attempt to evoke an emotional response from potential consumers that will encourage the purchase of a particular product or service.

Very early advertisements tended to be primarily descriptive, simply picturing the product. Later advertisements often told a story with pictures and words. In looking at the advertisements in this chapter, first determine whether the approach used is positive, negative, or a combination of both factors. What were the expected consequences of using (or not using) the product? How did the advertisement try to sell the product or service? What emotional response(s) were expected?

The preceding evaluation is not too difficult, but in this exercise you must go even further with your analysis. You are trying to determine what each advertisement can tell you about earlier generations of Americans and the times in which they lived. Look at (and read) each advertisement carefully. Does it reveal anything about the values of the time period in which the advertisements appeared? About the roles of men and women? About attitudes concerning necessities and luxuries? About people's aspirations or fears?

House plans also must be analyzed if they are to tell us something about how people used to live. At one time or another, you have probably looked at a certain building and thought, "That is truly an ugly, awful-looking building! Whatever possessed the lunatic who built it?" Yet when that building was designed and built, most likely it was seen as a truly beautiful structure and may have been widely praised by its occupants as well as by those who merely passed by. Why is this so? Why did an earlier generation believe the building was beautiful?

All of us are aware that standards for what is good art, good music, good literature, and good architecture change over time. What may be pleasing to the people of one era might be considered repugnant or even obscene by those of another time. But is this solely the result of changing fads, such as the sudden rises and declines in the popularity of movie and television stars, rock 'n' roll groups, or fashionable places to vacation?

The answer is partly yes, but only partly. Tastes do change, and fads such as the Hula-Hoop and the yo-yo come and inevitably go. However, we must still ask why a particular person or thing becomes popular or in vogue at a certain time. Do these changing tastes in art, music, literature, and architecture *mean* something? Can they tell us something about the people who embraced these various styles? More to the point, can they tell us something about the *values* of those who embraced them? Obviously, they can.

In examining these middle-class homes, you should first look for common exterior and interior features. Then look at the interior rooms and their functions, comparing them with rooms in American homes today. You also must try to imagine what impression these houses conveyed to people in the late nineteenth and early twentieth centuries. Finally, you will be thinking about all the evidence—the advertisements and the house plans—as a whole. What is the relationship between the material culture (in this case, the advertisements and the house plans) and the values and concerns of Americans in the late nineteenth and early twentieth centuries?

Sources 1 through 3 from Sears Roebuck & Co. catalogues, 1897 and 1902.

1. Children's Reefer Jackets (1897) and Children's Toys (1902).

SEARS ROEBUCK & CO. INC.

85¢

$1.50

24171

24172

◆◆◆◆ **REEFER JACKETS** FOR CHILDREN FROM 1 TO 5 YEARS OLD. ◆◆◆◆

Reefer Jackets for little toddlers, from one to four years, nobby, stylish little coats at little bits of prices. As usual S. R. & Co. will save you money on these goods.

Do not forget to mention age and color desired when ordering.

DRESSED SAILOR DOLLS.
Sailor Girl Dolls.
No. 29R735 Sailor Girl Doll, bisque head, flowing hair, solid eyes, dressed to represent a girl in sailor costume. A very pretty doll. Length, 13 inches.
Price, each.................50c

Sailor Boy Dolls.
No. 29R739 Sailor Boy Doll, dressed to represent a boy in sailor costume, companion doll to sailor girl. Length, 13 inches.
Price, each.....................50c

The Penny Saver.
No. 29R147 A perfect registering bank; no key, no combination. Each time a cent is dropped into the bank the bell rings and the register indicates. Opens automatically at each 50 cents. The total always in sight. They are attractive and interesting to children. The mechanism is made of steel, and will not break or get out of order. It is highly interesting to children, and for this reason will encourage them to save. Shipping weight, 5 pounds. Price, each.........85c

[199]

2. Boys' Wash Suits and Girls' Wash Dresses[3] (1902).

BOYS' WASH SUITS.

The extraordinary value we offer in Boys' Wash Suits can only be fully appreciated by those who order from this department. A trial order will surely convince you that we are able to furnish new, fresh, up to date, stylish and well made wash suits at much lower prices than similar value can be had from any other house.

NOTE.—Boys' wash suits can be had only in the sizes as mentioned after each description. Always state age of boy and if large or small of age.

Boy's Wash Crash Suit, 35 Cents.

38R2130
$1.39

38R2128
98c

38R2131
$1.48

Navy Blue and White Percale Wash Suit, 40 Cents.

GIRLS' WASH DRESSES.

AGES FROM 4 TO 14 YEARS.

WHEN ORDERING please state Age, Height, Weight and Number of Inches around Bust.

SCALE OF SIZES, SHOWING PROPORTION OF BUST AND LENGTH TO THE AGE OF CHILD

Age				4	6	8	10	12	14
Bust				24	27	28	29	30	31
Skirt length				18	20	22	24	26	28

No. 38R2126 GIRLS' DRESS. Some made of Madras and some made of gingham in fancy stripes and plaids, round yokes, "V" shape yokes, some trimmed with braid, ruffles and embroidery. We show no illustration of this number on account of the differ

3. Washable, casual clothing.

3. Hip Pad and Bustle, 1902.

Parisienne Hip Pad and Bustle.

No. 18R4880 The Parisienne Hip Pad and Bustle, made of best tempered, black enameled, woven wire with hip pads of padded cloth. Perfect in shape, and light in weight. Very durable.
Price, each...**40c**

If by mail, postage extra, each, **10 cents.**

Source 4 from 1893 advertisement.

4. Corset (1893).

DOCTORS RECOMMEND REAST'S PATENT

INVIGORATOR CORSETS.

FOR LADIES, MAIDS, BOYS, GIRLS, AND CHILDREN.

Dr. M. O. B. NEVILLE, L.R.C.P., Edin. Medical Officer of Health, says, Nov. 1st, 1890:—

"From a scientific point of view, I am of opinion that your Corset is the only one that gives support without unduly compressing important organs. Its elasticity, in a great measure, prevents this. I am satisfied, by its support of back and shoulders, that it is a material help to expanding the chest."

"Mrs. WELDON'S FASHION JOURNAL," says July '90:—

"Undoubtedly supplies a long-felt want for ensuring an upright form and graceful carriage, COMBINES ELEGANCE of FORM WITH COMFORT. It renders a corset what it should be, comfort, and support to the wearer, strengthening the spine, expanding the chest, and giving necessary support without tight lacing or undue pressure."

PRICES.

Child's under 5 years, 3/4; Boys' and Girls' over 5 years, 4/6; Maids, 5/6; Ladies', 6/6, 8/6, 12/9, 18/6, 22/6, 63/-.

SOLD BY ALL DRAPERS, OR SEND P.O. TO
REAST, 15, CLAREMONT, HASTINGS, ENGLAND.
FOR LICENSE FOR MANUFACTURING, OR SALE OF AMERICAN PATENT APPLY AS ABOVE.

Source 5 from an 1884 advertisement.

5. Beauty Advice Book.

A SCRAP-BOOK
FOR
"HOMELY WOMEN" ONLY.

We dedicate this collection of toilet secrets, not to the pretty women (they have advantages enough, without being told how to double their beauty), but to the plainer sisterhood, to those who look in the glass and are not satisfied with what they see. To such we bring abundant help.

CONTENTS. Part 1--Part 2.

Practical devices for ugly ears, mouths, fingertips, crooked teeth. To reduce flesh, etc. How to bleach and refine a poor skin. Freckles, Pimples, Moles, etc. Mask of Diana of Poictiers. Out of 100 Cosmetics, which to choose. How to make and apply them for daylight, evening, and the stage (one saves two thirds, and has a better article by making instead of buying Cosmetics). What goes to constitute a belle. Madame Vestris's methods for private Theatricals. How to sit for a photograph successfully, and other toilet hints.

Send $1.00, 2 two-cent stamps, and an envelope addressed to yourself.

BROWN, SHERBROOK, & CO.,
27 Hollis Street, Boston, Mass.

Source 6 from a 1912 advertisement.

6. Massage Cream for the Skin.

Source 7 from 1895, 1888, and 1912 advertisements.

7. Croup Remedy (1895), Garment Pins (1888), and Boys' Magazine (1912).

8. Ladies' and Men's Hats (1897).

LATEST DESIGNS IN STYLISH TRIMMED HATS.
AT 99 CENTS, $2.35, $3.25 AND UPWARDS.

WE SUBMIT ON THESE FOUR PAGES, the very newest effects in fashionable trimmed hats made especially for us from original designs, the same styles as will be shown by fashionable city milliners in large cities; styles that it will be impossible for you to secure in the stores in smaller towns, such goods as can be had only from the big millinery emporiums in metropolitan cities and there at two to three times our prices. These illustrations are made by artists direct from the hats, but it is impossible in a plain black and white drawing to give you a fair idea of the full beauty of these new hat creations. We ask you to read the descriptions carefully, note the illustrations and send us your order with the understanding that if the hat, when received, is not all and more than we claim for it, perfectly satisfactory, you are at liberty to return it to us at our expense and we will immediately return your money.

Wonderful Value.

99c

$1.95

No. 39R101 Is a black dress shape fancy straw, slightly raised on the left. Very tastefully trimmed in the front with six large muslin roses and shaded foliage. Trimmed high to the right is a large rosette consisting of silk finished pink mull in half wheel effect, same extending all around the crown and falling over the back and caught on bandeau with loops of the same material. A very stylish young or middle aged ladies' hat. Shape can be ordered only in black or white, trimmings in any color desired, but looks very handsome as described. Price, each............99c

No. 39R107 This is a hand made fancy straw braid dress hat, drooping slightly to front and back. The wire frame is covered with an imported hand made straw braid, trimmed fully to the left with artistically designed rosettes draped in plume effect. The entire crown is covered with an imported tinted foliage and buds. The facing is neat drawn work of narrow folds of pink silk finished mull, and the bandeau is covered with nicely made loops of the same material. An exceedingly becoming and effectively designed hat. Can be ordered in all colors, Price, each............$1.95

...HAT DEPARTMENT...

DO NOT BE SATISFIED WITH ANY STYLE HAT when you can have at no additional expense a hat that will be becoming and at the same time stylish and in good form. Different sections of the country have their styles, due mainly to their difference in occupation and environment. If you live on a ranch and want the proper hat for such a life, we have it. If you wish the fashionable derby or stiff hat, we can supply this.

OUR LINE OF SOFT AND FEDORA SHAPES CANNOT BE EXCELLED.

VALUE. We can sell you a hat at almost any price, but by our manufacturer to the wearer plan we are able to sell to you at almost the same price your home merchant pays for the same quality. We want your order, because we can save you 25 to 40 per cent, and at the same time fill your order with NEW, CLEAN, UP TO DATE GOODS.

MEN'S DERBY OR STIFF HATS, $1.50.

No. 33R2010 Young Men's Stiff Hat, in fashionable shape. Is a very neat block, not extreme, but stylish. Crown, 4¾ inches; brim, 1¾ inches. Fine silk band and binding. Colors, black or brown. Sizes, 6¾ to 7½.
Price, each.... $1.50
If by mail, postage extra, 34 cents.
A Fashionable Block in Men's Stiff Hats for $2.00.

Men's Large or Full Shape Stiff Hats.

No. 33R2040 A style particularly suited to large men. A shapely, staple hat, as shown in illustration. Crown, 5¼ inches; brim, 2¼ inches. Fine silk band and binding. Sizes, 6¾ to 7¾. Color, black only.
Each.... $1.50
If by mail, postage extra, 34 cents.

Our Men's $2.25 Quality Full Shape Hat.
No. 33R2046 Men's Full Shape Hat, same style and dimensions as the above, in the high grade non-breakable stock, with very fine silk band and binding; imported leather sweatband. Color, black only. Sizes, 6¾ to 7¾. Price, each............$2.25
If by mail, postage extra, 34 cents.

9. Men's Underwear (1902).

MEN'S UNDERWEAR.

ASTONISHING TEMPTATIONS FOR ALL MANKIND.

QUALITIES THAT WILL SURPRISE YOU,

PRICES THAT WILL CONVINCE YOU.

MAKE A CHANGE, Off with the Old, on with the New. Prudence suggests it, your health demands it. Our prices protect you from over profit paying. We handle more Underwear and Hosiery than any one concern in the World. We save you nearly 50 per cent. on your purchases and give you better values than you could possible obtain anywhere else either wholesale or retail. Every garment we quote is guaranteed to be exactly as represented or money refunded. **EVERY PRICE WE QUOTE IS A REVELATION.**

OUR TERMS ARE LIBERAL. All goods sent C. O. D., subject to examination, on receipt of $1.00, balance and express charges payable at express office. **Three** per cent. Discount allowed if cash in full accompanies your order. Nearly All Our Customers Send Cash in Full.

Ventilated Health Underwear.

Summer Weight Balbriggan.

No. 2830 Men's Ventilated Natural Gray Mixed Summer Undershirts. The most comfortable as well as the most healthful balbriggan underwear ever made; fine gauge and soft finish; fancy collarette neck, pearl buttons and ribbed cuffs; ventilated all over with small drop stitch openings. Highly recommended by the best physicians as conducive to good health. Sizes 34 to 42 only. Price each..**$0.58**

MEN'S FANCY UNDERWEAR.
Men's Striped Balbriggan Underwear, 41 Cents.
No. 16R5078 Men's Fine Fancy Balbriggan Undershirts, knit from fine Egyptian cotton, made in a very narrow ¼-inch alternating white and blue stripe. A very pretty garment that never fails to give satisfaction. Fast color. Trimmed with collarette neck and pearl buttons. Perfect fitting ribbed cuffs. Never retails for less than 50 to 65 cents. Stitched throughout with never-rip seams. Sizes, 34 to 44 breast measure.
Price, each......................41c

Source 10 from an 1893 advertisement.

10. Shaving Soaps.

WILLIAMS' SHAVING SOAPS have enjoyed an unblemished reputation for excellence— for over HALF A HUNDRED YEARS—and are to-day the *only* shaving soaps—of absolute purity, with well-established claims for healing and antiseptic properties.

"CHEAP" and impure Shaving Soaps—are composed largely of refuse animal fats—abound in scrofulous and other disease germs—and if used —are almost sure to impregnate the pores of the skin—resulting in torturing cutaneous eruptions and other forms of blood-poisoning.

 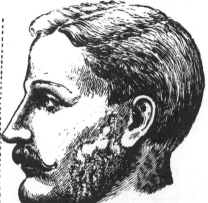

This view shows face—as shaved daily for years—with the famous WILLIAMS' Shaving Soap—always soft—fresh —bright and healthy. Not a sore or pimple in over 20 years of Shaving Experience.

This view shows the effect of being shaved ONCE with an impure—so-called "Cheap" Shaving Soap. Blood-poison— caused by applying impure animal fats to the tender cuticle of the face.

MR. CHAS. A. FOSTER,

34 SAVIN STREET,

BOSTON, MASS., writes:

"Never again will I allow a Barber to shave me unless I am *sure* he is using the only safe and reliable shaving soap made—namely WILLIAMS'. The other day—being in a hurry—I went into a shop near the Boston and Maine depot—to get a shave.

"I noticed a rank odor when the lather was put on my face, and asked the Barber if he used WILLIAMS' Shaving Soap. He said, 'No—I do not—because it costs a little more than other kinds.'

"A few days after this experience—my face was all broken out—terribly sore and smarting like fire.

"I consulted my Physician who told me it was a bad case of 'BARBER'S ITCH'—caused by the use of the Cheap Shaving Soap—containing diseased animal fats.

"I have suffered the worst kind of torture for two weeks—but I have learned a lesson."

Qu–?

Ask your Barber if *he* uses WILLIAMS'. Take no chances. Blood-poisoning—in some form or other is the almost sure result of using a cheaply made and impure Shaving Soap. While shaving—the pores of the Skin are open—and quickly drink in—any of the disease germs which may be contained in the diseased animal fats—so largely used in all "cheap"—inferior Toilet and Shaving Soaps. Ask for WILLIAMS'—and *insist* that you have it—and enjoy a feeling of SECURITY—as well as of comfort—while shaving or being shaved.

In providing for the safety and comfort of visitors—it has been officially ordered that

WILLIAMS' SHAVING SOAPS

shall be used EXCLUSIVELY—in all of the Barber Shops located on the Grounds of the World's Columbian Exposition. Thus AT THE VERY START—it receives the highest possible Honor.

WILLIAMS' "JERSEY CREAM" TOILET SOAP.

Something new with us. The result of 50 years of costly and laborious experiment. Send for circular. A most exquisite—healing and beautifying toilet soap. Containing the rich yellow cream of *our own herd* of imported Jersey Cattle. A full size cake mailed to any address for 25c. in stamps. Do not fail to try it. Ask your Druggist—or send to us.—Address,

The J. B. Williams Co., Glastonbury, Conn., U. S. A.

"WILLIAMS' SOAPS have for a foundation—over half a hundred years of unblemished reputation."

Source 11 from a 1908 advertisement.

11. Safety Razor.

"Shave Yourself"

"The man who shaves himself before breakfast in the morning has a pleasure which is never known by those whose faces are not familiar with the razor or for whom it is wielded by another.

"The operation creates a sense of cleanliness, opens one's eyes to things as they are, dissipates the cobwebs in the brain which accumulate during the night, and assists in establishing amicable relations with the world for the beginning of the day."

Well lathered, you can shave yourself with the "GILLETTE" in three to five minutes any and every morning in the year at a fraction of a cent per day. The blade of my Razor, the "GIL-LETTE," is the only new idea in Razor Blades for over 400 years. This double-edged, thin-as-a-wafer blade is held by the Gillette frame in a perfectly rigid manner (which avoids all possibility of vibration), thus ensuring a comfortable, safe and uniform shave — which conditions are not obtainable with any other make of razor.

With the "GILLETTE" a slight turn of the handle adjusts the blade (which is always in position) for a light or close shave with a soft or hard beard.

The "GILLETTE" holder triple silver plated will last you a lifetime, and when the blades become dull, throw away and buy—

10 Brand New Double-Edged "GILLETTE" Blades for 50c.

No blades re-sharpened or exchanged. The price of the "GILLETTE" set is $5.00 everywhere.

Sold by the leading Jewelry, Drug, Cutlery and Hardware Dealers.

Ask for the "GILLETTE" and booklet. Refuse all substitutes and write me to-day for special 30-day free trial order.

King C. Gillette

Care of Gillette Sales Co.

279 Times Building, New York City.

Gillette Safety **Razor**
NO STROPPING. NO HONING.

Source 12 from a 1912 advertisement.

12. Watch Chains.

Source 13 from 1916 advertisement.

13. Colt Revolver (1916).

Source 14 from an 1891 advertisement.

14. One-Volume Book.

NONE ARE TOO BUSY TO READ

IN ONE VOLUME.

"The Best Fifty Books of the Greatest Authors."

CONDENSED FOR BUSY PEOPLE.

BENJAMIN R. DAVENPORT, EDITOR.

NO EXCUSE FOR IGNORANCE.

Born 1564.   William Shakespeare.   Died 1616.

THIS WORK of 771 pages covers the whole range of Literature from Homer's Iliad, B. C. 1200 to Gen. Lew. Wallace's Ben Hur, A. D. 1880, including a Brief Biographical Sketch and FINE FULL-PAGE PORTRAIT OF EACH AUTHOR. Every one of the Fifty Books being so thoroughly reviewed and epitomized, as to enable the READERS OF THIS VOLUME TO DISCUSS THEM FULLY, making use of Familiar Quotations properly, and knowing the connection in which they were originally used by their Great Authors.

THIS BOOK is made from material furnished by Homer, Shakespeare, Milton, Bunyan, Dickens, Stowe, Gen. Lew. Wallace. and the other great authors of thirty centuries.

BY IT A LITERARY EDUCATION MAY BE ACQUIRED WITHIN ONE WEEK, ALL FROM ONE VOLUME.

A BOOK FOR BUSY AMERICANS.

TIME SAVED. MONEY SAVED.
KNOWLEDGE IN A NUTSHELL.

NEW YORK WORLD, March 15th.—"The book is one destined to have a great sale, because it supplies, IN THE FULLEST SENSE, A LONG FELT LITERARY WANT."

Born 1783.   Washington Irving.   Died 1859.

Opinions expressed by practical, busy and successful self-made men, as to the great value and merit of Mr. Davenport's condensations:

Mr. PHILIP D. ARMOUR writes: "I am pleased to own 'Fifty Best Books.' It certainly should enable the busy American, at small expenditure of time, to gain a fairly comprehensive knowledge of the style and scope of the authors you have selected."

GEN. RUSSELL A. ALGER writes: "I have received the beautiful volume. It is surely a very desirable work."

GOV. JOSEPH E. BROWN, of Georgia, writes: "You have shown great power of condensation. This is eminently a practical age; men engaged in the struggle for bread have no time to enter much into details in literature. What the age wants is to get hold of the substance of a book. This work entitles you to be understood as a benefactor."

Born 1812.   Charles Dickens.   Died 1870.

BOSTON DAILY GLOBE, April 2, 1891.—"Men of the present generation have not time to wade through from 2,000 to 3,000 pages of any of literature's standard volumes, and as a result they do not undertake it at all, and are often placed in an embarrassing position."

BUFFALO EXPRESS, March 1st.—"The Best Fifty Books of the Greatest Authors. Condensed for Busy People," edited by Benjamin R. Davenport, deserves high praise. It not only gives busy people an introduction to literature, but takes them to its very sanctum sanctorum and bids them be at home. The editor has selected his best fifty books with the advice of the most eminent literary men in England and America. These masterpieces, from Homer's 'Iliad' to Lew. Wallace's 'Ben Hur,' he has condensed into one volume of 771 pages, working in all of the famous passages and supplying a narrative in good, straightforward, unpretentious English. The story of each book is accompanied with a brief biographical sketch and a portrait of each author. No matter how familiar one is with any of these fifty books, be it for instance, 'Don Quixote,' 'Rasselas,' 'Les Miserables,' 'Paradise Lost,' or any other, he will be forced to admit, after reading the dozen pages devoted to each one in this condensation, that there is little, if anything, to add, either with regard to plot, characters, scenes, situations, quotations, or anything else that is ever discussed by people. The result of days or weeks of reading will be the possession of hardly one single bit of information or one tangible idea concerning the book in hand that is not to be acquired by reading the dozen pages in this condensation within a half hour."

SOLD BY SUBSCRIPTION ONLY.   AGENTS WANTED EVERYWHERE.

CANVASSERS who desire to represent a book which sells rapidly and without argument should send for CIRCULARS.   Books forwarded, postage paid, to any address upon receipt of price.

Fine English Muslin, Sprinkled Edges, $3 75.   Full Sheep, Library Style, Marbled Edges, $4.75.
Seal Russia, Gilt Edges, $6.75.

19th CENTURY BOOK CONCERN, 40 Exchange St., Buffalo, N. Y.

1891]

Source 15 from a 1906 advertisement.

15. Correspondence School.

What are You Worth
From The
NECK
UP?

It is estimated that the average man is worth $2.00 a day from the neck *down*—what is he worth from the neck *up?*

That depends entirely upon training. If you are trained so that you can plan and direct work you are worth ten times as much as the man who can work only under orders.

The **International Correspondence Schools** go to the man who is struggling along on small pay and say to him, "We will train you for promotion right where you are, or we will qualify you to take up a more congenial line of work at a much higher salary."

What the I. C. S. says it can do, it *will* do. It has already done it for others and will do it for *you,* if you only show the inclination.

Thousands of ambitious men, realizing this fact, have marked the I. C. S. coupon, and multiplied their wages many times. During March, 403 students voluntarily reported an increase in salary and position as the direct result of **I. C. S.** training.

In this day of demand for leaders, a young man ought to be ashamed to be satisfied with small wages when he has the I. C. S. ready to qualify him for a higher salary.

Mark the coupon at once and mail it. You need not leave your present work, or your own home, while the I. C. S. prepares you to advance.

Back your *trained hand* with a *trained head!* It pays big. This coupon is for you. *Will you use it?*

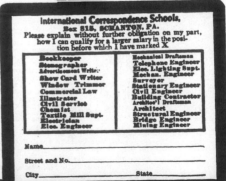

International Correspondence Schools,
Box 815, SCRANTON, PA.
Please explain without further obligation on my part, how I can qualify for a larger salary in the position before which I have marked X

Bookkeeper	Mechanical Draftsman
Stenographer	Telephone Engineer
Advertisement Writer	Elec. Lighting Supt.
Show Card Writer	Mechan. Engineer
Window Trimmer	Surveyor
Commercial Law	Stationary Engineer
Illustrator	Civil Engineer
Civil Service	Building Contractor
Chemist	Architect'l Draftsman
Textile Mill Supt.	Architect
Electrician	Structural Engineer
Elec. Engineer	Bridge Engineer
	Mining Engineer

Name_____

Street and No._____

City_____ State_____

Source 16 from a 1906 advertisement.

16. Typewriter.

A Course in Practical Salesmanship
Tuition FREE ~ All Expenses Paid

IN these times of keen business rivalry, the services of the Trained Salesman command a high premium.

The Oliver Sales Organization is the finest body of Trained Salesmen in the world. It is composed of picked men, and is under the guidance of Sales Experts.

In less than ten years it has placed the Oliver Typewriter where it belongs—in a position of absolute leadership.

Its aggregate earnings are enormous and the individual average is high.

The scope of its activities is as wide as civilization and the greatest prizes of the commercial world are open to its membership.

The organization is drilled like an army. It affords a liberal education in actual salesmanship, and increases individual earning power many per cent, by systematic development of natural talents.

Its ranks are recruited from every walk of life. Men who had missed their calling and made dismal failures in the over-crowded professions have been developed in the Oliver School of Practical Salesmanship into phenomenal successes.

The Oliver Typewriter puts the salesman in touch with the men worth knowing—the human dynamos who furnish the brain power of the commercial world.

Because every Business Executive is interested in the very things the Oliver stands for—economy of time and money—increase in efficiency of Correspondence and Accounting Departments.

The OLIVER Typewriter
The Standard Visible Writer

is simple in principle, compactly built, durable in construction, and its touch is beautifully elastic and most responsive.

In versatility, legibility, perfect alignment, visibility, etc., it is all that could be desired in a writing machine.

It's a constant source of inspiration to the salesman, as every day develops new evidence of its wide range of usefulness.

Just as the winning personality of a human being attracts and holds friends, so does the Oliver, by its responsiveness to all demands, gain and hold an ever-widening circle of enthusiastic admirers.

If you wish to learn actual salesmanship and become a member of the Oliver Organization, send in your application **immediately,** as the ranks are rapidly being filled.

You can take up this work in spare time, or give us your entire time, just as you prefer.

Whether you earn $300 a year, or **twelve times** $300 a year, depends entirely upon **yourself.**

We offer to properly qualified applicants the opportunity to earn handsome salaries and to gain a knowledge of salesmanship that will prove of inestimable value.

Can you afford to vegetate in a poorly-paid position, when the way is open to a successful business career?

Address at once.

THE OLIVER TYPEWRITER CO., 161 Wabash Ave., Chicago
WE WANT LOCAL AGENTS IN THE UNITED STATES AND CANADA.
PRINCIPAL FOREIGN OFFICE—75 QUEEN VICTORIA ST., LONDON.

Source 17 from a 1908 advertisement.

17. Life Insurance.

Don't Depend on Your Relatives When You Get Old

If you let things go kind o' slip-shod *now*, you may later have to get out of the 'bus and set your carpet-bag on the stoop of some house where your arrival will hardly be attended by an ovation.

If you secure a membership in the Century Club this sad possibility will be nipped in the bud. It is very, very comfortable to be able to sit under a vine and fig-tree of your own.

The Club has metropolitan headquarters and a national membership of self-respecting women and men who are building little fortunes on the monthly plan. Those who have joined thus far are a happy lot—it would do your heart good to read their letters.

We would just as soon send our particulars to you as to anybody else, and there is no reason in the world why you shouldn't know all about everything. You'll be glad if you do and sorry if you don't.

Be kind to those relatives—*and to yourself*.

Address, stating without fail your occupation and the exact date of your birth,

Century Life-Insurance Club
Section O

5, 7 and 9 East 42d Street, New York

RICHARD WIGHTMAN, Secretary

Source 18 from 1881 and 1885 advertisements.

18. Bicycles (1881) and Tricycles (1885).

COLUMBIA BICYCLES

The Art of wheelmanship is a gentlemanly and fascinating one, once acquired never forgotten, which no young man should neglect to acquire.

The Bicycle is practical everywhere that a buggy is, and enables you to dispense with the horse and the care and cost of keeping him. It is destined to be the prevailing light, quick, ready conveyance in country towns.

The Youth take to bicycles like ducks to water. They ride it quickly, easily, safely and gracefully. They can get more pleasure out of it than out of a horse, a boat, and a tennis or cricket outfit all together.

Parents should favor bicycle riding by their boys, because it gives them so much enjoyment, makes them lithe and strong, keeps them from evil associations, and increases their knowledge and their self-reliance. There is no out-door game or amusement so safe and wholesome.

The above paragraphs are but fragmentary suggestions; ask those who have ridden: read "The American Bicycler" (50 cts.), the "Bicycling World" (7 cts. a copy), our illustrated catalogue (3-ct. stamp).

The Columbia bicycles are of elegant design, best construction, fine finish, and are warranted. They may be had with best ball-bearings, finest nickel plate, and other specialties of construction and finish, according to choice.

The Mustang is a less expensive, plain and serviceable style of bicycle made by us for boys and youths.

Physicians, clergymen, lawyers, business men of every class, are riding our Columbias in nearly every State and Territory to-day, with profit in pocket, with benefit in health, and with delightful recreation. The L.A. W. Meet at Boston brought 800 men together on bicycles; but the **boys,** who outnumber them, and who have their own clubs and associations in so many places, were at school and at home. Why don't every boy have a bicycle?

Send 3-cent stamp for our 24-page illustrated catalogue and price-list, with full information.

THE POPE M'F'G CO.,
598 Washington Street,
BOSTON MASS.

COLUMBIA BICYCLES.

FOR HEALTH—BUSINESS—PLEASURE.

"Having examined somewhat carefully the 'wheels' of England and France, I do not believe that a better roadster is made in the world than the 'Expert Columbia.'"—ALONZO WILLIAMS, Professor of Mathematics, Brown University, Providence, R. I.

"A contractor and builder in Pennsylvania writes: 'I am using my 'wheel' night and day to make business calls, and conveying hardware and other things. . . . I would not exchange my bicycle for the best horse in the country.' "—*The Wheelman.*

"From the practical results which I determined by subjecting the different qualities of steel from which it is constructed to the recognized standard of Government tests, I am free to assert that you may justly claim that the 'Columbia' *has not its equal in quality of material and finish;* all of which is shown in the tabulated results in your possession."—F. J. DRAKE, U. S. Inspector of Material.

"A LADY'S TESTIMONY.—A recent recruit from the fair sex, in bearing evidence as to the utility of the tri cycle, writes: 'My sister and myself have just returned from a tour, having ridden from Leeds to Woodbridge (Suffolk), and home again by Halstead and Walden (Essex), or a total of 470 miles whilst we have been away; and, as we have had such a successful time of it in every respect, we intend having another tour next year.' "—*The C. T. C. Gazette.*

EVERY BOY AND MAN SHOULD HAVE A

COLUMBIA BICYCLE.

"I want to lift my voice in favor of the 'wheel' as a thing of beauty, as an instrument of pleasure, and as one of the most practical of modern inventions, looking towards practical ends."—REV. GEO. F. PENTECOST.

"But the bicycle and tricycle are not only enjoyable modes of locomotion, they are also without a peer in their hygienic capacity."—DR. S. M. WOODBURN.

EVERY LADY SHOULD RIDE A

COLUMBIA TRICYCLE.

"I am of the opinion that no exercise for women has ever been discovered that is to them so really useful. Young and middle-aged ladies can learn to ride the tri cycle with the greatest facility, and they become excellently skilful. The tricycle is, in fact, now with me a not uncommon prescription, and is far more useful than many a dry, formal, medicinal one which I had to write on paper."—B. W. RICHARDSON, M. D., F. R. S.

Illustrated Catalogue Sent Free.

THE POPE M'F'G CO., Principal Office, 597 Washington St., Boston, Mass.

[1885]   BRANCH HOUSES: 12 Warren St., New York; 179 Michigan Ave., Chicago.

Source 19 from 1896 and 1914 advertisements.

19. Gramophone (1896) and Victrola (1914).

20. Ford Automobile (1907) and Electric Car for Women (1912).

FORD RUNABOUT
"Built for Two"

Two's company and a crowd frequently spoils a motoring trip.

When you have a large car you feel like filling up the seats—seems stingy for two to usurp so much luxury; so your tonneau is always full. Everybody's happy but—

Did you ever feel as if you'd just like to go alone—you and she—and have a day all your own? Go where you please, return when you please, drive as fancy dictates, without having to consult the wishes or the whims of others?

Ford Runabouts are ideal for such trips. Just hold two comfortably; ride like a light buggy, control easily and you can jog along mile after mile and enjoy the scenery.

Of course you can scorch if you want to—40 miles an hour easily—but you won't want to. You'll get used to the soft purr of the motor and the gentle motion of the car over the rolling country roads and—well, it's the most luxurious sensation one can imagine.

"**We've enjoyed motoring** more since we've had the Ford Runabout than we ever did before," says one lady whose purse can afford anything she desires. "Got the big car yet, but 'two's company,' and most times that's the way we go."

$600,
F.O.B. Detroit

Model N. 4 Cyl. 15 H.P.

FORD MOTOR COMPANY,
25 Piquette Ave., - Detroit, Mich.

BRANCH RETAIL STORES—New York, Philadelphia, Boston, Chicago, Buffalo, Cleveland, Detroit and Kansas City. Standard Motor Co., San Francisco, Oakland and Los Angeles, distributors for California. Canadian trade supplied by Ford Motor Company of Canada, Walkerville, Ont.

The Automobile for Women

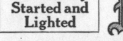

Electrically Started and Lighted

Controls Itself Pumps Its Own Tires

THE advent of the Inter-State, with its marvelously simple mechanism, its electrical self-starter and its self-controller has brought a revolution in motoring. Now the powerful and magnificent Inter-State starts and obeys the will of the woman driver as readily, as easily and as simply as an electric coupe. Without moving from the driver's seat or shifting gears she starts the engine by a turn of the switch — regulates the mixture by a simple movement of the lever on the steering column, and the magnificent Inter-State is under way and under perfect and absolute control, with no more trouble than turning on an electric light. The Inter-State electric self-starter is **part of the system and built into it,** and the motor dynamo turns the engine itself until it picks up under its own power.

No labor to start the Inter-State

Electric Lights as in Your Own Home

Any or all lights on by turning switch

ONE of the greatest features of the Inter-State is its electric light system—not a single light or two—but an entire and reliable system, front —side—rear, all correlated and so arranged that by a turn of the switch, without leaving the driver's seat, any or all of the lights may be turned on in all their brilliancy. No more gas tanks, no more oil filling, no more lamp trimming or adjusting. The system is simply perfect. The front headlights are provided with a dimming feature so that driving in city streets may be done with a medium diffused light.

Write Today for Art Catalog

This describes fully the six 40 and 50 H. P. completely equipped Models which cost from $2,400 to $3,400. Gives complete details of all the equipment and features, and also shows the Inter-State Models 30-A and 32-B, 40 H. P., costing $1,750 and $1,700 respectively.

THAT greatest nuisance of motoring—tire pumping—is *totally eliminated* with the Inter-State equipment. Any woman can attach the valve to the tire, turn on the pump and in a few minutes have tires just as solid and as perfectly filled as if done by the greatest tire expert in the world.

The Inter-State *does* the work. You *direct* it. There is nothing to it at all and you are forearmed for any emergency with the complete and thorough equipment of the Inter-State.

Inter-State Tire Pumping—No Work

Motoring Now All Pleasure

THIS great car performs all the labor itself—electrically self-started—electric lights and ignition, tire pumping and the automatic regulation of fuel consumption.

For the first time in the history of the automobile, electricity plays its *real part* in the entire mechanism. The Inter-State Electric System is really the *nerve system* commanding the energy and motion of the powerful steel muscles that make the Inter-State such a masterpiece of construction. Every conceivable accessory and feature is built into or included in the Inter-State. The Inter-State is truly the *only complete car* in this country or abroad —and this statement is made advisedly.

The Only Complete Car—Equipment and Features Unequalled

INTER-STATE AUTOMOBILE COMPANY, Dept. X, Muncie, Indiana
Boston Branch: 153 Massachusetts Avenue   *Omaha Branch:* 310 South 18th Street

Source 21 from a 1913 advertisement.

21. Auto Horn.

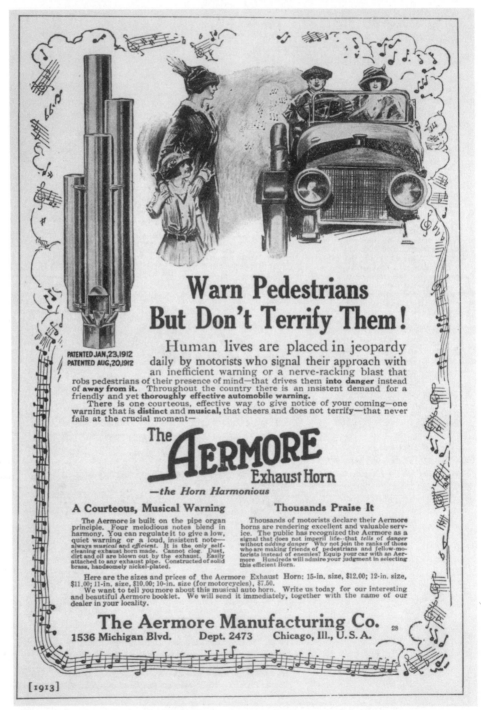

22. Stove (1884) and Washer and Wringer (1908).

ASK YOUR DEALER FOR THE
"GLENWOOD"

WITH PATENT MAGIC GRATE.

There is nothing more essential to the healthy happy home than well cooked food—which you may always be sure of by using the Glenwood Range. 100 styles! Illustrated Circular and Price List sent free.

WEIR STOVE CO., Taunton, Mass.

The Electric Washer and Wringer

YOU can now have your washings done by electricity. The 1900 Electric Washer Outfit (Washer, Wringer and Motor complete) does all the heavy work of washing and wrings out the clothes.

Any electric light current furnishes the power needed. You connect up the washer the same way you put an electric light globe into its socket. Then all there is to do to start the washer is—turn on the electricity. The motion of the tub (driven by the electricity) and the water and soap in the tub wash the clothes clean. Washing is done quicker and easier, and more thoroughly and economically this way than ever before.

Washing

30 Days' FREE Trial—Freight Prepaid

Servants will stay contented—laundry bills will be saved—clothes will last twice as long—where there is a 1900 Electric Washer to do the washing.

These washers save so much work and worry and trouble, that they *sell themselves.* This is the way of it—

We ship you an Electric Washer and *prepay the freight.*

Use the washer a month. Wash your linens and laces—wash your blankets and quilts—wash your rugs.

Then—when the month is up, if you are not convinced the washer is all we say—don't keep it. Tell us you don't want the washer and that will settle the matter. We won't charge anything for the use you have had of it.

This is the *only* washer outfit that does *all* the drudgery of the washing—*washes* and *wrings* clothes—saves them from wear and tear—and keeps your servants contented.

Our Washer Book tells how our washers are made and how they work. Send for this book today.

Don't mortgage your pleasure in life to dread of wash-day and wash-day troubles with servants. Let the 1900 Electric Washer and Wringer shoulder your wash-day burden—save your clothes and money, and keep your servants contented.

Write for our Washer Book at once. Address—

The 1900 Washer Co. 3133 Henry Street, Binghamton, N. Y. (If you live in Canada, write to the Canadian 1900 Washer Co., 355 Yonge Street, Toronto, Ont.)

Wringing

23. Vacuum Cleaner (1909) and Bathroom Closet (1913).

Why stir up the Dust Demon to Frenzy like this?

The Man
always wonders why some way of cleaning can't be found without tormenting him with choking clouds of dust.

You can Escape all this for $25

EVERY MAN AND WOMAN

The Woman
thinks she is performing praiseworthy and necessary work in an unavoidable manner.

should now realize that such laborious and tormenting "cleaning" methods, not only are absolutely unnecessary, but are a **relic of barbarism, a mockery and a farce.** "Cleaning" with broom and carpet-sweeper merely scatters more of the dirt over a wider area. Old dirt has to be *rehandled again and again.* The house is never thoroughly clean. Disease germs are left to multiply, then are sent flying to infect all those whose powers of resistance may be lowered.

THE IDEAL VACUUM CLEANER

(Fully Protected by Patents)

Operated by Hand puts no tax on the strength.

Price $25

"IT EATS UP THE DIRT"

literally sucks out all the dust, grit, germs, moths and eggs of vermin that are *at the object* as well as *in* it—gobbles them down into its capacious maw, never to trouble you again.

This machine places in your hands a method of cleaning carpets, rugs, curtains, upholstery, wall decorations, etc., that hitherto has been limited to the very rich. It does exactly the same work as the Vacuum Cleaning systems that cost from $500 up—*and does it better and with more convenience.*

The Ideal Vacuum Cleaner **is the perfection of the Vacuum Cleaning principle.**

Or by Electric Motor, at a cost of 2 cents per hour.
Price **$55** or **$60**

PRICE $35 and $60

OPERATED BY HAND

Weighs only 20 pounds. Anybody can use it. Everybody can afford it.
Compared with sweeping **it is ease itself.**

It is absolutely dustless.
Every machine guaranteed.

PRICE $25

Our Free Illustrated Booklet tells an interesting story of a remarkable saving in money, time, labor, health, and strength. Send for it to-day.

The American Vacuum Cleaner Company
225 Fifth Avenue, New York City

[1909]

The Noiselessness of the Siwelclo Is an Advantage Found in No Other Similar Fixture.

This appeals particularly to those whose sense of refinement is shocked by the noisy flushing of the old style closet. The Siwelclo was designed to prevent such embarrassment and has been welcomed whenever its noiseless feature has become known. When properly installed it cannot be heard outside of its immediate environment.

SIWELCLO Noiseless Siphon Jet CLOSET

Every sanitary feature has been perfected in the Siwelclo—deep water seal preventing the passage of sewer gas, thorough flushing, etc.

The Siwelclo is made of Trenton Potteries Co. Vitreous China, with a surface that actually repels dirt like a china plate. It is glazed at a temperature 1000 degrees higher than is possible with any other material.

The most sanitary and satisfactory materials for all bathroom, kitchen and laundry fixtures are Trenton Potteries Co. Vitreous China and Solid Porcelain. Your architect and plumber will recommend them. If you are planning a new house or remodeling, you ought to see the great variety and beauty of design such as are shown in our new free booklet S13 "Bathrooms of Character." Send for a copy now.

The Trenton Potteries Co.
Trenton, N. J., U. S. A.

The largest manufacturers of sanitary pottery in the U.S.A.

24. Musical Organ.

CARPENTER,

"LIBRARY ORGAN."

Containing the Celebrated Carpenter Organ Action.

Something Entirely New! The Æsthetic Taste Gratified!

THIS IS ONLY ONE OF ONE HUNDRED DIFFERENT STYLES.

THIS effective and beautiful design in the modern Queen Anne Style is intended to meet the demands of those desiring an instrument of special elegance, and in harmony with the fittings and furnishings of the Study or Library Room, combining as it does, in a substantial and tasteful manner, the Organ, the Library cases, and the cabinet for bric-a-brac and articles of virtu.

It is well adapted to find favor in homes of culture and refinement, and will be championed by the music lover and connoisseur.

The composition is one of well balanced proportions, chaste subordination of ornamentation, and of artistic arrangement in constructive details, imparting to the design a rich simplicity and substantial worth

This beautiful organ contains the Celebrated Carpenter Organ Action. The action is to an Organ what the works are to a watch. The merits of the Carpenter Organ were fully proved on page 158 of the YOUTH'S COMPANION of April 20th, to which special attention is directed.

A beautiful 80-page Catalogue, the finest of its kind ever published, is now ready and will be sent free to all applying for it.

Nearly all reliable dealers sell the Carpenter Organs, but if any do not have them to show you, write to us for a Catalogue and information where you can see them. DO NOT BUY ANY ORGAN UNTIL YOU HAVE EXAMINED "THE CARPENTER." In writing for a Catalogue always state that you saw this advertisement, in the *Youth's Companion.*

Address or call on E. P. CARPENTER. Worcester, Mass., U. S. A.

Source 25 from a 1909 advertisement.

25. Reed and Rattan Furniture.

ESTABLISHED 1826

Heywood-Wakefield

TRADE MARK

FACSIMILE OF OUR TAG

THE name *Heywood-Wakefield* appearing on Reed and Rattan Furniture signifies quality, style, and workmanship, that individualizes our brands of goods and has made them world-renowned. The best in Rattan Furniture is *not* the best unless it bears the tag *Heywood-Wakefield*

Our furniture enhances the beauty of any home. Its presence lends an influence of dignity, comfort, and artisticness that harmonizes with any color treatment or architectural effect. So numerous are the styles made by us in Reed and Rattan Furniture, covering every known desire for the household, club, or hotel, and to which our design creators are constantly adding new effects in shapes and patterns, that you are practically sure of possessing, when selecting our goods, ideas that are exclusive and original.

We are also producers of the well-known line of

Heywood *Wakefield*

go-carts and baby carriages. Made in every conceivable style, including our celebrated collapsible, room-saving go-carts.

We have prepared attractive illustrated catalogs showing and describing our Reed and Rattan Furniture. Before purchasing, *write for catalog G.*

We also furnish, free, interesting catalog of our go-carts and baby carriages. If interested, *write for catalog 7.*

Write to our nearest store.

HEYWOOD BROTHERS AND WAKEFIELD COMPANY

BOSTON, BUFFALO, NEW YORK, PHILADELPHIA, BALTIMORE, CHICAGO, SAN FRANCISCO, LOS ANGELES, PORTLAND, ORE.

J. C. PLIMPTON & CO., Agts. LONDON AND LIVERPOOL, ENG.

Style 6830 B

26. Houses in New York (1887) and Tennessee (1892). Exterior View and Floor Plan.

* * * This marvelous house has been built more than 300 times from our plans; *it is so well planned* that it affords ample room even for a large family. 1st floor shown above; on 2d floor are 4 bedrooms and in attic 2 more. Plenty of Closets. The whole warmed by one chimney.

Large illustrations and full description of the above as well as of 39 other houses, ranging in cost from $400 up to $6,500, may be found in "SHOPPELL'S MODERN LOW-COST HOUSES," a large quarto pamphlet, showing also how to select sites, get loans, &c. Sent postpaid on receipt of 50c. Stamps taken, or send $1 bill and we will return the change. Address, BUILDING PLAN ASSOCIATION. (Mention this paper.) 24 Beekman St. (Box 2702,) N. Y.

Source 27 from a *Ladies' Home Journal* advertisement, 1909.

27. Advice for Couples Buying a Home.

This is the house the young couple saved and paid for in five years.

A Young Couple
Were Married 5 Years Ago

He had a moderate salary. They started simply and saved. But they didn't skimp. They gave little dinners and heard the best lectures. In five years they had saved enough to pay for the house at the head of this page.

Another Young Couple Were Married, Too

They put by $7 a week, and the house at the bottom of this page is now theirs, —entirely paid for. A third young couple's income was $16 per week. They saved $8 of it, and bought and paid for the house at the bottom of this page.

How these and 97 others did it, step by step, dollar by dollar, is all told in the great series, "*How We Saved For a Home,*"— 100 articles by 100 people who saved for and now own their own homes on an

Average Salary of $15 a Week: None Higher Than $30

This great series will run for an entire year in

The Ladies' Home Journal

For ONE DOLLAR, for a year's subscription, you get the whole series.

THE CURTIS PUBLISHING COMPANY, PHILADELPHIA, PA.

This is the house saved for on $7 a week and now all paid for.

This is the house paid for out of a salary of $16 per week, saving $8.

Sources 28 through 31 from *Palliser's Model Homes,* 1878.

28. Cottage for a Mill Hand at Chelsea, Mass. (Cost $1,200).

This is a very attractive design, and intended to give ample accommodation at a low cost for an ordinary family.

The cellar is placed under the Kitchen and Hall, which was thought in this instance to be sufficient to meet all requirements, though it is generally considered, in the Eastern States at least, to be poor economy not to have a cellar under the whole house, as it only requires about one foot in depth of additional stone work to secure a cellar, it being necessary to put down the stone work in any case, so that it will be beyond the reach of frost. The Kitchen is without a fire-place, the cooking to be done by a stove, which, if properly contrived, is a very effective ventilator, and preferred by many housekeepers for all Kitchen purposes.

The Parlor and Dining-room or general Living-room are provided with the healthy luxury of an open fire-place, and we know of no more elegant, cleanly and effective contrivance for this purpose than the one adopted in this instance; they are built of buff brick, with molded jambs and segment arch, and in which a basket grate or fire dogs can be placed for the desired fire, and in this way large rooms are kept perfectly comfortable in cold weather without heat from any other source. These fire-places are also provided with neat mantels constructed of ash, and which are elegant compared with the marbelized slate mantel, which is a sham, and repulsive to an educated taste.

On entering nearly every house in the land we find the same turned walnut post at the bottom of the stairs with tapering walnut sticks all the way up, surmounted with a flattened walnut rail having a shepherd's crook at the top; however, in this instance it is not so, but the staircase is surmounted with an ash rail, balusters and newel of simple, though unique design; and now that people are giving more attention to this important piece of furniture, we may look for a change in this respect.

This house is supplied with a cistern constructed with great care, the Kitchen sink being supplied with water by a pump, and there is no more easy method of procuring good water for all purposes of the household.

For a compact, convenient Cottage with every facility for doing the work with the least number of steps, for a low-priced elegant Cottage, we do not know of anything that surpasses this. Cost, $1,200.

Mr. E. A. Jones of Newport, Ohio, is also erecting this Cottage with the necessary changes to suit points of compass. Such a house as this if taste-fully furnished, and embellished with suitable surroundings, as neat and well-kept grounds, flowers, etc., will always attract more attention than the uninviting, ill-designed buildings, no matter how much money may have been expended on them.

It is not necessary that artistic feeling should have always a large field for its display; and in the lesser works and smaller commissions as much art may find expression as in the costly façades and more pretentious structures.

29. Floor Plan of Cottage for a Mill Hand.

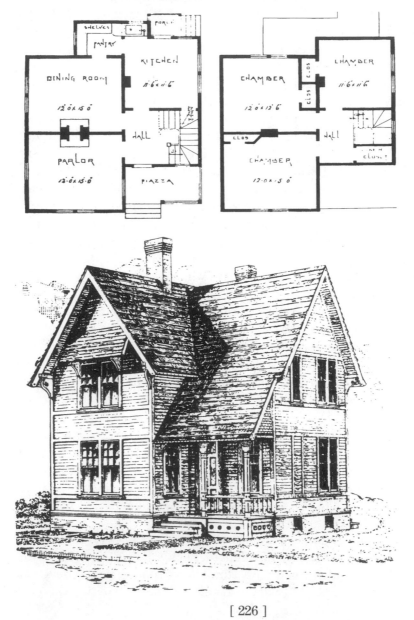

30. Residence of Rev. Dr. Marble, Newtown, Conn. (Cost $2,925).

This house commands a particularly fine view from both sides and the front, and is situated in one of the pleasantest country towns in New England, the hotels of this town being crowded during the summer months with people from the cities.

The exterior design is plain, yet picturesque, and at once gives one an idea of ease and comfort. The roofing over the Hall and Sitting-room is a particularly fine feature, and the elevation of the rear is very striking, the roof over the porch being a part of the main roof.

The interior arrangements are very nice, the Hall being very spacious, and in it we have a very easy and handsome stair-case of plain design, constructed of Georgia pine; the newel extends up to ceiling of first floor, while the other two posts extend up to ceiling of second floor. In all country houses one of the first things to be aimed at is to secure ample stair-cases, and until a man can afford space for an easy ascent to a second floor he should stay below; and to-day we find in houses, where there is no necessity for it, stairs that are little better than step-ladders, making a pretence of breadth at the bottom with swelled steps, and winding the steps on ap-proaching the floor above, thus making a trap for the old and for the children.

The corner fire-place between Parlor and Dining-room is a feature we indulge in to a great extent in these days of economy, sliding doors and fire-places, although we sometimes have clients who object to this, thinking it would not look as well as when placed in center of side wall; but when they are asked how this and that can be provided for with the best and most economical results, they readily give in.

There is no water-closet [toilet] in the house, but an Earth-Closet is provided in the rear Hall, which is thoroughly ventilated.

The Dining-room is a very cheerful room and the Kitchen is reached through a passage also connecting with side veranda. The pantry is lighted with a window placed above press; each fire-place is furnished with a neat hard-wood mantel, and the Hall is finished in Georgia pine, the floor being laid with this material, and finished in natural color.

The exterior is painted as follows: Ground, light slate; trimmings, buff, and chamfers, black. Cost, $2,925.

The sight of this house in the locality in which it is built is very refresh-ing, and is greatly in advance of the old styles of rural box architecture to be found there. When people see beautiful things, they very naturally covet them, and they grow discontented in the possession of ugliness. Handsome houses, other things equal, are always the most valuable. They sell quickest and for the most money. Builders who feign a blindness to beauty must come to grief.

31. Floor Plan of a Clergyman's Residence.

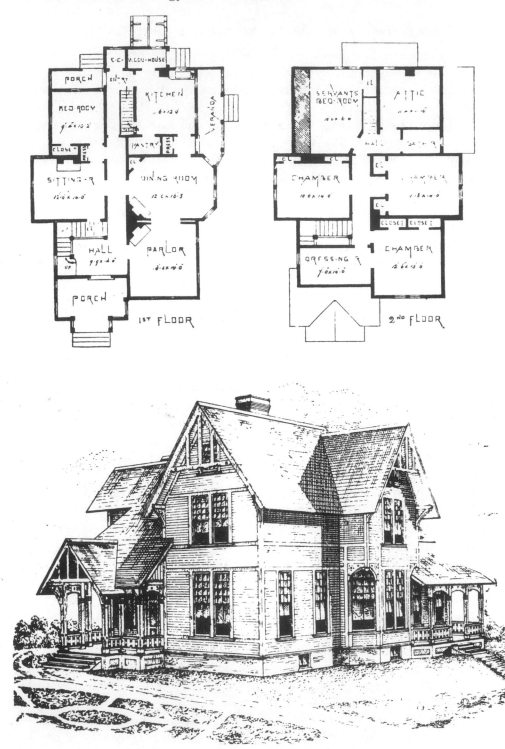

32. Perspective View and Floor Plans for a Suburban Middle-Class Home (Cost $3,600).

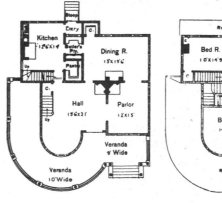

PERSPECTIVE.

DESCRIPTION.

For explanation of all symbols(* † etc.) see supplement page 120.

GENERAL DIMENSIONS: Width, including veranda, 43 ft.; depth, including veranda, 49 ft. 6 ins.

HEIGHTS OF STORIES: Cellar, 7 ft.; first story, 10 ft.; second story, 9 ft.; attic, 8 ft.

EXTERIOR MATERIALS: Foundation, brick; first story, clapboards; second story, gables, roofs and lower portion of veranda railing, shingles.

INTERIOR FINISH: Two coat plaster for papering; plaster, cornices and centers in hall, parlor and dining-room. Soft wood flooring and trim throughout. Main stairs, ash. Kitchen and bath-room, wainscoted. Chair-rail in dining-room. Picture molding in hall, parlor and dining-room. All interior woodwork grain filled and finished with hard oil.

COLORS: All clapboards, first story, Colonial yellow. Trim, including water-table, corner boards, casings, cornices, bands, veranda posts and rails, outside doors, conductors, etc., ivory white. Veranda floor and ceiling, oiled. Shingles on side walls and gables stained dark yellow. Roof shingles, dark red.

ACCOMMODATIONS: The principal rooms, and their sizes, closets, etc., are shown by the floor plans. Cellar under whole house with inside and outside entrances and concrete floor. One room finished in attic, remainder of attic floored for storage. Double folding doors between parlor and hall and parlor and dining-room. Direct communication from hall with dining-room, parlor and kitchen. Bathroom, with complete plumbing, in second story. Open fire-places in dining-room, parlor and hall. Wide veranda. Bay-window in hall and bedroom over. Two stationary wash-tubs in cellar under kitchen.

COST: $3,600, including mantels, range and heater. The estimate is based on † New York prices for labor and materials.

Price of working plans, specifications, detail drawings, etc., $35.
Price of †† bill of materials, ... 10.

FIRST FLOOR.

SECOND FLOOR.

FEASIBLE MODIFICATIONS: General dimensions, materials and colors may be changed. Cellar may be decreased in size or wholly omitted. Sliding doors may be used in place of folding doors. Portable range may be used instead of brick-set range. Servants' water-closet could be introduced in cellar. Fireplaces may be reduced in number.

The price of working plans, specifications, etc., for a modified design, varies according to the alterations required and will be made known upon application to the Architects.

Address, CO-OPERATIVE BUILDING PLAN ASSOCIATION, Architects, 203 Broadway and 164–6–8 Fulton Street, New York, N. Y.

33. The New Business of Advertising.

"Photographs in Advertising," *Printers' Ink,* August 17, 1898, p. 18.

It may have been noticed that the trend of modern magazine advertising is toward the use of photographs. . . . An advertisement that contains the photograph of a beautiful woman is certain to be attractive, and consequently its success is largely guaranteed. . . . But there are a host of articles on the market that can be advertised to great advantage by the introduction of a lady into the picture, and many advertisers have already seen this. . . .

But though the photographs of pretty women are only supposed to be attractive to the male sex, the picture of a baby or "cute" child will immediately captivate ninety-nine per cent of humanity. . . . Whatever he or she is supposed to advertise, we feel kindly toward, even if it is only for introducing us to the baby. . . .

Earnest Elmo Calkins, *The Business of Advertising* (New York: D. Appleton and Co., 1915 [1920 reprint]), pp. 1, 9.

It is hard to find a satisfactory definition of advertising. A picturesque way of putting it is to call it business imagination, an imagination that sees in a product possibilities which can be realized only by appealing to the public in new ways to create a desire where none existed before. . . .

Advertising modifies the course of the people's daily thoughts, gives them new words, new phrases, new ideas, new fashions, new prejudices and new customs. In the same way it obliterates old sets of words and phrases, fashions and customs. It may be doubted if any other one force, the school, the church and the press excepted, has so great an influence as advertising. To it we largely owe the prevalence of good roads, rubber tires, open plumbing, sanitary underwear, water filters, hygienic waters, vacuum cleaners, automobiles, kitchen cabinets, pure foods. These are only a few of the things which the public has been taught by advertising to use, to believe in, and to demand.

S. Roland Hall, *The Advertising Handbook: A Reference Work Covering the Principles and Practice of Advertising* (New York: McGraw-Hill, 1921), pp. 79–80, 101–103.

In other words, certain thoughts have become fixed in our minds in connection with certain other thoughts, and when we bring up one end of the connection the other is likely to follow. . . .

There is a motive, and a good one, in calling an automobile the "Lincoln," for that suggests sturdy, honest qualities.

No writer would undertake to make a real hero out of a character known as "Percy," for this name suggests "sissiness.". . .

Man is the stronger, as a rule. He is the bread-winner, to a large extent. His job is more in the outside world. He grows up to severer tasks, as a rule. He is more accustomed to rebuffs.

Though woman has progressed a long way in taking her place on an equal plane with that of man in business, politics and the professions, yet she is still to a large extent more sheltered than man. Her affairs are more within the home. Her sex makes her interest in clothes, home-furnishings, and the like keener than man's as a general thing. . . .

Because of her years of comparative non-acquaintance with mechanical matters, woman is generally less apt in understanding mechanical description and directions, and such advertisers must use greater care when appealing to women. . . .

On the other hand it is generally admitted that men are more democratic, more gregarious, than women—that women move more within their own circle or "clique."

A man is not likely to care if several other men in his circle have a hat exactly like his own. A woman would hardly care to buy a hat exactly like one worn by several other women in her town or community. A woman ordinarily will think nothing of shopping at several places to look at hats. A man is likely to visit only one shop. . . .

Claude C. Hopkins, *My Life in Advertising* (1927), reprinted as Claude C. Hopkins, *My Life in Advertising and Scientific Advertising* (Chicago: Advertising Publications, 1966), pp. 8–9, 119.

I am sure that I could not impress the rich, for I do not know them. I have never tried to sell what they buy. . . . But I do know the common people. I love to talk to laboring-men, to study housewives who must count their pennies, to gain the confidence and learn the ambitions of poor boys and girls. Give me something which they want and I will strike the responsive chord. My words will be simple, my sentences short. Scholars may ridicule my style. The rich and vain may laugh at the factors which I feature. But in millions of humble homes the common people will read and buy. They will feel that the writer knows them. And they, in advertising, form 95 per cent of our customers. . . .

People are like sheep. They cannot judge values, nor can you and I. We judge things largely by other's impressions, by popular favor. We go with

the crowd. So the most effective thing I have ever found in advertising is
the trend of the crowd.

❧ QUESTIONS TO CONSIDER ❧

For convenience, the evidence is divided into three sections. Sources 1 through 25 are advertisements from popular magazines and the 1897 and 1902 Sears Roebuck & Co. catalogues. The prices probably seem ridiculously low to you, but these items were reasonably priced and affordable—although not really cheap—for most middle-class Americans in cities and towns and on farms. Sources 26 through 32 all deal with houses and buying a house, including house plans readily available by mail and through pattern books. Again, the prices seem very low, but working-class homes could be built for less than one thousand dollars (excluding the cost of the land) and middle-class homes for as little as two thousand dollars during this period.

As you read each advertisement, you will find it helpful to jot down notes. First, try to determine the message of the ad. What is the advertiser trying to sell? What emotion(s) does the ad appeal to? What fears? What hopes? Then ask what the ad tells you about society during that time. Does it tell you anything about men's roles? About women's roles? About the relationships between men and women? Does it tell you anything about children or young people? About adults' concerns about young people? About old people? Finally, do you see any changes occurring during the time pe-

riod—for example, in the two ads for the Gramophone and the Victrola (Source 19) or in the ads for automobiles (Source 20)? If so, what do these changes tell you about the roles of men, women, and young people between the 1880s and 1917?

Source 26 contains two advertisements for houses. Source 27 is an advertisement for a magazine series giving advice on how to buy a home. What do they tell you about people's needs and wants with regard to housing? What advice is offered to young married people? What values are emphasized by these advertisements for housing? Sources 28 through 32 consist of house plans and descriptions from architectural pattern books, arranged chronologically from 1878 to 1900. Look carefully at the exterior features of these houses. How would you describe them to a student who had not seen the pictures? Next, look at the interior rooms and their comparative sizes. What use or uses would each room probably have had? What rooms did these houses have that our own modern houses do not have? Do modern houses have rooms that these houses lacked? What similarities do you find in all the houses, from the mill hand's cottage ($1,200) in Source 28 to the suburban middle-class home ($3,600) in Source 32? What differences are there? Finally, what kinds of things seemed to be important to the owners of these houses? What kind of impression did they wish to make on other people?

The excerpts in Source 33 are drawn from an advertising journal, two textbooks, and the autobiography of a famous advertising pioneer. *Printers' Ink* was a weekly journal of advertising founded in the second half of the nineteenth century. What kinds of photographs does the author recommend using? Why? What is the relationship between the photographs and the item being sold? Earnest Calkins first published a book on "modern" advertising in 1895, which he later rewrote as a textbook, *The Business of Advertising*. How does he define advertising? In what ways does he believe that advertising affects people?

S. Roland Hall had worked in advertising and later taught both salesmanship and advertising. Why does he believe that the names of products are important? What does he think are the major differences between men and women? How might these differences affect people who wrote advertisements? Finally, Claude Hopkins was a self-made man who became one of the highest-paid advertising copywriters of the late nineteenth and early twentieth centuries, at one time earning over $100,000 a year. In this excerpt from his autobiography, he explains the basic elements in his approach to advertising. To what factors does he attribute his success?

To conclude, consider what you have learned from the evidence as a whole. Can you describe how white middle-class Americans lived during this period? How the new business of advertising promoted material goods and houses? What these advertisements reveal about white middle-class values, hopes, and fears during this era of rapid changes?

∽ EPILOGUE ∽

Of course, not all Americans could live like the middle-class families you just studied. The poor and the immigrants who lived in the cities were crowded into windowless, airless tenement buildings that often covered an entire block. Poor rural black and white sharecroppers in the South lived in one- or two-room shacks, and many farmers in the western plains and prairies could afford to build only sod houses. During the Great Depression of the 1930s, many people, including middle-class families, lost their homes entirely through foreclosure, and the 1960s and 1970s saw the price of houses increase so rapidly that many families were priced out of the housing market. Even today, the problem of the homeless has not been solved.

The early twentieth century saw the captains of industry come under attack for what many came to believe were their excesses. Evidence of their disdain for and defiance of the public good, as well as of their treatment of workers, their political influence, and their ruthless business practices, came more and more to light due to the efforts of reformers and muckraking journalists. The society that once had venerated the industrial barons began to worry that they had too much power and came to believe that such power should be restricted.

Architecture also was undergoing a rapid transformation. Neoclassical, Georgian, colonial, and bungalow styles signaled a shift toward less ostentation and increased moderation in private dwellings. Perhaps the most striking work was done by Chicago architect Frank Lloyd Wright, who sought to give functional and social meaning to his designs and to make each structure blend into its unique landscape. According to Wright's concepts, there was no standard design for the "perfect house." Wright's ideas formed the basis for a series of movements that ultimately changed the perspective and direction of American architecture.

Progressive muckrakers also criticized advertising, particularly the claims of patent medicine advertisements. Such salesmanship, however, was described as "the brightest hope of America" by the 1920s. Bruce Barton, a talented salesman and founder of a huge advertising agency, even discovered "advertisements" in the Bible, which he described as the first "best seller." Although its image was slightly tarnished by the disillusionment accompanying the Great Depression, advertising helped "sell" World War II to the American public by encouraging conservation of scarce resources, and it emerged stronger and more persuasive than ever in the 1950s. Americans were starved for consumer goods after wartime rationing, and their rapid acceptance of a new entertainment medium—television—greatly expanded advertising opportunities.

But advertising still had (and has) its critics. Writing in 1954, historian David Potter, in *People of Plenty,* characterized advertising as the basic "institution of abundance." Advertising, he maintained, had become as powerful as religion or education had been in earlier eras. Advertising, he said, now actually *created* the standards and values of our society. Because advertising lacked social goals or social responsibility, however, he believed that its power was dangerous. We must not forget, Potter warned, "that it ultimately regards man as a consumer and defines its own mission as one of stimulating him to consume."

CHAPTER 9

THE "NEW" WOMAN OF THE 1920s: IMAGE AND REALITY

∽ THE PROBLEM ∾

With the publication of his novel *Main Street* in 1920, American author Sinclair Lewis produced the first of several best sellers. This novel was especially popular among college students, perhaps because many of them identified with the young protagonist, Carol, a so-called new woman of the early twentieth century: college educated, young, attractive, idealistic, ambitious, and "modern." The novel begins as Carol, who has graduated from a coeducational college in the Midwest and then drifted into library school in Chicago, returns to St. Paul, Minnesota, as a librarian. Bored, lonely, and dissatisfied with her job, she soon meets Dr. Will Kennicott, more than twelve years her senior. After a brief courtship, they marry and return to his hometown of Gopher Prairie.

In the small town of Gopher Prairie, the young bride finds narrow-mindedness, conformity, vicious gossip, and rigid insistence on traditional male and female roles. None of her efforts to improve her situation—town beautification plans, a community theater, a reading and discussion group—is successful. With the birth of a child, Carol feels more trapped and desperate. Finally, determined to find a better life, she separates from her husband and moves to Washington, D.C., with her young son. There she works as a government clerk, rents an apartment, and makes a lively new circle of friends. After a year, her husband comes to visit her, and five months later, pregnant again, she returns to Gopher Prairie for good.

At the end of the novel, Carol Kennicott passionately defends her rebellion and her aspirations for women, crying out that she may have failed, but she tried her best. "Sure. . . . feels like it might snow tomorrow," her husband replies. "Have to be thinking about putting up the storm windows pretty soon."

Was there a "new" woman who came of age in the 1920s? Were young women liberated from outmoded expectations based on gender? In this chapter, the central question asks you to analyze both the images and the realities of the new woman as portrayed in best sellers, nonfiction, and films from the 1920s.

☙ BACKGROUND ❧

The 1920s have caught the imaginations of both historians and the general public, who have, nevertheless, found the period difficult and elusive to characterize. Marked at its beginning by the conclusion of the Great War (which we now call World War I) and at its end by the disastrous stock market crash of 1929, this decade seemed special even to those people living at the time. Many of them called it the Jazz Age. It was in some ways an era of incredibly rapid changes, most noticeably in the economic and cultural aspects of American life. Some of these changes raised very real questions about the values and assumptions of an older, more rural way of life. Indeed, one useful way to examine the decade is in terms of the strains and conflicts between pre–World War I attitudes, beliefs, and behaviors and those of twentieth-century modernism.

Economically, after some postwar dislocations in 1920 and 1921, the country seemed to be enjoying enormous prosperity. Mass production of new goods fed consumer demand fueled by seductive advertising, and personal worth increasingly became identified with possessing up-to-date material goods. Business practices and values were widely admired, imitated, and accepted by the general public, as corporate mergers and the development of chain stores standardized and homogenized the goods and services available to customers in all sections of the country. Like Henry Ford, corporate leaders soon came to understand that better-paid workers could buy more products and that more satisfied workers produced more. Management transformed its hostility toward organized labor into "corporate paternalism," an approach to labor relations that reduced labor union membership during the decade. Technological breakthroughs in both pure and applied science, as well as in medicine, seemed to promise better and healthier lives for all Americans. That farming, mining, and a few other sectors of the economy were not sharing in this prosperity did not seem very important.

Continuity rather than change characterized the politics of the decade. With the exception of the presidential election of 1928, which pitted old stock American, Protestant, "dry," Republican, rural, small-town candidate Herbert Hoover against Democrat Alfred Smith, who seemed to represent the newer, ethnic, Catholic, "wet" immigrants from urban areas, American politics was business as usual. The three conservative Republican presidents—Warren Harding, Calvin Coolidge, and Herbert Hoover—in theory opposed intervening in the economy but in practice were pro-business in their actions. From the scandalous, graft-ridden administration of Warren Harding, the farm bill veto and strikebreaking activities of Calvin Coolidge, and the anti-Progressive decisions of the U.S. Supreme Court, to the short-lived flurry of hope for a new Progressive party under the leadership of Senator Robert La Follette, little positive change was achieved.

What seemed most obvious to the majority of people were the rapid cultural changes taking place in American society. Urbanization, along with the radio and movies, made possible the rise of a truly national mass culture. Radio listeners in all parts of the country could enjoy the new music, especially jazz, and the new spectator sports, such as baseball and football. Even small cities had movie theaters. In Muncie, Indiana (population 35,000 in 1920), there were nine theaters that showed more than twenty different films every week. Because of the rapidity of communication, such varied individuals as baseball player George Herman "Babe" Ruth, aviator Charles Lindbergh, and English Channel swimmer Gertrude Ederle became widely admired national heroes. The

proliferation and popularity of mass-circulation magazines for both middle- and working-class readers were paralleled by the success of the new middle-class book clubs, which created instant best sellers, in both fiction and nonfiction. Some serious writers of the Lost Generation[1] left the country; others stayed home and wrote critically of the materialism and values of the era. And in the Harlem Renaissance, a new generation of African American authors found their voice and wrote about the strengths of their heritage.

Perhaps the single most important factor in changing the way Americans lived in this era was the automobile. When asked about changes that had taken place in his lifetime, one long-time Muncie resident replied, "I can tell you what's happening in just four letters: A-U-T-O!" The automobile offered the freedom to live farther away from one's place of work, visit other nearby towns, and go away for a vacation. For young people, access to an automobile meant freedom from chaperons or curious neighbors, as serious courtship was replaced by casual dating. By the 1920s, the automobile also had become an important status symbol for both youths and their parents.

Such sweeping changes were not without opposition, and the twenties witnessed a series of reactions against the forces of modernism. Feeling overwhelmed by the late nineteenth- and early twentieth-century influx of poorer immigrants from southern and

1. Writers such as Ernest Hemingway and Sinclair Lewis who had been disillusioned by World War I and whose work questioned the old prewar values.

eastern Europe, Congress established a temporary and then a permanent quota system to bar them. These laws marked the abandonment of the traditional American policy of welcoming those who immigrated for economic opportunity.

The twenties also saw the rise of a new Ku Klux Klan, for the first time popular in urban areas and outside the South, dedicated to "100 percent Americanism" and devoted to enforcing the values of a nineteenth-century rural America. Two famous trials of the decade, the Sacco and Vanzetti case against Italian anarchists convicted of committing a murder during a payroll robbery and the Scopes case, in which a teacher was found guilty of breaking Tennessee law by teaching about evolution, highlighted the social and cultural strains inherent in the conflict between the older values of rural, small-town America and modernism.

Perhaps nowhere were these strains more evident than in the heated debates of the decade about the proper place and roles of women. There was no doubt in the minds of contemporary observers that women's roles were changing. The Nineteenth Amendment, granting women the vote, had been ratified in 1920, setting off wild speculations about the impact women voters might have on politics. Transforming their organization into the League of Women Voters, the leaders of the National American Woman's Suffrage Association urged citizenship education and took a neutral, bipartisan position on candidates. Thus voting patterns did not change much. So-

cial feminists did successfully lobby for the Sheppard-Towner maternal and infant health care bill, although their efforts to ratify the child labor amendment met with defeat. The more radical feminists of the National Woman's Party surveyed the remaining legal discriminations against women and, in 1923, proposed an equal rights amendment (ERA), which would have required that all laws apply equally to men and women. Those women who favored protective labor laws for women opposed the ERA, however, and feminists, all of whom wanted to expand women's opportunities and choices, were once again divided over goals and strategies.

Economically, women continued to enter the work force but were clustered in "women's jobs." Approximately one in four women worked for pay. Most women workers were young and unmarried, although more married women were taking paid employment during the twenties. Openings for women in the service sector expanded, as did clerical jobs and a limited number of professional positions. But women in general were not taken seriously as workers. Employers believed that they worked only to earn "pin money" for unnecessary purchases and that they would quit their jobs as soon as they could. Married women who worked carried the double burden of paid employment and unpaid housework and often faced public disapproval as well. In spite of unequal pay and limited employment opportunities, many "new" women of the twenties worked diligently and expected to rise to higher positions on the basis of their merit. This was especially true of women with high school and college educations.

Culturally, there were noticeable changes in the appearance and behavior of younger women. The new woman had begun to emerge well before World War I, but in the 1920s, popularized by the media and the cartoons of John Held, Jr., a single stereotype began to dominate: the flapper. The flapper, so called because of the short-lived fad of wearing unbuckled galoshes that flapped when she walked, had short "bobbed" hair and wore cosmetics, short skirts, and dangling beads. She often smoked and even drank in public, and she presented herself as a "good sport" and "pal" to men of her own age. Flirting with and dating many different young men, she often seemed to care only about dancing and having fun. Older Americans were appalled by the appearance and outraged by the behavior of this 1920s woman. Worried and upset about the practice of "petting" (engaging in sexual intimacies that usually stopped just short of sexual intercourse), Americans complained that the new woman was completely immoral.

Of course, as historian Paul Carter has pointed out, there was another side to the twenties, and only a small minority of women were flappers. Nevertheless, fashion responded to the flapper style, middle-aged married women adopted variations of it, and even mail-order catalogues intended for rural and small-town consumers featured models with short hair and skimpy skirts. Films, novels, nonfiction, mass-circulation magazines, and advertisements all portrayed the new woman, investigated the dilemmas she faced, and reached conclusions about her life based on their own presuppositions and value judgments.

In this chapter, you will be analyzing both best-selling fiction and some selected nonfiction, as well as the images presented by two popular film stars, to determine the degree to which there was a new woman who came of age in the 1920s. To do so, you will need to compare the image of the new woman with some of the realities of her life.

∞ THE METHOD ∞

Historians must always be aware of the possibility that an *image*—how a person or a particular time appeared—may be quite different from its historical *reality*—how that person or era actually was. The independent ethical cowboy, the docile and happy slave, and the passive, oppressed Victorian wife and mother are all examples of historically inaccurate images. Such images are usually culturally constructed. Sometimes, as in the case of the new woman of the 1920s, the image is created by contemporaries who are attempting to understand their own times. The image may also be created at a later time. For example, the story of George Washington, who was so honest that he would not lie about chopping down his father's cherry tree, is a consciously developed and accepted image created by Americans who were seeking national heroes in an uncertain and difficult period of history.

The image of the new woman of the 1920s came from many sources, including journalism, films, and advertising. In this chapter, you will primarily be using fiction and nonfiction to determine both the image of the new woman—how she was portrayed—and the reality—how different from previous women she actually was. You will be supplementing your analysis of the image of the new woman with some visual evidence, photographs of two popular female film stars.

Since the nineteenth century, women have provided the bulk of the readership for popular novels, often those written by other women. In the 1920s, book clubs patronized by middle-class subscribers chose book-of-the-month selections on the basis of their potential appeal to club members and, in the process, helped to create widely read and discussed best sellers. Another phenomenon of the 1920s was the influx of students on college campuses. Certain books became fads, and most students read them. The excerpts from the novels that you will be analyzing here are examples of these kinds of popular fiction. Describe the image of the new woman portrayed in each novel: How does she look? What do others think about her? How does she feel about herself? What does she do? What happens to her?

When a resident of Muncie submitted a story to *Live Stories,* the magazine rejected it, stating that "stories should embody picturesque settings for action; they should also present situations of high emotional character, rich in sentiment. A moral conclusion is essential." Although our own modern fiction often does not contain a "moral conclusion" or message, popular fiction in the 1920s almost always did. When you analyze the excerpts from the best-selling novels of the twenties, also ask yourself questions about the conclusions: Who wins? Who loses? Why?

It would be a mistake, however, to depend solely on fiction to understand the past. In this chapter, you will also be reading three nonfiction excerpts from two books and an article. Reformers, especially Progressives of the late nineteenth and early twentieth centuries, used nonfiction and documentary photographs extensively to educate the public about problems created by rapid industrialization and urbanization. By the 1920s, there was a large middle-class audience for nonfiction. Serious books such as H. G. Wells's *Outline of History* and Will Durant's *The Story of Philosophy* each sold over a million copies. These books were obviously educational. Other nonfiction, such as *Woman and the New Race,* tried to persuade readers to support a particular course of action. *Middletown* documented conditions and attitudes through direct field research, and "Feminist—New Style" sought to explain the times in which its readers were living. Nonfiction should be both compared to and contrasted with fiction from the same historical period to provide a more complete understanding of U.S. history.

Finally, you will compare and contrast the public images of movie stars Mary Pickford and Clara Bow. Nicknamed "America's Sweetheart," Pickford was born in 1893 and began making films as a teenager. She was extremely popular among Americans of all ages and socioeconomic classes in the years immediately preceding and following World War I. A shrewd businesswoman, Pickford married the handsome and famous film star Douglas Fairbanks and continued to make films during the 1920s. But she was narrowly typecast, often playing young or teenage "girl" roles even when she was in her thirties, in wholesome, family-oriented movies.

Born in 1905, Clara Bow was a red-haired, seventeen-year-old beauty contest winner who was discovered by Hollywood. She got her start in films in 1923, playing a series of "ordinary girls" such as waitresses, theater usherettes, salesgirls, and manicurists. In all these films, she portrayed a modern working "girl," a flapper who loves dancing, wild parties, and flirting with men. Her real fame came after she was chosen by the English romance writer Elinor Glyn to star in the film adaptation of *IT*. As a result, Clara Bow became the "It Girl" and a role model for thousands of young, female moviegoers. Offstage, her life was very much like that of the flappers she portrayed.

∽ THE EVIDENCE ∽

FICTION

Source 1 from E. M. Hull, *The Sheik* (Boston: Small, Maynard and Company, 1921), pp. 1–2, 4, 10–11, 35, 259, 272–273, 275.

1. Excerpts from E. M. Hull's *The Sheik*.

[*The novel begins at a hotel in French Africa, where a farewell dance is being held for the young Diana Mayo, a "new" woman who is about to leave on a month-long trip through the desert. Lady Conway is talking with a young man about Diana's proposed trip.*]

. . . "I thoroughly disapprove of the expedition of which this dance is the inauguration. I consider that even by contemplating such a tour alone into the desert with no chaperon or attendant of her own sex, with only native camel drivers and servants, Diana Mayo is behaving with a recklessness and impropriety that is calculated to cast a slur not only on her own reputation, but also on the prestige of her country. I blush to think of it. . . . The girl herself seemed, frankly, not to understand the seriousness of her position, and was very flippant and not a little rude. I wash my hands of the whole affair. . . ."

[*Diana, who has a reputation for arrogance, is there with her older brother, who looks bored.*]

. . . By contrast, the girl at his side appeared vividly alive. She was only of medium height and very slender, standing erect with the easy, vigorous carriage of an athletic boy, her small head poised proudly. Her scornful mouth and firm chin showed plainly an obstinate determination, and her deep blue eyes were unusually clear and steady. The long, curling black lashes that shaded her eyes and the dark eyebrows were a foil to the thick crop of loose, red-gold curls that she wore short, clubbed about her ears. . . .

[*At the dance, one of Diana's admirers begs her not to take the trip, confessing that he is in love with her and worried about her safety because she is so beautiful. When he tries to hold her hand, she pulls away.*]

. . . "Please stop. I am sorry. We have been good friends, and it has never occurred to me that there could be anything beyond that. I never thought that you might love me. I never thought of you in that way at all. . . . I am very content with my life as it is. Marriage for a woman means the end of independence, that is marriage with a man who is a man, in spite of all that the most modern woman may say. I have never obeyed any one in my life; I do not wish to try the experiment. I am very sorry to have hurt you. You've been a splendid pal, but that side of life does not exist for me. . . . A man to me is just a companion with whom I ride or shoot or fish; a pal, a comrade, and that's just all there is to it." . . .

[*In spite of everyone's objections, Diana sets off on horseback with an Arab guide and servants she has hired. Before they have gone very far, a large caravan passes them.*]

. . . One of two of the camels carried huddled figures, swathed and shapeless with a multitude of coverings, that Diana knew must be women. The contrast between them and herself was almost ridiculous. It made her feel stifled even to look at them. . . . The thought of those lives filled her with aversion. . . .

[*When night falls, Diana's party is attacked by a group of Arabs, and she is kidnapped and taken to their camp, where Sheik Ahmed Ben Hassan, who masterminded the kidnapping, has sex with her against her will. In spite of herself, she gradually falls in love with him during the next two months. But she pretends to be*

*cold and uncaring for fear he will get tired of her and leave her. Out for a ride with
a servant, she is captured by the Sheik's enemy, and when the Sheik tries to rescue
her, he is badly wounded. While the Sheik is still unconscious, Diana learns that he
is not really an Arab but the son of an English aristocrat and a Spanish noble-
woman, adopted by the Arabs after his mother died in the desert.]*

. . . He must live, even if his life meant death to her hopes of happiness;
that was nothing compared with his life. She loved him well enough to
sacrifice anything for him. If he only lived she could even bear to be put out
of his life. It was only he that mattered, his life was everything. . . . If she
could only die for him. . . .

*[The Sheik recovers. Convinced that he has grown tired of her, Diana gives in to
depression.]*

She wondered numbly what would become of her. It did not seem to
matter much. Nothing mattered now that he did not want her any more.
The old life was far away, in another world. She could never go back to it.
She did not care. It was nothing to her. It was only here in the desert, in
Ahmed Ben Hassan's arms, that she had become alive, that she had learned
what life really meant, that she had waked both to happiness and sorrow. . . . If she could have had the promise of a child. . . . A child that would
be his and hers, a child—a boy with the same passionate dark eyes, the
same crisp brown hair, the same graceful body, who would grow up as tall
and strong, as brave and fearless as his father. Surely he must love her
then. . . . Beside her love, everything dwindled into nothingness. He was
her life, he filled her horizon. Honour itself was lost in the absorbing
passion of her love. He had stripped it from her and she was content that
it should lie at his feet. He had made her nothing, she was his toy, his
plaything, waiting to be thrown aside. . . .

*[At the end of the novel, after Diana tries to kill herself rather than be sent back, the
Sheik admits that he loves her.]*

Source 2 from Percy Marks, *The Plastic Age* (New York: The Century Company,
1924), pp. 157, 174, 212–213, 216–217, 223–224, 244–245, 248–249, 265, 288,
320, 322.

2. Excerpts from Percy Marks's *The Plastic Age*.

*[The novel begins as Hugh Carver, a high school track star and likable, clean-cut
young man, arrives for his freshman year at the all-male college of Sanford. He
pledges the same fraternity to which his father belonged, studies just enough to get*

by with average grades, and spends endless hours discussing life and "girls" with his friends. When one of the upperclassmen suggests that if they went out with "cheap women" it would take their minds off sex, another student disagrees.]

. . . "The old single standard fight," he said, propping his head on his hand. "I don't see any sense in scrapping about that any more. We've got a single standard now. The girls go just as fast as the fellows."

"Oh, that's not so," Hugh exclaimed. "Girls don't go as far as fellows."

Ferguson smiled pleasantly at Hugh and drawled; "Shut up, innocent; you don't know anything about it. I tell you the old double standard has gone all to hell." . . .

[*In his sophomore year, Hugh—who has just started drinking alcohol—and his roommate, Carl, get drunk and go into town, where two prostitutes try to pick them up.*]

. . . They were crude specimens, revealing their profession to the most casual observer. If Hugh had been sober they would have sickened him, but he wasn't sober; he was joyously drunk and the girls looked very desirable. . . .

[*A football player prevents Hugh from going with the prostitutes, but Carl goes anyway. A few weeks later, Carl and seven others are diagnosed with venereal disease and expelled from Sanford. Hugh's next adventure takes place at a fraternity dance. He doesn't have a date, but he sees a young woman, Hester, whom he has met before. He dances with her.*]

"Hot stuff, isn't it?" she asked lazily.

Hugh was startled. Her breath was redolent of whisky. . . .

As the evening wore on he danced with a good many girls who had whisky breaths. One girl clung to him as they danced and whispered, "Hold me up, kid; I'm ginned." He had to rush a third, a dainty blond child, to the porch railing. She wasn't a pretty sight as she vomited into the garden; nor did Hugh find her gasped comment, "The seas are rough to-night," amusing. Another girl went sound asleep in a chair and had to be carried up-stairs and put to bed. . . .

[*Later that evening, Hester drags Hugh into the darkened dining room of the fraternity house and tells him she wants to pet. Going to get one of the chaperon's coats, he walks in on a couple in bed. Disgusted, he leaves the dance.*]

He thought of Hester Sheville, of her whisky breath, her lascivious pawing—and his hands clenched. "Filthy little rat," he said aloud, "the stinkin', rotten rat."

Then he remembered that there had been girls there who hadn't drunk anything, girls who somehow managed to move through the whole orgy calm and sweet. His anger mounted. It was a hell of a way to treat a decent girl, to ask her to a dance with a lot of drunkards and soused rats.

[*The summer of his junior year, Hugh visits his friend Norry Parker, whose family has a cottage on Long Island. There Hugh meets lots of "new" women.*]

. . . They flirted with him, perfected his "petting" technique, occasionally treated him to a drink, and made no pretense of hiding his attraction for them.

At first Hugh was startled and a little repelled, but he soon grew to like the frankness, the petting, and the liquor; and he was having a much too exciting time to pause often for criticism of himself or anybody else. . . .

[*Just before he leaves, Hugh meets Cynthia Day and falls in love with her.*]

. . . Suddenly Hugh was attracted by a girl he had never seen before. She wore a red one-piece bathing-suit that revealed every curve of her slender, boyish figure. . . . Her hair was concealed by a red bathing-cap, but Hugh guessed that it was brown; at any rate, her eyes were brown and very large. She had an impudent little nose and full red lips. . . .

[*After returning to college that fall, Hugh and Cynthia write to each other regularly, and she accepts his invitation to come to Sanford for prom week.*]

When Hugh eventually saw Cynthia standing on a car platform near him, he shouted to her and held his hand high in greeting. She saw him and waved back, at the same time starting down the steps.

She had a little scarlet hat pulled down over her curly brown hair, and she wore a simple blue traveling-suit that set off her slender figure perfectly. Her eyes seemed bigger and browner than ever, her nose more impudently tilted, her mouth more supremely irresistible. Her cheeks were daintily rouged, her eyebrows plucked into a thin arch. She was New York from her small pumps to the expensively simple scarlet hat. . . .

[*Later, Norry Parker has a talk with Hugh.*]

"I never expected you to fall in love with Cynthia, Hugh," he said in his gentle way. "I'm awfully surprised. . . ."

Hugh paused in taking off his socks. "Why not?" he demanded. "She's wonderful."

"You're so different."

[245]

"How different? . . ."

Norry was troubled. "I don't think I can explain exactly," he said slowly. "Cynthia runs with a fast crowd, and she smokes and drinks—and you're —well, you're idealistic."

Hugh pulled off his underclothes and laughed as he stuck his feet into slippers and drew on a bathrobe. "Of course, she does. All the girls do now. She's just as idealistic as I am." . . .

[*That night at the prom, Hugh and Cynthia dance to a "hot" jazz band, get drunk, and go back to Norry's dorm room. Just as they are about to make love, Norry comes in and escorts Cynthia back to her room. Hugh is ashamed and hungover the next morning; Cynthia decides to return to New York. When she asks if he loves her, Hugh says yes, but she knows that he's lying.*]

"I'm twenty and lots wiser about some things than you are. I've been crazy about you—I guess I am kinda yet—and I know that you thought you were in love with me. I wanted you to have hold of me all this time. That's all that mattered. It was—was your body, Hugh. You're sweet and fine, and I respect you, but I'm not the kid for you to run around with. I'm too fast. I woke up early this morning, and I've done a lot of thinking since. You know what we came near doing last night? Well, that's all we want each other for. We're not in love." . . .

[*After prom week, Hugh goes into training for a big track meet and applies himself to his studies. Elected to the prestigious senior council, Hugh begins to plan for his future: graduate school at Harvard and teaching. When Norry returns from Christmas holidays, he tells Hugh that he saw Cynthia and that she looked terrible.*]

. . . "What's the matter? Is she sick?"

Norry shook his head. "No, I don't think she is exactly sick," he said gravely, "but something is the matter with her. You know, she has been going an awful pace, tearing around like crazy. I told you that, I know, when I came back in the fall. Well, she's kept it up, and I guess she's about all in. I couldn't understand it. Cynthia's always run with a fast bunch, but she's never had a bad name. She's beginning to get one now." . . .

[*After this conversation, Hugh writes a brief note to Cynthia asking what's wrong. She replies that she loves him and had tried to give him up because she knew she was bad for him. Confused, Hugh continues to correspond with her and just before graduation asks her to meet him in New York. He can stay only two hours, so they go to a coffee shop to talk. Hugh asks her to marry him, then changes his mind. They discuss prom night, and Hugh tells Cynthia that he has not been drunk at all since then and has regained his self-respect. Cynthia thinks about her own partying.*]

She did not say that she knew that he did not love her; she did not tell him how much his quixotic chivalry moved her. Nor did she tell him that she knew only too well that she could lead him to hell, as he said, but that that was the only place she could lead him. . . .

[*Again, Hugh asks her to marry him after he has completed his graduate education and become established. She refuses his offer, lying and saying that she does not love him. She also points out that he shouldn't marry her if he doesn't love her.*]

"Of course not." He looked down in earnest thought and then said softly, his eyes on the table, "I'm glad that you feel that way, Cynthia." She bit her lip and trembled slightly. "I'll confess now that I don't think that I love you either. You sweep me clean off my feet when I'm with you, but when I'm away from you I don't feel that way. I think love must be something more than we feel for each other." He looked up and smiled boyishly. "We'll go on being friends anyhow, won't we?"

Somehow she managed to smile back at him. "Of course," she whispered, and then after a brief pause added: "We had better go now. Your train will be leaving pretty soon." . . .

NONFICTION

Source 3 from Margaret Sanger, *Woman and the New Race* (New York: Brentano's, 1920), pp. 93–95.

3. Excerpt from Margaret Sanger's *Woman and the New Race.*

The problem of birth control has arisen directly from the effort of the feminine spirit to free itself from bondage. Woman herself has wrought that bondage through her reproductive powers and while enslaving herself has enslaved the world. The physical suffering to be relieved is chiefly woman's. Hers, too, is the love life that dies first under the blight of too prolific breeding. Within her is wrapped up the future of the race—it is hers to make or mar. All of these considerations point unmistakably to one fact—it is woman's duty as well as her privilege to lay hold of the means of freedom. Whatever men may do, she cannot escape the responsibility. For ages she has been deprived of the opportunity to meet this obligation. She is now emerging from her helplessness. Even as no one can share the suffering of the overburdened mother, so no one can do this work for her. Others may help, but she and she alone can free herself.

The basic freedom of the world is woman's freedom. A free race cannot be born of slave mothers. A woman enchained cannot choose but give a measure of that bondage to her sons and daughters. No woman can call herself free who does not own and control her body. No woman can call herself free until she can choose consciously whether she will or will not be a mother.

It does not greatly alter the case that some women call themselves free because they earn their own livings, while others profess freedom because they defy the conventions of sex relationship. She who earns her own living gains a sort of freedom that is not to be undervalued, but in quality and in quantity it is of little account beside the untrammeled choice of mating or not mating, of being a mother or not being a mother. She gains food and clothing and shelter, at least, without submitting to the charity of her companion, but the earning of her own living does not give her the development of her inner sex urge, far deeper and more powerful in its outworkings than any of these externals. In order to have that development, she must still meet and solve the problem of motherhood.

Source 4 from Robert S. Lynd and Helen M. Lynd, *Middletown: A Study in American Culture* (New York: Harcourt, Brace and Company, 1929), pp. 256–257, 112, 114–117, 120–121, 123, 131, 241, 266–267.

4. Excerpts from Robert S. and Helen M. Lynd's *Middletown.*

The general attitude reflected in such characteristic school graduation essays of the 1890 period as "Woman Is Most Perfect When Most Womanly" and "Cooking, the Highest Art of Woman" contrasts sharply with the idea of getting one's own living current among the Middletown high school girls of today: 89 per cent. of 446 girls in the three upper classes in 1924 stated that they were planning to work after graduation, and 2 per cent. more were "undecided"; only 3 per cent. said definitely that they did not expect to work. . . .

[*The Lynds reported that married working women were not as accepted as readily as single working women. Nevertheless, they noted that the 1920 census had shown that 28 percent of the working women of Middletown were married.*]

A heavy taboo, supported by law and by both religious and popular sanctions, rests upon sexual relationships between persons who are not married. There appears to be some tentative relaxing of this taboo among the younger generation, but in general it is as strong today as in the county-seat of forty years ago. There is some evidence that in the smaller community of the eighties [1880s] in which everybody knew everybody else, the group prohibition was outwardly more scrupulously observed than today. A man who was a young buck about town in the eighties says, "The fellows nowadays don't seem to mind being seen on the street with a fast woman, but you bet we did then!" . . .

. . . Theoretically, it is the mysterious attraction of two young people for each other and that alone that brings about a marriage, and actually most of Middletown stumbles upon its partners in marriage guided chiefly by "romance." Middletown adults appear to regard romance in marriage as something which, like their religion, must be believed in to hold society together. Children are assured by their elders that "love" is an unanalyzable mystery that "just happens"—"You'll know when the right one comes along," they are told with a knowing smile. . . .

And yet, although theoretically this "thrill" is all-sufficient to insure permanent happiness, actually talks with mothers revealed constantly that, particularly among the business group, they were concerned with certain other factors; the exclusive emphasis upon romantic love makes way as adolescence recedes for a pragmatic calculus. Mothers of the business group give much consideration to encouraging in their children friendships with the "right" people of the other sex, membership in the "right" clubs, deftly warding off the attentions of boys whom they regard it as undesirable for their daughters to "see too much of," and in other ways interfering with and directing the course of true love.

[Mothers generally looked for "good providers" as husbands for their daughters, and young women who not only could keep house but could be a social asset as wives for their sons, the Lynds found.]

Not unrelated to this social skill desired in a wife is the importance of good looks and dress for a woman. In one of Marion Harland's *Talks*,[2] so popular in Middletown in the nineties, one reads, "Who would banish from our midst the matronly figures so suggestive of home, comfort, and motherly love?" Today one cannot pick up a magazine in Middletown without seeing in advertisements of everything from gluten bread to reducing tablets' instructions for banishing the matronly figure and restoring "youthful beauty." "Beauty parlors" were unknown in the county-seat of the nineties; there are seven in Middletown today.

2. Popular advice essays aimed at women.

"Good looks are a girl's trump card," says Dorothy Dix, though she is quick to add that much can be done without natural beauty if you "dress well and thereby appear 50 per cent. better-looking than you are . . . make yourself charming," and "cultivate bridge and dancing, the ability to play jazz and a few outdoor sports."

[*In general, the Lynds noted, Middletown men did not value "brains" in women, believing that although women were purer and more moral than men, they were not as intelligent. Most Middletown citizens were concerned about the striking increase in the divorce rate.*]

The frequency of divorces and the speed with which they are rushed through have become commonplaces in Middletown. "Anybody with $25 can get a divorce" is a commonly heard remark. Or as one recently divorced man phrased it, "Any one with $10 can get a divorce in ten minutes if it isn't contested. All you got to do is to show non-support or cruelty and it's a cinch." . . .

[*The Lynds reported that middle-class women were more likely to use some form of birth control than working-class women.*]

Child-bearing and child-rearing are regarded by Middletown as essential functions of the family. Although the traditional religious sanction upon "fruitfulness" has been somewhat relaxed since the nineties, and families of six to fourteen children, upon which the grandparents of the present generation prided themselves, are considered as somehow not as "nice" as families of two, three, or four children, child-bearing is nevertheless to Middletown a moral obligation. Indeed, in this urban life of alluring alternate choices, in which children are mouths instead of productive hands, there is perhaps a more self-conscious weighting of the question with moral emphasis; the prevailing sentiment is expressed in the editorial dictum by the leading paper in 1925 that "married persons who deliberately refuse to take the responsibility of children are reasonable targets for popular opprobrium." But with increasing regulation of the size of the family, emphasis has shifted somewhat from child-bearing to child-rearing. The remark of the wife of a prosperous merchant, "You just can't have so many children now if you want to do for them. We never thought of going to college. Our children never thought of anything else," represents an attitude almost universal today among business class families and apparently spreading rapidly to the working class.

Although, according to the city librarian, increased interest in business and technical journals has been marked, as in its reading of books Middletown appears to read magazines primarily for the vicarious living in fictional form they contain. Such reading centers about the idea of romance underlying the institution of marriage; since 1890 there has been a trend toward franker "sex adventure" fiction. It is noteworthy that a culture which traditionally taboos any discussion of sex in its systems of both religious and secular training and even until recently in the home training of children should be receiving such heavy diffusion of this material through its periodical reading matter. The aim of these sex adventure magazines, diffusing roughly 3,500 to 4,000 copies monthly throughout the city, is succinctly stated. . . .

. . . "Middletown is amusement hungry," says the opening sentence in a local editorial; at the comedies Middletown lives for an hour in a happy sophisticated make-believe world that leaves it, according to the advertisement of one film, "happy convinced that Life is very well worth living."

Next largest are the crowds which come to see the sensational society films. The kind of vicarious living brought to Middletown by these films may be inferred from such titles as: "*Alimony*—brilliant men, beautiful jazz babies, champagne baths, midnight revels, petting parties in the purple dawn, all ending in one terrific smashing climax that makes you gasp"; "*Married Flirts—Husbands:* Do you flirt? Does your wife always know where you are? Are you faithful to your vows? *Wives:* What's your hubby doing? Do you know? Do you worry? Watch out for *Married Flirts.*" So fast do these flow across the silver screen that, e.g., at one time *The Daring Years, Sinners in Silk, Women Who Give,* and *The Price She Paid* were all running synchronously, and at another "*Name the Man*—a story of betrayed womanhood" *Rouged Lips,* and *The Queen of Sin.* While Western "action" films and a million-dollar spectacle like *The Covered Wagon* or *The Hunchback of Notre Dame* draw heavy houses, and while managers lament that there are too few of the popular comedy films, it is the film with burning "heart interest" that packs Middletown's motion picture houses week after week. Young Middletown enters eagerly into the vivid experience of *Flaming Youth:* "neckers, petters, white kisses, red kisses, pleasure-mad daughters, sensation-craving mothers, by an author who didn't dare sign his name; the truth bold, naked, sensational"—so ran the press advertisement—under the spell of the powerful conditioning medium of pictures presented with music and all possible heightening of the emotional content, and the added factor of sharing this experience with a "date" in a darkened room. Meanwhile, *Down to the Sea in Ships,* a costly spectacle of whaling adventure, failed at the leading theater "because," the exhibitor explained, "the whale is really the hero in the film and there wasn't enough 'heart interest' for the women."

Source 5 from Dorothy Dunbar Bromley, "Feminist—New Style," *Harper's Monthly* (October 1927), pp. 552, 554–556, 558–559.

5. Excerpts from Dorothy Dunbar Bromley's "Feminist—New Style."

Is it not high time that we laid the ghost of the so-called feminist?

"Feminism" has become a term of opprobrium to the modern young woman. For the word suggests either the old school of fighting feminists who wore flat heels and had very little feminine charm, or the current species who antagonize men with their constant clamor about maiden names, equal rights, woman's place in the world, and many another cause . . . *ad infinitum.* Indeed, if a blundering male assumes that a young woman is a feminist simply because she happens to have a job or a profession of her own, she will be highly—and quite justifiably—insulted: for the word evokes the antithesis of what she flatters herself to be. . . .

. . . Why, then, does the modern woman care about a career or a job if she doubts the quality and scope of women's achievement to date? There are three good reasons why she cares immensely: first, she may be of that rare and fortunate breed of persons who find a certain art, science, or profession as inevitable a part of their lives as breathing; second, she may feel the need of a satisfying outlet for her energy whether or no she possesses creative ability; third, she may have no other means of securing her economic independence. And the latter she prizes above all else, for it spells her freedom as an individual, enabling her to marry or not to marry, as she chooses—to terminate a marriage that has become unbearable, and to support and educate her children if necessary. . . .

But even though Feminist—New Style may not see her own course so clearly marked out before her, and even if she should happen to have an income, she will make a determined effort to fit her abilities to some kind of work. For she has observed that it is only the rare American of either sex who can resist the mentally demoralizing effect of idleness. She has seen too many women who have let what minds they have go to seed, so that by the time they are forty or forty-five they are profoundly uninteresting to their husbands, their children, and themselves. . . .

. . . Nor has she become hostile to the other sex in the course of her struggle to orient herself. On the contrary, she frankly likes men and is grateful to more than a few for the encouragement and help they have given her. . . .

When she meets men socially she is not inclined to air her knowledge and argue about woman's right to a place in the sun. On the contrary, she either talks with a man because he has ideas that interest her or because she finds it amusing to flirt with him—and she will naturally find it doubly amusing if the flirtation involves the swift interplay of wits. She will not waste many engagements on a dull-witted man, although it must be admitted that she finds fewer men with stagnant minds than she does women. . . .

. . . As for "free love," she thinks that it is impractical rather than immoral. With society organized as it is, the average man and woman cannot carry on a free union with any degree of tranquillity.

Incidentally, she is sick of hearing that modern young women are cheapening themselves by their laxity of morals. As a matter of fact, all those who have done any thinking, and who have any innate refinement, live by an aesthetic standard of morals which would make promiscuity inconceivable. . . .

. . . She readily concedes that a husband and children are necessary to the average woman's fullest development, although she knows well enough that women are endowed with varying degrees of passion and of maternal instinct. Some women, for instance, feel the need of a man very intensely, while others want children more than they want a husband, want them so much, in fact, that they vow they would have one or two out of wedlock if it were not for the penalty that society would exact from the child, and if it were not for the fact that a child needs a father as much as a mother.

But no matter how much she may desire the sanction of marriage for the sake of having children, she will not take any man who offers. First of all a man must satisfy her as a lover and a companion. And second, he must have the mental and physical traits which she would like her children to inherit. . . .

. . . But even while she admits that a home and children may be necessary to her complete happiness, she will insist upon *more freedom and honesty within the marriage relation.*

She considers that the ordinary middle-class marriage is stifling in that it allows the wife little chance to know other men, and the husband little chance to know other women—except surreptitiously. It seems vital to her that both should have a certain amount of leisure to use exactly as they see fit, without feeling that they have neglected the other. . . .

Feminist—New Style would consider it a tragedy if she or her husband were to limit the range of each other's lives in any way. Arguing from the fact that she herself can be interested in other men without wanting to exchange them for her husband, she assumes that she has something to give him that he may not find in other women. But if the time should come when it was obvious that he preferred another woman to her or that he preferred to live alone, she would accept the fact courageously, just as she would expect him to accept a similar announcement from her; although she would hope that they would both try to preserve the relationship if it were worth preserving, or if there were children to be considered. But if the marriage should become so inharmonious as to make its continuation a nightmare, she would face the tragedy, and not be submerged by it. For life would still hold many other things—and people—and interests.

6. Still Photographs of Mary Pickford and Clara Bow.

Source 6a: Archive Photos.

6a. Mary Pickford, Photo Portrait.

6b. Pickford in *Tess of Storm Country* (1922).

Source 6c: Archive Photos/American Stock.

6c. Clara Bow, Publicity Still.

Source 6d: Museum of Modern Art Film Archive.

6d. Bow in *Mantrap* (1926).

∽ QUESTIONS TO CONSIDER ∽

The first part of the evidence (Sources 1 and 2) consists of excerpts from two best sellers: the enormously popular novel *The Sheik* (1921), which went into fifty printings in the first year of its publication and was later made into an equally popular film starring Rudolph Valentino, and *The Plastic Age* (1924), a novel that became a fad on college campuses across the country. Although both of these sources are fiction, historians often analyze the images portrayed in popular novels and stories for clues to understanding the everyday culture of a society. How are the "new" women in these novels portrayed? What do people think about them? How do they feel about themselves? What happens to them? Are any moral messages contained in the ways these novels conclude?

The second part of the evidence (Sources 3 through 5) is from two nonfiction books widely discussed by middle-class readers and an article by a "new" woman published in the middle-class magazine *Harper's Monthly*. Because of the social purity laws of the late nineteenth and early twentieth centuries, birth control information and devices were illegal in many states. Through women's clinics, pamphlets, and books, Margaret Sanger struggled to make birth control legal and acceptable. What did she want women to do? Why did she believe that access to birth control was so important for women?

In 1925, sociologists Robert and Helen Lynd, along with three female field researchers, conducted in-depth interviews in a medium-size city they called Middletown (Muncie, Indiana). They were interested in the changes that had occurred since the 1890s, particularly the changes in the way people lived and what they believed. These interviews (Source 4) have become a valuable resource for social historians and were of great interest to people living at the time. What trends did the Lynds identify with respect to working women? What did people think about women who worked outside the home? What were the attitudes of the residents toward premarital sex? Marriage? Divorce? Birth control? Child rearing? How did the citizens react to the new emphasis on sex and sexuality in mass culture?

Dorothy Bromley's article (Source 5) is an attempt to describe the young women whom she called "New Style" feminists. According to Bromley, why didn't young women like to be called feminists? In what ways were they independent? What were their attitudes toward men? Toward marriage and children? What were their goals for themselves?

Finally, consider the contrasting film images of Mary Pickford (Sources 6a and 6b), whose popularity began before World War I and continued into the 1920s, and Clara Bow (Sources 6c and 6d), a new star of the 1920s who was called the "It Girl" because of a film in which she had played a flapper with a lot of sex appeal. What impression did each woman give? What sort of traits did each seem to represent? In what ways did the "ideal" type of young woman as portrayed in films seem to change in the 1920s? How can you explain the continuing popularity of Mary Pickford among audiences of all ages in the 1920s?

Now you are ready to summarize what you have found. From the fiction and nonfiction you have read, as well as the photos of the movie stars you have compared, how would you describe the image of the new woman of the 1920s? What were the realities that affected her? What were the limits of her freedom? And finally, to what degree was the young woman of the 1920s actually new or different from young women of the previous generation?

⟳ EPILOGUE ⟳

For all practical purposes, the stock market crash of 1929 and the deep depression that lasted throughout the 1930s ended the fascination with the new woman and replaced it with sympathy and concern for the "forgotten man." Women who worked, especially married women, were perceived as taking jobs away from unemployed men who desperately needed to support their families. In hard times, people clung to traditional male and female roles: Men should be the breadwinners, and women should stay home and take care of the family. Women's fashions changed just as dramatically. Clothing became more feminine, hemlines dropped, and hair styles were no longer short and boyish.

Yet women, including married women, continued to move into paid employment throughout the 1930s, and with the United States' entry into World War II, millions of women who had never held paying jobs before went to work in factories and shipyards, motivated by patriotism and a desire to aid the war effort. By the 1950s, women workers, having been replaced by returning veterans, were once again being urged to stay at home and fulfill their destinies as wives and mothers. Women's educational achievements and age at marriage dropped, while the white middle-class birthrate nearly doubled. Women were still entering the work force, but in feminized clerical and retail jobs and in professions such as elementary school teaching and nursing. Fashions changed from knee-length tailored suits and dresses and "Rosie the Riveter" slacks to puff-sleeved, tiny-waisted, full-skirted, ankle-length dresses.

The problem of image versus reality, so prominent in the 1920s, was also present in the 1960s. By the mid-1960s, another new woman was emerging. Wearing jeans, T-shirts, jewelry, and long hair, young women were dressing like young men. New feminist organizations were founded, a revised version of the ERA was passed by Congress (but not ratified by the states), and millions of women entered universities, paid jobs, and professions. Older Americans expressed a dislike for unisex clothing, were concerned about the easy birth control available with oral contraceptives, and questioned the morality of young women and the popularity of primitive-sounding music. Films, best-selling novels, nonfiction, and advertising all portrayed images of these newest "new" women, but almost never analyzed the realities of their lives.

CHAPTER 10

DOCUMENTING THE DEPRESSION: THE FSA PHOTOGRAPHERS AND RURAL POVERTY

∽ THE PROBLEM ∽

On a cold, rainy afternoon in the spring of 1936, Dorothea Lange was driving home from a month-long field trip to central California. One of several young photographers hired by the Historical Section of the Farm Security Administration (FSA), Lange had been talking with migrant laborers and taking photographs of the migrants' camps.

After passing a hand-lettered road sign that read PEA PICKERS CAMP, Lange drove on another twenty miles. Then she stopped, turned around, and went back to the migrant camp. The pea crop had frozen, and there was no work for the pickers, but several families were still camped there. She ap-

proached a woman and her daughters, talked with them briefly, asked to take a few pictures, and left ten minutes later. The result was one of the most famous images of the Great Depression, "Migrant Mother" (see Source 8). This photograph and others like it moved Americans deeply and helped to create support for New Deal legislation and programs to aid migrant workers, sharecroppers, tenant farmers, and small-scale farmers.

In this chapter, you will be analyzing some of the documentary photographs from the FSA to determine how and why they were so effective in creating support for New Deal legislation.

∽ BACKGROUND ∾

In 1930, President Herbert Hoover was at first bewildered and then defensive about the rapid downward spiral of the nation's economy. Hoover, like many other Americans, believed in the basic soundness of capitalism, advocated the values of individualism, and maintained that the role of the federal government should be limited. Nevertheless, Hoover was a compassionate man. As private relief sources dried up, he authorized public works projects and some institutional loans, at the same time vetoing other relief bills and trying to convince the nation that prosperity would return soon. The media, especially newspapers and middle-class magazines, followed Hoover's lead.

Americans turned out at the polls in record numbers for the election of 1932—and voted for the Democratic candidate, Franklin D. Roosevelt, in equally record numbers. As unemployment increased dramatically along with bank and business failures, Congress reacted by rapidly passing an assortment of programs collectively known as the New Deal. Calling together a group of experts (mainly professors and lawyers) to form a "brain trust," the newly elected president acted quickly to try to restore the nation's confidence. In his fireside radio chats, as well as in his other speeches, Roosevelt consistently reassured the American public that the country's economic institutions were sound.

Like her husband, first lady Eleanor Roosevelt was tireless in her efforts to mitigate the effects of the depression. With boundless energy, she traveled throughout the country, observing conditions firsthand and reporting back to her husband. One of the few New Dealers deeply committed to civil rights for African Americans, she championed both individuals and the civil rights movement whenever she could. Although she was criticized and ridiculed for her nontraditional behavior as first lady, to millions of Americans, Eleanor Roosevelt was the heart of the New Deal. In fact, during the depression, more than 15 million Americans wrote directly to the president and first lady about their personal troubles and economic difficulties.

In an emergency session early in 1933, Congress began the complicated process of providing immediate relief for the needy and legislation for longer-term recovery and reform. Banking, business, the stock market, unemployed workers, farmers, and young people were targets of this early New Deal legislation.

The New Deal administration soon realized that the problems of farmers were going to be especially difficult to alleviate. To meet the unusual European demand for farm products during World War I, many American farmers had overexpanded. They had mortgaged their farms and borrowed money to buy expensive new farm equipment, but most had not shared in the profits of the so-called prosperous decade of the 1920s.

Unfortunately, the New Deal's Agricultural Adjustment Act (AAA) bene-

CHAPTER 10

DOCUMENTING
THE
DEPRESSION:
THE FSA
PHOTOGRAPHERS
AND RURAL
POVERTY

fited only relatively large, prosperous farmers. Intended to reduce farm production and thus improve the prices farmers received for their goods, the AAA unintentionally encouraged large farmers to accept payment for reducing their crops, use the money to buy machinery, and evict the sharecroppers and tenants who had been farming part of their land. Explaining to Dorothea Lange why his family was traveling to California, one farmer simply said they had been "tractored out." With no land of their own to farm, sharecroppers and tenants packed their few belongings and families into old trucks and cars and took to the road looking for seasonal agricultural work in planting, tending, or picking produce.

In so doing, they joined thousands of other American farm families who lived in the Dust Bowl—the plains and prairie states where unwise agricultural practices and a long drought had combined to create terrifying dust storms that blotted out the sun, blew away the topsoil, and actually buried some farms in dust. These Dust Bowl refugees, along with former tenants and sharecroppers, joined Mexican Americans already working as migrant laborers in California. For those left behind, especially in the poverty-stricken areas of the rural Midwest and South, conditions were almost as terrible as in the migrant camps.

It was to aid these displaced farmers that President Roosevelt created the Resettlement Administration (RA), which two years later became the Farm Security Administration (FSA). The RA was headed by Rexford Tugwell, an economics professor from Columbia University. A former Progressive, Tugwell was an optimist who believed that if the public was educated about social and economic problems, they would support legislation to correct whatever was wrong. To accomplish this task, he hired Roy Stryker, a former graduate student of his, to direct the Historical Section of the agency.

Stryker in turn hired a small group of photographers to travel around the country and take photos illustrating the difficulties faced by small farmers, tenants, and sharecroppers and, to a lesser extent, the FSA projects intended to ameliorate these problems. Hoping to mobilize public opinion in support of FSA-funded projects such as model migrant camps, rural cooperatives, health clinics, and federal relief for the poorest families, Stryker made the photographs widely available to national middle-class magazines and local newspapers. The Historical Section also organized traveling exhibits and encouraged authors to use the photographs in their books.

How did Americans feel when they saw these images? What qualities did the photographs portray? Why were they so effective in creating support for New Deal legislation?

◯ THE METHOD ◯

By the end of the nineteenth century, technological advances had made using cameras and developing photographs easier, but both the equipment and the developing methods were still cumbersome and primitive by today's standards. Nevertheless, people were fascinated by photography, and many talented amateurs, such as E. Alice Austen, spent hours taking pictures of their families, friends, and homes. Indeed, these photographs are an important source of evidence for social historians trying to reconstruct how Americans lived in the past.

Documentary photography, however, has a different purpose: reform. During the Progressive era of the late nineteenth and early twentieth centuries, middle-class Americans increasingly became concerned about the growing number of poor families who depended on the labor of their children to supplement their meager standard of living. First Jacob Riis, the author of *How the Other Half Lives* (1890), and then Lewis Hine, in his work for the National Child Labor Committee, photographed the living and working conditions of young children and documented the ill effects of child labor. These photographs were used to persuade the public to support the abolition of child labor. In states that were unwilling to end child labor completely, the pictures were used to convince people to support the strict regulation of young people's work. Although this effort was successful in some states, it failed on the national level when the U.S. Supreme Court struck down a federal law regulating child labor in 1919 (*Hammer v. Dagenhart*).

Roy Stryker was impressed by the power of such photographs and had used many of Hine's images to illustrate Rexford Tugwell's reform-oriented economics textbook in the 1920s. The dozen or so talented photographers whom Stryker hired to work for the Historical Section of the FSA were relatively young (most were in their twenties or thirties) and came from a variety of backgrounds. Most, like Dorothea Lange, Walker Evans, Jack Delano, Carl Mydans, John Collier, Marion Post (Wolcott), and Theodor Jung, were already either established professionals or serious amateurs. Others took their first professional photographs for the Historical Section: Ben Shahn and Russell Lee had been painters, and Arthur Rothstein and John Vachon were unemployed college students. All the photographers were white, except Gordon Parks, a twenty-nine-year-old African American fashion photographer who joined the Historical Section in 1941. Parks never photographed farmers while at the FSA; instead, he sensitively documented the lives of African Americans and racial discrimination in Washington, D.C.

Although the Progressive photographers such as Lewis Hine often posed their subjects or emphasized their dirt and poverty, the FSA photographers generally did not. Working in the field, they relied on taking vast quantities of photographs and sending them to

CHAPTER 10

DOCUMENTING
THE
DEPRESSION:
THE FSA
PHOTOGRAPHERS
AND RURAL
POVERTY

Stryker, who selected what he wanted for the files. Walker Evans, who worked briefly for the FSA, was an exception, however. When he and James Agee were in Alabama photographing tenant farmers for their book *Let Us Now Praise Famous Men* (1941), Evans rearranged furniture, posed and reposed people, and cleaned up what he thought was clutter. Working with a huge eight-by-ten view camera, Evans considered himself an artist who saw the potential for beauty in the poverty and hard lives of the tenant farmers. According to historian James Curtis, Evans also thought middle-class viewers would react more sympathetically to his vision of the rural poor than to the actual realities of their poverty.

Stryker himself was not a photographer but an able administrator who planned the field trips, developed background reading lists for the photographers, and wrote "shooting scripts" to guide them once they were in the field. "As you are driving through the agricultural areas . . . ," Stryker wrote to Dorothea Lange in California, "would you take a few shots of various types of farm activities such as your picture showing the lettuce workers?" But beyond these kinds of general suggestions, Stryker gave his photographers remarkable freedom while he concentrated on coordinating their activities, promoting the wide use of their photos, and defending the Historical Section against congressional criticism and budget cuts.

When analyzing these pictures, you must remember that documentary photographs are not intended to present a balanced or an unbiased view. Instead, these photographs are intended to appeal to viewers' emotions and motivate viewers to work for and support change. As a student looking at these photographs, you will need to be specific about *what* you feel and then try to determine *why* the photograph makes you feel that way. Finally, try to make some connections between the photographs and the federal programs sponsored by the RA and the FSA.

∽ **THE EVIDENCE** ∽

Sources 1 through 17 from United States Farm Security Administration,
Historical Division, Library of Congress, Washington, D.C.

1. Abandoned Farm Home, Ward County, North Dakota, 1940 (John Vachon).

CHAPTER 10

DOCUMENTING
THE
DEPRESSION:
THE FSA
PHOTOGRAPHERS
AND RURAL
POVERTY

2. "Tractored-Out" Farm, Hall County, Texas, 1938 (Dorothea Lange).

3. Skull, South Dakota Badlands, 1936 (Arthur Rothstein).

4. Farmer and Sons in Dust Storm, Cimarron County, Oklahoma, 1936 (Arthur Rothstein).

5. Family Moving to Krebs, Oklahoma, from Idabel, Oklahoma, 1939 (Dorothea Lange).

CHAPTER 10

DOCUMENTING
THE
DEPRESSION:
THE FSA
PHOTOGRAPHERS
AND RURAL
POVERTY

6. Migrant Family Living in a Shack Built on an Abandoned Truck Bed, Highway 70, Tennessee, 1936 (Carl Mydans).

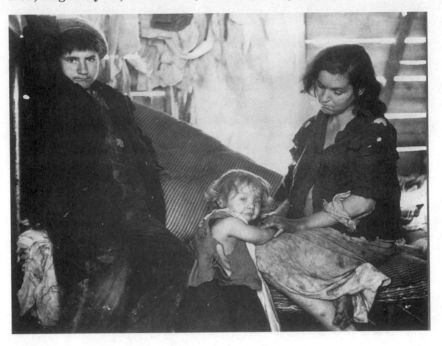

7. Migrants from Oklahoma, Blyth, California, 1936 (Dorothea Lange).

8. Migrant Mother, Nipomo, California, 1936 (Dorothea Lange).

9. Mexican Migrant Worker's Home, Imperial Valley, California, 1937 (Dorothea Lange).

CHAPTER 10

DOCUMENTING
THE
DEPRESSION:
THE FSA
PHOTOGRAPHERS
AND RURAL
POVERTY

10. Living Quarters of Fruit-Packing House Workers, Berrien, Michigan, 1940 (John Vachon).

11. Plantation Owner and Field Hands, Clarksdale, Mississippi, 1936 (Dorothea Lange).

12. Cotton Pickers, Pulaski County, Arkansas, 1935 (Ben Shahn).

13. Owner of the General Store, Bank, and Cotton Gin, Wendell, North Carolina, 1939 (Marion Post Wolcott).

CHAPTER 10

DOCUMENTING
THE
DEPRESSION:
THE FSA
PHOTOGRAPHERS
AND RURAL
POVERTY

14. FSA Client and His Family, Beaufort, South Carolina, 1936 (Carl Mydans).

15. Mule Dealer, Creedmoor, North Carolina, 1940 (Arthur Rothstein).

16. Bud Fields and His Family, Tenant Farmers, Hale County, Alabama, 1936 (Walker Evans).

17. Christmas Dinner, Tenant Farmer's Home, Southeastern Iowa, 1936 (Russell Lee).

CHAPTER 10

DOCUMENTING
THE
DEPRESSION:
THE FSA
PHOTOGRAPHERS
AND RURAL
POVERTY

⬿ QUESTIONS TO CONSIDER ⬾

Sources 1 through 4 are photographs taken to illustrate what had happened to the once-fertile farmlands of the plains and prairies. How would you describe these pictures to someone who could not see them? What had happened to the land? How do these photos make you feel?

Sources 5 through 8 are photographs of farm families who were on the road. They had left or been evicted from the farms where they had lived and were looking for jobs as migrant workers. How would middle-class Americans have felt when they saw these pictures? Which photograph do you think is the most effective? Why?

Sources 9, 10, 12, 14, 16, and 17 show the living and working conditions at migrant camps and for the tenant and sharecropper families who did not leave their homes. What do you notice most when you look at these photographs? How do these pictures make you feel? Why? In contrast, Sources 11, 13, and 15 are of men who were relatively well off during the depression. How are they portrayed? How do you feel about these men? Why?

Finally, think about the photographs as a whole. What messages did they send to the middle-class Americans who saw them in newspapers, magazines, books, or traveling exhibits? What major problems did the photographs portray, and what kinds of programs did the FSA propose to try to aid the poorer farmers? Why do you think these documentary photographs were so effective in creating sympathy and support for aid to these farmers?

⬿ EPILOGUE ⬾

By 1941, the FSA photographs were well known to millions of Americans, and the Historical Section had justified its existence. That year also saw the publication of the classic book *Let Us Now Praise Famous Men: Three Tenant Families,* written by James Agee and illustrated with photos by FSA photographer Walker Evans. After the Japanese attack on Pearl Harbor in December 1941 and the United States' subsequent entry into World War II, the direction of the Historical Section changed. The buildup of defense industries and the effects of the war on everyday Ameri-cans dominated the photographers' assignments. Eventually, the Historical Section was moved to the Office of War Information, and in 1943, after transferring more than 130,000 FSA photographs to the Library of Congress, Roy Stryker resigned from government service.

America's participation in World War II finally brought an end to the Great Depression—and an end to the New Deal as well. Stryker spent the next decade working for Standard Oil of New Jersey, and most of the former FSA photographers did freelance work, taught courses, or found permanent jobs in photojournalism with magazines such as *Life* and *Look*. Ben Shahn went back to his first love, painting, and became a well-known artist. Marion Post (Wolcott) got married and raised a family, returning to photography only when she was in her sixties. The plight of the rural poor was once again forgotten, and middle-class materialism and conformity dominated the cold war years of the 1950s.

Yet a whole new generation was soon to rediscover the work of the FSA photographers. In 1962, Edward Steichen, head of the photography department at the New York Museum of Modern Art and a photographer himself, mounted a major exhibition of the FSA images called "The Bitter Years, 1935–1941." By the end of the 1960s, young Americans also had rediscovered some of the same problems the New Deal photographers had captured in their pictures: rural poverty, racial discrimination, and social injustice. Once again, Americans demanded reform, especially during the presidencies of John F. Kennedy and Lyndon Johnson.

CHAPTER 11

THE BURDENS OF POWER: THE DECISION TO DROP THE ATOMIC BOMB, 1945

∽ THE PROBLEM ∽

At 2:45 A.M. on August 6, 1945, three B-29 bombers took off from an American air base in the Marianas, bound for Japan. Two of the airplanes carried cameras and scientific instruments; the third carried an atomic bomb, a new type of weapon with the destructive power of 20,000 tons of TNT.

In the Japanese city of Hiroshima, residents were so undisturbed by the sight of so few enemy planes that most did not bother to go to air raid shelters. When the bomb exploded 2,000 feet above the city, 80,000 people were killed instantly, and at least that many died soon afterward of radiation poisoning.[1] More than 80 percent of Hi-

roshima's buildings were destroyed, and the flash of light was so intense that shadowlike "silhouettes" of people who disappeared were "photographed" onto the walls of buildings and rubble.

The decision to drop the atomic bomb on Hiroshima ultimately rested with President Harry S Truman, who had been in office only 116 days when

---

1. The actual number of bomb-related deaths in Hiroshima has been the subject of much debate. The U.S. Strategic Bombing Survey estimated the number of people who were killed instantly at 80,000. An August 1946 survey placed the total number killed (instantly and soon after, from radiation poisoning) at more than 122,000. A 1961 Japanese study contended that the true figure was about 166,000. In the late 1970s, a careful estimate by Japanese officials placed the total bomb-related deaths (as of November 1945) at 130,000. The total population of Hiroshima at the time the bomb was dropped was 300,000.

the bomb was dropped and, indeed, had known of its existence only since April 25. The war in Europe ended with the surrender of Nazi Germany in early May of 1945. But Japan was still to be conquered, and there was enormous hostility against the Japanese in the United States. Truman's military advisers told him that an invasion of the Japanese mainland could cost the United States between 500,000 and 1,000,000 casualties. At the same time, however, the situation in Europe was grave, as it was becoming increasingly clear that the wartime alliance between the United States and the Soviet Union was rapidly deteriorating. As for President Truman, he had been suspicious of the Russians since 1941, and the eroding alliance confirmed his worst fears. To what extend might the dropping of the atomic bomb on Hiroshima have been used to threaten the Soviets with American military prowess in the postwar years? Moreover, at the Yalta Conference, Soviet premier Joseph Stalin promised to enter the war against Japan approximately three months after the fall of Germany. To what extent was the atomic bomb used to end the war in the Pacific before the Russians could become involved and thus increase the Soviet Union's power in Asia?

In this chapter, you will be analyzing the evidence to answer four major questions: (1) Why did President Truman decide to drop the atomic bomb on Hiroshima? (2) What principal factors went into that decision? (3) Were there any alternatives to using the atomic bomb? If so, why did President Truman not choose one of the alternatives? (4) Who were the key figures who helped President Truman make up his mind? Why did he heed the words of some advisers but not others?

Even though you will have to go beyond the evidence provided here, you also should be willing to ponder the important question of whether President Truman's decision to use the atomic bomb on Hiroshima was the proper one. To answer that question (a controversial one even today), you will have to combine the evidence with material in the Background section of this chapter and with other reading.

∞ BACKGROUND ∞

In 1918, New Zealand physicist Ernest Rutherford was criticized for his failure to attend a meeting of a British committee of scientists trying to create a defense against German submarines during World War I. Rutherford's excuse for his absence shocked his fellow scientists: "Talk softly, please. I have been engaged in experi- ments which suggest that the atom can be artificially disintegrated. If it is true, it is of far greater importance than a war."

By the 1920s, separate research centers investigating the splitting of the atom had been established at Göttingen (Germany), Cambridge (England), and Copenhagen (Denmark). Physi-

CHAPTER 11

THE BURDENS
OF POWER: THE
DECISION TO
DROP THE
ATOMIC BOMB,
1945

cists and chemists from all over the Western world came to these centers to study and perform research, encouraging each other and sharing their ideas in what was, briefly, a true international community of scientists. Experiments were carried out using comparatively crude equipment as scientists groped in the dark for the essence of matter itself and how that matter could be transformed. Some researchers had used alpha particles[2] to bombard atoms of nitrogen, thereby changing the atoms into oxygen and hydrogen. When others asked the scientists the practical usefulness of their work, most of them simply shrugged; they did not know. Yet they felt that they were on the brink of an important scientific breakthrough in unlocking the riddles of the universe.

In 1932, scientists at Cambridge discovered the neutron,[3] a subatomic particle that could be used to bombard and split atoms. That important discovery speeded up atomic research considerably. Neutrons were used to split atoms in Paris, Cambridge, Rome, Zurich, and Berlin. In 1934, building on those experiments, scientists in Rome created the first chain reaction, in which the split atoms themselves released neutrons, which in turn split other atoms. In late 1938, two German physicists at Berlin's Kaiser Wilhelm Institute used neutrons

to split atoms of uranium. That type of uranium (U-235) was a highly unstable element that, when split by neutrons, created significant amounts of radioactivity.

At this point, politics entered the realm of science. In early 1933, Adolf Hitler came to power in Germany as an avowed nationalist, expansionist, and anti-Semite. Czechoslovakia, occupied by Germany in 1938, was the only place in Europe that held large stocks of high-grade uranium. Although Hitler himself was cool toward atomic research, officers in the German War Department recognized that a chain reaction of uranium could produce an extremely powerful weapon and urged scientists in Berlin to push forward. Interestingly, those scientists purposely slowed down their work, fearing the uses Hitler might make of such an atomic device. Scientists working in Germany who were unsympathetic to or fearful of Hitler fled the country, principally to England and the United States. One such person was Leo Szilard, a Hungarian who recognized that a possible race over the production of atomic weapons might develop between Germany and other nations. At Columbia University in New York, Szilard urged upon his fellow émigrés a self-imposed moratorium on publishing the results of their atomic research in scientific journals. At the same time, in October 1939, Szilard was instrumental in getting world-famous mathematician and scientist Albert Einstein to write a letter to President Roosevelt proposing a speed-up of American atomic research. Roosevelt gave his vague go-

2. Alpha particles are positively charged composite particles consisting of two protons and two neutrons that are indistinguishable from the nucleus of a helium atom.

3. Rutherford predicted the existence of the neutron in 1915. Fittingly, it was his laboratory that proved his theoretical hunch correct.

ahead, although funds were not made available to the scientists, most of whom were centered at Columbia University, until December 6, 1941 (ironically, one day before the Japanese attacked Pearl Harbor).

Once the United States was officially in World War II, President Roosevelt gave his full support to the top-secret project to develop atomic weaponry, a project that in the end cost more than $2 billion (carefully hidden from Congress). In 1942, British and United States scientists merged their efforts to create the Manhattan Project, the code name for the building of an atomic bomb.

To direct the Manhattan Project, Roosevelt chose General Leslie Groves, forty-eight years old in 1942 and a career military officer well-known for his skill in administration. An FBI investigation of Groves showed only that he had an incredible weakness for chocolate (he stored his private supply of chocolate in the same safe that contained some of the world's most vital nuclear secrets). He often called the scientists "my crackpots" but was an able administrator who provided his "crackpots" with everything they desired. Ultimately, the Manhattan Project employed more than 150,000 people (only a dozen or so of whom knew of the whole operation) who worked at the University of Chicago, Oak Ridge (Tennessee), Hanford (Washington), and Los Alamos (New Mexico).[4]

The Manhattan Project was given its urgency by the fear that Hitler would have his hands on the atomic bomb before the Allies. As noted, what the scientists of the West did not know was that German physicists, because they hated Hitler and feared nuclear weaponry, had purposely slowed down their efforts. In 1944, soldiers of American general George Patton's advancing armies captured the papers of one of the German scientists engaged in nuclear research. These papers showed that Germany was at least two years behind the West in the development of atomic weapons.

This fact presented American scientists with a real dilemma. The entire goal of the Manhattan Project was to beat Hitler to the atomic bomb, but now it was clear that nuclear research, purposely retarded by German physicists, was years away from building a successful nuclear device for the Third Reich. As Albert Einstein said, "If I had known that the Germans would not succeed in constructing the atomic bomb, I would never have lifted a finger." Several other scientists agreed with Einstein and hoped that, even if the bomb was developed, it would never be used.

Yet, as seen above, political and military considerations rarely were far

---

4. Columbia University scientists were transferred to the University of Chicago, away from the coast, where they continued their experiments and calculations. Oak Ridge was a city built by the Manhattan Project in an isolated area of eastern Tennessee; there U-235 was extracted from the more passive U-238. Hanford was where plutonium (used in the bomb dropped on Nagasaki) was produced, a new element that Chicago scientists discovered by using neutrons to bombard U-238. Los Alamos was where the bombs were assembled and tested.

CHAPTER 11

THE BURDENS
OF POWER: THE
DECISION TO
DROP THE
ATOMIC BOMB,
1945

from nuclear research. Even with Nazi Germany close to defeat, President Truman, who assumed the presidency upon Roosevelt's death on April 12, 1945, looked upon a world filled with dangers. Japan remained unconquered, and Truman's military advisers predicted a fearful toll if the Japanese mainland was invaded. Relations with the Soviet Union, an ally in the war against Germany, also were deteriorating rapidly. To what extent might Truman have seen the atomic bomb as the military and political solution to both these problems?

It is important to note that what eventually became the cold war between the Soviet Union and the West actually had its origins in World War II itself, long before it was known that the atomic bomb would work. In many ways, the only factor that brought the Soviet Union and the West together as allies was their mutual enemy, Hitler's Germany. Soviet premier Joseph Stalin, whose nation had been invaded twice by Germany in the twentieth century, viewed the West as a constant threat. To Stalin, the Soviet Union had carried the burden of the fight against Hitler since 1941 (until the 1944 Allied landing at Normandy, in France, to create a "second front" against Germany), had suffered staggering casualties, and had seen whole areas of the Soviet Union utterly devastated.[5] To guard against another such invasion, Stalin believed that the Soviet Union must dominate the nations of eastern Europe and not let a strong Germany emerge from World War II. Increasingly suspicious of Great Britain and the United States, Stalin believed that he needed to keep those nations as unaware as possible of his country's economic and military vulnerability, a belief that resulted in a policy of secrecy toward the West.

Many policymakers in Great Britain and the United States were as suspicious of the Soviet Union as Stalin was of them. Britain's prime minister Winston Churchill had distrusted the Russians since the Bolshevik Revolution of 1917, believed that Russian communists had a master plan for world domination, and urged that a hard line be taken against Stalin. On the other hand, President Franklin Roosevelt, although harboring few illusions about the Soviet Union, hoped that by making some concessions he could lessen Stalin's fears and gain the Soviet premier's cooperation in the postwar world and in forming the United Nations. At the Yalta Conference in February 1945, Roosevelt, Churchill, and Stalin agreed that the postwar governments of eastern Europe would be freely elected but pro-Russian. The three powers also agreed on the temporary partition of Germany into three zones of occupation to be governed cooperatively by the three victorious powers, who eventually would merge these zones into

---

5. Russian military deaths are estimated to have exceeded 7 million. In contrast, Germany suffered approximately 3.5 million military deaths, China 2.2 million, Japan 1.3 million, Great Britain and the Commonwealth 500,000, and the United States 350,000. Indeed, when civilian deaths are added to military deaths, the Soviet Union lost a total of 40 percent of all people killed in World War II, or approximately 20 of 50 million.

one reconstructed and reformed German state. The city of Berlin, well within the projected Soviet zone, likewise would be divided into three administrative sectors. In addition, the Soviet Union was given the right to exact heavy reparations from a defeated Germany, which ultimately amounted to the dismantling of German industry within the Russian zone for shipment to the Soviet Union. Stalin agreed to enter the war against Japan three months after the fall of Germany and also promised to conclude a treaty with China's Chiang Kai-shek, the person the United States hoped would lead China after the defeat of Japan. Even amid these joint declarations for unity at Yalta, however, considerable distrust remained.

Roosevelt's death brought Truman to the presidency. Truman's views of the Soviet Union were closer to those of Churchill than to Roosevelt's. Although Truman honored agreements [on reparations, the partitioning of Germany and Berlin, and the return of Russian "traitors" (deserters) to the Soviet government] and ordered the United States Army (which had advanced beyond the line Roosevelt, Churchill, and Stalin had agreed on earlier) to draw back, in other ways he made it clear that his policy toward the Soviet Union would be different from that of Roosevelt. Immediately after the surrender of Germany, Truman cut off aid to the Soviet Union, reasoning that the war in Europe had ended and that further assistance was unnecessary. Stalin was outraged. Furthermore, at the Potsdam Conference, Truman demanded that free elections be held immediately in eastern Europe, a demand that Stalin unhesitatingly rejected. Also at Potsdam, Truman informed Stalin that the United States had developed a new weapon of enormous destructive power, a fact Stalin probably already knew through espionage.

Thus it is evident that even before the end of World War II, the alliance between the Soviet Union and the West had eroded badly. Deep suspicions and distrust on both sides caused leaders of the United States and the Soviet Union to view the other as a dangerous threat to peace and stability. As Truman confronted his first weeks in office and considered whether to use the atomic bomb against Japan, he faced other difficult decisions with regard to the Soviet Union. Should the bomb be used on Japan to save American lives? Could the bomb's secrets be used as a "bargaining chip" with the Soviet Union?

⟨⟩ THE METHOD ⟨⟩

Although personal memoirs are sometimes written several years after a particular event has occurred, historians nevertheless treat them as *primary sources* (evidence that is contemporary to the event being analyzed), principally because the authors of these memoirs were present when the

CHAPTER 11

THE BURDENS
OF POWER: THE
DECISION TO
DROP THE
ATOMIC BOMB,
1945

event was taking place. Indeed, as seen in this chapter, some of those people were more than mere eyewitnesses—some were key figures in the event itself. Therefore, personal memoirs can be invaluable tools for those seeking to understand the past, a particular decision someone made in the past, and the factors that went into the making of that decision.

Yet one always must be cautious when using personal diaries, memoirs, and reminiscences. The historian must keep in mind that each memoir is only one person's view or perspective of the event or decision. Was the author in a good position to see how a particular event unfolded or how a particular decision was made? Was the author aware of all the factors and people involved? Was the author trying to make himself or herself "look good" to future generations (as British prime minister Winston Churchill clearly tried to do in his history of the Second World War)? Generally, the farther away from the event or decision the author was, the less reliable that author's memories are considered to be. Therefore, as you examine each piece of evidence, ask yourself this question: Was the person in a good position to see what she or he is reporting?

The next thing you must look for is the author's *intent* in writing down recollections in the first place. Does the author of the memoir have a bias? If so, what is it? Is the author seeking to justify, defend, attack, or exonerate? Does the author magnify or minimize his or her role in the decision? Why? Be alert for the author's intent, stated or hidden, and possible biases.

Sometimes authors of memoirs either accidentally or purposely omit vital information or distort the facts. Did any of the authors of the memoirs in this chapter do so? How can you tell? Aside from simple forgetfulness or having a poor vantage point, can you think of any other reasons why this might have been done?

As you read each selection carefully, keep a chart like the one below to help you recall the main points. And as you examine each piece of evidence, keep the central questions you are to answer firmly in mind:

1. Why did President Truman decide to drop the atomic bomb on Hiroshima?
2. What principal factors went into that decision?

Author	Position	What Author Should Be Expected to Know	Biases?	Agreement or Disagreement with Other Memoirs (Omissions?)

3. Were there any alternatives to using the atomic bomb? If so, why didn't President Truman choose one of them?
4. Who were the key figures who helped Truman with his decision? Why did he heed the words of some advisers but not those of others?
5. Do you think the decision President Truman made to drop the atomic bomb on Hiroshima was the proper one?

Keep in mind that alternatives to dropping an atomic bomb on Japan were open to President Truman. Those alternatives included urging Japan to surrender and offering a guarantee that the emperor would retain his throne; an American invasion of the Japanese mainland; the continued (or increased) use of conventional bombs; a joint United States–Soviet Union assault on Japan; and inviting Japanese government and military leaders to witness a test demonstration of an atomic bomb in the hope that it would convince Japan to surrender. As you examine the evidence, you might well get a clearer picture of why Truman ultimately made the decision he did if you keep in mind the alternatives open to him. As you will see in the evidence, many of these alternatives were advocated by others.

∞ THE EVIDENCE ∞

Source 1 from Harry S Truman, *Memoirs: Year of Decisions* (Garden City, N.Y.: Doubleday and Company, 1955), pp. 10–11, 416–423.

1. Harry S Truman (President of the United States, April 12, 1945–January 1953).[6]

My own knowledge of these developments had come about only after I became President, when Secretary Stimson had given me the full story. He had told me at that time that the project was nearing completion and that a bomb could be expected within another four months. It was at his suggestion, too, that I had then set up a committee of top men and had

6. We have rearranged Truman's recollections to put events closer to chronological order.

CHAPTER 11

THE BURDENS
OF POWER: THE
DECISION TO
DROP THE
ATOMIC BOMB,
1945

asked them to study with great care the implications the new weapon might have for us. . . .[7]

[*Here Truman identifies the eight-man Interim Committee, chaired by Secretary of War Stimson and composed of leading figures in government, business, and education. Truman then names the three scientists from the Manhattan Project who would consult with the committee and reports that the Interim Committee's recommendations were brought to him by Stimson on June 1, 1945.*]

It was their recommendation that the bomb be used against the enemy as soon as it could be done. They recommended further that it should be used without specific warning and against a target that would clearly show its devastating strength. I had realized, of course, that an atomic bomb explosion would inflict damage and casualties beyond imagination. On the other hand, the scientific advisers of the committee reported, "We can propose no technical demonstration likely to bring an end to the war; we see no acceptable alternative to direct military use." It was their conclusion that no technical demonstration they might propose, such as over a deserted island, would be likely to bring the war to an end. It had to be used against an enemy target.

The final decision of where and when to use the atomic bomb was up to me. Let there be no mistake about it. I regarded the bomb as a military weapon and never had any doubt that it should be used. The top military advisers to the President recommended its use, and when I talked to Churchill he unhesitatingly told me that he favored the use of the atomic bomb if it might aid to end the war.

In deciding to use this bomb I wanted to make sure that it would be used as a weapon of war in the manner prescribed by the laws of war. That meant that I wanted it dropped on a military target. I had told Stimson that the bomb should be dropped as nearly as possible upon a war production center of prime military importance. . . .

[*Here Truman describes how the four potential targets of Hiroshima, Kokura, Niigata, and Nagasaki were chosen by Truman, Stimson, and the president's military advisers. The Strategic Air Forces were given the latitude to choose from among those four cities the one where the first atomic bomb would be dropped, with weather as the primary consideration.*]

A month before the test explosion of the atomic bomb the service Secretaries and the Joint Chiefs of Staff had laid their detailed plans for the

7. This was the Interim Committee, referred to below and in other memoirs.

defeat of Japan before me for approval. There had apparently been some differences of opinion as to the best route to be followed, but these had evidently been reconciled, for when General Marshall had presented his plan for a two-phase invasion of Japan, Admiral King[8] and General Arnold had supported the proposal heartily.

The Army plan envisaged an amphibious landing in the fall of 1945 on the island of Kyushu, the southernmost of the Japanese home islands. This would be accomplished by our Sixth Army, under the command of General Walter Krueger. The first landing would then be followed approximately four months later by a second great invasion, which would be carried out by our Eighth and Tenth Armies, followed by the First Army transferred from Europe, all of which would go ashore in the Kanto plains area near Tokyo. In all, it had been estimated that it would require until the late fall of 1946 to bring Japan to her knees.

This was a formidable conception, and all of us realized fully that the fighting would be fierce and the losses heavy. But it was hoped that some of Japan's forces would continue to be preoccupied in China and others would be prevented from reinforcing the home islands if Russia were to enter the war.

There was, of course, always the possibility that the Japanese might choose to surrender sooner. Our air and fleet units had begun to inflict heavy damage on industrial and urban sites in Japan proper. Except in China, the armies of the Mikado had been pushed back everywhere in relentless successions of defeats.

Acting Secretary of State Grew had spoken to me in Late May[9] about issuing a proclamation that would urge the Japanese to surrender but would assure them that we would permit the Emperor to remain as head of the state. Grew backed this with arguments taken from his ten years' experience as our Ambassador in Japan, and I told him that I had already given thought to this matter myself and that it seemed to me a sound idea. Grew had a draft of a proclamation with him, and I instructed him to send it by the customary channels to the Joint Chiefs and the State-War-Navy Coordinating Committee in order that we might get the opinions of all concerned before I made my decision.

On June 18 Grew reported that the proposal had met with the approval of his Cabinet colleagues and of the Joint Chiefs. The military leaders also

8. Admiral Ernest J. King (1878–1956) was chief of naval operations. He favored using the bomb on Hiroshima.
9. This was the important May 28 meeting. See Joseph C. Grew, *Turbulent Era: A Diplomatic Record of Forty Years, 1904–1945,* ed. Walter Johnson (Boston: Houghton Mifflin Company, 1952), Vol. II, pp. 1421–1428.

CHAPTER 11

THE BURDENS
OF POWER: THE
DECISION TO
DROP THE
ATOMIC BOMB,
1945

discussed the subject with me when they reported the same day. Grew, however, favored issuing the proclamation at once, to coincide with the closing of the campaign on Okinawa, while the service chiefs were of the opinion that we should wait until we were ready to follow a Japanese refusal with the actual assault of our invasion forces.

It was my decision then that the proclamation to Japan should be issued from the forthcoming conference at Potsdam. This, I believed, would clearly demonstrate to Japan and to the world that the Allies were united in their purpose. By that time, also, we might know more about two matters of significance for our future effort: the participation of the Soviet Union and the atomic bomb. We knew that the bomb would receive its first test in mid-July. If the test of the bomb was successful, I wanted to afford Japan a clear chance to end the fighting before we made use of this newly gained power. If the test should fail, then it would be even more important to us to bring about a surrender before we had to make a physical conquest of Japan. General Marshall told me that it might cost half a million American lives to force the enemy's surrender of his home grounds. . . .

At Potsdam, as elsewhere, the secret of the atomic bomb was kept closely guarded. We did not extend the very small circle of Americans who knew about it. Churchill naturally knew about the atomic bomb project from its very beginning, because it had involved the pooling of British and American technical skill.

On July 24 I casually mentioned to Stalin that we had a new weapon of unusual destructive force. The Russian Premier showed no special interest. All he said was that he was glad to hear it and hoped we would make "good use of it against the Japanese.". . .

On July 28 Radio Tokyo announced that the Japanese government would continue to fight. There was no formal reply to the joint ultimatum of the United States, the United Kingdom, and China. There was no alternative now. The bomb was scheduled to be dropped after August 3 unless Japan surrendered before that day.

On August 6, the fourth day of the journey home from Potsdam, came the historic news that shook the world. I was eating lunch with members of the *Augusta*'s crew when Captain Frank Graham, White House Map Room watch officer, handed me the following message:

TO THE PRESIDENT
FROM THE SECRETARY OF WAR
Big bomb dropped on Hiroshima August 5 at 7:15 P.M. Washington time. First reports indicate complete success which was even more conspicuous than earlier test.

I was greatly moved. I telephoned Byrnes aboard ship to give him the news and then said to the group of sailors around me, "This is the greatest thing in history. It's time for us to get home.". . .

Source 2 from Henry L. Stimson and McGeorge Bundy, *On Active Service in Peace and War* (New York: Harper and Brothers, 1948), pp. 613–633.

2. Henry L. Stimson (Secretary of War, 1941–1945).[10]

The policy adopted and steadily pursued by President Roosevelt and his advisers was a simple one. It was to spare no effort in securing the earliest possible successful development of an atomic weapon. The reasons for this policy were equally simple. The original experimental achievement of atomic fission had occurred in Germany in 1938, and it was known that the Germans had continued their experiments. In 1941 and 1942 they were believed to be ahead of us, and it was vital that they should not be the first to bring atomic weapons into the field of battle. Furthermore, if we should be the first to develop the weapon, we should have a great new instrument for shortening the war and minimizing destruction. At no time, from 1941 to 1945, did I ever hear it suggested by the President, or by any other responsible member of the government, that atomic energy should not be used in the war. All of us of course understood the terrible responsibility involved in our attempt to unlock the doors to such a devastating weapon; President Roosevelt particularly spoke to me many times of his own awareness of the catastrophic potentialities of our work. But we were at war, and the work must be done. I therefore emphasize that it was our common objective, throughout the war, to be the first to produce an atomic weapon and use it. The possible atomic weapon was considered to be a new and tremendously powerful explosive, as legitimate as any other of the deadly explosive weapons of modern war. The entire purpose was the production of a military weapon; on no other ground could the wartime expenditure of so much time and money have been justified. The exact circumstances in which that weapon might be used were unknown to any of us until the middle of 1945, and when that time came, as we shall presently see, the military use of atomic energy was connected with larger questions of national policy. . . .

10. Parts of this chapter appeared earlier as "The Decision to Use the Atomic Bomb" in the February 1947 issue of *Harper's* magazine.

CHAPTER 11

THE BURDENS
OF POWER: THE
DECISION TO
DROP THE
ATOMIC BOMB,
1945

As time went on it became clear that the weapon would not be available in time for use in the European theater, and the war against Germany was successfully ended by the use of what are now called conventional means. But in the spring of 1945 it became evident that the climax of our prolonged atomic effort was at hand. By the nature of atomic chain reactions, it was impossible to state with certainty that we had succeeded until a bomb had actually exploded in a full-scale experiment; nevertheless it was considered exceedingly probable that we should by midsummer have successfully detonated the first atomic bomb. This was to be done at the Alamogordo Reservation in New Mexico. It was thus time for detailed consideration of our future plans. What had begun as a well-founded hope was now developing into a reality.

On March 15, 1945 I had my last talk with President Roosevelt. . . .

I did not see Franklin Roosevelt again. The next time I went to the White House to discuss atomic energy was April 25, 1945, and I went to explain the nature of the problem to a man whose only previous knowledge of our activities was that of a Senator who had loyally accepted our assurance that the matter must be kept a secret from him. Now he was President and Commander-in-Chief, and the final responsibility in this as in so many other matters must be his. President Truman accepted this responsibility with the same fine spirit that Senator Truman had shown before in accepting our refusal to inform him. . . .

[*Here Stimson summarizes his report to Truman and reproduces a nine-point memorandum on postwar atomic policy, the high points of which were Stimson's belief that atomic bomb secrets should not be shared with any other nation and his corresponding fear that eventual nuclear proliferation constituted a serious threat to civilization. Stimson then summarizes the work and recommendations of the Interim Committee, which agree with Truman's recollections on page 207.*]

In reaching these conclusions the Interim Committee carefully considered such alternatives as a detailed advance warning or a demonstration in some uninhabited area. Both of these suggestions were discarded as impractical. They were not regarded as likely to be effective in compelling a surrender of Japan, and both of them involved serious risks. Even the New Mexico test would not give final proof that any given bomb was certain to explode when dropped from an airplane. Quite apart from the generally unfamiliar nature of atomic explosives, there was the whole problem of exploding a bomb at a predetermined height in the air by a complicated mechanism which could not be tested in the static test of New Mexico. Nothing would have been more damaging to our effort to obtain surrender than a warning or a demonstration followed by a dud—and this was a real possibility. Furthermore, we had no bombs to waste. It was vital that a sufficient effect be quickly obtained with the few we had. . . .

The principal political, social, and military objective of the United States in the summer of 1945 was the prompt and complete surrender of Japan. Only the complete destruction of her military power could open the way to lasting peace.

Japan, in July, 1945, had been seriously weakened by our increasingly violent attacks. It was known to us that she had gone so far as to make tentative proposals to the Soviet Government, hoping to use the Russians as mediators in a negotiated peace. These vague proposals contemplated the retention by Japan of important conquered areas and were therefore not considered seriously. There was as yet no indication of any weakening in the Japanese determination to fight rather than accept unconditional surrender. If she should persist in her fight to the end, she had still a great military force. . . .

[*Here Stimson summarizes the military strength of the Japanese, which was believed to include an armed force of 5 million men and 5,000 suicide aircraft. Stimson then recalls that his military advisers estimated that an assault on the Japanese mainland would result in more than 1 million casualties to American forces alone. With those considerations in mind, Stimson wrote a memorandum to President Truman on July 2 reporting that Japan might be close to surrender and that a properly worded call to Japan to lay down its arms (and including an American promise that Emperor Hirohito could remain on his throne) might avoid the inevitably bloody combat on the Japanese mainland. The atomic bomb, untested as of July 2, was not mentioned in the memorandum for security reasons.*]

The adoption of the policy outlined in the memorandum of July 2 was a decision of high politics; once it was accepted by the President, the position of the atomic bomb in our planning became quite clear. I find that I stated in my diary, as early as June 19, that "the last chance warning . . . must be given before an actual landing of the ground forces in Japan, and fortunately the plans provide for enough time to bring in the sanctions to our warning in the shape of heavy ordinary bombing attack and an attack of S-1." S-1 was a code name for the atomic bomb.

There was much discussion in Washington about the timing of the warning to Japan. The controlling factor in the end was the date already set for the Potsdam meeting of the Big Three. It was President Truman's decision that such a warning should be solemnly issued by the U.S. and the U.K. from this meeting, with the concurrence of the head of the Chinese Government, so that it would be plain that *all* of Japan's principal enemies were in entire unity. This was done, in the Potsdam Ultimatum of July 26,

CHAPTER 11

THE BURDENS
OF POWER: THE
DECISION TO
DROP THE
ATOMIC BOMB,
1945

which very closely followed the above memorandum of July 2, with the exception that it made no mention of the Japanese Emperor.[11]

On July 28 the Premier of Japan, Suzuki, rejected the Potsdam ultimatum by announcing that it was "unworthy of public notice." In the face of this rejection we could only proceed to demonstrate that the ultimatum had meant exactly what it said when it stated that if the Japanese continued the war, "the full application of our military power, backed by our resolve, will mean the inevitable and complete destruction of the Japanese armed forces and just as inevitably the utter devastation of the Japanese homeland.". . .

As I read over what I have written, I am aware that much of it, in this year of peace, may have a harsh and unfeeling sound. It would perhaps be possible to say the same things and say them more gently. But I do not think it would be wise. As I look back over the five years of my service as Secretary of War, I see too many stern and heartrending decisions to be willing to pretend that war is anything else than what it is. The face of war is the face of death; death is an inevitable part of every order that a wartime leader gives. The decision to use the atomic bomb was a decision that brought death to over a hundred thousand Japanese. No explanation can change that fact and I do not wish to gloss it over. But this deliberate, premeditated destruction was our least abhorrent choice. The destruction of Hiroshima and Nagasaki put an end to the Japanese war. It stopped the fire raids, and the strangling blockade; it ended the ghastly specter of a clash of great land armies. . . .

Source 3 from Dwight D. Eisenhower, *The White House Years: Mandate for Change, 1953–1956* (Garden City, N.Y.: Doubleday and Company, 1963), pp. 312–313.

3. General Dwight D. Eisenhower (Supreme Commander, Allied Military Forces in Europe).

. . . The incident took place in 1945 when Secretary of War Stimson, visiting my headquarters in Germany, informed me that our government was preparing to drop an atomic bomb on Japan. I was one of those who felt that there were a number of cogent reasons to question the wisdom of such an act. I was not, of course, called upon, officially, for any advice or

11. Keep this point in mind, for it will be very important later.

counsel concerning the matter, because the European theater, of which I was the commanding general, was not involved, the forces of Hitler having already been defeated. But the Secretary, upon giving me the news of the successful bomb test in New Mexico, and of the plan for using it, asked for my reaction, apparently expecting a vigorous assent.

During his recitation of the relevant facts, I had been conscious of a feeling of depression and so I voiced to him my grave misgivings, first on the basis of my belief that Japan was already defeated and that dropping the bomb was completely unnecessary, and secondly because I thought that our country should avoid shocking world opinion by the use of a weapon whose employment was, I thought, no longer mandatory as a measure to save American lives. It was my belief that Japan was, at that very moment, seeking some way to surrender with a minimum loss of "face." The Secretary was deeply perturbed by my attitude, almost angrily refuting the reasons I gave for my quick conclusions. . . .

Source 4 from William D. Leahy, *I Was There* (New York: Whittlesey House, 1950), pp. 440–442.

4. Admiral William D. Leahy (Chief of Staff to Presidents Roosevelt and Truman).

In the spring of 1945 President Truman directed Mr. Byrnes to make a special study of the status and prospects of the new atomic explosive on which two billion dollars already had been spent. Byrnes came to my home on the evening of June 4 to discuss his findings. He was more favorably impressed than I had been up to that time with the prospects of success in the final development and use of this new weapon.

Once it had been tested, President Truman faced the decision as to whether to use it. He did not like the idea, but was persuaded that it would shorten the war against Japan and save American lives. It is my opinion that the use of this barbarous weapon at Hiroshima and Nagasaki was of no material assistance in our war against Japan. The Japanese were already defeated and ready to surrender because of the effective sea blockade and the successful bombing with conventional weapons.

It was my reaction that the scientists and others wanted to make this test because of the vast sums that had been spent on the project. Truman knew that, and so did the other people involved. However, the Chief Executive made a decision to use the bomb on two cities in Japan. We had only

CHAPTER 11

THE BURDENS
OF POWER: THE
DECISION TO
DROP THE
ATOMIC BOMB,
1945

produced two bombs at that time. We did not know which cities would be the targets, but the President specified that the bombs should be used against military facilities. . . .

One of the professors associated with the Manhattan Project told me that he had hoped the bomb wouldn't work. I wish that he had been right. . . .

Source 5 from Joseph C. Grew, *Turbulent Era: A Diplomatic Record of Forty Years, 1904–1945,* ed. Walter Johnson (Boston: Houghton Mifflin Company, 1952), Vol. II, pp. 1421–1428.

5. Joseph C. Grew (Former Ambassador to Japan and in 1945 Under Secretary of State and Briefly Acting Secretary of State).

For a long time I had held the belief, based on my intimate experience with Japanese thinking and psychology over an extensive period, that the surrender of the Japanese would be highly unlikely, regardless of military defeat, in the absence of a public undertaking by the President that unconditional surrender would not mean the elimination of the present dynasty if the Japanese people desired its retention. I furthermore believed that if such a statement could be formulated and issued shortly after the great devastation of Tokyo by our B-29 attacks on or about May 26, 1945, the hands of the Emperor and his peace-minded advisers would be greatly strengthened in the face of the intransigent militarists and that the process leading to an early surrender might even then be set in motion by such a statement. Soviet Russia had not then entered the war against Japan, and since the United States had carried the major burden of the war in the Pacific, and since the President had already publicly declared that unconditional surrender would mean neither annihilation nor enslavement, I felt that the President would be fully justified in amplifying his previous statement as suggested. My belief in the potential effect of such a statement at that particular juncture was fully shared and supported by those officers in the Department of State who knew Japan and the Japanese well. . . .

In my own talk with the President on May 28, he immediately said that his own thinking ran along the same lines as mine, but he asked me to discuss the proposal with the Secretaries of War and Navy and the Chiefs of Staff and then to report to him the consensus of that group. A conference was therefore called and was held in the office of the Secretary of War in the Pentagon Building on May 29, 1945, and the issue was discussed for an hour. According to my memorandum of that meeting it became clear in the course of the discussion that Mr. Stimson, Mr. Forrestal, and General

Marshall (Admiral King was absent) were all in accord with the principle of the proposal but that for certain military reasons, not then divulged, it was considered inadvisable for the President to make such a statement at that juncture. It later appeared that the fighting on Okinawa was still going on, and it was felt that such a declaration as I proposed would be interpreted by the Japanese as a confession of weakness. The question of timing was the nub of the whole matter, according to the views expressed. I duly reported this to the President, and the proposal for action was, for the time being, dropped.

When Mr. Byrnes became Secretary of State over a month later, I endeavored to interest him in the importance and urgency of a public statement along the lines proposed, but during those few days he was intensely occupied in preparing for the Potsdam Conference, and it was only on the morning of his departure for Potsdam that I was able to hand him a draft on which a declaration might be based. This was the draft I had shown to the President. Mr. Byrnes was already on his way out of his office to drive to the airport, and his last action before leaving was to place our draft in his pocket. Mr. Stimson was then already in Europe and I urged Jack McCloy, Assistant Secretary of War, when he met him over there, to tell Mr. Stimson how strongly I felt about the matter.

Mr. Stimson did take energetic steps at Potsdam to secure the decision by the President and Mr. Churchill to issue the proclamation. In fact, the opinion was expressed to me by one American already in Potsdam, that if it had not been for Mr. Stimson's wholehearted initiative, the Potsdam Conference would have ended without any proclamation to Japan being issued at all. But even Mr. Stimson was unable to have included in the proclamation a categorical undertaking that unconditional surrender would not mean the elimination of the dynasty if the Japanese people desired its retention.

The main point at issue historically is whether, if immediately following the terrific devastation of Tokyo by our B-29s in May, 1945,[12] "the President had made a public categorical statement that surrender would not mean the elimination of the present dynasty if the Japanese people desired its retention, the surrender of Japan could have been hastened.

"That question can probably never be definitively answered but a good deal of evidence is available to shed light on it. From statements made by a number of the moderate former Japanese leaders to responsible Americans after the American occupation, it is quite clear that the civilian advisers to the Emperor were working toward surrender long before the Potsdam

12. The following quotation is taken from a letter from Grew to Stimson, February 12, 1947.

CHAPTER 11

THE BURDENS
OF POWER: THE
DECISION TO
DROP THE
ATOMIC BOMB,
1945

Proclamation, even indeed before my talk with the President on May 28, for they knew then that Japan was a defeated nation. The stumbling block that they had to overcome was the complete dominance of the Japanese Army over the Government, and even when the moderates finally succeeded in getting a decision by the controlling element of the Government to accept the Potsdam terms, efforts were made by the unreconciled elements in the Japanese Army to bring about nullification of that decision. The Emperor needed all the support he could get, and in the light of available evidence I myself and others felt and still feel that if such a categorical statement about the dynasty had been issued in May, 1945, the surrender-minded elements in the Government might well have been afforded by such a statement a valid reason and the necessary strength to come to an early clear-cut decision.

"If surrender could have been brought about in May, 1945, or even in June or July, before the entrance of Soviet Russia into the war and the use of the atomic bomb, the world would have been the gainer.

"The action of Prime Minister Suzuki in rejecting the Potsdam ultimatum by announcing on July 28, 1945, that it was 'unworthy of public notice' was a most unfortunate if not an utterly stupid step.[13] Suzuki, who was severely wounded and very nearly assassinated as a moderate by the military extremists in 1936, I believe from the evidence which has reached me was surrender-minded even before May, 1945, if only it were made clear that surrender would not involve the downfall of the dynasty. That point was clearly *implied* in Article 12 of the Potsdam Proclamation that 'the occupying forces of the Allies shall be withdrawn from Japan as soon as . . . there has been established in accordance with the freely expressed will of the Japanese people a peacefully inclined and responsible government.' This however was not, at least from the Japanese point of view, a categorical undertaking regarding the dynasty, nor did it comply with your [Henry L. Stimson's] suggestion that it would substantially add to the chances of acceptance if the ultimatum should contain a statement that we would not exclude a constitutional monarchy under the present dynasty. Suzuki's reply was typical of oriental methods in retaining his supposed bargaining position until he knew precisely what the Potsdam Proclamation meant in that respect. The Asiatic concern over the loss of assumed bargaining power that might arise from exhibiting what might be interpreted as a sign of weakness is always uppermost in Japanese mental processes. He can seldom be made to realize that the time for compromise has passed if it ever

13. See Truman memoirs, p. 209, and Stimson memoirs, p. 212.

existed. This explains but certainly does not excuse Suzuki's reply, and the result of his reply was to release the atom bomb to fulfill its appointed purpose. Yet I and a good many others will always feel that had the President issued as far back as May, 1945, the recommended categorical statement that the Japanese dynasty would be retained if the Japanese people freely desired its retention, the atom bomb might never have had to be used at all. . . ."

Source 6 from John L. McCloy, *The Challenge to American Foreign Policy* (Cambridge, Mass.: Harvard University Press, 1953), pp. 40–44.

6. John L. McCloy (Assistant Secretary of War, 1941–1945).

[*McCloy was present at the meeting of Truman and his military advisers in late June. As he recalled, the "prospect of an attack on the main Japanese islands, even at that late date, was not too attractive." Nevertheless, the Joint Chiefs of Staff unanimously recommended an amphibious assault on the islands of Kyushu and Honshu, and Truman gave his tentative approval, even though the president had been sobered by the estimates of American casualties.*]

After the President's decision had been made and the conference was breaking up, an official, not theretofore participating,[14] suggested that serious attention should be given to a political attempt to end the war. The meeting fell into a tailspin, but after control was recovered, the idea appealed to several present. It appealed particularly to the President, and to one member of the Joint Chiefs of Staff, who, by the way, was the one member of that body who had no responsibility to a particular service.

It was also at this meeting that the suggestion was first broached that warning be given the Japanese of our possession of the bomb before we dropped it. Although all present were "cleared," the uninhibited mention of the "best-kept secret of the war" caused a sense of shock, even among that select group.

Now this incident indicates that at this time everyone was so intent on winning the war by military means that the introduction of political considerations was almost accidental. It cannot be charged against the military that they did not initially put forward the suggestion of political action. It was not their job to do so. Nor did any one of them oppose the thought of political action, though several of the Chiefs were not too happy about it. Not one of the Chiefs nor the Secretary thought well of a bomb warning,

14. As it turns out, "an official" was McCloy himself. See Forrestal memoirs, p. 223.

CHAPTER 11

THE BURDENS
OF POWER: THE
DECISION TO
DROP THE
ATOMIC BOMB,
1945

an effective argument being that no one could be certain, in spite of the assurances of the scientists, that the "thing would go off." At that time, we had not yet had the benefit of the Alamogordo test.

As a result of the meeting, a rather hastily composed paper was drawn up. It embodied the idea which later formed the basis of the appeal to the Japanese to surrender. That proposal, it will be recalled, was refused brusquely by the Japanese Government. Yet, as we now know, it did provoke considerable discussion and divergence of opinion among the Japanese military leaders and politicians. It is interesting to speculate whether, better prepared, this proposal might not have included statements of the policy which we put into effect in Japan almost immediately after the war ended. Such a proposal might well have induced surrender without the use of the bomb. What effect that might have had on postwar developments is a subject worthy of conjecture.

Although no one from the State Department was present at the conference which has been described, Mr. Joseph Grew for some time had been most energetically urging a political approach to the Japanese, but his thoughts never seemed effectively to have gotten to the White House, at least prior to the June meeting. . . .

Source 7 from James F. Byrnes, *All in One Lifetime* (New York: Harper and Brothers, 1958), pp. 282–287, 290–291, 300–301.

7. James F. Byrnes (Secretary of State, 1945–1947).

[*Byrnes was Truman's personal representative on the Interim Committee, and Truman soon would name him secretary of state. Byrnes's recollections begin with the formation and work of the Interim Committee.*]

As I heard these scientists and industrialists predict the destructive power of the weapon, I was thoroughly frightened. I had sufficient imagination to visualize the danger to our country when some other country possessed such a weapon. Thinking of the country most likely to become unfriendly to us, I asked General Marshall and some of the others at the meeting how long it would take the Soviets to develop such a bomb. The consensus was that they would have the secret in two or three years, but could not actually produce a bomb in less than six or seven years. One or two expressed the opinion that Soviet progress would depend upon whether or not they had taken German scientists and production experts as prisoners of war for the purpose of having them work on such weapons. No one seemed too alarmed at the prospect because it appeared that in seven years we should be far ahead of the Soviets in this field; and, of course, in 1945 we could not believe that after their terrible sacrifices, the Russians would think of making war for many years to come.

A few days after the committee was appointed, President Truman referred to me a letter addressed to President Roosevelt by Dr. Albert Einstein, dated March 25, which was in President Roosevelt's office at the time of his death at Warm Springs. In it Dr. Einstein requested the President to receive Dr. L. Szilard,[15] "who proposes to submit to you certain considerations and recommendations." After citing Dr. Szilard's reputation in the scientific field, Dr. Einstein went on to say that Dr. Szilard was concerned about the lack of adequate contact between the atomic scientists and the Cabinet members who were responsible for determining policy. Dr. Einstein concluded with the hope that the President would give his personal attention to what Dr. Szilard had to say.

President Truman asked me to see Szilard, who came down to Spartanburg, bringing with him Dr. H. C. Urey and another scientist. As the Einstein letter had indicated he would, Szilard complained that he and some of his associates did not know enough about the policy of the government with regard to the use of the bomb. He felt that scientists, including himself, should discuss the matter with the Cabinet, which I did not feel desirable. His general demeanor and his desire to participate in policy making made an unfavorable impression on me, but his associates were neither as aggressive nor apparently as dissatisfied. . . .

[*Here Byrnes recalls that, with the exception of Robert Oppenheimer, Szilard was critical of the scientific consultants to the Interim Committee, presumably because of what Szilard feared was their overenthusiasm to use the bomb. Byrnes reported to General Leslie Groves (director of the Manhattan Project) the visit of Szilard and his colleagues, whereby Groves replied that he already knew of the meeting, because he had had the scientists followed. Byrnes then summarizes the recommendations of the Interim Committee, recalls plans to cover up the test firing of the atomic bomb at Alamogordo, New Mexico, voices his concern about the estimated losses an assault on the Japanese mainland would inflict, and remembers Stimson arguing at Potsdam for an ultimatum to the Japanese before either an assault or the dropping of an atomic bomb.*]

15. Leo Szilard was a physicist working on the Manhattan Project. According to Szilard's reminiscences, Byrnes was especially concerned about the Soviet Union's postwar behavior and believed that a show of America's nuclear power would frighten the Soviets and make them "more manageable" after the war was over. Szilard recalled that he was "flabbergasted" by Byrnes's "rattling the bomb" as a diplomatic weapon. See Leo Szilard, "Reminiscences," in *The Intellectual Migration: Europe and America, 1930–1960,* ed. Donald Fleming and Bernard Bailyn (Cambridge, Mass.: Harvard University Press, 1969), pp. 122–133.

CHAPTER 11

THE BURDENS
OF POWER: THE
DECISION TO
DROP THE
ATOMIC BOMB,
1945

On our arrival[16] we were informed that Stalin, who traveled by train for health reasons, would be delayed for a day. However, the Prime Minister was already in residence; his quarters, about a mile away, he had designated as "10 Downing Street, Potsdam," this address appearing on the dinner menus when he entertained. Stalin's quarters were more remote, located in the vast wooded park surrounding Cecilienhof Palace, where the meetings were to be held. Though we received official invitations to visit his quarters on several occasions, it was obvious that their location was a well-guarded secret to the Conference personnel generally.

We spent a morning with our military advisers, and in the afternoon the President, Admiral Leahy, and I drove into Berlin. Here we saw what remained of the German Chancellery and other relics of the broken regime. But our small party had no monopoly on sightseeing. On our return I heard from Will Clayton and Ed Pauley (our representative on the reparations Committee) that they had seen machinery from a manufacturing plant which had been moved from the U.S. zone of Germany into the Soviets' shortly before our arrival. It was now standing in an open field. They also had heard stories of all kinds of materials and even herds of cattle being taken to Russia. We knew that in our quarters the original bath fixtures had vanished, others having been hurriedly substituted for our use, and there was plain evidence that the Soviets were unilaterally awarding themselves reparations, both in large and small quantities.

About noon the next day, July 17, Stalin called on the President. It was, of course, their first meeting. Molotov accompanied him and from that moment things began to happen. For more than an hour the four of us remained in conference, Chip Bohlen and Pavlov doing the interpreting. After an exchange of greetings, and some remarks on his long and tiresome train journey, Stalin launched into a discussion of Russia's entry into the Japanese war. He reported that the Japanese had already made overtures to him to act as mediator, to which he had given no definite reply since they did not provide for an unconditional surrender. But he left me with the distinct impression that he was not anxious to see an end to the fighting until Soviet entry into the war could help secure the concessions he expected of China. He said he had not yet reached an agreement with the Chinese Premier, T. V. Soong, on certain matters, and that this was necessary before he could declare war. Negotiations had been halted until after the Potsdam meeting, he said, and mentioned, among other unsettled questions, arrangements for the Port of Dairen. The President commented that the United States wanted to be certain that Dairen was maintained as an

16. At the Potsdam Conference, July 1945.

open port, and Stalin said that would be its status, should the Soviets obtain control of it.

Not having been at Yalta on the day the so-called secret agreement was arrived at, and having been out of government service for three months, I could make no statement of my own knowledge, but having heard a few days before that there had been an understanding between President Roosevelt and Stalin that Dairen should be an open port, I supported the President's statement in a general way, saying that our people understood that at Yalta President Roosevelt had taken the same position. Stalin merely repeated that that would be its status under Soviet control. Nevertheless, I was disturbed about what kind of bargain he might coerce China into making, for the very fact that they had not reached agreement made me suspect that Stalin was increasing his demands. The President told Stimson that night that "he had clinched the Open Door in Manchuria." I was encouraged but not quite that confident. However, the President and I felt that, without appearing to encourage Chiang to disregard any pledges made by Roosevelt at Yalta, we should let him know that the United States did not want him to make additional concessions to the Soviets. Then the President received from Chiang a cable stating that China had gone the limit to fulfill the Yalta agreement. I prepared a message which the President approved and on the 23rd sent to Chiang Kai-shek: "I asked that you carry out the Yalta agreements, but I have not asked that you make any concessions in excess of that agreement. If you and Generalissimo Stalin differ as to the correct interpretation of the Yalta agreement, I hope you will arrange for Soong to return to Moscow and continue your efforts to reach complete understanding."

Our purpose was stated in the first sentence. The second sentence was to encourage the Chinese to continue negotiations after the adjournment of the Potsdam Conference. I had some fear that if they did not, Stalin might immediately enter the war, knowing full well that he could take not only what Roosevelt and Churchill, and subsequently Chiang, had agreed to at Yalta, but—with China divided and Chiang seeking Soviet support against Chinese Communists—whatever else he wanted. On the other hand, if Stalin and Chiang were still negotiating, it might delay Soviet entrance and the Japanese might surrender. The President was in accord with that view. . . .

The President and I discussed whether or not we were obligated to inform Stalin that we had succeeded in developing a powerful weapon and shortly would drop a bomb in Japan. Though there was an understanding that the Soviets would enter the war with Japan three months after Germany surrendered, which would make their entrance about the middle of August,

CHAPTER 11

THE BURDENS
OF POWER: THE
DECISION TO
DROP THE
ATOMIC BOMB,
1945

with knowledge of the Japanese peace feeler and the successful bomb test in New Mexico, the President and I hoped that Japan would surrender before then. However, at luncheon we agreed that because it was uncertain, and because the Soviets might soon be our allies in that war, the President should inform Stalin of our intention, but do so in a casual way.

He then informed the British of our plan, in which they concurred. Upon the adjournment of the afternoon session, when we arose from the table, the President, accompanied by our interpreter, Bohlen, walked around to Stalin's chair and said, substantially, "You may be interested to know that we have developed a new and powerful weapon and within a few days intend to use it against Japan." I watched Stalin's expression as this was being interpreted, and was surprised that he smiled blandly and said only a few words. When the President and I reached our car, he said that the Generalissimo had replied only, "That's fine. I hope you make good use of it against the Japanese."

I did not believe Stalin grasped the full import of the President's statement, and thought that on the next day there would be some inquiry about this "new and powerful weapon," but I was mistaken. I thought then and even now believe that Stalin did not appreciate the importance of the information that had been given him; but there are others who believe that in the light of later information about the Soviets' intelligence service in this country, he was already aware of the New Mexico test, and that this accounted for his apparent indifference. . . .

Source 8 from James Forrestal, *The Forrestal Diaries,* ed. Walter Millis and E. S. Duffield (New York: Viking Press, 1951), pp. 55, 70–71, 74–78, 80–81.

8. James Forrestal (Secretary of the Navy).

[*Forrestal recalls a meeting that took place on May 11, 1945, between himself, a few high-ranking naval officers, and United States ambassador to the Soviet Union Averell Harriman, the main topic of which was the threat of the Soviet Union's postwar power in Asia. There was some talk of making a separate peace with Japan before the Soviets entered the Pacific war (as they had promised to do at Yalta). The fear that a weak postwar China would be an invitation to the Russians to "move in quickly" also was expressed.*]

8 March 1947   *Meeting with McCloy*

. . . McCloy recalled the meeting with President Truman at the White House at which the decision was taken to proceed with the invasion of Kyushu. He said this for him illustrated most vividly the necessity for the civilian voice in military decisions even in time of war. He said that what he had to say was pertinent not merely to the question of the invasion of the Japanese mainland but also to the question of whether we needed to get Russia in to help us defeat Japan. At this particular meeting, which occurred in the summer of 1945, before the President went to Potsdam, where, under the pressure of Secretary Byrnes, he states his principal mission would be to get the Russians into the war against the Japs, the President made the rounds of his military advisers and asked them to tell him whether the Japanese mainland invasion was necessary. They all agreed it was. He finally left it that they would proceed with the plannings for the invasion of Kyushu but that they were to raise the question with him again before its execution and he would reserve decision on whether or not the attack should be carried into the Tokyo plan [plain?].

As the meeting broke up, McCloy said he had not been asked but wanted to state his views.[17] (Neither Stimson nor I was at this meeting.) He said that he thought before the final decision to invade Japan was taken or it was decided to use the atomic bomb political measures should be taken; the Japanese should be told of what had happened to Germany, particularly in view of the fact that some of their people who had been in Germany were back in Japan and would be able to report on the destruction and devastation which they had witnessed; that the Japs should be told, furthermore, that we had another and terrifyingly destructive weapon which we would have to use if they did not surrender; that they would be permitted to retain the Emperor and a form of government of their own choosing. He said the military leaders were somewhat annoyed at his interference but that the President welcomed it and at the conclusion of McCloy's observations ordered such a political offensive to be set in motion.

13 July 1945   *Japanese Peace Feeler*

The first real evidence of a Japanese desire to get out of the war came today through intercepted messages from Togo, Foreign Minister, to Sato, Jap Ambassador in Moscow, instructing the latter to see Molotov if possible before his departure for the Big Three meeting [the Potsdam Conference], and if not then, immediately afterward, to lay before him the Emperor's strong desire to secure a termination of the war. This he said arose not only out of the Emperor's interest in the welfare of his own subjects but out of his interest toward mankind in general. He was anxious, he said, to see cessation of bloodshed on both sides. Togo said to convey to the Russians the fact that they wanted to remain at peace with Russia, that the Japanese did not desire permanent annexation of any of the territories they had

17. See McCloy memoirs, p. 218.

CHAPTER 11

THE BURDENS
OF POWER: THE
DECISION TO
DROP THE
ATOMIC BOMB,
1945

conquered in Manchuria. Togo said further that the unconditional surrender terms of the Allies was about the only thing in the way of termination of the war and he said that if this were insisted upon, of course the Japanese would have to continue the fight.

Sato's response . . . was to protest that the proposals were quite unrealistic; looked at objectively it was clear that there was no chance now of dividing Russia from the other Allies.

15 July 1945   *Japanese Peace Feeler*

Messages today on Japanese–Russian conversations. Togo, Foreign Minister, insisted that Sato present to Molotov the request of the Emperor himself. Sato's replies insistently pointed out the lack of reality in Togo's apparent belief that there is a chance of persuading Russia to take independent action on the Eastern war. He stated very bluntly and without any coating how fantastic is the hope that Russia would be impressed by Japanese willingness to give up territory which she had already lost. . . . Throughout Sato's message ran a note of cold and realistic evaluation of Japan's position; and he said that the situation was rapidly passing beyond the point of Japan's and Russia's cooperating in the security of Asia but [that the question was] rather whether there would be any Manchukuo or even Japan itself left as entities. The gist of his final message was that it was clear that Japan was thoroughly and completely defeated and that the only course open was quick and definite action recognizing such fact. . . .

It is significant that these conversations began before there could have been much effect from the thousand-plane raids of the Third Fleet and several days before the naval bombardment of Kamaishi.

24 July 1945   *Japanese Peace Feeler*

. . . Finally, on the first of July, Sato sent a long message outlining what he conceived to be Japan's position, which was in brief that she was now entirely alone and friendless and could look for succor from no one. . . . He strongly advised accepting any terms, including unconditional surrender, on the basis that this was the only way of preserving the entity of the Emperor and the state itself. . . .

The response to his message was that the Cabinet in council had weighed all the considerations which he had raised and that their final judgment and decisions was that the war must be fought with all the vigor and bitterness of which the nation was capable so long as the only alternative was the unconditional surrender.

28 July 1945

. . . Talked with Byrnes [now at Potsdam as American Secretary of State, having succeeded Mr. Stettinius on the conclusion of the San Francisco Conference]. . . . Byrnes said he was most anxious to get the Japanese affair over with before the Russians got in, with particular reference to Dairen and Port Arthur. Once in there, he felt, it would not be easy to get them out. . . .

29 July 1945

. . . On the way back to our headquarters we passed the equipment of an American armored division drawn up alongside the road. It included tanks and light armored vehicles and must have extended for about three miles. Commodore Schade said the Russians were much impressed by it. There came back to my mind the President's remark about Stalin's observation about the Pope: When Churchill suggested that the Pope would still be a substantial influence in Europe, Stalin snorted and said, "How many divisions has the Pope got?" . . .

⚭ QUESTIONS TO CONSIDER ⚭

The selections begin with the memoirs of President Harry S Truman because he ultimately had to make the decision to drop the atomic bomb on Hiroshima. According to Truman, what figures were most influential in his thinking? What alternatives did Truman himself think he had?

Truman's July 26 proclamation calling on the Japanese to surrender is a crucial piece of evidence. According to Truman (based on his conversations with Acting Secretary of State Joseph Grew), what was the nature of the proclamation to be? Did Truman offer any more details about that proclamation? Keep these points in mind because they will be of some importance later. Secretary of War Henry Stimson was one of Truman's key advisers. How did Stimson enhance Truman's memories with regard to the April 25 meeting (where the president received his first full briefing on the bomb)? Did Stimson add important information about the Interim Committee?

Stimson's recollection of the July 26 proclamation to Japan (he called it the Potsdam Ultimatum) adds one vital piece of information Truman does not mention. What is it? How important was this piece of information? How important was its omission by Truman?

The memoirs of Eisenhower and Leahy were included to give you the views of two military men concerning the detonation of the atomic bomb. Both men seem to have been opposed.

CHAPTER 11

THE BURDENS
OF POWER: THE
DECISION TO
DROP THE
ATOMIC BOMB,
1945

Why? According to Eisenhower, what was Stimson's reaction? Why? According to Leahy, who was "pushing" the bomb? Why?

Joseph Grew probably knew Japanese thinking better than anyone in Truman's inner circle, having been ambassador to Japan for several years. According to Grew, what was the situation in Japan in early July 1945? In his view, would Japan have surrendered if the atomic bomb had *not* been dropped? What did Grew think of the July 26 Potsdam Ultimatum (it was, after all, his idea)?

According to John McCloy, how did the Potsdam Ultimatum originate? McCloy calls the document a "rather hastily composed paper." Why? Did McCloy see any alternatives? More important, how influential did McCloy think Grew was in Truman's "inner circle"? Why? In a larger sense, what point was McCloy trying to make?

James Byrnes was Truman's personal observer on the Interim Committee and soon after his secretary of state. What apparently was one of Byrnes's important concerns with regard to dropping the bomb? How influential would you say this view was?

Byrnes's meeting with scientist Leo Szilard and H. C. Urey apparently went badly, a fact corroborated by Szilard's reminiscences. Why? What does this tell you about Byrnes?

According to Byrnes, what were the United States' alternatives in July 1945? Reporting on the Potsdam Conference, how did Byrnes portray Stalin? Furthermore, Byrnes raised a key point with regard to the Soviet Union's entrance into the war against Japan. It had been agreed earlier that the Soviets would reach an agreement with the Chinese *before* entering the war. How did Byrnes view these negotiations? Why did he hope the Soviets and the Chinese would take a long time in reaching an agreement? What does this tell you about Byrnes's thinking? His biases? How does Forrestal's diary help us understand Byrnes's thinking? How did Forrestal clarify the situation in Japan? Did he offer any clues as to how United States officials believed the Soviet Union should be dealt with?

Now return to the central questions. Why did President Truman decide to drop the atomic bomb on Hiroshima? What factors went into his decision? Were there any alternatives to dropping the bomb? If so, why did Truman not pursue them? What advisers were and were not influential with Truman? Finally, do you think Truman's decision was the proper one?

⚭ EPILOGUE ⚭

Two days after the United States dropped the uranium bomb on Hiroshima, the Soviet Union declared war on Japan and invaded Manchuria. Meanwhile, Japanese scientists, realizing the magnitude of what had happened at Hiroshima, begged their government to surrender. Japanese military leaders stubbornly refused. Therefore, the next day (August 9), the United States dropped a second atomic bomb (this one using plutonium instead of uranium) on Nagasaki, with equally devastating results. On August 10, the Japanese emperor asserted himself against the military and agreed to surrender on the terms announced in the Potsdam Ultimatum of July 26. On September 2, the formal surrender took place, and the Second World War came to an end, with a total loss of life of approximately 50 million military personnel and civilians.

The scientists who worked on the Manhattan Project were of two minds concerning Hiroshima and Nagasaki. American physicist Robert Brode probably spoke for the majority when he said, "But if I am to tell the whole truth I must confess that our relief was really greater than our horror," principally because the war at last was over. Yet American electronics specialist William Higinbotham spoke for others when he wrote to his mother, "I am not a bit proud of the job we have done . . . perhaps this is so devastating that man will be forced to be peaceful." As for Robert Oppenheimer, the director of the Los Alamos operation and popularly known as the "father of the bomb," he feared that Hiroshima and Nagasaki were only the beginning and that a nuclear arms race between the United States and the Soviet Union was almost inevitable.

Most other Americans also were of two minds about the bomb. Even as they enthusiastically celebrated the end of the war, at the same time the atomic bomb frightened them and made their collective future insecure. A few years later, when *Time* magazine asked an eight-year-old boy what he wanted to be when he grew up, the boy replied, "Alive!"

Some Americans criticized Truman's decision to drop atomic bombs on Hiroshima and Nagasaki. Several African American newspaper editors were especially critical, claiming that no such horrible device would ever have been dropped on "white" Germans and that Japanese were victims because they were not Caucasians. For example, the *Chicago Defender,* a weekly newspaper with a national circulation primarily to African American readers, reacted angrily to a public opinion poll that reported a 12 to 1 margin in favor of dropping more atomic bombs on Japan: "Would the people . . . have voted 12 to 1 for the use of the bomb against Germany or any other white race?" the newspaper asked. For the most part, however, African Americans were more worried about keeping their newly won jobs once white veterans returned from the war. And, like white Americans, African Americans rejoiced at the war's end, even as they feared the weapon that had ended it.

Oppenheimer was prophetic that the postwar years would witness a nuclear arms race between the United States and the Soviet Union. Both nations had scooped up as many German scientists as they could to supplement their own atomic weapons research.

CHAPTER 11

THE BURDENS
OF POWER: THE
DECISION TO
DROP THE
ATOMIC BOMB,
1945

Moreover, the Soviet Union tried to pierce American atomic secrecy through espionage. Neither side seems to have been fully committed to international control (through the United Nations) of atomic research. The Soviets rejected such a plan in 1946,[18] and in 1947 President Truman issued his "loyalty order," which placed government employees, including nuclear scientists, under rigid scrutiny.

In August 1949, a United States Air Force "flying laboratory" picked up traces of radioactive particles in the atmosphere in East Asia, a clear indication that the Soviet Union had detonated an atomic device. In January 1950, Truman gave orders for the United States to proceed with the development of a hydrogen bomb, nicknamed "Super" by some scientists. That bomb was tested on November 1, 1952. By 1953, however, the Soviet Union had announced that it, too, possessed such a bomb. The nuclear arms race was well under way, given even more urgency by the cold war mentality that gripped both superpowers in the late 1940s and 1950s.[19]

By the 1980s, several other nations possessed atomic devices, thus increasing world tensions. Yet the two superpowers appeared to be acting more responsibly, gradually moving toward arms limitation treaties and agreements providing for the elimination of certain weapons in their nuclear arsenals. In December 1987, President Ronald Reagan and Soviet premier Mikhail Gorbachev signed a historic treaty that eliminated enough medium- and short-range nuclear missiles to have destroyed Hiroshima thirty-two thousand times. Moreover, the successors to these two men, President George Bush and Russian president Boris Yeltsin, acted with equal responsibility in decreasing nuclear arms, even in the face of political opposition (in Bush's case, a negative reaction by conservatives in his own party; in Yeltsin's case opposition from a strong but frustrated military establishment).

In spite of those initiatives, tensions remain. The collapse of the Soviet Union has created the troubling possibility that nuclear scientists from the former superpower might sell their technology, secrets, and services to less responsible nations, thereby heightening the threat of nuclear proliferation. Indeed, the concern that Iraq was close to developing a nuclear device was one of the major factors behind Operation Desert Storm in early 1991.

18. The plan, conceived by the United States, forbade the Soviet Union from developing its own atomic weapon and would have created an international agency to control nuclear raw materials.

19. Robert Oppenheimer had opposed the development of the hydrogen bomb. In late 1953, he was accused of having had "associations" with Communists and of being disloyal. A closed-door hearing (April 12 to May 6, 1954) ended with Oppenheimer's security clearance being removed.

CHAPTER 12

A GENERATION IN WAR AND TURMOIL: THE AGONY OF VIETNAM

∽ THE PROBLEM ∽

When the middle-class readers of *Time* magazine went to their mailboxes in January 1967, they were eager to find out who the widely read newsmagazine had chosen as "Man of the Year." To their surprise, they discovered that the "Inheritors"—the whole generation of young people under twenty-five years of age—had been selected as the major newsmakers of the previous year. *Time*'s publisher justified the selection of an entire generation by noting that, in contrast to the previous "silent generation," young people of the late 1960s were dominating history with their distinctive lifestyles, music, and beliefs about the future of the United States.

Those who wrote to the editor about this issue ranged from a writer who thought the selection was a long-overdue honor to one who called it an "outrageous choice," from a correspondent who described contemporary young people as "one of our best generations" to one who believed the choice of a generation was "eloquent nonsense." Furthermore, many writers were frightened or worried about their children, and some middle-aged correspondents insisted that they themselves belonged to the "put-upon" or "beaten" generation.

There is no doubt that there was a generation gap in the late 1960s, a kind of sharp break between the new generation of young people comprising nearly half the population and their parents. The first segment of the "baby-boom" generation came to adulthood during the mid- to late 1960s,[1] a time marked by the high

1. Although the birthrate began to climb during World War II (from 19.4 births per 1,000 in 1940 to 24.5 in 1945), the term *baby boom* generally is used to describe the increase in the birthrate between 1946 and the early 1960s.

CHAPTER 12

A GENERATION
IN WAR AND
TURMOIL: THE
AGONY OF
VIETNAM

point of the civil rights movement, the rise of a spirit of rebellion on college campuses, and serious divisions in America over the United States' participation in the Vietnam War. For most baby boomers, white and black alike, the war was the issue that concerned them most immediately, for this was the generation that would be called on to fight or to watch friends, spouses, or lovers called to military service.

Your task in this chapter is to identify and interview at least one member of the baby-boom generation (prefer-ably born between 1946 and 1956)[2] about his or her experiences during the Vietnam War era. Then, using your interview, along with those of your classmates and those provided in the Evidence section of this chapter, determine the ways in which the baby-boom generation reacted to the Vietnam War. On what issues did baby boomers agree? On what issues did they disagree? Finally, how can a study of birth cohorts (groups of people of the same generation) help historians to understand a particular era in the past?

⚭ BACKGROUND ⚭

The year 1945 was the beginning of the longest sustained economic boom in American history. Interrupted only a few times by brief recessions, the boom lasted from 1945 to 1973. And although there were still pockets of severe poverty in America's deteriorating inner cities and in some rural areas such as Appalachia, most Americans had good cause to be optimistic about their economic situations.

The pent-up demand of the depression and war years broke like a tidal wave that swept nearly every economic indicator upward. Veterans returning from World War II rapidly made the transition to the civilian work force or used the GI Bill to become better educated and, as a result, secure better jobs than they had held before the war. Between 1950 and 1960, real wages increased by 20 percent, and disposable family income rose by a staggering 49 percent. The number of registered automobiles more than doubled between 1945 and 1955, and the American automobile industry was virtually unchallenged by foreign competition. At the same time, new home construction soared, as 13 million new homes were built in the 1950s alone—85 percent of them in the new and mushrooming suburbs.[3]

New homes were financed by new types of long-term mortgage loans that required only a small down payment (5 to 10 percent) and low monthly payments (averaging $56 per month for a tract house in the suburbs). And these new homes required furniture and appliances, which led to

2. A person born during the late 1950s and early 1960s would technically be considered a baby boomer but would probably have been too young to remember enough to make an interview useful.
3. There were 114,000 housing starts in 1944. In 1950, housing starts had climbed to 1,692,000.

sharp upturns in these industries. Between 1945 and 1950, the amount spent on household furnishings and appliances increased 240 percent, and most of these items were bought "on time" (installments).[4] Perhaps the most coveted appliance was a television set, a product that had been almost nonexistent before the war. In 1950 alone, 7.4 million television sets were sold in the United States, and architects began designing homes with a "family room," a euphemism for a room where television was watched.

This new postwar lifestyle could best be seen in America's burgeoning suburbs. Populated to a large extent by new members of the nation's mushrooming middle class, suburbanites (as they were called) for the most part were better educated, wealthier, and more optimistic than their parents had been. Most men commuted by train, bus, or automobile back to the center city to work, while their wives remained in the suburbs, having children and raising them. It was in these suburbs that a large percentage of baby boomers were born.

Sociologist William H. Whyte called America's postwar suburbs the "new melting pot," a term that referred to the expectation that new middle-class suburbanites should leave their various class and ethnic characteristics behind in the cities they had abandoned and become homogeneous. Men were expected to work their way up

the corporate ladder, tend their carefully manicured lawns, become accomplished barbecue chefs, and serve their suburban communities as Boy Scout leaders or Little League coaches. For their part, women were expected to make favorable impressions on their husband's bosses (to aid their husbands in their climb up the corporate ladder), provide transportation for the children to accepted after-school activities (scouts, athletics, music and dance lessons), and make a happy home for the family's breadwinner. Above all, the goal was to fit in with their suburban neighbors. Thus suburbanites would applaud the 1956 musical *My Fair Lady,* which was based on the premise that working-class flower seller Eliza Doolittle would be accepted by "polite society" as soon as she learned to speak properly.

The desire for homogeneity (or conformity) would have a less beneficial side as well. The cold war and the McCarthy era meant that the demand for homogeneity could be enforced by the threat of job loss and ostracism. In addition, many suburban women had met their husbands in college and hence had had at least some college education.[5] But the expectation that they be primarily wives and mothers often meant that they were discouraged from using their education in other ways. As a result, one survey of suburban women revealed that 11 per-

4. Between 1946 and 1956, short-term consumer credit rose from $8.4 billion to almost $45 billion, most of it to finance automobiles and home furnishings. The boom in credit card purchases ("plastic money") did not occur until the 1960s.

5. One midwestern women's college boasted that "a high proportion of our graduates marry successfully," as if that was the chief reason for women to go to college in the first place. Indeed, in many cases it was. See Elaine Tyler May, *Homeward Bound: American Families in the Cold War Era* (New York: Basic Books, 1988), p. 83.

CHAPTER 12

A GENERATION
IN WAR AND
TURMOIL: THE
AGONY OF
VIETNAM

cent of them felt that they experienced a "great deal of emotional disturbance." At the same time, men were expected to be good corporate citizens and good team players at work. It was rumored that IBM employees began each day by gathering together, facing the home office, and singing the praises of IBM and its executive vice president C. A. Kirk (to the tune of "Carry Me Back to Old Virginny"):

Ever we praise our able leaders,
And our progressive C. A. Kirk is one
  of them,
He is endowed with the will to go for-
  ward,
He'll always work in the cause of IBM.

Finally, homogeneity meant that suburbanites would have to purchase new cars, furniture, television sets, and so on to be like their neighbors (it was called "keeping up with the Joneses"), even though monthly payments already were stretching a family's income pretty thin.

There was an underside to the so-called affluent society. Indeed, many Americans did not share in its benefits at all. As middle-class whites fled to the suburbs, conditions in the cities deteriorated. Increasingly populated by the poor—African Americans, Latin American immigrants, the elderly, and unskilled white immigrants—urban areas struggled to finance essential city services such as police and fire protection. Moreover, poverty and its victims could be found in rural areas, as Michael Harrington pointed out in his classic study *The Other America,* published in 1962. Small farmers, tenants, sharecroppers, and migrant workers not only were poor but often

lacked any access to even basic educational opportunities and health care facilities.

Young people who lacked the money or who were not brought up with the expectation of earning a college degree tended to continue in more traditional life patterns. They completed their education with high school or before, although others attended a local vocationally oriented community college or trade school for a year or two. They often married younger than their college counterparts, sought stable jobs, and aspired to own their own homes. In other words, they rarely rejected the values of their parents' generation.

The baby boomers began leaving the suburbs for college in the early 1960s. Once away from home and in a college environment, many of these students began questioning their parents' values, especially those concerned with materialism, conformity, sexual mores and traditional sex roles, corporate structure and power, and the kind of patriotism that could support the growing conflict in Vietnam. In one sense, they were seeking the same thing that their parents had sought: fulfillment. Yet to the baby boomers, their parents had chased false gods and a false kind of fulfillment. Increasingly alienated by impersonal university policies and by the actions of authority figures such as college administrators, political leaders, and police officers, many students turned to new forms of religion, music, and dress and to the use of drugs to set themselves apart from the older generation. The term *generation gap* could be heard across the American landscape as bewildered, hurt, and angry parents confronted their children, who (in the parents' view) had "gotten everything." Nor could the children seem to communicate to their confused parents how bankrupt they believed their parents' lives and values actually were. In the midst of this generational crisis, the Vietnam War was becoming a major conflict.

The Japanese defeat of Western colonial powers, particularly Britain and France, in the early days of World War II had encouraged nationalist movements[6] in both Africa and Asia. The final surrender of Japan in 1945 left an almost total power vacuum in Southeast Asia. As Britain struggled with postwar economic dislocation and, within India, the independence movement, both the United States and the Soviet Union moved into this vacuum, hoping to influence the course of events in Asia.

Vietnam had long been a part of the French colonial empire in Southeast Asia and was known in the West as French Indochina. At the beginning of World War II, the Japanese had driven the French from the area. Under the leadership of Vietnamese nationalist (and communist) Ho Chi Minh, the Vietnamese had cooperated with American intelligence agents and fought a guerrilla-style war against the Japanese. When the Japanese were finally driven from Vietnam in 1945, Ho Chi Minh declared Vietnam independent.

The Western nations, however, did not recognize this declaration. At the end of World War II, France wanted to reestablish Vietnam as a French colony. But seriously weakened by war, France could not reassert itself in Vietnam without assistance. At this point, the United States, eager to gain France as a postwar ally and member of the North Atlantic Treaty Organization, and viewing European problems as being more immediate than problems in Asia, chose to help the French reenter Vietnam as colonial masters. From 1945 to 1954, the United States gave more than $2 billion in financial aid to France so that it could regain its former colony. U.S. aid was contingent upon the eventual development of self-government in French Indochina.

Ho Chi Minh and other Vietnamese felt that they had been betrayed. They believed that in return for fighting against the Japanese in World War II, they would earn their independence. Many Vietnamese viewed the reentry of France, with the United States' assistance, as a broken promise. Almost immediately, war broke out between the French and their Westernized Vietnamese allies and the forces of Ho Chi Minh. In the cold war atmosphere of the late 1940s and early 1950s, the United States gave massive aid to the French, who, it was maintained, were fighting against monolithic communism.

The fall of Dien Bien Phu in 1954 spelled the end of French power in Vietnam. The U.S. secretary of state, John Foster Dulles, tried hard to convince Britain and other Western allies of the need for "united action" in Southeast Asia and to avoid any use of American ground troops (as President Truman had authorized earlier in Ko-

6. Those in nationalist movements seek independence for their countries.

CHAPTER 12

A GENERATION
IN WAR AND
TURMOIL: THE
AGONY OF
VIETNAM

rea). The allies were not persuaded, however. Rather than let the area fall to the communists, President Eisenhower and his secretary of state eventually allowed the temporary division of Vietnam into two sections: South Vietnam, ruled by Westernized Vietnamese formerly loyal to the French, and North Vietnam, governed by the communist Ho Chi Minh.

Free and open elections to unify the country were to be held in 1956. However, the elections were never held because American policymakers feared that Ho Chi Minh would easily defeat the unpopular but pro–United States Ngo Dinh Diem, the United States' choice to lead South Vietnam. From 1955 to 1960, the United States supported Diem with more than $1 billion of aid as civil war between the South Vietnamese and the Northern Vietminh (later called the Vietcong) raged across the countryside and in the villages.

President Kennedy did little to improve the situation. Facing his own cold war problems, among them the building of the Berlin Wall and the Bay of Pigs invasion,[7] Kennedy simply poured more money and more "military advisers" (close to seventeen thousand by 1963) into the troubled country. Finally, in the face of tremendous Vietnamese pressure, the United States turned against Diem, and in 1963 South Vietnamese generals, encouraged by the Central Intelligence Agency, overthrew the corrupt and repressive Diem regime. Diem was as-

sassinated in the fall of 1963, shortly before Kennedy's assassination.

Lyndon Johnson, the Texas Democrat who had succeeded Kennedy in 1963 and won election as president in 1964, was an old New Dealer[8] who wished to extend social and economic programs to needy Americans. The "tragedy" of Lyndon Johnson, as the official White House historian, Eric Goldman, saw it, was that the president was increasingly drawn into the Vietnam War. Actually, President Johnson and millions of other Americans still perceived Vietnam as a major test of the United States' willingness to resist the spread of communism.

Under Johnson, the war escalated rapidly. In 1964 the Vietcong controlled almost half of South Vietnam, and Johnson obtained sweeping powers from Congress[9] to conduct the war as he wished. Bombing of North Vietnam and Laos was increased, refugees were moved to "pacification" camps, entire villages believed to be unfriendly were destroyed, chemical defoliants were sprayed on forests to eliminate Vietcong hiding places, and troops increased until by 1968 about 500,000 American men and women were serving in Vietnam.

As the war effort increased, so did the doubts. In the mid-1960s, the chair of the Senate Foreign Relations Committee, J. William Fulbright, raised important questions about whether

7. The Berlin Wall was a barricade created to separate East Berlin (communist) from West Berlin. The Bay of Pigs invasion was a United States–sponsored invasion of Cuba in April 1961 that failed. The American role was widely criticized.

8. Johnson served in Congress during the 1930s and was a strong supporter of New Deal programs.
9. The Tonkin Gulf Resolution gave Johnson the power to "take all necessary measures to repel any armed attack against the forces of the United States and to prevent further aggression."

the Vietnam War was serving our national interest. Several members of the administration and foreign policy experts (including George Kennan, author of the original containment policy) maintained that escalation of the war could not be justified. Television news coverage of the destruction and carnage, along with reports of atrocities such as the My Lai massacre,[10] disillusioned more and more Americans. Yet Johnson continued the bombing, called for more ground troops, and offered peace terms that were completely unacceptable to the North Vietnamese.

Not until the Tet offensive—a coordinated North Vietnamese strike across all of South Vietnam in January 1968, in which the communists captured every provincial capital and even entered Saigon (the capital of South Vietnam)—did President Johnson change his mind. Two months later, Johnson appeared on national television and announced to a surprised nation that he had ordered an end to most of the bombing, asked North Vietnam to start real peace negotiations, and withdrawn his name from the 1968 presidential race. Although we now know that the Tet offensive was a setback for Ho Chi Minh, in the United States it was seen as a major setback for the West, evidence that the optimistic press releases about our imminent victory simply were not true.

As the United States' role in the Vietnam War increased, the government turned increasingly to the conscription of men for military service (the draft). Early in the war, all college men up to age twenty-six could get automatic deferments, which allowed them to remain in school while noncollege men (disproportionately poor and black) were drafted and sent to Vietnam. As the demand for men increased, however, such deferments became somewhat more difficult to obtain. College students had to maintain good grades, graduate student deferments were ended, and draft boards increasingly were unsympathetic to pleas for conscientious objector status.[11] Even so, the vast majority of college students who did not want to go to Vietnam were able to avoid doing so, principally by using one of the countless loopholes in the system (ROTC [Reserve Officers' Training Corps] duty, purposely failing physical examinations, getting family members to pull strings, obtaining conscientious objector status, and so on). Only 12 percent of the college graduates between 1964 and 1973 served in Vietnam (21 percent of high school graduates and an even higher percentage of high school dropouts served).

As the arbitrary and unfair nature of the draft became increasingly evident, President Richard Nixon finally replaced General Lewis Hershey (who had headed the Selective Service System since 1948) and instituted a new system of conscription: a lottery. In this system, draft-age men were assigned numbers and were drafted in order from lowest to highest number until the draft quota was filled. With

---

10. This incident occurred in March 1968, when American soldiers destroyed a Vietnamese village and killed many of the inhabitants, including women and children.

11. Conscientious objectors are those whose religious beliefs are opposed to military service (such as the Society of Friends, or Quakers).

CHAPTER 12

A GENERATION
IN WAR AND
TURMOIL: THE
AGONY OF
VIETNAM

this action, the very real threat of the draft spread to those who had previously felt relatively safe. Already divided, an entire generation had to come face to face with the Vietnam War.

❧ THE METHOD ❧

Historians often wish they could ask specific questions of the participants in a historical event—questions that are not answered in surviving diaries, letters, and other documents. Furthermore, many people, especially the poor, uneducated, and members of minority groups, did not leave written records and thus often are overlooked by historians.

But when historians are dealing with the comparatively recent past, they do have an opportunity to ask questions by using a technique called oral history. Oral history—interviewing famous and not-so-famous people about their lives and the events they observed or participated in—can greatly enrich knowledge of the past. It can help the historian capture the "spirit of an age" as seen through the eyes of average citizens, and it often bridges the gap between impersonal forces (wars, epidemics, depressions) and personal and individual responses to them. Furthermore, oral history allows the unique to emerge from the total picture: the conscientious objector who would not serve in the army, the woman who did not marry and devote herself to raising a family, and so forth.

Oral history is both fascinating and challenging. It seems easy to do, but it is really rather difficult to do well. There is always the danger that the student may "lead" the interview by imposing his or her ideas on the subject. Equally possible is that the student may be led away from the subject by the person being interviewed.

Still other problems sometimes arise: The student may miss the subtleties in what is being said or may assume that an exceptional person is representative of many people. Some older people like to tell only the "smiling side" of their personal history—that is, they prefer to talk about the good things that happen to them, not the bad things. Others actually forget what happened or are influenced by reading or television. Some older people cannot resist sending a message to younger people by recounting how hard it was in the past, how few luxuries they had when they were young, how far they had to walk to school, and so forth. Yet oral history, when used carefully and judiciously along with other sources, is an invaluable tool that helps one re-create a sense of our past.

Recently, much attention has been paid—and rightly so—to protecting the rights and privacy of human subjects. For this reason, the federal government requires that the interviewee consent to the interview and be fully aware of how the interview is to be used. The interviewer must explain the purpose of the interview, and the person being interviewed must sign a release form (for samples, see Sources 1 through 3). Although these requirements are intended to apply mostly to psychologists and sociologists, historians who use oral history are included as well.

When you identify and interview an individual of the baby-boom generation, you will be speaking with a member of a *birth cohort*. A birth cohort comprises those people born within a few years of one another who form a historical generation. Members of a birth cohort experience the same events—wars, depressions, assassinations, as well as personal experiences such as marriage and childbearing—at approximately the same age and often have similar reactions to them. Sociologist Glen Elder showed that a group of people who were relatively deprived as young children during the Great Depression grew up and later made remarkably similar decisions about marriage, children, and jobs. Others have used this kind of analysis to provide insights into British writers of the post–World War I era and to explain why the Nazi party appealed to a great many young Germans.

Yet even within a birth cohort, people may respond quite differently to the same event(s). *Frame of reference* refers to an individual's *personal background,* which may influence that person's beliefs, responses, and actions. For example, interviews conducted with Americans who lived during the Great Depression of the 1930s reveal that men and women often coped differently with unemployment, that blacks and whites differed in their perceptions of how hard the

times were, and that those living in rural areas had remarkably different experiences from city dwellers.

In this chapter, all the interviewees belong to the generation that came of age during the Vietnam War. Thus, as you analyze their frames of reference, age will not give you any clues. However, other factors, such as gender, race, socioeconomic class, family background, values, region, and experiences, may be quite important in determining the interviewees' frames of reference and understanding their responses to the Vietnam War. When a group of people share the same general frame of reference, they are a generational subset who tend to respond similarly to events. In other words, it may be possible to form tentative generalizations from the interviewees about how others with the same general frames of reference thought about and responded to the Vietnam War. To assist you in conducting your own interview of a member of the baby-boom generation (or birth cohort), we have included some instructions for interviewers and a suggested interview plan.

Instructions for Interviewers

1. Establish the date, time, and place of the interview well in advance. You may wish to call and remind the interviewee a few days before your appointment.
2. Clearly state the purpose of the interview *at the beginning*. In other words, explain why the class is doing this project.

CHAPTER 12

A GENERATION
IN WAR AND
TURMOIL: THE
AGONY OF
VIETNAM

3. Prepare for the interview by carefully reading background information about the 1960s and by writing down and arranging the questions you will be asking to guide the interview.

4. It is usually a good idea to keep most of your major questions broad and general so the interviewee will not simply answer with a word or two ("How did you spend your leisure time?"). Specific questions such as, "How much did it cost to go to the movies?" are useful for obtaining more details.

5. Avoid "loaded" questions, such as, "Everyone hated President Lyndon Johnson, didn't they?" Instead, keep your questions neutral: "What did you think about President Lyndon Johnson and his Vietnam strategy?"

6. If any of your questions involve controversial matters, it is better to ask them toward the end of the interview, when the interviewee is more comfortable with you.

7. Always be courteous, and be sure to give the person enough time to think, remember, and answer. Never argue, even if he or she says something with which you strongly disagree. Remember that the purpose of the interview is to find out what *that person* thinks, not what you think.

8. Always take notes, even if you are tape-recording the interview. Notes will help clarify unclear portions of the tape and will be essential if the recorder malfunc-

tions or the tape is accidentally erased.

9. Many who use oral history believe that the release forms should be signed at the beginning of the interview; others insist that this often inhibits the person who is to be interviewed and therefore should not be done until the end of the session. Although students who are using the material only for a class exercise are not always held strictly to the federal requirements, it is still better to obtain a signed release. Without such a release, the tape cannot be heard and used by anyone else (or deposited in an oral history collection), and the information the tape contains cannot be published or made known outside the classroom.

10. Try to write up the results of your interview as soon as possible after completing it. Even in rough form, these notes will help you capture the sense of what was said as well as the actual information that was presented.

A Suggested Interview Plan

Remember that the person you have chosen to interview is a *person*, with feelings, sensitivities, and emotions. If you intend to tape-record the interview, ask permission first. If you believe that a tape recorder will inhibit the person you have selected, leave it at home and rely on your ability to take notes.

The following suggestions may help you get started. People usually remember the personal aspects of their lives more vividly than they remember national or international events. That is a great advantage in this exercise because what you are attempting to find out is how this person lived during the 1960s. Begin by getting the following important data on the interviewee:

1. Name
2. Age in 1968
3. Race, sex
4. Where the person lived in the 1960s and what the area was like then
5. Family background (what the interviewee's parents did for a living; number of brothers and sisters; whether the interviewee considered himself or herself rich, middle class, or poor)
6. Educational background

Then move on to the aspects of the person's life that will flesh out your picture of the 1960s and early 1970s.

1. Was the person in college at any time? What was college life like during the period?
2. If the person was not in college, what did he or she do for a living? Did he or she live at home or away from home?
3. How did the person spend his or her leisure time? If unmarried, did the person go out on dates? What was dating like? Did he or she go to the movies (if so, which ones)? Did he or she watch much television (if so, which shows)?

These questions should give you a fairly good idea of how the person lived during the period. Now move on to connect the interviewee with the Vietnam War.

1. Did the person know anyone who volunteered or was drafted and sent to Vietnam? How did the interviewee feel about that? Did the person lose any relatives or friends in Vietnam? What was his or her reaction to that?
2. (Male) Was the person himself eligible for the draft? Did he volunteer for the service or was he drafted? Was he sent to Vietnam? If so, what were some memorable Vietnam experiences? What did the person's family think of his going to Vietnam? (Female) If you intend to interview a female who went to Vietnam as a nurse, alter the above questions.
3. Was the person a Vietnam War protester? If so, what was that experience like? If not, did the person know any Vietnam War protesters? What did the person think of them?
4. Did the person know anyone who tried to avoid going to Vietnam? What did the person think of that?

Finally, review the national events and people of the Vietnam era and develop some questions to ask your interviewee about these events and people. As you can see, you have guided the interview through three stages, from personal information and background to the interviewee's reactions to a widening sphere of experiences and events.

CHAPTER 12
A GENERATION
IN WAR AND
TURMOIL: THE
AGONY OF
VIETNAM

⌒ THE EVIDENCE ⌒

Sources 1 and 2 from Collum Davis, Kathryn Back, and Kay MacLean, *Oral History: From Tape to Type* (Chicago: American Library Association, 1977), pp. 14, 15.

1. Sample Unconditional Release for an Oral Interview.

<u>Tri-County Historical Society</u>

For and in consideration of the participation by <u>Tri-County Historical Society</u> in any programs involving the dissemination of tape-recorded memories and oral history material for publication, copyright, and other uses, I hereby release all right, title, or interest in and to all of my tape-recorded memoirs to <u>Tri-County Historical Society</u> and declare that they may be used without any restriction whatsoever and may be copyrighted and published by the said <u>Society,</u> which may also assign said copyright and publication rights to serious research scholars.

In addition to the rights and authority given to you under the preceding paragraph, I hereby authorize you to edit, publish, sell and/or license the use of my oral history memoir in any other manner which the <u>Society</u> considers to be desirable and I waive any claim to any payments which may be received as a consequence thereof by the <u>Society.</u>

PLACE   <u>Indianapolis,</u>
            <u>Indiana</u>
DATE   <u>July 14, 1975</u>

<u>Harold S. Johnson</u>
(Interviewee)

<u>Jane Rogers</u>
(for <u>Tri-County Historical Society</u>)

2. Sample Conditional Release for an Oral Interview.

__Tri-County Historical Society__

I hereby release all right, title, or interest in and to all or any part of my tape-recorded memoirs to __Tri-County Historical Society,__ subject to the following stipulations:

That my memoirs are to be *closed* until five years following my death.

PLACE Indianapolis,
Indiana
DATE   July 14, 1975

Harold S. Johnson
(Interviewee)

Jane Rogers
(for   Tri-County Historical Society   )

Source 3 from the University of Tennessee.

3. Form Developed by a Large U.S. History Survey Class at the University of Tennessee, Knoxville, 1984.

This form is to state that I have been interviewed by _____ on
(Interviewer)
_____ on my recollections of the Vietnam War era. I understand that
(date)
this interview will be used in a class project at the University of Tennessee, and that the results will be saved for future historians.

Signature

Date

CHAPTER 12

A GENERATION
IN WAR AND
TURMOIL: THE
AGONY OF
VIETNAM

Sources 4 through 10 are from interviews conducted by the authors. Photographs were supplied by the interviewees.

4. Photograph of John and His Family. Left to Right: John's Father, John, John's Mother, and John's Brother.

John

[*John was born in 1951. His father was a well-to-do and prominent physician, and John grew up in a midwestern town that had a major university. He graduated from high school in 1969 and enrolled in a four-year private college. John dropped out of college in 1971 and returned home to live with his parents. He found work in the community and associated with students at the nearby university.*]

My earliest memory of Vietnam must have been when I was in the seventh grade [1962–1963] and I saw things in print and in *Life* magazine. But I really don't remember much about Vietnam until my senior year in high school [1968–1969].

I came from a repressive private school to college. College was a fun place to hang out, a place where you went after high school. It was just expected of you to go.

At college there was a good deal of apprehension and fear about Vietnam—people were scared of the draft. To keep your college deferments, you had to keep your grades up. But coming from an admittedly well-to-do family, I somehow assumed I didn't have to worry about it too much. I suppose I was outraged to find out that it *could* happen to me.

No, I was outraged that it could happen to *anyone*. I knew who was going to get deferments and who weren't going to get them. And even today my feelings are still ambiguous. On one hand I felt, "You guys were so dumb to get caught in that machine." On the other, and more importantly, it was wrong that *anyone* had to go.

Why? Because Vietnam was a bad war. To me, we were protecting business interests. We were fighting on George III's side, on the wrong side of an anticolonial rebellion. The domino theory didn't impress me at all.[12]

I had decided that I would not go to Vietnam. But I wasn't really worried for myself until Nixon instituted the lottery. I was contemplating going to Canada when my older brother got a CO.[13] I tried the same thing, the old Methodist altar boy gambit, but I was turned down. I was really ticked when I was refused CO status. I thought, "Who are you to tell me who is a pacifist?"

My father was conservative and my mother liberal. Neither one intervened or tried to pressure me. I suppose they thought, "We've done the best we could." By this time I had long hair and a beard. My dad had a hard time.

The antiwar movement was an intellectual awakening of American youth. Young people were concentrated on college campuses, where their maturing intellects had sympathetic sounding boards. Vietnam was part of that awakening. So was drugs. It was part of the protest. You had to be a part of it. Young people were waking up as they got away from home and saw the world around them and were forced to think for themselves.

I remember an argument I had with my father. I told him Ho Chi Minh was a nationalist before he was a Communist, and that this war wasn't really against communism at all. It's true that the Russians were also the bad guys in Vietnam, what with their aid and support of the North Vietnamese, but they had no business there either. When people tried to compare Vietnam to World War II, I just said that no Vietnamese had ever bombed Pearl Harbor.

The draft lottery certainly put me potentially at risk. But I drew a high number, so I knew that it was unlikely that I'd ever be drafted. And yet, I

12. The domino theory, embraced by Presidents Eisenhower, Kennedy, and Johnson, held that if one nation fell to the communists, the result would be a toppling of other nations, like dominoes.
13. CO stands for conscientious objector.

CHAPTER 12

A GENERATION
IN WAR AND
TURMOIL: THE
AGONY OF
VIETNAM

wasn't concerned just for myself. For example, I was aware, at least intellectually, that blacks and poor people were the cannon fodder in Vietnam. But I insisted that *no one,* rich or poor, had to go to fight this war.

Actually I didn't think much about the Vietnamese people themselves. The image was of a kid who could take candy from you one day and hand you a grenade the next. What in hell were we doing in that kind of situation?

Nor did I ever actually know anyone who went to Vietnam. I suppose that, to some extent, I bought the "damn baby napalmers" image. But I never had a confrontation with a veteran of Vietnam. What would I think of him? I don't know. What would he think of me?

Kent State was a real shock to me. I was in college at the time, and I thought, "They were students, just like me." It seemed as if fascism was growing in America.

I was part of the protest movement. After Kent State, we shut down the campus, then marched to a downtown park where we held a rally. In another demonstration, later, I got a good whiff of tear gas. I was dating a girl who collapsed because of the gas. I recall a state policeman coming at us with a club. I yelled at him, telling him what had happened. Suddenly he said, "Here, hold this!" and gave me his club while he helped my date to her feet.

But there were other cops who weren't so nice. I went to the counter-inaugural in Washington in June 1973. You could see the rage on the cops' faces when we were yelling, "One, two, three, four, we don't want your f——ing war!" It was an awakening for me to see that much emotion on the subject coming from the other side. I know that I wasn't very open to other opinions. But the other side *really* was closed.

By '72 their whole machine was falling apart. A guy who gave us a ride to the counter-inaugural was a Vietnam vet. He was going there too, to protest against the war. In fact, he was hiding a friend of his who was AWOL,[14] who simply hid rather than go to Vietnam.

Then Watergate made it all worthwhile—we really had those f——ers scared. I think Watergate showed the rest of the country exactly what kind of "Law and Order" Nixon and his cronies were after!

I have no regrets about what I did. I condemn them all—Kennedy, Johnson, Nixon—for Vietnam. They all had a hand in it. And the war was wrong, in every way imaginable. While I feel some guilt that others went and were killed, and I didn't, in retrospect I feel much guiltier that I wasn't a helluva lot more active. Other than that, I wouldn't change a thing. I can still get angry about it.

14. AWOL is an acronym for "absent without leave."

How will I explain all that to my sons? I have no guilt in terms of "duty towards country." The *real* duty was to fight *against* the whole thing. I'll tell my sons that, and tell them that I did what I did so that no one has to go.

[*John chose not to return to college. He learned a craft, which he practices today. He married a woman who shared his views ("I wouldn't have known anyone on the other side, the way the country was divided"), had two children, and shared the responsibilities of child care. John and his wife are now divorced.*]

5. Photograph of Mike in Vietnam.

CHAPTER 12

A GENERATION
IN WAR AND
TURMOIL: THE
AGONY OF
VIETNAM

Mike

[Mike was born in 1948. His family owned a farm in western Tennessee, and Mike grew up in a rural environment. He graduated from high school in 1966 and enrolled in a community college not far from his home. After two quarters of poor grades, Mike left the community college and joined the United States Marine Corps in April 1967. He served two tours in Vietnam, the first in 1967–1969 and the second in 1970–1971.]

I flunked out of college my first year. I was away from home and found out a lot about wine, women and song but not about much else. In 1967 the old system of the draft was still in effect, so I knew that eventually I'd be rotated up and drafted—it was only a matter of time before they got me.

My father served with Stilwell in Burma and my uncle was career military. I grew up on a diet of John Wayne flics. I thought serving in the military was what was expected of me. The Marines had some good options—you could go in for two years and take your chances on the *possibility* of not going to Vietnam. I chose the two-year option. I thought what we were doing in Vietnam was a noble cause. My mother was against the war and we argued a lot about it. I told her that if the French hadn't helped us in the American Revolution, then we wouldn't have won. I sincerely believed that.

I took my six weeks of basic training at Parris Island [South Carolina]. It was sheer hell—I've never been treated like that in my life. Our bus arrived at Parris Island around midnight, and we were processed and sent to our barracks. We had just gotten to sleep when a drill instructor threw a thirty-two gallon garbage can down the center of the barracks and started overturning the metal bunks. We were all over the floor and he was screaming at us. It was that way for six weeks—no one ever talked to us, they shouted. And all our drill instructors geared our basic training to Vietnam. They were always screaming at us, "You're going to go to Vietnam and you're gonna f—— up and you're gonna die."

Most of the people in basic training with me were draftees. My recruiter apologized to me for having to go through boot camp with draftees. But most of the guys I was with were pretty much like me. Oh, there were a few s—— birds, but not many. We never talked about Vietnam—there was no opportunity.

There were a lot of blacks in the Corps and I went through basic training with some. But I don't remember any racial tension until later. There were only two colors in the Marine Corps: light green and dark green. My parents drove down to Parris Island to watch me graduate from basic training, and they brought a black woman with them. She was from Memphis and was the wife of one of the men who graduated with me.

After basic training I spent thirteen weeks in basic infantry training at Camp Lejeune [North Carolina]. Lejeune is the armpit of the world. And the harassment didn't let up—we were still called "scumbag" and "hairbag" and "whale——." I made PFC [private first class] at Lejeune. I was an 03-11 [infantry rifleman].

From Lejeune [after twenty days' home leave] I went to Camp Pendleton [California] for four-week staging. It was at Pendleton where we adjusted our training at Parris Island and Lejeune to the situation in Vietnam. I got to Vietnam right after Christmas 1967.

It was about this time that I became aware of antiwar protests. But as far as I was concerned they were a small minority of malcontents. They were the *protected,* were deferred or had a daddy on the draft board. I thought, "These people are disloyal—they're selling us down the drain."

We were not prepared to deal with the Vietnamese people at all. The only two things we were told was don't give kids cigarettes and don't pat 'em on the heads. We had no cultural training, knew nothing of the social structure or anything. For instance, we were never told that the Catholic minority controlled Vietnam and they got out of the whole thing—we did their fighting for them, while they stayed out or went to Paris or something. We had a Catholic chaplain who told us that it was our *duty* to go out and kill the Cong,[15] that they stood against Christianity. Then he probably went and drank sherry with the top cats in Vietnam. As for the majority of Vietnamese, they were as different from us as night and day. To be honest, I still hate the Vietnamese SOBs.

The South Vietnamese Army was a mixed bag. There were some good units and some bad ones. Most of them were bad. If we were fighting alongside South Vietnam units, we had orders that if we were overrun by Charley[16] that we should shoot the South Vietnamese first—otherwise we were told they'd turn on us.

I can't tell you when I began to change my mind about the war. Maybe it was a kind of maturation process—you can only see so much death and suffering until you begin to wonder what in hell is going on. You can only live like a nonhuman so long.

I came out of country[17] in January of 1969 and was discharged not too long after that. I came home and found the country split over the war. I thought, "Maybe there *was* something to this antiwar business after all." Maybe these guys protesting in the streets weren't wrong.

15. "Cong" was short for the Vietcong, also known as the VC.
16. "Charley" was a euphemism for the Vietcong.
17. "Country" meant Vietnam.

CHAPTER 12

A GENERATION
IN WAR AND
TURMOIL: THE
AGONY OF
VIETNAM

But when I got back home, I was a stranger to my friends. They didn't want to get close to me. I could feel it. It was strange, like the only friends I had were in the Marine Corps. So I re-upped[18] in the Marines and went back to Vietnam with a helicopter squadron.

Kent State happened when I was back in Vietnam. They covered it in *Stars and Stripes*.[19] I guess that was a big turning point for me. Some of the other Marines said, "Hooray! Maybe we should kill more of them!" That was it for me. Those people at Kent State were killed for exercising the same rights we were fighting for for the Vietnamese. But I was in the minority—most of the Marines I knew approved of the shootings at Kent State.

Meanwhile I was flying helicopters into Cambodia every day. I used pot to keep all that stuff out of my mind. Pot grew wild in Vietnam, as wild as the hair on your ass. The Army units would pick it and send it back. The first time I was in Vietnam nobody I knew was using. The second time there was lots of pot. It had a red tinge, so it was easy to spot.

But I couldn't keep the doubts out of my mind. I guess I was terribly angry. I felt betrayed. I would have voted for Lyndon Johnson—when he said we should be there, I believed him. The man could walk on water as far as I was concerned. I would've voted for Nixon in '68, the only time I ever voted Republican in my life. I believed him when he said we'd come home with honor. So I'd been betrayed twice, and Kent State and all that was rattling around in my head.

I couldn't work it out. I was an E5 [sergeant], but got busted for fighting and then again for telling off an officer. I was really angry.

It was worse when I got home. I came back into the Los Angeles airport and was spit on and called a baby killer and a mother raper. I really felt like I was torn between two worlds. I guess I was. I was smoking pot.

I went back to school. I hung around mostly with veterans. We spoke the same language, and there was no danger of being insulted or ridiculed. We'd been damn good, but nobody knew it. I voted for McGovern in '72—he said we'd get out no matter what. Some of us refused to stand up one time when the national anthem was played.

What should we have done? Either not gotten involved at all or go in with the whole machine. With a different attitude and tactics, we could have *won*. But really we were fighting for just a minority of the Vietnamese, the westernized Catholics who controlled the cities but never owned the back-country. No, I take that back. There was no way in hell we could have won that damned war and won anything worth winning.

18. "Re-upped" means reenlisted.
19. *Stars and Stripes* is a newspaper written and published by the armed forces for service personnel.

I went to Washington for the dedication of the Vietnam Veterans Memorial. We never got much of a welcome home or parades. The dedication was a homecoming for me. It was the first time I got the whole thing out of my system. I cried, and I'm not ashamed. And I wasn't alone.

I looked for the names of my friends. I couldn't look at a name without myself reflected back in it [the wall].

One of the reasons I went back to school was to understand that war and myself. I've read a lot about it and watched a lot of TV devoted to it. I was at Khe Sanh and nobody could tell about that who wasn't there. There were six thousand of us. Walter Cronkite said we were there for seventy-two days. I kept a diary—it was longer than that. I'm still reading and studying Vietnam, trying to figure it all out.

[Mike returned to college, repeated the courses he had failed, and transferred to a four-year institution. By all accounts, he was a fine student. Mike is now employed as a park ranger. He is married, and he and his wife have a child. He is considered a valuable, respected, and popular member of his community. He rarely speaks of his time in the service.]

CHAPTER 12

A GENERATION
IN WAR AND
TURMOIL: THE
AGONY OF
VIETNAM

6. Photograph of MM, Boot Camp Graduation.

MM[20]

[*MM was born in 1947 and grew up in a midsize southern city. He graduated from high school in 1965. A standout in high school football, he could not get an athletic scholarship to college because of low grades. As a result, he joined the United States Army two months after graduating from high school to take advantage of the educational benefits he would get upon his discharge. He began his basic training in early September 1965.*]

I went into the service to be a soldier. I was really gung ho. I did my basic training at Fort Gordon [Georgia], my AIT [advanced infantry training] at

---

20. Since MM's first name also is Mike, his initials are used to avoid confusion.

Ford Ord [California], and Ranger school and Airborne at Fort Benning [Georgia].

All of this was during the civil rights movement. I was told that, being black, I had a war to fight at home, not in Vietnam. That got me uptight, because that wasn't what I wanted to do—I'd done some of that in high school.[21] I had one mission accomplished, and was looking for another.

A lot of guys I went into the service with didn't want to go to Nam—they were afraid. Some went AWOL. One guy jumped off the ship between Honolulu and Nam and drowned. Another guy shot himself, trying to get a stateside wound. He accidentally hit an artery and died. Most of us thought they were cowards.

I arrived in Nam on January 12, 1966. I was three days shy of being eighteen years old. I was young, gung ho, and mean as a snake. I was with the Twenty-fifth Infantry as a machine gunner and rifleman. We went out on search and destroy missions.

I did two tours in Vietnam, at my own request. You could make rank[22] faster in Nam and the money was better. I won two silver stars and three bronze stars. For my first silver star, I knocked out two enemy machine guns that had two of our platoons pinned down. They were drawing heavy casualties. The event is still in my mind. Two of the bronze stars I put in my best friend's body bag. I told him I did it for him.

I had a friend who died in my arms, and I guess I freaked a little bit. I got busted[23] seven times. They [the army] didn't like the way I started taking enemy scalps and wearing them on my pistol belt. I kept remembering my friend.

I didn't notice much racial conflict in Nam. In combat, everybody seemed to be OK. I fought beside this [white] guy for eleven months; we drank out of the same canteen. When I got home, I called this guy's house. His mother said, "We don't allow our son to associate with niggers." In Vietnam, I didn't run into much of that.

The Vietnamese hated us. My first day in Vietnam, Westmoreland[24] told us that underneath every Vietnamese was an American. I thought, "What drug is he on?" But they hated us. When we weren't on the scene, the enemy would punish them for associating with us. They would call out to us, "G.I. Number Ten."[25] They were caught between a rock and a hard place.

21. MM participated in sit-ins to integrate the city's lunch counters and movie theaters.
22. Earn promotions.
23. Demoted.
24. General William Westmoreland, American commander in Vietnam.
25. "Number Ten" meant bad; no good.

CHAPTER 12

A GENERATION
IN WAR AND
TURMOIL: THE
AGONY OF
VIETNAM

We could have won the war several times. The Geneva Convention[26] wouldn't let us, and the enemy had the home court advantage. To win, it would have taken hard soldiering, but we could have done it. America is a weak country because we want to be everybody's friend. We went in there as friends. We gave food and stuff to the Vietnamese and we found it in the hands of the enemy. We just weren't tough enough.

I got out of the Army in 1970. I was thinking about making the Army a career, and was going to re-enlist. But when they wanted me to go back for a third tour in Vietnam, I got out. Hell, everybody told me I was crazy for doing two.

[*MM used his GI Bill benefits to obtain three years of higher education: two years at two four-year colleges and one in a business school. According to him, however, jobs have been "few and far between." He describes himself as "restless" and reports that automobile backfires still frighten him. He has been married and divorced twice.*]

7. Photograph of Eugene (Second from Right) Marching.

26. The Geneva Convention refers to international agreements for the conduct of war and the treatment of prisoners. The agreements began to be drawn up in the 1860s.

Eugene

[Eugene was born in 1948 in a large city on the West Coast. He graduated from high school in June 1967 and was drafted in August. Initially rejected because of a hernia, he had surgery to correct that problem and then enlisted in the Marine Corps.]

It was pretty clear from basic training on, no ifs, ands, or buts, that we were going to Vietnam. The DIs[27] were all Vietnam vets, so we were told what to expect when we got there. They'd tell us what to do and all we had to do was do it.

I got to Vietnam in June of 1968. Over there, the majority of blacks stuck together because they had to. In the field was a different story, but in the rear you really caught it. Blacks would catch hell in the rear—fights and things like that. When we went to the movies with Navy guys, they put us in the worst seats. Sometimes they just wanted to start a fight. My whole time in Vietnam I knew only two black NCOs[28] and none above that.

We were overrun three times. You could tell when we were going to get hit when the Vietnamese in our camp (who cleaned up hooches) disappeared. Usually Charley had informants inside our base, and a lot of info slipped out. They were fully aware of our actions and weapons.

When we were in the rear, we cleaned our equipment, wrote letters home, went to movies, and thought a lot about what we'd do when we got out. I had training in high school as an auto mechanic, and I wanted to start my own business.

You had to watch out for the rookies until they got a feel for what was going on. We told one new L.T.,[29] "Don't polish your brass out here or you'll tip us off for sure." He paid us no mind and Charley knocked out him and our radio man one night.

You could get anything over there you wanted [drugs]. Marijuana grew wild in the bush. Vietnamese kids would come up to you with a plastic sandwich bag of twenty-five [marijuana] cigarettes for five dollars. It was dangerous, but we smoked in the bush as well as out. At the O.P.s,[30] everybody knew when the officer would come around and check. We'd pass the word: "Here comes the Man." That's why a lot of guys who came back were so strung out on drugs. And opium—the mamasans[31] had purple teeth because of it.

27. Drill instructors.
28. Noncommissioned officers; sergeants.
29. Lieutenant.
30. Outposts.
31. Old Vietnamese women.

CHAPTER 12

A GENERATION
IN WAR AND
TURMOIL: THE
AGONY OF
VIETNAM

We could have won the war anytime we wanted to. We could have wiped that place off the map. There was a lot of talk that that's what we should have done. But we didn't because of American companies who had rubber and oil interests in Vietnam, and no telling what else. To them, Vietnam was a money-making thing. We were fighting over there to protect those businesses.

It was frustrating. The Army and Marines were ordered to take Hill 881 and we did, but it was costly. A couple of weeks later we just up and left and gave it back.

When I got out [in January 1970], I was a E5.[32] I couldn't find a job. So I talked to an Air Force recruiter. I got a release from the Marines[33] and joined the Air Force. I rigged parachutes and came out in 1975.

I stayed in L.A.[34] until 1977. Then I became a long-distance truck driver. I was doing pretty good when I got messed up in an accident. My truck jackknifed on ice in Pennsylvania and I hit the concrete barrier.

[*Eugene has not worked regularly since the accident. A lawsuit against the trucking company is pending. He is divorced.*]

32. Sergeant.
33. Eugene had four years of reserve obligation.
34. Los Angeles, California.

8. Photograph of Helen at an Army Hospital in Phu Bai, South Vietnam.

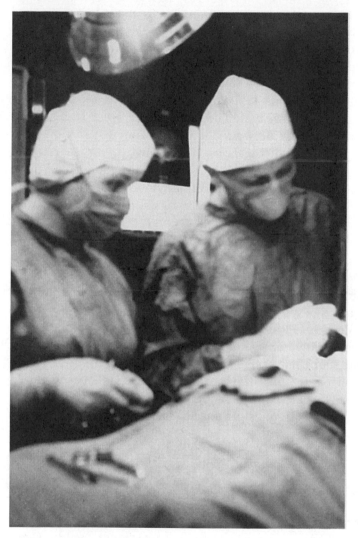

Helen

[*Helen was born in 1942 in Cleveland, Ohio, and grew up there. Since grade school, she had wanted to be a nurse. After graduation from high school, she spent three years in nurses' training to become a registered nurse. She worked for three years in the operating rooms of a major medical facility in Cleveland. In 1966, she joined the United States Navy.*]

[335]

CHAPTER 12

A GENERATION
IN WAR AND
TURMOIL: THE
AGONY OF
VIETNAM

I joined the Navy in 1966 and reported to Newport, Rhode Island, for basic training. Our classes consisted of military protocol, military history, and physical education. There was only a passing reference made to our medical assignments and what was expected of us.

I was assigned to the Great Lakes Naval Hospital [outside Chicago]. Although I had been trained and had experience as an operating room surgical nurse, at first I was assigned to the orthopedic wards. It was there that I got my first exposure to mass casualties [from Vietnam]. Depending on the extent of their injuries, we would see patients at Great Lakes about seven to ten days after them being wounded in Vietnam.

I became attached to some of the boys—they were young, scared and badly injured. I remember a Negro who in tears asked for his leg to be taken off—he couldn't stand the smell of it anymore and had been to surgery once too often for the removal of dead tissue. He was in constant pain.

On the wards, we always kept nightlights on. If someone darkened a ward by accident, it produced a sense of terror in the patients. Many were disoriented, and a lot had nightmares.

When I made the decision to go to Vietnam, I volunteered in 1968 and requested duty aboard a hospital ship. It was necessary to extend my time on active duty in order to go. I felt I had a skill that was needed and it was something I felt I personally had to do. I didn't necessarily agree with our policy on being there, but that wasn't the point.

The median age of our troops in Vietnam was nineteen years old. It was like treating our kid brothers. I would have done as much for my own brothers. I know this sounds idealistic, but that's the way I felt then.

The troops got six weeks of staging, preparing them for duty in Vietnam. Most of the nurses were given no preparation, no orientation as to what to expect when you go into a war zone. No one said, "These are the things you'll see," or "These are the things you'll be expected to do."

I was assigned to the U.S.S. *Sanctuary,* which was stationed outside of Da Nang harbor. The *Sanctuary* was a front-line treatment facility. Casualties were picked up in the field combat areas and then brought by Medevac choppers to the ship. During our heaviest months, we logged over seven hundred patient admissions per month. That was at the height of the Tet offensive in January through March, 1968. I had just gotten to Vietnam.

It was terribly intense. There was nothing to shelter you, no one to hold your hand when mass casualties came in. If you had time to think, you'd have thought, "My God, how am I to get through this?" We dealt with multiple amputations, head injuries, and total body trauma. Sometimes injuries were received from our own people caught in crossfires. When all hell breaks loose at night in the jungle, a nineteen-year-old boy under ambush will fire at anything that moves.

How do you insulate yourself against all this? We relaxed when we could, and we put a lot of stock in friendships (the corpsmen were like our kid brothers). We played pranks and sometimes took the launch ashore to Da Nang. Occasionally we were invited to a party ashore and a helicopter came out for the nurses. The men wanted American women at their parties.

There were some people who had the idea that the only reason women were in the service was to be prostitutes or to get a man. Coming back from Vietnam, I was seated next to a male officer on the plane who said to me, "Boy, I bet you had a great time in Vietnam." I had my seat changed. When I got home and was still in uniform I was once mistaken for a police officer.

On the *Sanctuary,* we had Vietnamese patients too. But our guys were distrustful of them, especially children who had been observed planting mines (probably in exchange for a handful of rice). The Vietnamese were often placed under armed guard. I have friends who were nurses in country who harbor a real hatred for the Vietnamese.

I heard a story of a Vietnamese child running up to a chopper that was evacuating casualties and tossing a grenade into it. Everyone on board was killed in a split second; both crew and casualties, because they paused to help a child they thought needed them. A soldier I knew said, "If they're in the fire zone, they get killed." War really takes you to the lowest level of human dignity. It makes you barbaric.

After Vietnam, I was stationed at the Naval Academy in Annapolis to finish out my duty. There I dealt basically with college students—measles and sports injuries. It was a hard adjustment to make.

In Vietnam, nurses had a great deal of autonomy, and we often had to do things nurses normally aren't allowed to do. You couldn't do those things stateside. Doctors saw it as an encroachment on their areas of practice. I'd been a year under extreme surgical conditions in Vietnam, and then in Annapolis someone would ask me, "Are you sure you know how to start an IV?"[35] It was hard to tame yourself down. Also, in the civilian setting, mediocrity was tolerated. I heard people say, "That's not my job." Nobody would have said that in Vietnam. There, the rules were put aside and everybody did what they could. When we got back to the states, there was no one to wind us down, deprogram us, tell us that Vietnam was an abnormal situation. . . . It was as if no one cared, we were just expected to cope and go on with our lives. . . .

I guess the hardest thing about nursing in Vietnam was the different priorities. Back home, if we got multiple-trauma cases from, say, an auto-

35. Intravenous mechanism.

CHAPTER 12

A GENERATION
IN WAR AND
TURMOIL: THE
AGONY OF
VIETNAM

mobile accident, we always treated the most seriously injured first. In Vietnam, it was often the reverse. I remember working on one soldier who was not badly wounded, and he kept screaming for us to help his buddy, who was seriously wounded. I couldn't tell him that his buddy didn't have a good chance to survive, and so we were passing him by. That was difficult for a lot of us, went against all we'd been trained to do. It's difficult to support someone in the act of dying when you're trained to do all you can to save a life. Even today, I have trouble with patients who need amputations or who have facial injuries.

It is most important to realize that there is a great cost to waging war. Many men are living out their lives in veterans' hospitals as paraplegics or quadriplegics, who in World War II or Korea would not have survived. Most Americans will never see these people—they are hidden away from us. But they are alive.

Maybe the worst part of the war for many of these boys was coming home. The seriously wounded were sent to a military hospital closest to their own homes. Our orthopedic ward at Great Lakes Naval Hospital had forty beds, and it was like taking care of forty kid brothers. They joked around and were supportive of each other. But quite a few of them got "Dear John"[36] letters while they were there. Young wives and girlfriends sometimes couldn't deal with these injuries, and parents sometimes had trouble coping too. All these people were "casualties of war," but I believe that these men especially need our caring and concern today, just as much as they did twenty years ago.

[*On her discharge from the United States Navy in August 1969, Helen returned to nursing. She married in 1972. She and her husband, an engineering physicist, have two children. Helen returned to school and received her B.S. degree in nursing. She is now a coordinator of cardiac surgery and often speaks and writes of her Vietnam experience. She also actively participates in a local veterans' organization. Recently, her daughter offered her mother's services to speak on Vietnam to a high school history class, but she was rebuffed by the teacher, who said, "Who wants to hear about that? We lost that war!" Both Helen and her daughter (who is proud of what her mother did) were offended.*]

36. A "Dear John" letter is one that breaks off a relationship.

9. Photograph of Nick (on Right) with Some Buddies in Vietnam.

Nick

[Nick was born in 1946 in a midsize southern city. Both his parents were skilled factory workers. Nick graduated from high school in 1964 and wanted to work for the fire department, but he was too young for the civil service. He got a job at the local utility company and got married in 1966. Nick was drafted in 1967. He served with the First Cavalry Division.]

CHAPTER 12

A GENERATION
IN WAR AND
TURMOIL: THE
AGONY OF
VIETNAM

I suppose I could have gotten a deferment, but I didn't know they were available. My wife was pretty scared when I got drafted, but neither of us ever imagined that I would shirk my duty.

I did my boot camp at Fort Benning [Georgia]. About 80 percent of the people in boot camp with me were draftees. A number of the draftees were black. I had worked with blacks before the Army, had many black friends, and never saw any racial problems. We were then sent to Fort Polk, Louisiana, for advanced infantry training. They had built simulated Vietnamese villages that were very similar to what we later encountered in Vietnam. Overall, we were trained pretty well, but we were still pretty scared.

I arrived in Vietnam on December 12, 1967, and was assigned to go out on "search and destroy" missions. Even though I was prepared mentally, I was still very frightened. I was wounded once when we got ambushed while we were setting up an ambush of our own. Another time I got hit with some shrapnel from a 60 mm mortar. That was at 3:00 A.M. and the medics didn't arrive until 7:30.

I'm not proud of everything I did in Vietnam, but I won't run away from it either. You got so hard at seeing friends killed and things like that. We desecrated their dead, just as they did ours. We used to put our unit's shoulder patches on the VC dead (we nailed 'em on) to get credit for it.

I didn't like the Vietnamese themselves. Most of the civilians were VC sympathizers, and the South Vietnamese army just wouldn't fight. I was in some kind of culture shock. Here we were, trying to help these people, and some of them were living in grass huts. Once I asked myself, "What am I doing here?"

The highest rank I made was sergeant, but I was demoted when I caught a guy in my unit asleep on guard duty and busted him with a shotgun. I was demoted for damaging the shotgun, government property.

I got back to the States in December 1968. There were some protesters at the Seattle airport, but they just marched with signs and didn't harass us at all. Over time, I lost my hostility to the antiwar protesters, although at the time I despised them. Except for Jane Fonda[37] (who went too far), I have no bad feelings for them at all. I have a friend who threatened to run his daughter off because she had a Jane Fonda workout tape.

I'm no hero and didn't do anything special. But college students today need to know that the people who fought in that war are no less important than people who fought in World War I, World War II, or Korea.

---

37. Movie star and antiwar activist Jane Fonda organized shipments of food and medical supplies to North Vietnam and traveled to Vietnam during the war.

[*Nick returned to his position with the utility company. He and his wife have two sons, born in 1969 and 1972. He never talked about Vietnam and wanted to throw his medals out, but his wife made him keep them. When his sons started asking questions, he told them about Vietnam. They convinced him to bring his medals out and display them. Since returning from Vietnam, he has never voted "and never will. . . . I have no use for politicians at all." He is now enjoying retirement.*]

10. Photograph of Robyn as a College Student.

Robyn

[*Robyn was born in 1955 and raised in a Wisconsin farming town of around fifteen hundred people. Her father owned a small construction business and, like many other men in town, had proudly served in World War II. Her mother was a high school teacher. Robyn has three sisters and three brothers, none of whom served in Vietnam.*]

CHAPTER 12

A GENERATION
IN WAR AND
TURMOIL: THE
AGONY OF
VIETNAM

I remember starting to watch the war on television when I was about ten. I asked my mother, "How come they're killing each other?" She said that America was the land of freedom and that we were in Vietnam to help make the people free. As a teacher, though, she always encouraged us to think for ourselves and find our own answers.

The guys in town started going away [to Vietnam], and, in a town that size, everybody knows. When my ninth-grade algebra teacher suddenly disappeared, no adults would talk about it. Later, we found out that he had received CO status. In my town, that wasn't much different from being a Communist. The peer pressure was tremendous.

I have always believed the United States is the greatest country in the world, but it's not perfect. The more I heard about the war, the more I realized something was wrong. Although only in high school, I felt obligated to let the government know that I thought it was in the wrong. And yet at no time while I was protesting the war was I *ever* against the guys fighting it. My quarrel was with how the government was running the war.

I recall one of my first "protests." I was in the high school band and we were playing "The Star-Spangled Banner" at a basketball game. Although I stood and played with the rest of the band, I turned my back to the flag. When I came home that night, my father hit me for being disrespectful. So much for the right to free speech we were fighting to protect.

When I left for college in 1973, one brother had just gotten a medical deferral, and another would soon be registering for the draft. The war was becoming more and more personal. I skipped classes to attend rallies and antiwar events, and I wrote lots of letters to politicians. When the POW-MIA bracelets[38] came out, I helped sell them. There were quite a few heated discussions with some protesters who thought that wearing a bracelet (my guy is still MIA) was contrary to the cause. In those days, I tended to "discuss" things in decibels.

My second year of college ended with me skipping classes to watch the televised returns of our POWs. I would have loved to hug each one, so this was my way of saying "Welcome home" and to bear witness. I cried the whole time—for them, for their families, and for all the agony we'd all gone through during the war. Then I dropped out of school and just "vegetated" for a year. My idealistic perceptions of humanity had been severely challenged, and I was drained.

After Vietnam, I got involved in some projects that were targets to help Vietnam vets. One of my best and proudest experiences will always be my

---

38. Bracelets were worn to show that Prisoners of War and Missing in Action were remembered by the public; they also were intended to urge government action in returning these soldiers.

work at the Vietnam Veterans Memorial in Washington, D.C. I worked at the wall as a volunteer every week for almost ten years. Unlike past memorials, this one doesn't honor the war. It's the Vietnam *Veterans* Memorial, not War Memorial, and it honors those who fought it.

I have seen firsthand its healing effects on vets and their families. And on me. At the wall, the former protester and the Vietnam veteran share something in common—our great sadness for those who were lost and those who haven't yet returned. Vietnam vets also don't seem to have the glorified view of war that older vets do.

The government's lack of support for Vietnam vets (during and after the war) might be part of the reason. If more people were aware of the other side of war, the side the vets saw, they'd have a lot more incentive to work things out. Instead of seeing war as an alternative solution, people would finally realize that war is simply the result of our failure to find a solution.

[*Robyn returned to college and eventually graduated from law school. She worked in Washington, D.C., for a nonprofit education organization and as a government relations consultant. Robyn now works at a public and government relations firm. She continues to work with Vietnam veterans and, in particular, on the POW-MIA issue.*]

∞ QUESTIONS TO CONSIDER ∞

The interviews in this chapter were conducted between 1985 and 1992. As you read through the seven interviews, try to get a sense of the tone and general meaning of each one. Then try to establish the respective frames of reference for each interviewee by comparing and contrasting their backgrounds. From which socioeconomic class does each person come? From what region of the country? What do you know about their parents and friends? What did they think was expected of them? Why?

After high school, all the interviewees' experiences diverged greatly. Eventually, Mike, MM, Eugene, and Helen enlisted in the armed services.

What reason did each person give (if any) for enlisting? How different were their reasons? For his part, Nick was drafted. What was his reaction to being drafted?

Both John and Robyn became involved in antiwar protests, but for very different reasons. Why did each become involved? Would John and Robyn have agreed on why the war should have been opposed?

Return to the five veterans. What were their feelings about the Vietnamese people? What did they believe were the reasons for American involvement in the war? What were their reactions to events of the times—the draft, antiwar protests, Kent State, race rela-

CHAPTER 12

A GENERATION
IN WAR AND
TURMOIL: THE
AGONY OF
VIETNAM

tions in the armed services, what they actually did in Vietnam? What did each one think about the situation of returning veterans? Some of the interviewees seem to have made the adjustment to civilian life better than others. Can you think of why that might have been so? Finally, what do you think each person (veterans and civilians alike) learned from his or her personal experiences during the Vietnam War era?

Now look at the photographs carefully. Are they posed or unposed? For whom might they have been intended? What image of each person is projected? How does each person help to create that image?

The majority of the interviewees have never met one another. Do you think they could meet and talk about the Vietnam era today? What might such a conversation be like?

✑ EPILOGUE ✑

In the spring of 1971, fifteen thousand antiwar demonstrators disrupted daily activities in the nation's capital by blocking the streets with trash, automobiles, and their own bodies. Twelve thousand were arrested, but the protest movement across the country continued. In June, the Pentagon Papers, a secret 1967 government study of the Vietnam War, was published in installments by the *New York Times*. The Pentagon Papers revealed that government spokespersons had lied to the American public about several important events, particularly about the Gulf of Tonkin incident.

As part of his reelection campaign in 1972, President Nixon traveled first to China and then to the Soviet Union and accelerated the removal of American troops from Vietnam. "Peace," his adviser Henry Kissinger announced, "is at hand." Withdrawal was slow and painful and created a new group of refugees—those Vietnamese who had supported the Americans in South Vietnam. Nixon became mired in the Watergate scandal and resigned from office in 1974 under the threat of impeachment. The North Vietnamese entered Saigon in the spring of 1975 and began a "pacification" campaign of their own in neighboring Cambodia. Nixon's successors, Gerald Ford and Jimmy Carter, offered amnesty plans that a relatively small number of draft violators used. Many who were reported Missing in Action (MIA) in Vietnam were never found, either dead or alive. The draft was replaced by a new concept, the all-volunteer army.

The Vietnam veterans who never had their homecoming parades and had been alternately ignored and maligned finally got their memorial. A stark, simple, shiny black granite wall engraved with the names of 58,000 war dead, the monument is located on the mall near the Lincoln Memorial in Washington, D.C. The idea came from Jan Scruggs (the son of a milkman), a Vietnam veteran who was wounded and decorated for bravery when he was nineteen years old. The winning design was submitted by twenty-year-old Maya Lin, an undergraduate architecture student at Yale University. A representational statue designed by thirty-eight-year-old Frederick Hart, a former antiwar protester, stands near the wall of names. All one hundred United States senators cosponsored the gift of public land, and the money to build the memorial was raised entirely through 650,000 individual public contributions. Not everyone was pleased by the memorial, and some old emotional wounds were reopened. Yet more than 150,000 people attended the dedication cere-monies on Veterans Day 1982, and the Vietnam veterans paraded down Constitution Avenue. Millions of Americans have already viewed the monument, now one of Washington's most visited memorials.

As for the baby boomers, many have children old enough to have served in Operation Desert Storm. Many have put their Vietnam-era experiences behind them as they pursue careers, enjoy middle age, and wait for grandchildren (a new birth cohort). For many, however, Vietnam is a chapter in American history that will never be closed.

CHAPTER 13

DEMOCRACY AND DIVERSITY: AFFIRMATIVE ACTION IN CALIFORNIA

⬭ THE PROBLEM ⬭

On November 5, 1996, Californians who went to the polls for the presidential election were asked to vote on several other questions as well. The most controversial was Proposition 209, a proposal to ban all California state programs involving gender preference or race. If the proposal was approved, affirmative action in such areas as state university admissions, state jobs, and state contracts would end. There had been intense campaigning by both supporters and opponents of affirmative action, with both sides invoking ideals of equality and justice. Proposition 209 did pass, with 54 percent of the voters, or over 4.5 million people, approving it.

A coalition of California civil rights groups, joined by the U.S. Department of Justice with President Clinton's support, immediately filed a lawsuit, arguing that Proposition 209 was un-

constitutional. As a result of the suit, a California federal district court issued an injunction preventing the implementation of Proposition 209 until the case could be tried and the constitutional question decided.

Is California's situation unique? Not at all, as contemporary observer and author Haynes Johnson has noted. California has always been a "mirror" for what is happening in America, "the pacesetter, the place where national cultural and political trends started."[1] In fact, during the 1990s, affirmative action programs everywhere began to encounter opposition.

What has happened? How has the meaning of equality changed over time? What are the arguments for and

1. Haynes Johnson, *Divided We Fall* (New York: Norton, 1994), p. 98.

[346]

against affirmative action? In this chapter, you will examine California as a test case to determine why affirmative action is so controversial today.

∽ BACKGROUND ∾

California became part of the United States as a result of the Mexican-American War (1846–1848). The Treaty of Guadalupe Hidalgo, which ended the war, ceded some two million square miles of Mexican land to the United States. In return, the United States paid Mexico $15 million and also assumed another $3.25 million of American citizens' claims against the Mexican government.

Gold had been discovered earlier, in 1842, by a Mexican rancher who lived about 35 miles north of Los Angeles, but it was a small strike that seemed to run out quickly. Not so the discovery of gold at Sutter's Mill in the Sierra Madre foothills in 1848. The resulting rush of miners and settlers populated California so rapidly that it skipped a territorial stage and became a state as part of the Compromise of 1850.

Rich also in natural resources such as lumber, fish, salt, borax, and range land, California continued to grow rapidly in the second half of the nineteenth century. Immigrants from Japan and China arrived by ship (until the Chinese Exclusion Act of 1882), while settlers from the eastern and midwestern United States arrived via the new transcontinental railroad. In spite of earthquakes and fires, droughts and floods, California was a magnet whose population doubled every twenty years until the mid-

1920s, with one-third of the increase due to the birth rate and the remainder from immigration and in-migration from states. Ethnic tensions and violence against minority groups were common.

The early twentieth century also witnessed the growth of new sectors of California's economy, such as the birth of the Hollywood film industry, the development of the oil industry, the establishment of wineries, and the rise of the agribusinesses of the Central Valley. At the same time, Progressive reformers moved to restrain the political influence of railroads and big business and began efforts to conserve some of the natural beauty of the state, such as that of the Yosemite area. Ethnic tensions were still evident, however, as Chinese residents were confined to Chinatowns, and Japanese were denied access to property ownership and education. During the depression of the 1930s, Mexican Americans along with Mexican citizens were forcibly returned to Mexico. Even the displaced Okies and other Americans fleeing the dust bowl of the plains states were often barred from California towns and cities.

The two worst outbreaks of prejudiced behavior in California occurred during World War II. The forced relocation and internment of over 100,000 Japanese, two-thirds of whom were U.S. citizens, caused them enormous

CHAPTER 13

DEMOCRACY
AND DIVERSITY:
AFFIRMATIVE
ACTION IN
CALIFORNIA

psychological and financial hardship. Although most returned to California after the war, only about 10 percent of their assets remained; the majority had to start all over again. The other instance, called the "zoot suit riots" because of the gangster-style clothes worn by some young Mexican Americans, took place in 1943, when about two hundred U.S. Navy sailors went on a rampage in East Los Angeles, attacking members of the neighborhood Hispanic gangs. The Los Angeles Police Department stood by and watched, maintaining that it was the job of the shore patrol and the military police to control the rioters. Only after a formal protest by the Mexican government did the riots finally end.

The cold war that followed World War II brought prosperity to large areas of California. Between the 1940s and the 1970s, the U.S. government poured $100 billion into defense-related industries such as aircraft and electronics. By the 1960s, the golden state was also known for its youth culture, which encompassed surfers, hippies, and a music scene as varied as the folksongs of Joan Baez, the surfer sound of the Beach Boys, and the hard rock of Jefferson Airplane. A decade later, California had established a well-regarded system of higher education: 8 state universities, 21 state colleges, and 100 junior or community colleges. During the 1960s, the U.S. government had promoted civil rights through a series of initiatives such as affirmative action, the Civil Rights Act of 1964, and the Voting Rights Act of 1965. California, with its increasingly diverse population, also struggled to provide its minority groups

and women with increased access to jobs, to government contracts, and to higher education.

But the sixties, a decade that seemed in some ways to hold out the promise of a better life for all, had a darker side, even in California. Militant Native Americans occupied Alcatraz Island in San Francisco Bay as a symbolic gesture of cultural and economic protest. Cesar Chavez, leader of the United Farm Workers, exposed the terrible living conditions and exploitation of the migrant agricultural workers whom he was trying to organize. The *bracero* (day laborer) program that had permitted "temporary" work by immigrant Mexicans ended in 1964, but illegal (or "undocumented") workers continued to pour across the border. At the same time, more public concern focused on the young people in the barrios who were deeply involved in gangs. The rock concerts, protest marches, and demonstrations of the sixties were increasingly marked by violence.

Preceded by smaller riots in eastern cities and followed by riots in other major cities, the Watts riot of 1965 in Los Angeles shocked many Americans with its violence and revealed poverty and despair in the midst of what had appeared to be prosperity and optimism. After an incident involving a drunk-driving arrest, African American rioters looted and burned buildings in that inner-city ghetto, where the population was ten times greater in 1965 than it had been in 1940. During the six days that the riot lasted, it spread to adjoining areas, and the National Guard was called out to help contain it. Thirty-four people were killed; more than a thousand were injured; and $40 million worth of property was damaged or destroyed. In 1970, riots broke out in the Hispanic section of Los Angeles. Rioting occurred again in Los Angeles in 1992, after the acquittal of several white police officers who had been videotaped while brutally beating a black motorist.

During the 1970s, 1980s, and 1990s, California experienced major changes in its economy, population patterns, and politics. The economy, particularly the large sector dependent upon federal defense spending, plunged into a recession as cold war tensions decreased and American foreign policy changed. Blue-collar jobs contracted; low-paying jobs in the service sector expanded only slightly; and as technical and communications skills became more important for job seekers, access to good education became crucial.

Equally striking were changes in the population. After 1965, when the United States began to loosen immigration restrictions, the country experienced another "new" immigration: from Latin America, especially Mexico, and from Asia and the Pacific Islands. For example, between 1970 and 1983, over one million Hispanics, Asians, and other foreign-born people moved to the county of Los Angeles. Although African Americans are currently the largest minority group in the United States (about 12.5 percent of the population, according to the 1990 census), Hispanics and Asians and Pacific Islanders are the fastest-growing groups. In California, in 1990, the 7.6 million Hispanics were the largest minority group, followed by the 2.8 million Asian and Pacific Islanders and the 2.2 million African

Americans. It is estimated that in the year 2000, Hispanics will make up over 30 percent of California's population; Asians, 14 percent; and African Americans, just under 7 percent. Combined, these groups will compose 51 percent of the state's population. Because of immigration, California has grown so rapidly that Hispanics and Asians have often crowded into poorer inner-city areas such as Watts, where African Americans were already living. Conflicts have increased between the African Americans and some of the newer immigrants, such as Korean store owners, and even occur at times between earlier immigrants such as the Chinese and the newer arrivals. Since the late 1960s, politics has reflected the new ethnic and racial identities and awareness.

As the California economy worsened and the racial and ethnic composition of the state's population continued to change, the practice of affirmative action came under increasingly critical scrutiny, especially with regard to access to the better universities and colleges. As Professor Steven Cahn[2] has pointed out, two different kinds of affirmative action have developed during the past thirty-six years. In a 1961 executive order, President Kennedy called for *procedural* affirmative action to ensure that job applicants would not be discriminated against because of national origin, race, religion, or creed. By 1965, President Johnson had prohibited discrimination on the basis of gender and called for the development of affirmative action plans to promote full employment of women

2. Steven Cahn, "Two Concepts of Affirmative Action," *Academe*, January–February, 1997, pp. 14, 16.

CHAPTER 13

DEMOCRACY
AND DIVERSITY:
AFFIRMATIVE
ACTION IN
CALIFORNIA

and minorities. During President Nixon's administration in the 1970s, *preferential* affirmative action required goals and timetables to correct the "under-utilization"[3] of women and minorities. In some instances, separate lists of African Americans, Asian Americans, Hispanic Americans,[4] and Caucasian Americans have been used for job openings, promotions, and college admissions in a conscious effort to provide such diversity.

Thus, the intent of affirmative action has been to provide more nearly equal economic and educational opportunities for two very different categories of people who have previously suffered discrimination: members of racial and ethnic minority groups, and women. There is no doubt that affirmative action programs have offered women new options in the areas of employment and government contracts. However, women still do not earn as much as men with similar levels of education and experience, nor are women usually found in upper-management or administrative positions. Sexism, like racism, remains in many areas of American society and institutions. Nevertheless, gender is a category that includes females of all classes, races, and ethnic groups.

Although issues of gender and affirmative action are very important, this chapter focuses on affirmative action for members of racial and ethnic minority groups, and to a lesser extent, on some related socioeconomic issues. As we have seen, California already has a very diverse population and is the home of many different cultures. What happens in California also tends to reflect what is happening in the nation as a whole. On the basis of the 1990 census, population experts estimate that by the year 2020, Hispanics will make up 16 percent of the U.S. population; African Americans, 14 percent; and Asian Americans, 7 percent. By 2050, these groups, along with Native Americans, will be approximately 50 percent of the U.S. population. The problems in reconciling democracy and diversity, in providing equality and justice for all Americans, raise some very difficult and sensitive issues. Underlying these issues, of course, are our own attitudes about other races and cultures. How has the meaning of equality changed since 1776? What are the pros and cons of affirmative action? Why is affirmative action so controversial?

☜ THE METHOD ☞

One definition of racism is expecting certain kinds of thought patterns or

behavior just because of a person's racial background. Or racism may mean treating a person differently merely because of his or her race. However it may be expressed, racism is still pre-

3. Under-utilization means that there are fewer people in an employment category—for example, African American history professors—than the number of African Americans receiving doctorates in history would lead you reasonably to expect.

4. Hispanics may be of any race.

sent in American society. Prejudice against members of ethnic minority groups, whether Hispanics, Asians, Pacific Islanders, or others, sometimes is blatant and direct, as in incidents involving name-calling on college campuses and even in corporate boardrooms. At other times it is subtle, absorbed almost unthinkingly from images in television, films, newspapers, books, and so forth. Unfortunately, as one professor of American history noted recently, discussing racial or ethnic issues in the classroom is very difficult, "like walking on eggshells."[5] Many white students are afraid that they will say something that will offend minority students; some politically conservative students believe that their ideas will be dismissed as "racist" without any discussion; some minority students either doubt that such discussions are worthwhile or fear that they will get angry with their classmates. Yet we *must* talk about race, ethnicity, equality, and justice because what makes American democracy work is not simply a representative system of government, but also what Americans think and believe as well as how they act in their daily lives.

In this chapter, you will be using some analytical skills that you learned in previous chapters and practicing the skills necessary for discussing sensitive issues. You will begin by analyzing how the American concept or ideal of equality has changed over time. (California's Proposition 209 illustrates the challenge to affirmative ac-

tion.) Next, you will identify arguments for and against affirmative action in the 1990s. You will see those arguments in a variety of sources including speeches, articles, statistics, and opinion polls.

Describing historical changes in the meanings of words and listing pro-and-con arguments from historical evidence can be done by most students fairly easily and dispassionately. Inevitably, however, the evidence in this problem leads into the present and one's own value systems and judgments. These beliefs are very important to each of us and involve our convictions and emotions.

When we analyze a historical person's words or actions, we try to understand why that individual in that place or time might have spoken or acted a particular way. As you learned in the preceding chapter, frame of reference (unique, personal background), as well as the times in which one lives, can be very influential in forming value systems and judgments. In the same way, each of your classmates has developed attitudes and beliefs from a particular place, background, and time period. Recognizing that others around you may not share your beliefs, try to listen to others fully and respectfully, allowing them sufficient uninterrupted time to express their points of view. The goal of this kind of discussion is to hear and to understand—although not necessarily to share or to approve of—other people's ideas about diversity, equality, and justice.

The evidence is divided into three sections: (1) the changing meanings of equality (Sources 1–5); (2) the challenge to affirmative action in Cali-

---

5. Robbie Lieberman, "Walking on Eggshells? Teaching Recent U.S. History in the 1990s," *Organization of American Historians' Newsletter*, November 1995, p. 3.

CHAPTER 13

DEMOCRACY
AND DIVERSITY:
AFFIRMATIVE
ACTION IN
CALIFORNIA

fornia (Source 6); and (3) arguments for and against affirmative action (Sources 8–15). Sources 1 through 3 are the classic statements of American ideals. In Source 4, Abraham Lincoln tries to explain his understanding of equality between whites and blacks on the eve of the Civil War. Over one hundred years later, President Lyndon Johnson describes what he thinks equality means (Source 5). Source 6 consists of Proposition 209, called by its supporters the California Civil Rights Initiative.

Source 7 consists of excerpts from a landmark decision of the U.S. Supreme Court, in the case of *Regents of the University of California v. Bakke.* Alan Bakke was an aerospace engineer who wanted to become a physician. He applied twice to the University of California medical school at Davis and was rejected both times. After discovering that the school had reserved for members of racial minorities sixteen of the one hundred admissions places, Bakke sued, claiming that there was now "reverse discrimination" because less-qualified members of minority groups were being admitted instead of better-qualified whites. Sources 8 through 11 present differing opinions about affirmative action from four prominent African Americans: Ward Connerly is a well-to-do land consultant, member of the Board of Regents of the University of California, and leader of the campaign to pass Proposition 209. Retired

General Colin Powell commanded American forces during the Gulf War and was widely suggested as a potential vice-presidential candidate in 1996. Shelby Steele is a professor at San Jose State University, California, and Thomas Sowell is a nationally syndicated newspaper columnist and fellow at the Hoover Institution in Stanford, California.

Scholastic Aptitude Test (SAT) scores (see Source 12), along with high school grades, are used by nearly all colleges and universities to predict success in college. Responding to criticism of the SATs, the College Board has worked in recent years to reduce cultural or racial biases in the questions, although standardized test-taking itself may be culturally biased. Other factors, such as possessing athletic skills or being the child of an alumnus or of a generous donor to the school, may also be considered for admissions. However, SAT scores are still a major factor in determining most admissions to top colleges and universities. Source 12 is a chart presenting SAT scores by racial and ethnic group as well as by family income.

Finally, you will be reading a public opinion poll (Source 14) and excerpts from two speeches about affirmative action: Republican presidential candidate Bob Dole's speech in San Diego, California, in 1996 and President Bill Clinton's speech in the same city in 1997 (Sources 13 and 15).

⬯ THE EVIDENCE ⬯

THE CHANGING MEANINGS OF EQUALITY

1. Excerpt from the Declaration of Independence, 1776.

We hold these truths to be self-evident: That all men are created equal; that they are endowed by their Creator with certain unalienable rights; that among these are life, liberty, and the pursuit of happiness. . . .

2. The Motto of the United States.

E Pluribus Unum ("From many, one")

3. The Pledge of Allegiance, 1942.[6]

I pledge allegiance to the flag of the United States of America, and to the Republic for which it stands, one nation, under God, indivisible, with liberty and justice for all.

Source 4 quoted in Arthur Zilversmit, ed., *Lincoln on Black and White: A Documentary History* (Belmont, Calif.: Wadsworth, 1971), pp. 47–48.

4. Excerpts from Abraham Lincoln's Fourth Debate with Stephen A. Douglas, at Charleston, Illinois, 1858.

I have never hesitated to say, and I do not now hesitate to say, that I think, there is a physical difference between the white and black races which I believe will for ever forbid the two races living together on terms of social and political equality. And inasmuch as they cannot so live, while they do remain together there must be the position of superior and inferior, and I as much as any other man am in favor of having the superior position

---

6. Originally published in 1892 in a boys' magazine, the Pledge was reworded in the 1920s and became official in 1942. The words "under God" were added in 1954.

[353]

CHAPTER 13
DEMOCRACY
AND DIVERSITY:
AFFIRMATIVE
ACTION IN
CALIFORNIA

assigned to the white race. I say upon this occasion I do not perceive that because the white man is to have the superior position the negro should be denied everything. I do not understand that because I do not want a negro woman for a slave I must necessarily want her for a wife. . . . My understanding is that I can just let her alone. . . . I will add to this that I have never seen to my knowledge a man, woman or child who was in favor of producing a perfect equality, social and political, between negroes and white men.

Source 5 quoted in Lee Rainwater and William L. Yancey, eds., *The Moynihan Report and the Politics of Controversy* (Cambridge, Mass.: MIT Press, 1967), pp. 126–127.

5. Excerpts from President Lyndon Johnson's Speech at Howard University, 1965.

But freedom is not enough. You do not wipe away the scars of centuries by saying: Now you are free to go where you want, do as you desire, and choose the leaders you please.

You do not take a person who, for years, has been hobbled by chains and liberate him, bring him up to the starting line of a race and then say, "you are free to compete with all the others," and still justly believe that you have been completely fair.

Thus it is not enough just to open the gates of opportunity. All our citizens must have the ability to walk through those gates. . . .

To this end, equal opportunity is essential, but not enough. Men and women of all races are born with the same range of abilities. But ability is not just the product of birth. Ability is stretched or stunted by the family you live with, and the neighborhood you live in, by the school you go to and the poverty or the richness of your surroundings. It is the product of a hundred unseen forces playing upon the infant, the child, and the man. . . .

THE CHALLENGE TO AFFIRMATIVE ACTION

Source 6 from "Text of Proposition 209," *San Jose Mercury News*, September 20, 1996.

6. Excerpts from Proposition 209, the California Civil Rights Initiative, 1996.

a) The state shall not discriminate against, or grant preferential treatment to, any individual or group on the basis of race, sex, color, ethnicity, or national origin in the operation of public employment, public education, or public contracting. . . .

    c) Nothing in this section shall be interpreted as prohibiting bona fide qualifications based on sex which are reasonably necessary to the normal operation of public employment, public education, or public contracting. . . .

    e) Nothing in this section shall be interpreted as prohibiting action which must be taken to establish or maintain eligibility for any federal program, where ineligibility would result in a loss of federal funds to the state.

    f) For the purposes of this section, *state* shall include, but not necessarily be limited to, the state itself, any city, county, city and county, public university system, including the University of California, community college district, school district, special district, or any other political subdivision or governmental instrumentality of or within the state. . . .

ARGUMENTS FOR AND AGAINST AFFIRMATIVE ACTION

Source 7 from *Regents of the University of California v. Bakke*, 438 U.S. 265 (1978).

7. Excerpts from *Regents of the University of California v. Bakke*, 1978.

If petitioner's [the University of California's] purpose is to assure within its student body some specified percentage of a particular group merely because of its race or ethnic origin, such a preferential purpose must be rejected. . . . Preferring members of any one group for no reason other than race or ethnic origin is discrimination for its own sake. This the Constitution forbids. . . .

    Physicians serve a heterogeneous population. An otherwise qualified medical student with a particular background—whether it be ethnic, geographic, culturally advantaged or disadvantaged—may bring to a profes-

CHAPTER 13

DEMOCRACY
AND DIVERSITY:
AFFIRMATIVE
ACTION IN
CALIFORNIA

sional school of medicine experiences, outlook, and ideas that enrich the training of its student body and better equip its graduates to render with understanding their vital service to humanity.

Ethnic diversity, however, is only one element in a range of factors a university may properly consider in attaining the goal of a heterogeneous student body. . . .

Justice Lewis Powell

Source 8 quoted in *New York Times,* April 18, 1996, p. A1; April 29, 1996, p. A27.

8. Ward Connerly, 1996.

Nobody ever gave me any race or sex preferences when I came into the cold world 56 years ago, and I made it anyway—high school, college, my own big business, important friends. If I could make it, anybody can, because the playing field is a lot closer to level now. The truth is that preferences at this point are not just reverse discrimination, they're degrading to people who accept them. They've got to go.

The greatest harm caused by lowering the admission requirements for blacks is the personal damage done to students who are the "beneficiaries" of such policies. Do we not understand that these young men and women will soon be required to compete in a world that will not give them any concessions? . . .

People tend to perform at the level of competition. When the bar is raised, we will rise to the occasion. That is exactly what black students will do in a society that has equal standards for all.

Source 9 from Shelby Steele, *The Content of Our Character* (New York: Harper Perennial, 1990), pp. 94–96, 143–144.

9. Shelby Steele, 1990.

Black though I may be, it is impossible for me to sit in my single-family house with two cars in the driveway and a swing set in the backyard and *not* see the role class has played in my life. . . .

What became clear to me is that people like myself, my friend, and middle-class blacks in general are caught in a very specific double bind that keeps two equally powerful elements of our identity at odds with each other. The middle-class values by which we were raised—the work ethic, the importance of education, the value of property ownership, of respectability, of "getting ahead," of stable family life, of initiative, of self-reliance, et cetera—are, in themselves, raceless and even assimilationist. They urge us toward participation in the American mainstream, toward integration, toward a strong identification with the society, and toward the entire constellation of qualities that are implied in the word individualism. . . .

But the particular pattern of racial identification that emerged in the sixties and that still prevails today urges middle-class blacks (and all blacks) in the opposite direction. This pattern asks us to see ourselves as an embattled minority, and it urges an adversarial stance toward the mainstream and an emphasis on ethnic consciousness over individualism. It is organized around an implied separatism.

The opposing thrust of these two parts of our identity results in the double bind of middle-class blacks. There is no forward movement on either plane that does not constitute backward movement on the other. . . .

Most of the white students I talked with spoke as if from under a faint cloud of accusation. There was always a ring of defensiveness in their complaints about blacks. A white student I spoke to at UCLA told me: "Most white students on this campus think the black student leadership here is made up of oversensitive crybabies who spend all their time looking for things to kick up a ruckus about." A white student at Stanford said, "Blacks do nothing but complain and ask for sympathy when everyone really knows that they don't do well because they don't try. If they worked harder, they could do as well as everyone else."

That these students felt accused was most obvious in their compulsion to assure me that they were not racist. . . . I think it was the color of my skin itself that accused them.

. . . My skin not only accused them; it judged them. And this judgment was a sad gift of history that brought them to account whether they deserved such accountability or not. It said that wherever and whenever blacks were concerned, they had reason to feel guilt. And whether it was earned or unearned, I think it was guilt that set off the compulsion in these students to disclaim. I believe it is true that, in America, black people make white people feel guilty.

CHAPTER 13

DEMOCRACY
AND DIVERSITY:
AFFIRMATIVE
ACTION IN
CALIFORNIA

Source 10 quoted in *New York Times,* June 8, 1996, p. B8.

10. Colin Powell, 1996.

There are those who rail against affirmative action preferences, while living lives of preference, who do not understand that the progress achieved over the past generation must be continued if we wish to bless future generations. . . . We must fight misguided government efforts that seek to shut it all down. . . . When one black man graduates from college for every one hundred who go to jail, we still need affirmative action. When half of all African American men between 24 and 35 years of age are without full-time employment, we need affirmative action.

Source 11 quoted in *Knoxville News Sentinel,* July 12, 1997, p. A8.

11. Thomas Sowell, 1997.

Crucial facts have been left out in much of the hysteria about declining black enrollments at the University of California at Berkeley in the wake of the end of affirmative action policies there. . . .

During the decade of the 1980s, Berkeley's rapid increase in the number of black students on campus did not translate into comparable increases in the number of blacks actually graduating. . . .

Where group body count has been the overriding consideration, minority students who were perfectly capable of graduating from a good college have been artificially turned into failures by being admitted to high-pressure campuses where only students with exceptional academic backgrounds can survive. . . .

Despite much hysteria over the fact that there is only one black student entering Berkeley's law school this year [in 1997, after affirmative action admissions were discontinued], 15 were admitted—and 14 chose to go somewhere else. These other places included Harvard, Stanford, and the like, so don't shed tears over these students, either.

Not only have double standards produced needless educational failures among minority students, they have polarized the races by producing great resentments among white students. It has been a policy under which both groups have lost, though in different ways—and in which the country as a whole has lost. . . .

Source 12 from the College Entrance Examination Board. Cited in Dana Y. Takagi, *The Retreat from Race* (New Brunswick, N.J.: Rutgers University Press, 1992), p. 200.

12. SAT Scores by Race and Class, 1991.

Mean SAT Scores by Race and by Class, 1991

Income	Black		Asian		White	
	Verbal	Math	Verbal	Math	Verbal	Math
Less than $10,000	321	358	340	485	407	452
$10,000–$20,000	334	370	353	499	416	457
$20,000–$30,000	348	381	393	512	423	466
$30,000–$40,000	361	392	414	523	429	474
$40,000–$50,000	371	403	435	535	437	484
$50,000–$60,000	376	408	449	546	445	494
$60,000–$70,000	386	417	456	556	454	502
$70,000 or more	413	447	482	590	471	526

Source 13 quoted in *New York Times,* October 29, 1996, p. A21.

13. Excerpts from Presidential Candidate Bob Dole's Speech, San Diego, California, 1996.

Now we've reached another turning point, this time for quality and opportunity in America. And the California Civil Rights Initiative allows the voters of this state to endorse a great principle, the principle that racial distinctions have no place in our lives or in our laws. . . .

. . . We believe it's wrong to use quotas, set-asides[7] and other preferences that serve only to pit one American against another American, or group against group. . . .

It is true that many of us in the years following 1964—and I did—supported some race-conscious measures designed to speed the process of inclusion, a measure that was supposed to be transitional, transitional and temporary. But it didn't work. . . .

But this was a blind alley in the search for equal justice. . . . Programs that started as temporary and limited have become permanent and broad. . . .

7. A set-aside is a percentage of the contract or subcontracts on public projects that is reserved for minority businesses to bid on.

CHAPTER 13

DEMOCRACY
AND DIVERSITY:
AFFIRMATIVE
ACTION IN
CALIFORNIA

And I just want to end this on a positive note. We must bring quality education to every child in every community. And I believe the surest route to economic mobility for all Americans lies in the access to a good school. Letting parents choose the best school for their children is perhaps the most urgent civil rights issue of our time. . . .

And finally, we must bring a growing economy to every community. . . . Give people an opportunity to make it in the private sector. They don't need quotas and preferences.

Source 14 from Gallup Organization, "Black/White Relations," June 10, 1997. <http://gallup.com/poll/special race>.

14. Summary of Gallup Poll on Black-White Relations, June 10, 1997.

There are major differences in the perceptions of blacks and whites about the status of race relations in this country today. Whites are more positive than blacks on a variety of perceptual measures of how well blacks are faring in our society, and how they are treated in the local community. These gaps are in some instances smaller than they were in the 1960's, but have not narrowed in recent years.

Whites also tend to view themselves as having very little personal prejudice against blacks, but perceive that "other" whites in their area have much higher levels of prejudice against blacks. Blacks also ascribe to whites significantly higher levels of racial prejudice than whites give themselves. Blacks claim that they have little prejudice against whites. . . .

. . . There has thus been a significant decline in the past several decades in the number of whites who express overtly prejudicial sentiments.

Whites and blacks have distinctly different views on the role of the government—perhaps building off of their differential perceptions of the status of race relations in the U.S. today. Whites want the number of affirmative action programs to decrease or at the least stay the same, and feel that blacks should help themselves rather than relying on the government. Blacks hold the contrary views.

The average white American tends to live, work and send their child to school in environments which are mostly or all white. Blacks, on the other hand, have relatively high degrees of contact in these everyday settings with whites. Less than a majority of blacks live in mostly or all black neighborhoods, and only a fourth send their children to schools that are mostly or all black. Both blacks and whites, however, are very highly likely to worship only with members of their race.

Source 15 from "Remarks of the President at University of California at San Diego Commencement," June 14, 1997 (The White House, Office of the Press Secretary).

15. Excerpts from President Bill Clinton's Speech in San Diego, California, June 14, 1997.

To be sure, there is old, unfinished business between black and white Americans, but the classic American dilemma has now become many dilemmas of race and ethnicity. We see it in the tension between black and Hispanic customers and their Korean or Arab grocers; in a resurgent anti-Semitism even on some college campuses; in a hostility toward new immigrants from Asia to the Middle East to the former communist countries to Latin America and the Caribbean—even those whose hard work and strong families have brought them success in the American Way.

We see a disturbing tendency to wrongly attribute to entire groups, including the white majority, the objectionable conduct of a few members. If a black American commits a crime, condemn the act—but remember that most African Americans are hard-working, law-abiding citizens. If a Latino gang member deals drugs, condemn the act—but remember that the vast majority of Hispanics are responsible citizens who also deplore the scourge of drugs in our life. If white teenagers beat a young African American boy almost to death just because of his race, for God's sakes [sic] condemn the act—but remember the overwhelming majority of white people will find it just as hateful. If an Asian merchant discriminates against her customers of another minority group, call her on it—but remember, too, that many, many Asians have borne the burden of prejudice and do not want anyone else to feel it. . . .

In our efforts to extend economic and educational opportunity to all our citizens, we must consider the role of affirmative action. I know affirmative action has not been perfect in America—that's why two years ago we began an effort to fix the things that are wrong with it—but when used in the right way, it has worked.

It has given us a whole generation of professionals in fields that used to be exclusive clubs. . . . There are more African American, Latino and Asian American lawyers and judges, scientists and engineers, accountants and executives than ever before.

But the best example of successful affirmative action is our military. Our armed forces are diverse from top to bottom. . . . And, more important, no one questions that they are the best in the world. . . .

There are those who argue that scores on standardized tests should be the sole measure of qualification for admissions to colleges and universities.

[361]

CHAPTER 13

DEMOCRACY
AND DIVERSITY:
AFFIRMATIVE
ACTION IN
CALIFORNIA

But many would not apply the same standard to the children of alumni or those with athletic ability. . . .

I believe a student body that reflects the excellence and the diversity of the people we will live and work with has independent educational value. . . .

And beyond the educational value to you, it has a public interest because you will learn to live and work in the world you will live in better. When young people sit side by side with people of many different backgrounds, they do learn something that they can take out into the world. And they will be more effective citizens.

Many affirmative action students excel. They work hard, they go out and serve the communities that need them for their expertise and role model. If you close the door on them, we will weaken our greatest universities and it will be more difficult to build the society we need in the 21st century. . . .

Let me say, I know that the people of California voted to repeal affirmative action without any ill motive. The vast majority of them simply did it with a conviction that discrimination and isolation are no longer barriers to achievement. But consider the results. Minority enrollments in law school and other graduate programs are plummeting for the first time in decades. . . .

. . . To those who oppose affirmative action, I ask you to come up with an alternative. I would embrace it if I could find a better way. And to those of us who still support it, I say we should continue to stand for it, we should reach out to those who disagree or are uncertain and talk about the practical impact of these issues, and we should never be thought unwilling to work with those who disagree with us to find new ways to lift people up and bring people together. . . .

❧ QUESTIONS TO CONSIDER ❧

What do you think the word *equal* meant to the authors of the Declaration of Independence in 1776 (Source 1)? What groups of people were probably excluded, and why? Do you think it is possible to relate the United States motto "From many, one" (Source 2) to our diverse population? Should we try? Why or why not? What, if anything, should the government do to ensure "liberty and justice for all" (Source 3)? What are Lincoln's views on equality between whites and blacks (Source 4)? Why did he use the example of the African American woman? Do you think that he was viewed as a liberal or as a conservative in 1858? Why? President Johnson's speech (Source 5) was intended especially for African Americans but obviously has implications for all Americans. Why did he say that "freedom is not enough"?

In this chapter, we have represented the challenge to affirmative action by California's Proposition 209, although Texas, Mississippi, and several other states have recently proposed similar measures. Why, do you think, did Proposition 209's supporters call it the California Civil Rights Initiative? Sections we have omitted explain that the law would not be retroactive, that the remedies would be the same as they currently were for discrimination cases, and that any section in conflict with a federal law could be dropped. What exactly would the law cover? What do you think section c means?

When Alan Bakke sued for admission to medical school, claiming that he was being discriminated against because he was white, the U.S. Supreme Court had to consider the constitutionality of "racially conscious" university admissions programs. Reread the excerpts from Justice Powell's opinion carefully. What is he saying about racial quotas? about the relationship between race and diversity? about the needs of society?

Sources 8, 9, 10, and 11 represent the beliefs of four middle-class or upper-class professional African American men. What major points does each make? On what issues do they disagree?

What is the relationship between SAT scores and income (Source 12)? If *only* SAT combined math and verbal scores were used, which group would have the most college admissions? the second-most? the fewest? Would giving preference to students from families whose income is below $10,000 and using combined SAT scores change these results? If so, how? What factors might account for these differences in the scores?

What major reasons does Bob Dole give for opposing affirmative action? What do you think are the most significant findings of the 1997 Gallup Poll on race relations? What major reasons does President Bill Clinton give for supporting affirmative action? What do *you* think about affirmative action? Finally, having studied all the evidence, can you describe how the meaning of *equality* has changed since the American Revolution? Why is affirmative action so controversial today?

∽ EPILOGUE ∽

One of the major reasons that we study American history is to understand how we, as a nation, reached where we are today. Although all Americans agree that a democracy like ours must provide equality and justice for all, we often disagree among ourselves about what these goals mean

and how we can best achieve them. Furthermore, the historical record of the relationships between the dominant white Euro-American society and Native Americans, African Americans, Hispanic Americans, and Asian Americans is filled with shocking examples of injustice and inequality.

CHAPTER 13

DEMOCRACY
AND DIVERSITY:
AFFIRMATIVE
ACTION IN
CALIFORNIA

There are no easy answers to the complex issues raised by this chapter. Yet a democracy is not simply a static form of representative government, but rather a dynamic, constantly changing political, economic, and social system based on shared, deeply held beliefs. In the twenty-first century, there is no doubt that the very concept of "minority groups" will be altered by changes in the composition of our population. What will not be altered is our commitment to achieving equality and justice for all.

TEXT CREDITS

Source 8: Reprinted with permission of the copyright holder, International Herald Tribune, Paris.

CHAPTER TWELVE

Page 259: "Ever we praise . . ." Reprinted by permission from *The IBM Songbook*, copyright 1935 by International Business Machines Corporation.

CHAPTER THIRTEEN

Source 9: Copyright © 1990 by Shelby Steele from *The Content of Our Character*. Reprinted by permission of St. Martin's Press, Inc.

Source 11: Excerpts from a column by Thomas Sowell dated July 12, 1997, are reprinted by permission of the author.

Source 14: (Internet) Gallup Organization, "Black/White Relations," published 10 June 1997. Reprinted with permission.